Leonardo da Vinci

Aspects of the Renaissance Genius

Leonardo da Vinci

Aspects of the Renaissance Genius

SELECTED, EDITED, AND INTRODUCED BY

MORRIS PHILIPSON

GEORGE BRAZILLER / NEW YORK

THIS VOLUME IS DEDICATED
TO THE MEMORY OF

Jenny R. Alderman

(1867–1950)

Socrates:

"Beloved Pan, and all ye other gods who haunt this place, give me beauty in the inward soul; and may the outward and the inward man be at one. May I reckon the wise to be the wealthy, and may I have such a quantity of gold as a temperate man and he only can bear and carry.—Anything more? The prayer, I think, is enough for me."

—Plato's *Phaedrus*

Preface

Leonardo da Vinci, the man, has become as symbolic, evocative, and enigmatic as a work of art—as *Hamlet,* for example, or *Don Quixote,* or *Faust.* Not that there is any reason to believe one might come to know even a quite ordinary man any more easily than one might understand a thoroughly extraordinary man. Here the complexity compounds the difficulty; but the assumption is the same—by their works ye shall know them. And it is the fabulous range of Leonardo's works, added to the impression of excellence of his character, which initiates the power of his image. It is "fabulous" to us because only something mythical, fantastic, imaginary, could seem to account for so great a scope in our own experience of grimly sensible, pragmatically effective specialization. Our grandparents were women who could raise children, clean and cook, and sew and mend, and weave—design and execute; men who could build and plant, make music, and run the church, the town, and their own minds. They may have known *about* less, but they knew how to *do* more than we know.

We find that Leonardo as a man takes on the attributes of a work of art because we cannot easily believe anyone actually lived such a life; we can grasp the idea of him only as if it were the creation of a richly imaginative intelligence. And, for this reason, he functions in the top-heavy world of our excessive specialization—"the universal genius"—as a compensation: as an ideal of fulfillment in an age of frequent frustration, as an idea of completeness in an era of fragmentation, as a joyous expression of how optimistic-dreamer and practical-planner might be combined in this world of narrow specialties giving lip-service to the gods of "creativity."

Nothing could have convinced me of this more than when a friend of mine, who was then a psychiatrist at Yale University, mentioned the fact (which he found remarkable) that students who came to the clinic for help made reference—in their fantasies or in recounting their

vii

dreams—to Leonardo da Vinci even more often than to Albert Schweitzer. Of course, Schweitzer represents the idea of self-sacrifice in the service of humanity to a society raised to believe in only self-seeking and service to its own social class and the status quo; but Leonardo was something of a puzzle to my friend. Was it the all-encompassing but amorphous quality of his career that attracted the young?—the apparent unwillingness to be "limited." The specific contributions he had made to the arts, let alone his research into the physical sciences, were, for all practical purposes, a mystery to his patients. It was not history and biography that functioned in their psyches; it was an "archetype."

How much difference would it make if they were to know the best of what has been thought in this century about the life and work of Da Vinci? Only a little, I suspect; because the "facts" themselves offer only a little. But that minimum is still better than pure fancy. A revery founded on accurate information and suggestive interpretations is no less a revery, but it is infinitely more likely to be useful.

And so the most stimulating elements for an understanding of Leonardo have been gathered together here: Hauser on the social and economic conditions of the artist's time and place; Wölfflin, Valentiner, Berenson, and Read on various aspects of his contributions to the graphic and plastic arts; Koyré, Sarton, De Santillana, and Clark on the varieties of his research into what are now the physical sciences; Farrell and Eissler on the ways of understanding him psychologically; and, finally, Valéry and Shattuck on the philosophical implications of his method(s) and his "meaning."

This is about as close as one can get to the truth concerning his "secrets." Even these studies are not enough, but they are indispensable. It is incalculably more significant for reality to stimulate our imaginations than for make-believe to lead us astray.

1966   M. P.

Contents

PLATES

Numbers 1–10 *follow* page 6.
Numbers 11–34 *follow* page 95.
Numbers 35–59 *follow* page 171.
Numbers 60–70 *follow* page 275.
Numbers 71–82 *follow* page 339.
Numbers 83–93 *follow* page 388.

Introduction

The Fascination of Leonardo da Vinci

HY IS IT THAT practically no one offers a satisfying way of understanding Leonardo da Vinci? The intellectual, who would like to appreciate Leonardo, has been spoiled by his own good training. He is the graduate of a university, taught to examine evidence, analyze, compare, test hypotheses, and support theories with logically ordered arguments. He is victimized by the advantages of systematic thought. For him, Leonardo must remain an enigma or a failure because, no matter how he looks at "the fascination" in the hope of interpreting his life's work systematically, there is no system, no simple unity bringing together the variety of what he left behind.

The effort to understand Leonardo in this sense of intellectual comprehension is necessarily self-defeating. While his art may be evaluated by connoisseurs, critics, and historians, and his scientific reflections may be similarly interpreted, the fact remains that it is neither of these nor the sum of them which constitute "the fascination." The cultural value of Leonardo rests in how the image of his personality functions for us, not merely in what he did. In effect—Leonardo is infinitely more significant as a myth than as a man. From the time that the myth first began to be elaborated by the Romanticists a hundred years ago, Leonardo has gained increasing importance; he has gone from being the essence of the free creative spirit to standing as the existential model for everyman.

According to the myth—five hundred years ago, there lived a man who was, uniquely, a universal genius. He was handsome, manly, and entertaining. For his friends and patrons he played music and sang, made up riddles both verbal and visual, wrote fables and ironic morality tales. His interest in everything was equaled by his spontaneous originality in response to everything that interested him. For a living he worked as a painter, sculptor, civil and military engineer, architect, decorator, and stage manager-designer for all sorts of ceremonies. His energy appears to have been boundless. When not at work on one of his commissions—such as *The Last Supper* or the *Mona Lisa*—he studied the movements of water or the proportions of recently unearthed antiquities; the stratifications of rock or the anatomy of the human body; the natures of plants and animals or the intricacies of mathematics; and, from his examination of the flight of birds and the movements of air, he attempted to construct a machine that would *enable man to fly*. It seems that no one person has ever, before or since, been endowed with such an extraordinary range of talent. He might be thought of as combining the potential powers of Aristotle and Rembrandt. He remained unmarried, footloose, and free-lance. Born a love-child in a tiny provincial north Italian town, and having been acquainted with many of the greatest artists, intellectuals, and statesmen of his time, he ended his life as the honored guest of the King of France.

Since the heyday of the Romantic movement, which first sketched this portrait of him, this is the vision of Leonardo which has persisted. He is *the* genius, *the* artist, and in a sense—the only *intellectual bohemian*.

But for those who have tried to know the man and not only the myth, all the conventional standards of evaluation immediately bring shadows into the picture.

Although one has no reason to imagine he was unhappy about it, in all likelihood Leonardo was homosexual. As a court artist he was without the steady, fruitful patronage of a prince or pope who commissioned him to use his talents for their most valuable potentialities. Unlike Michelangelo or Raphael, who were respected exclusively as artists from the time of their youths, Leonardo was used by his patrons to fix the palace plumbing as often as he was expected to execute a portrait. As a brilliant mind trying to explore the variety of meanings to be grasped he was hampered by a lack of formal education; he did not even learn Latin—and then imperfectly—until his middle age. The worse that is said about him is that (for a variety of possible reasons) he left most of his paintings incomplete; many of them and other works of his art were destroyed—so that there is no full-blown body of completed works of his art comparable with other masters who lived as long as he. As a scientist he was without influence in the course of intellectual history, for (although now it can be clearly ascertained that he was "ahead of his time") he did not systematize the findings in his numerous *Notebooks;* he did not publish them; and for centuries they were unknown to all other researchers. The conclusion from that line of thought is to mourn for Leonardo as for a poet dying young— for he seems more fascinating in his potentiality than in his positive achievements.

The narrow idea of Leonardo as a *failure,* which is to be found in a number of scholarly books, is one of the most revealing commentaries on the very intellectuals themselves who offer that objective evaluation of him. It requires that one examine the most important presuppositions implicit in their values of "completeness" and "influence."

To bemoan the lack of an extensive body of *completed* paintings by which to judge an artist not only disregards the respect for drawing which has developed since the eighteenth century but demonstrates a form of wishful thinking. This hardly scholarly attitude of mind prefers to dwell on what is absent rather than concentrate on what is present. It is the prissy attitude which implies that something promised has not been delivered. But no one can answer the historical "if" question of what might have been delivered had Leonardo specialized in painting and ignored his research; nor would it make sense to presume what the history of science might have been had he specialized in his research and ignored his works of art. To cavil over lack of such completeness is even less forgivable than criticizing Columbus for not finding his promised route to the Indies. What point is there in saying that Columbus did not dig the Panama Canal? Still, the criticism of Columbus can be made with regard to his explicitly stated, and realizable, intention. But with an artist, intention cannot be anticipated: achievement and intention are ultimately identical. Significant questions may be asked only about what an artist accomplishes, not about what he left undone. The rest is make-believe.

If the maudlin complaint of "incompleteness" ends in pure sentimentality, the argument about "influence" shows the essential characteristics of greed.

When an original mind makes his discoveries available to all who may be interested in the subject of his studies then the individual's private thought becomes common property, commonly testable, a contribution to the ongoing progress of a discipline of thought. Depending upon how fruitful are the suggestions in method or how useful the conclusions that such a man offers—effecting future developments in one direction or another—it is possible to gauge his influence. In a rather schoolmarmish way, the historian of culture may "grade" the man's work and declare that he is of such-or-such a magnitude of greatness. It is a purely pedantic exercise, rhetorical in nature, of no intrinsic value, and necessarily open to constant revision as the course of the history of a line of thought takes different turns under the influences of others.

With respect to the concept of "influence" one is aware not only of the quality of make-believe that colors meditations on "completeness" but of another attitude of mind as well. Consider the implications of the statement by Charles Singer, an authority on the history of medicine, writing about Leonardo: "Had he produced the anatomical textbook which he had planned in collaboration with the Pavean Professor, Marc Antonio della Torre, the progress of anatomy and physiology would have been advanced by centuries." By indulging in such retrospective prophecy, what is being *held against* Leonardo (or Fate, or Chance)—and thereby raised as a warning to be respected by future investigators—is that his findings remained his alone; they were not contributed to the public fund of common knowledge and therefore not able to influence a community endeavor of assumed social importance.

The principle involved here is that social value has a priority over private interest. The historian who takes this position naively assumes that a man is to be regretfully but most distinctly reprimanded for not having been more socially responsible. It is the greed of the completely socialized, mass-minded man concerned only with what is good for man-in-general not with what is best for the individual. It is the disbelief of the team worker at the sight of the genuine loner. And it becomes more paradoxical as the convictions of our century become more materialistic. As the world of science grows more communal and less fun, and there is no commonly held belief in the ultimate purpose or aim of scientific progress —only the idea of progress itself is spotlessly admirable. Under these conditions, the fact that Leonardo's insights did not become common property in his own time, and thereby contribute to the teamwork progress in fields where his research was original and might have been valuable to others, leads the historian to make his judgment on behalf of mass-man and on the basis of his idea of intellectual economy. For him: Leonardo was a failure.

This peculiarly peevish conclusion simply ignores the main purpose for progressively improving life in general, namely: to make any one individual's life more significant for himself. Whether as a consequence of any one man's interests the rest of the world comes to be better off—is purely coincidental. The narrow judgment of historians amounts to saying that Leonardo's genius gave him an opportunity to contribute to the possible progress of a number of sciences; but, instead, *all* he did was to *enjoy himself.*

On the other hand, this self-enjoyment is precisely what makes Leonardo valuable as a paradigm: fascinating, mythical, and, therefore, still a living example to stimulate the imagination. In a world striving to press all effort into the possible service of mass-man, a world in which the significance of any and every activity is under the pressure of evaluation only in its *consequences to others*—Leonardo's image functions as an occasion to consider what it is for a life's activities to have *intrinsic value.*

A man framed by a sense of mystery, the body of whose art seems to fade off into "incompleteness," and whose scientific originality remained without "influence," Leonardo is a man whose lifework is either to be understood in respect to what it meant *to him*—or not appreciated at all.

The heart of the mythical power in this image is the idea of the universal genius. This means only that, attracted by an enormous number of things, he responded with the pleasure of understanding them in *his* way, on his own, by himself. What else does originality mean?

It may appear as though it is the great range of interests that fascinates us about Leonardo, but as soon as one reflects on the matter, it is not the breadth of attractions that impresses so much as the very fact of attraction itself. What makes a man *interested?*—not only in so much; what makes a man *interested* in anything at all? Nothing whatsoever in our science or in our art explains individual interest; and nothing but the *ex post facto* idea of "talent" offers even a verbal appearance of an explanation for the originality of response. The fascination of Leonardo's personality rests on this fact: that the essence of self-enjoyment is directly related to the interest one takes in the attractions of the rest of the world— in nature as well as in one's own spirit, in matter as in ideas, in the actual as in the possible, in the past and present as in the future.

As our socially and scientifically progressive culture exerts ever greater pressure against individuality, against independent responsiveness, singular evaluations and "loner" creativity—the idea of Leonardo may become even more powerful an archetype, because it will grow increasingly difficult to find examples demanding the effort to understand intrinsic values. Almost everyone else will have accommodated to the community. We know all too well that specialization is opposed to encyclopedic range but makes positive achievement more likely; that positive accomplishments make influence possible; and such influence is the only obvious measurement of the power that an individual can exert on the history of the social body. But is the individual's responsibility to society the prime responsibility he has? Ignoring the reciprocal relationship between one's debt to others and what one owes to himself—for those to whom the answer is "yes," Leonardo is a failure, and the progressive life of society does have priority over the values of anyone's life to himself.

But those who find attraction in this "mystery" are appealed to by the very lures that can make their lives more valuable to themselves, and which remain the primary conditions for intrinsic values. They recognize that the essence of all education is to be self-taught; and that the greatest source of pleasure is the capacity for self-entertainment. To be interested in the pursuit of beauty in art, truth in thought, and goodness in behavior—*to be interested*—is an investment independent of the judgment of others. The special example of Leonardo will continue to be useful to the sensitive but uncertain mind as long as it is possible to grasp the idea that, for one's own life, it is not so important to achieve the impersonal and objective status of being unique in history as it is to appreciate the intrinsic value of being unique to yourself.

1. Manner of Leonardo, *Head of a Girl*. Silverpoint drawing.
Florence, Uffizi.

2. Leonardo, *The Last Supper*. Milan, S. Maria delle Grazie. *Photo: Alinari-Art Reference Bureau.*

3. Raphael Morghen, *The Last Supper*. Etching after Leonardo. New York, The Metropolitan Museum of Art, Gift of Miss L. Chauncey, 1935.

4. Domenico Ghirlandaio, *The Last Supper*. Florence, Ognissanti.
Photo: Alinari-Art Reference Bureau.

5. Marcantonio Raimondi, *The Last Supper*. Engraving after Raphael.
London, British Museum.   *Photo: Art Reference Bureau.*

6. Desiderio da Settignano, *Bust of a Girl*. Florence, Museo Nazionale.
Photo: Alinari-Art Reference Bureau.

7. Leonardo, *Mona Lisa*. Paris, Louvre.
Photo: Agraci-Art Reference Bureau.

8. Leonardo, *The Virgin and Child with St. Anne*. Paris, Louvre.
Photo: Alinari-Art Reference Bureau.

9. After Leonardo, *Leda and the Swan*.
Rome, Galleria Borghese.
Photo: Alinari-Art Reference Bureau.

10. Giampietrino, *Abundance*.
Milan, Galleria Borromeo.
Photo: Alinari-Art Reference Bureau.

1/
THE MATRIX
OF CREATIVITY

"... In time of peace I believe that I can give you as complete satisfaction as anyone else in architecture pertaining to the construction of buildings both public and private, and in conducting water from one place to another. Also, I can execute sculpture in marble, bronze, or clay, likewise painting, in which my work will stand comparison with that of anyone else, whoever he may be.... Having now, Most Illustrious Lord, sufficiently seen and considered the proofs of all those who proclaim themselves masters and inventors of instruments of war, and finding that their inventions and use of the said instruments are nothing different from common practice, I am emboldened, without prejudice to anyone else, to put myself in communication with Your Excellency, in order to acquaint you with my secrets."

—from Leonardo's Letter to
Ludovico il Moro, 1483

The Social Status of the Renaissance Artist

by Arnold Hauser

HE INCREASED DEMANDS for works of art in the Renaissance leads to the ascent of the artist from the level of the petty bourgeois artisan to that of the free intellectual worker, a class which had previously never had any roots but which now began to develop into an economically secure and socially consolidated, even though by no means uniform group. The artists of the early Quattrocento are still entirely small folk; they are regarded as higher-grade craftsmen and their social origins and education do not make them any different from the petty bourgeois elements of the guilds. Andrea del Castagno is a peasant's son, Paolo Uccello the son of a barber, Filippo Lippi the son of a butcher, the Pollajuoli the sons of a poulterer. They are named after the occupation of their father, their birthplace or their master, and they are treated as familiarly as domestics. They are subject to the rules of the guild, and it is by no means their talent which entitles them to practise as professional artists, but the course of instruction completed according to guild regulations. Their education is based on the same principles as that of the ordinary craftsmen; they are trained not in schools, but in workshops, and the instruction is practical, not theoretical. After having acquired the rudiments of reading, writing and arithmetic, they are apprenticed to a master while still children and they usually spend many years with him. We know that even Perugino, Andrea del Sarto and Fra Bartolommeo

From *The Social History of Art* by Arnold Hauser (New York: Alfred A. Knopf, Inc., 1952), tr. by Stanley Godman in collaboration with the author. Reprinted by permission of the publisher. All rights reserved.

were apprenticed for eight to ten years. Most of the artists of the Renaissance, including Brunelleschi, Donatello, Ghiberti, Uccello, Antonio Pollajuolo, Verrocchio, Ghirlandajo, Botticelli and Francia, started in the goldsmith's workshop, which has rightly been called the art school of the century. Many sculptors begin work with stonemasons and ornamental carvers just as their medieval predecessors had done. Even when he is received into the Luke Guild, Donatello is still described as a "goldsmith and stonemason," and what he himself thinks about the relation between art and craft is best shown by the fact that he plans one of his last and most important works, the group of Judith and Holofernes, as a decoration for the fountain in the courtyard of the Palazzo Riccardi. But the leading artists' shops of the early Renaissance introduce, despite their still fundamentally artisan-like organization, more individual teaching methods. That applies, above all, to the workshop of Verrocchio, Pollajuolo and Ghirlandajo in Florence, of Francesco Squarcione in Padua and Giovanni Bellini in Venice, of which the leaders are just as important and famous as teachers as they are as artists. Apprentices no longer enter the first workshop that they come across, but go to a particular master, by whom they are received in greater numbers the more famous and sought after he is as an artist. For these boys are, if not always the best, at least the cheapest source of labour; and that is probably the main reason for the more intensive art education which is to be observed from now on, not the masters' ambition to be considered good teachers.

The course of instruction begins, still following the medieval tradition, with all kinds of odd jobs, such as the preparation of colours, repairing brushes and the priming of the pictures; it then extends to transferring the individual compositions from the cartoon to the panel, the execution of the various parts of garments and the less important parts of the body, and finishes with the completion of whole works from mere sketches and instructions. Thus the apprentice develops into the more or less independent assistant, who must be differentiated, however, from the pupil. For not all the assistants of a master are his own pupils, and not all pupils remain with their teacher as assistants. The assistant is often on the same level at the master, but also often merely an impersonal tool in the hands of the workshop-owner. As a consequence of the various combinations of these possibilities and the frequent co-operation of the master, the assistants and the pupils, there arises not only a mixture of styles which is difficult to analyse, but sometimes even an actual balancing of the individual differences, a communal form, on which, above all, the tradition of craftsmanship has a decisive influence. The circumstance which is familiar—whether it is truth or fiction—from artists' biographies of the Renaissance, that the master gives up painting because one of his pupils has outstripped him (Cimabue-Giotto, Verrocchio-Leonardo, Francia-Raphael), must either represent a later stage of development in which the workshop community was already in process of dissolution, or, as for example in the case of Verrocchio and Leonardo, there must be a more realistic explanation than is given in the anecdotes about these artists. Verrocchio probably stops painting and restricts himself to the execution of plastic works, after he has convinced himself that he can safely entrust the painting commissions to an assistant like Leonardo.[1]

The artist's studio of the early Renaissance is still dominated by the communal spirit of the masons' lodge and the guild workshop; the work of art is not yet the expression of an independent personality, emphasizing his individuality and excluding himself from all extraneous influences. The claim independently to shape the whole work from the first stroke to the last and the inability to co-operate with pupils and assistants are first noticeable in Michelangelo, who, in this respect too, is the first modern artist. Until the end of the fifteenth century the artistic labour process still takes place entirely in collective forms.[2] In order to cope with extensive undertakings, above all, great works of sculpture, factory-like organizations are started with many assistants and handymen. Thus in Ghiberti's studio up to twenty assistants are employed during the work on the Baptistry doors, which are among the greatest tasks to be commissioned in the Quattrocento. Of the painters, Ghirlandajo and Pinturicchio maintain a whole staff of assistants while they are working on their great frescoes. Ghirlandajo's workshop, in which above all his brothers and brother-in-law are engaged as permanent collaborators, is, along with the studios of the Pollajuoli and the della Robbia, one of the great family businesses of the century. There also exist owners of studios who are more business men than artists, and who usually accept commissions only in order to have them carried out by a suitable painter. Evangelista da Predis in Milan seems to have been one of these. For a time, he also employed Leonardo. Apart from these business-like forms of collective labour, we encounter in the Quattrocento the partnership of two usually still young artists, running a common workshop, because they cannot afford the expense of an independent undertaking. Thus, for example, Donatello and Michelozzo, Fra Bartolommeo and Albertinelli, Andrea del Sarto and Franciabigio, work together. Everywhere we still find superpersonal forms of organization preventing the atomization of artistic work. The tendency to intellectual amalgamation makes itself felt both in the horizontal and in the vertical direction. The representative personalities of the age form long uninterrupted successions of names which, as, for example, in the case of the master-pupil sequence: Fra Angelico—Benozzo Gozzoli—Cosimo Rosselli —Piero di Cosimo—Andrea del Sarto—Pontormo—Bronzino, make the main development seem to be that of an absolutely continuous tradition.

The spirit of craftsmanship which dominates the Quattrocento is expressed, above all, in the fact that the artists' studios often take on minor orders of a purely technical nature. From the records of Neri di Bicci we learn what a vast amount of handicraft goods is produced in one busy painter's workshop; apart from pictures, armorial bearings, flags, shop signs, tarsia-works, painted wood-carvings, patterns for carpet weavers and embroiderers, decorative objects for festive occasions and many other things are turned out. Even after he has become a distinguished painter and sculptor, Antonio Pollajuolo runs a goldsmith's workshop and in his studio, apart from sculpture and goldsmith work, cartoons for tapestries and sketches for engravings are drafted. Even at the height of his career, Verrocchio takes on the most varied terracotta work and wood-carving. For his patron Martelli, Donatello makes not only the well-known coat of arms but also a silver mirror. Luca della Robbia manufactures majolica tiles for churches and private houses, Botticelli draws patterns for embroideries and Squarcione is the owner of an embroidery workshop. Of course, one must discriminate both according to the stage of historical development and the standing of the individual artists and not run away with the idea that Ghirlandajo and Botticelli painted shop signs for the baker or the butcher round the corner; such orders will no longer have been executed in their workshop at all. On the other hand, the painting of guild flags, wedding chests and bridal plates was not felt to be a degrading occupation for the artist. Botticelli, Filippino Lippi, Piero di Cosimo, are active as painters of *cassoni* right into the period of the Cinquecento. A fundamental change in the generally accepted criteria of artistic work does not begin to make itself felt until the period of Michelangelo. Vasari no longer considers the acceptance of mere handicraft work compatible with the self-respect of an artist. This stage also signifies the end of the dependence of artists on the guilds. The outcome of the proceedings of the Genoese painters' guild against the painter Giovanni Battista Poggi, who was to be prevented from practising his art in Genoa, because he had not undergone the prescribed seven-years course of instruction there, is of symptomatic importance. The year 1590, in which this case took place and which brought the fundamental decision that the guild statutes were not binding on artists who did not keep an open shop, brings to a close a development of nearly two hundred years.[3]

The artists of the early Renaissance are also economically on an equal footing with the petty bourgeois tradesman. Their situation is in general not brilliant, but neither is it exactly precarious. No artist is as yet in a position to live like a lord, but, on the other hand, there exists nothing that one could call an artistic proletariat. It is true that in their income-tax declarations the painters are constantly complaining about their difficult financial circumstances, but such documents can certainly not be considered the most trustworthy of historical sources. Masaccio asserts that he cannot even pay his apprentice, and we know for a fact that he died poor and in debt.[4] According to Vasari, Filippo Lippi could not buy himself a pair of stockings, and in his old age, Paolo Uccello complains that he owns nothing, cannot work any longer and has a sick wife. Those artists were still best off who were in the service of a court or a patron. For example, Fra Angelico received fifteen ducats a month at the curia, at a time when on 300 a year one could live in grand style in Florence, where the cost of living was anyhow somewhat lower.[5] It is characteristic that prices remained in general on a medium level and that even the well-known masters were not much better paid than the average artist and the higher-grade craftsman. Personalities like Donatello probably received somewhat higher fees, but "fancy prices" were still non-existent.[6] Gentile da Fabriano received 150 florins for his "Adoration of the Magi," Benozzo Gozzoli 60 for an altar-piece, Filippo Lippi 40 for a Madonna, but Botticelli already received 75 for his.[7] Ghiberti drew a fixed salary of 200 florins a year while he was working on the doors of the Baptistry, whereas the Chancellor of the Signoria received 600 florins out of which he was also obliged to pay four clerks. In the same period, a good copyist of manuscripts received 30 florins in addition to full board. Artists were, accordingly, not exactly badly paid, even though not anything like so well as the famous literati and university teachers, who often received 500 to 2000 florins per annum.[8] The whole art market still moved within comparatively narrow limits; the artists had to demand interim payments during the work and even the employer could often pay for the materials only by instalments.[9] The princes also had to fight against shortage of ready money, and Leonardo complains repeatedly to his patron Ludovico Moro about not having received his fee.[10] The handicraft character of artistic work was expressed not least in the fact that the artists were in receipt of a regular wage from their employers. In the case of larger-scale artistic undertakings, all cash expenditure, that is to say, both the cost of the materials, the wages and often even the board and lodging of the assistants and apprentices, was borne by the employer, and the master himself was paid according to the time spent on the work. Wage-work remained the general rule in painting until the end of the fifteenth century; only later was this method of compensation limited to purely artisan jobs, such as restorations and copying.[11]

As the artistic profession breaks away from pure craftsmanship, all the conditions set down in work contracts are gradually altered. In a contract with Ghirlandajo, dated 1485, the price of the colours to be used is still particularized; but according to a contract with Filippino Lippi, dated 1487, the artist already has to bear the cost of the materials, and a similar agreement is made with Michelangelo in 1498. It is, of course, impossible to draw an absolute dividing-line here, but the change occurs, at any rate, towards the end of the century, and is again connected most conspicuously with the person of Michelangelo. In the Quattrocento it was still the general custom to require the artist to provide a guarantor to stand surety for the observance of the contract; with Michelangelo this guarantee becomes a mere formality. Thus, in one case, the writer of the contract himself acts as a guarantor for both sides.[12] The other obligations binding on the artist are defined more and more loosely and vaguely in the contracts. In a contract of the year 1524, Sebastiano del Piombo is left free to choose any subject he likes for a painting, on the sole condition that it shall not be the picture of a saint; and in 1531, the same collector orders a work from Michelangelo and it is left entirely to the artist to decide whether it shall be a painting or a piece of sculpture.

From the very beginning, artists were better placed in Renaissance Italy than in other countries, not so much as a result of the more highly developed forms of urban life—the bourgeois milieu in itself offered them no better opportunities than the ordinary craftsmen—but because the Italian princes and despots were better able to use and appreciate their gifts than foreign rulers. The fact that the Italian artists were less dependent on the guilds, which was the basis of their favoured position, is above all the result of their being frequently employed at the courts. In the North the master is tied to one city, but in Italy the artist often moves from court to court, from city to city, and this nomadic life already leads to a certain relaxation of guild regulations, which are based on local conditions and are only workable within local limits. As the princes attached importance to attracting to their courts not only highly skilled masters in general, but also particular artists who were often foreign to the locality, the latter had to be freed from the restrictions of guild statutes. They could not be forced to take local craft regulations into consideration in the execution of their commissions, to apply for a labour permit from the local guild authority and to ask how many assistants and apprentices they were allowed to employ. After they had finished their work for one employer, they went with their assistants into the employment and protection of another and again enjoyed the same exceptional rights. These travelling court painters were beyond the reach of the guilds from the very outset. But the privileges which artists enjoyed at the courts could not remain without effect on the way they were treated in the towns, particularly as the same masters were often employed in both places and the towns had to keep pace with the competition of the courts if they wanted to attract the best artists. The emancipation of the artists from the guilds is, therefore, not the result of their own heightened self-respect and the acknowledgement of their claim to be considered on an equal footing with the poets and scholars, but results from the fact that their services are needed and have to be competed for. Their self-respect is merely the expression of their market-value.

The social ascent of the artists is expressed first of all in the fees they receive. In the last quarter of the fifteenth century relatively high prices begin to be paid in Florence for fresco paintings. In 1485, Giovanni Tornabuoni agrees to pay Ghirlandajo a fee of 1,100 florins for painting the family chapel in S. Maria Novella. For his frescoes in S. Maria sopra Minerva in Rome, Filippino Lippi receives 2,000 gold ducats, which corresponds approximately to the same sum in florins. And Michelangelo receives 3,000 ducats for the paintings on the ceiling of the Sistine Chapel.[13] Towards the end of the century several artists are already doing well financially; Filippino Lippi even amasses a considerable fortune. Perugino owns houses, Benedetto da Majano an estate. Leonardo draws an annual salary of 2,000 ducats in Milan and in France he receives 35,000 francs per annum.[14] The celebrated masters of the Cinquecento, especially Raphael and Titian, enjoy a considerable income and lead a lordly life. Michelangelo's way of life is outwardly modest, it is true, but his income, too, is high, and when he refuses to accept payment for his work in S. Peter's, he is already a wealthy man. In addition to the increasing demand for works of art and the general rising of prices, the fact that round the turn of the century the papal curia comes more into prominence on the art market, and becomes a more serious rival to the Florentine public interested in art, must have had the biggest influence on the ascending scale of artists' fees. A whole series of artists now move from

Florence to magnanimous Rome. Naturally, those left behind profit from the high offers of the papal court—that is to say, only the more distinguished artists really profit, those whom an effort is made to keep back. The prices paid to the others lag considerably behind the fees paid in the best market, and now, for the first time, there begin to be real differences in the payments made to artists.[15]

The emancipation of the painters and sculptors from the fetters of the guilds and their ascent from the level of the artisan to that of the poet and scholar has been attributed to their alliance with the humanists; the humanists' support for them, on the other hand, has been explained by the fact that the literary and artistic monuments of antiquity formed an indivisible unity in the eyes of these enthusiasts, and that they were convinced that the poets and artists of classical antiquity were held in equal regard.[16] In fact, they would have considered it unthinkable that the creators of the works which they regarded with a common reverence because of their common origin should have been judged differently by their contemporaries. And they made their own age—and the whole of posterity right into the nineteenth century—believe that the artist, who had never been anything more than a mere mechanic in the eyes of antiquity, shared the honours of divine favour with the poet. There is no question that the humanists were very useful to the artists of the Renaissance in their efforts to achieve emancipation; the humanists confirmed them in the position they had won for themselves thanks to the favourable market, and they gave them the weapons with which to assert their claims against the guilds, and partly also against the resistance of the conservative, artistically inferior and, therefore, vulnerable elements in their own ranks. But the protection of the literati was by no means the reason for the social ascent of the artist; it was rather itself merely a symptom of the development which followed from the fact that—as a consequence of the rise of new seigniories and principalities, on the one hand, and the growth and enriching of the towns, on the other—the disproportion between supply and demand on the art market became ever smaller and began to achieve a perfect balance. It is a well-known fact that the whole guild movement had its origin in the attempt to prevent such a disproportion in the interest of the producers; the guild authorities only connived at the infringement of their statutes when shortage of work no longer seemed a menace. The artists owed their independence not to the goodwill of the humanists, but to the fact that this danger became increasingly insignificant. They also desired the friendship of the humanists, not in order to break the resistance of the guilds, but to justify the economic position they had already won for themselves in the eyes of the humanistically-minded upper class and in order to enlist the scientific advisers, whose help they needed in their fashioning of marketable mythological and historical subjects. For the artists the humanists were the guarantors of their intellectual status, and the humanists themselves recognized the value of art as a means of propaganda for the ideas on which their own intellectual supremacy was based. It was this mutual relationship which first gave rise to that conception of the unity of the arts which we take for granted, but which was unknown before the Renaissance. Plato is not the only one to make a fundamental distinction between the visual arts and poetry; even in the later years of classical antiquity and the Middle Ages, it occurred to no one to assume that there was any closer relationship between art and poetry than there was between science and poetry or between philosophy and art.

Medieval literature on art was limited to recipe books. No hard-and-fast line of any kind was drawn between art and craft in these practical manuals. Even Cennino Cennini's treatise on painting was still dominated by the ideas of the guilds and based on the guild conception of excellence in craftsmanship; he exhorted the artists to be industrious, obedient and persevering, and saw in the "imitation" of the paragons the most certain way to mastery. All this was on the old medieval-tradition-alist lines. The replacing of the imitation of the masters by the study of nature is first accomplished theoretically by Leonardo da Vinci, but he was merely expressing the victory of naturalism and rationalism over tradition which had been won long since in practise. His theory of art, which is based on the study of nature, shows that in the interim the relationship between master and pupil has completely changed. The emancipation of art from the spirit of pure craftsmanship had to begin with the alteration of the old system of apprenticeship and the abolition of the teaching monopoly of the guilds. As long as the right to practise as a professional artist was conditional on apprenticeship under a guild master, neither the influence of the guilds nor the supremacy of the craft tradition could be broken.[17] The education of the rising generation in art had to be transferred from the workshop to the school, and practical had to yield partly to theoretical instruction, in order to remove the obstacles which the old system put in the way of young talent. Of course, the new system gradually created new ties and new obstacles. The process begins by the authority of the masters being replaced by the ideal of nature, and ends with the finished body of doctrine represented by academic instruction, in which the place of the old discredited models is taken by new, just as strictly limited, but from now on scientifically based ideals. Incidentally, the scientific method of art education begins in the workshops themselves. Already in the early Quattrocento apprentices are made familiar with the rudiments of geometry, perspective and anatomy in addition to the practical instruction, and introduced to drawing from life and from puppets. The masters organize courses in their workshops and this institution gives rise, on the one hand, to the private academies with their combination of practical and theoretical instruction,[18] and, on the other, to the public academies in which the old workshop community and craft tradition are abolished and replaced by a purely intellectual teacher-pupil relationship. Workshop instruction and the private academies maintain themselves through the whole Cinquecento, but they gradually lose their influence on the formation of style.

The scientific conception of art, which forms the basis of instruction in the academies, begins with Leon Battista Alberti. He is the first to express the idea that mathematics is the common ground of art and the sciences, as both the theory of proportions and of perspective are mathematical disciplines. He is also the first to give clear expression to that union of the experimental technician and the observing artist which had already been achieved in practise by Masaccio and Uccello.[19] Both try to comprehend the world empirically and to derive rational laws from this experience of the world; both endeavour to know and to control nature; both are distinguished from the purely contemplative, scholastically confined university teacher by reason of their creative activity—a *poiein*. But if the technician and the natural scientist now has a claim to be considered an intellectual on the basis of his mathematical knowledge, the artist, who is often identical with the technician and the scientist, may also well expect to be distinguished from the craftsman and to have the medium in which he expresses himself regarded as one of the "free arts."

Leonardo does not add any new basic ideas to Alberti's statements, in which art is raised to the stature of a science and the artist placed on a level with the humanist; he merely stresses and increases the claims of his predecessor. Painting, he maintains, is, on the one hand, a kind of exact natural science; on the other, it is superior to the sciences, for these are "imitable," that is, impersonal, whereas art is tied to the individual and his inborn abilities.[20] Leonardo, therefore, justifies the claim of painting to be considered one of the "free arts" not only on the basis of the artist's mathematical knowledge but also on account of his talent, which, according to Leonardo, is equal to that of the poetic genius. He renews the dictum attributed to Simonides, which refers to painting as a "silent poetry" and poetry as a "speaking painting," and he thereby opens

that long controversy about the order of precedence in the arts to which
Lessing was later to contribute. Leonardo thinks that if the muteness of
painting is regarded as a defect, then one might just as well speak of the
blindness of poetry.[21] An artist in closer touch with the humanists would
never have had the presumption to make such a heretical assertion.

A higher assessment of the value of painting, rising above the
medieval workmanlike point of view, is to be noted even in the early
forerunners of humanism. Dante erects an imperishable monument to
the masters Cimabue and Giotto (*Purg.* XI, 94/96), and compares them
with poets like Guido Guinicelli and Guido Cavalcanti. In his sonnets,
Petrarch praises the painter Simone Martini, and in his eulogy of Florence,
Filippo Villani also mentions several artists among the famous men of
the city. The *novelle* of the Italian Renaissance, above all those of Boccaccio and Sacchetti, contain a wealth of anecdotes about artists. And
although art itself plays the smallest part in these stories, it is characteristic that the artists as such seem to be interesting enough to the story-tellers
to warrant their being lifted out of the anonymous existence of the
ordinary craftsman and treated as individual personalities. The first half
of the Quattrocento already sees the beginnings of the artist's biography,
which is such a typical product of the Italian Renaissance. Brunelleschi
is the first artist to have his life written by a contemporary; such a
distinction had previously been confined to princes, heroes and saints.
Ghiberti writes the first autobiography which we possess by an artist. In
honour of Brunelleschi the commune has a sepulchral monument erected
in the Cathedral, and Lorenzo desires the remains of Filippo Lippi to be
brought home from Spoleto and to be buried with full honours. He is
told in reply, however, that it is regretted, but Spoleto is much poorer
in great men than Florence and his wish cannot, therefore, be fulfilled.
All this is the expression of an unmistakable shift of attention from the
works to the personality of the artist. Men begin to be conscious of
creative power in the modern sense and there are increasing signs of the
rising self-respect of the artist. We possess signatures of nearly all the
important painters of the Quattrocento, and Filarete actually expresses a
wish that all artists should sign their works. But even more characteristic than this custom is the fact that most of these painters also leave behind
self-portraits, although they are not always self-contained pictures. The
artists portray themselves and sometimes their family as well as bystanders
beside the founders and patrons, the Madonna and her saints. Thus on
a fresco in the church of S. Maria Novella, Ghirlandajo depicts his own
relations opposite the founder and his wife, and the city of Perugia even

commissions Perugino to put his self-portrait beside his frescoes in the Cambio. Gentile da Fabriano receives the patrician toga from the republic of Venice; the city of Bologna elects Francesco Francia to the office of Gonfaloniere; Florence bestows on Michelozzo the exalted title of Member of the Council.[22]

One of the most significant tokens of the new self-consciousness of artists and of their changed attitude to their own work is the fact that they begin to emancipate themselves from direct commissions, and, on the one hand, no longer carry out their orders with the old conscientiousness, and, on the other, often undertake artistic tasks of their own accord without any outside commission. Filippo Lippi is already known not always to have kept to the continuous and uniform rate which was the general rule in craft work and to have left certain commissions on one side for a time, in order to apply himself to others on the spur of the moment. After his time, we come across this rhapsodic method of working more and more frequently,[23] and in Perugino we already meet a spoilt "star" who treats his employers quite badly; neither in the Palazzo Vecchio nor in the Ducal Palace in Venice does he carry out the work he has taken on and he makes Orvieto wait so long for the promised painting of the Chapel of the Madonna in the Cathedral that the commune finally entrusts Signorelli with the execution of the work. The gradual ascent of the artist is mirrored most clearly of all in the career of Leonardo, who is, no doubt, esteemed in Florence but still not particularly busy there, who then becomes the pampered court painter of Ludovico Moro, and Cesare Borgia's first military engineer, whilst he ends his life as the favourite and intimate friend of the French king. The fundamental change occurs at the beginning of the Cinquecento. From then onwards the famous masters are no longer the protégés of patrons, but great lords themselves. According to Vasari, Raphael leads the life of a grand seigneur, not that of a painter; he resides in his own palace in Rome, associates with princes and cardinals as equals; Baldassare Castiglione and Agostino Chigi are his friends, a niece of Cardinal Bibbiena is his bride. And Titian climbs even higher up the social ladder. His reputation as the most sought-after master of his time, his way of life, his rank, his titles, raise him into the highest circles of society. Emperor Charles V appoints him a Count of the Lateran Palace and a member of the Imperial Court, makes him a Knight of the Golden Spur and bestows on him a whole series of privileges together with a hereditary nobility. Rulers make a great effort, often without success, to have their portraits painted by him; he has, as Aretino mentions, a princely income; every time he is painted by him, the Emperor gives him costly presents; his daughter Lavinia receives a magnificent dowry; Henry III pays the aged master a personal visit, and when he falls a victim to the plague in 1576, he is buried in the church of the Frari with the greatest honours the Republic can offer, in spite of the strict prohibition, otherwise always observed without exception, against burying a victim of the plague in a church. Michelangelo, finally, rises to absolutely unprecedented heights. His supremacy is so obvious that he can afford wholly to forego all public honours, titles and distinctions. He scorns the friendship of princes and popes; he can dare to be their opponent. He is neither a count, nor a state councillor, nor a papal superintendent, but he is called the "Divine." He does not wish to be described as a painter or sculptor in letters addressed to him: he says he is simply Michelangelo Buonarroti, no more and no less; he desires to have young noblemen as his pupils, and, in his case, this must not be ascribed simply to snobbery; he maintains that he paints "col cervello" and not "colla mano," and would like best of all to conjure forth the figures from the marble block by the mere magic of his vision. This is more than the artist's inborn pride, more than the consciousness of being superior to the craftsman, the mere mechanic, the philistine; it is really evidence of a fear of coming into contact with ordinary reality. He is the first example of the modern, lonely, demonically impelled artist—the first to be completely possessed by his idea and for whom nothing exists but his idea—who feels a deep sense of responsibility towards his gifts and sees a higher and superhuman power in his own artistic genius. A degree of sovereignty is attained here, in the light of which all earlier conceptions of artistic freedom fade into nothingness. Now, for the first time, the full emancipation of the artist is achieved; now, for the first time, he becomes the genius such as we have known him to be since the Renaissance. The final change is now accomplished: it is no longer his art, but the man himself who is the object of veneration and who becomes a vogue. The world, whose glory it was his task to proclaim, now proclaims his glory; the cult of which he was the instrument is now applied to him; the state of divine favour is now transferred from his patrons and protectors to himself. At all times there had really existed a certain reciprocity of praise between the hero and the artist who proclaimed his glory, between the patron and the artist;[24] the greater the fame of the panegyrist, the greater was the value of the glory which he proclaimed. But now the relationship is so sublimated that the patron is exalted by the very act of exalting the artist and praises the artist instead of being praised by him. Charles V stoops to recover the brush which Titian drops, and thinks that nothing is more natural than that a master like Titian should be waited on by an emperor. The legend of the artist is complete. There is doubtless still an element of coquetry about it: the artist is allowed to swim in the light, so that the patron can shine in the reflection. But will the reciprocity of appreciation and praise, the mutual valuation and rewarding of services, the mutual protection of the other's interest, ever wholly cease? At the most, it will only become more veiled.

The fundamentally new element in the Renaissance conception of art is the discovery of the concept of genius, and the idea that the work of art is the creation of an autocratic personality, that this personality transcends tradition, theory and rules, even the work itself, is richer and deeper than the work and impossible to express adequately within any objective form. This idea remained foreign to the Middle Ages, which recognized no independent value in intellectual originality and spontaneity, recommended the imitation of the masters and considered plagiarism permissible, and which was, at the most, superficially touched but in no sense dominated by the idea of intellectual competition. The idea of genius as a gift of God, as an inborn and uniquely individual creative force, the doctrine of the personal and exceptional law which the genius is not only permitted to but must follow, the justification of the individuality and wilfulness of the artist of genius—this whole trend of thought first arises in Renaissance society, which, owing to its dynamic nature and permeation with the idea of competition, offers the individual better opportunities than the authoritarian culture of the Middle Ages, and which, owing to the increased need for publicity felt by the holders of power, creates a greater demand in the art market than the supply had had to meet in the past. But just as the modern idea of competition reaches back deep into the Middle Ages, so the medieval idea of art as determined by objective, superpersonal factors continues to have an after-effect for a long time and the subjectivist conception of artistic activity makes only very slow progress even after the end of the Middle Ages. The individualistic conception of the Renaissance, therefore, requires correction in two directions. Burckhardt's thesis is not, however, to be dismissed out of hand, for if strong personalities already existed in the Middle Ages,[25] yet to think and act individually is one thing and to be conscious of one's individuality, to affirm and deliberately to intensify it, is another. One cannot speak of individualism in the modern sense of the term until a reflexive individual consciousness takes the place of a mere individual reaction. The self-recollection of individuality does not begin until the Renaissance, but the Renaissance does not itself begin with the self-recollecting individuality. The expression of personality in art had been sought after and appreciated long before anyone had realized that art was based no longer on an objective What but on a subjective How. Long after it had become a self-confession, people still continued to talk about the objective truth in art, although it was precisely the self-expressionism in art which enabled it to win through to general recognition. The power of personality, the intellectual energy and spontaneity of the individual, is the great experience of the Renaissance; genius as the embodiment of this energy and spontaneity becomes the ideal, in which it finds the supreme expression of the nature of the human mind and its power over reality.

The development of the concept of genius begins with the idea of intellectual property. In the Middle Ages both this conception and the desire for originality are lacking; both are directly interrelated. As long as art is nothing but the representation of the Divine and the artist only the medium through which the eternal, supernatural order of things is made visible, there can be no question of autonomy in art nor of the artist actually owning his work. The obvious suggestion is to connect the idea of intellectual property with the beginnings of capitalism, but to do so would only be misleading. The idea of intellectual productivity and intellectual property follows from the disintegration of Christian culture. As soon as religion ceases to control and unite within itself all the spheres of spiritual life, the idea of the autonomy of the various forms of intellectual expression appears, and an art which bears its meaning and purpose within itself becomes conceivable. In spite of all attempts to base the whole of culture, including art, on religion, no later age has ever succeeded in restoring the cultural unity of the Middle Ages and depriving art of its autonomy. Even when it is placed in the service of extra-artistic purposes, art now remains enjoyable and significant in itself. But if one ceases to regard the separate intellectual moulds as so many different forms of one and the same truth, then the idea also occurs of making their individuality and originality the criterion of their value. The Trecento is still completely under the spell of *one* master—Giotto—and of his tradition; but in the Quattrocento individualistic efforts begin to make their mark in all directions. Originality becomes a weapon in the competitive struggle. The social process now seizes on an instrument which it has not itself produced, but which it adapts to its purposes and of which it heightens the effectiveness. As long as the opportunities on the art market remain favourable for the artist, the cultivation of individuality does not develop into a mania for originality—this does not happen until the age of mannerism, when new conditions on the art market create painful economic disturbances for the artist. But the ideal of the "original genius" itself does not appear until the eighteenth century, when, in the transition from private patronage to the free, unprotected market, artists have to wage a sterner fight for their material existence than ever before.

The most important step in the development of the concept of the genius is from the idea of actual achievement to that of the mere capacity to achieve, from the work to the person of the artist, from the appreciation of full success to that of mere intention and idea. This step could only have been taken by an age which had come to regard a personal style as interesting and instructive in itself. The fact that the Quattrocento already contained certain preconditions of this attitude is shown by a passage in Filarete's treatise, where the forms of a work of art are compared to the pen-strokes of a manuscript, which immediately betray the hand of the writer.[26] The appreciation of and growing fondness for drawings, rough drafts, sketches, the *bozzetto,* for the unfinished work generally, is a further step in the same direction. The origin of the taste for the fragment is likewise to be found in the subjectivist conception of art based on the idea of the genius; the philosophy of art developed by a study of classical torsi merely intensified it. For the Renaissance, the drawing and the sketch became momentous not merely as artistic forms, but also as documents and records of the creative process in art; they were recognized to be a particular form of expression on their own, distinct from the finished work; they were valued because they revealed the process of artistic invention at its starting point, where it was almost completely merged with the subjectivity of the artist. Vasari mentions that Uccello left behind so many drawings that they filled whole chests. From the Middle Ages, on the contrary, hardly any drawings have come down to us. Apart from the fact that the medieval artist certainly did not ascribe the same importance to his momentary brain-waves as did later masters, and probably did not consider it worth while to record every fleeting idea, the reason for the rarity of extant medieval drawings may well be the fact that drawing only became widespread when usable and reasonably priced stocks of paper became available[27] and that only a comparatively small proportion of the drawings actually done have survived. Old age is certainly not the only reason for their disappearance; it is obvious that less importance was attached to their preservation than later, and the whole difference between the art philosophy of the Middle Ages with its matter-of-fact, objective ways of thought and that of the subjectivistic Renaissance is cogently expressed in the medieval lack of interest in drawings. For the Middle Ages the value of the work of art was purely objective, whereas the Renaissance also attributed a personal value to it. The drawing became the direct formula of artistic creation, for it gave the most striking expression possible to the fragmentary, uncompleted and uncompletable element which adheres, in the final analysis, to every work of art. The raising of the mere capacity for achievement above the achievement itself, this fundamental feature of the concept of the genius, means that genius is regarded as not wholly realizable, and this explains why the incomplete drawing is considered a typical form of art.

It was only one step from the inability of the genius to communicate himself fully, to the misunderstood genius and to the appeal to posterity against the verdict of the contemporary world. The Renaissance never made this step. Not because it had more understanding of art than later ages against whose judgement unsuccessful artists have appealed, but because the artist's struggle for existence was still expressed in relatively harmless forms. Nevertheless, the concept of the genius already acquires certain dialectical characteristics; it already allows us a glimpse of the defensive machinery which the artist was to set in motion later on against the philistine to whom art is a closed book, on the one hand, and against the bunglers and dilettanti, on the other. Against the first named he was to shelter behind the mask of the eccentric, and against the latter he was to emphasize the inborn quality of his talent and the fact that art cannot be acquired by learning. Francisco de Hollanda already remarks in his *Conversations on Painting* (1548) that every important personality has something peculiar about him, and the idea that the genuine artist must be born was not even completely new at that time. The theory of the inspired quality of the genius, of the super-personal and irrational nature of his performance, shows that it is an intellectual aristocracy which is in process of constitution here, an aristocracy which prefers to forego personal merit, *virtù*, in the sense in which the early Renaissance used the term, in order to define itself the more sharply against others.

The autonomy of art gives expression in an objective form—from the standpoint of the work—to the same idea which the concept of the genius expresses in a subjective form—from the standpoint of the artist. The idea that cultural forms are independent of external laws is the counterpart of the idea of the spontaneity of the mind. On the other hand, the autonomy of art signifies for the Renaissance merely independence of the Church and of the metaphysics propounded by the Church, it does not imply an absolute and universal autonomy. Art emancipates itself from ecclesiastical dogmas, but remains closely connected with the scientific philosophy of the age, just as the artist breaks away from the clergy but enters all the more intimately into relationship with the humanists and their followers. But art is far from becoming a servant of science in the sense in which it was the "servant of theology" in the Middle Ages. It is and remains rather a sphere in which it is possible, in seclusion from the rest of the world, to organize one's intellectual life and indulge in intellectual pleasures of a quite peculiar kind. As one moves about in this world of art, one is separated both from the transcendent world of faith and from the world of practical affairs. Art can be made to serve the purposes of faith and be given problems to solve which are also the concern of science, but whatever extra-artistic functions it fulfils, it can always be considered as if it were itself its own object. This is the new point of view which the Middle Ages was not yet able and prepared to make its own. It does not mean, however, that before the Renaissance there was no feeling for and no enjoyment of the formal quality of a work of art, only such feeling and enjoyment was still unconscious and the work of art was judged, as soon as the transition had been made from a purely emotional to a conscious reaction, according to the intellectual content and symbolical value of the representation. The medieval interest in art was confined to the subject-matter, and it was not only in contemporary Christian art that the attention was concentrated on the meaning of the contents of the work, for even classical art was judged purely according to its spiritual content.[28] The change in the Renaissance attitude to classical art and literature is to be ascribed not to the discovery of new works and new authors, but to the transference of interest from the material content to the formal elements of the representation, whether it was a question of newly discovered or already familiar monuments, made no difference.[29] It is typical of the new attitude that the public now adopted the artistic approach of the artists themselves, and judged art not from the standpoint of life and religion but from that of art itself. Medieval art aimed at interpreting life and elevating man, Renaissance art at enriching life and delighting man. To the empirical and the transcendental sphere of life to which the medieval world was restricted, it added a new province, in which both the secular and metaphysical prototypes of existence acquired a new and hitherto undreamt-of meaning of their own.

The idea of an autonomous, non-utilitarian art, enjoyable in itself, was already familiar to the classical age; after being forgotten in the Middle Ages, it was simply rediscovered by the Renaissance. But it had never occurred to anyone before the Renaissance that a life devoted to the enjoyment of art might represent a higher and nobler form of existence. Plotinus and the Neoplatonists had ascribed a higher purpose to art, but had, at the same time, deprived it of its autonomy and made it a mere vehicle of intelligible knowledge. The idea of an art preserving the autonomy of its aesthetic nature and becoming an educational force despite its independence of the rest of the intellectual world, in fact merely as a result of its sovereign beauty, an idea already foreshadowed by Petrarch,[30] is just as unmedieval as it is unclassical. The whole aestheticism of the Renaissance is unmedieval and unclassical, for even though the application to life itself of the standpoint and standards of art was not wholly foreign to classical antiquity, yet it would be impossible to find a parallel in any other age to the episode reported from the Renaissance of a believer refusing to kiss a crucifix handed to him on his death-bed because it was ugly and asking for a more beautiful one.[31]

The Renaissance conception of aesthetic autonomy is not a purist idea; the artist strives to emancipate himself from the fetters of scholastic thinking, but he is not particularly eager to stand on his own feet and it does not occur to him to make the independence of art a question of principle. On the contrary, he stresses the scientific nature of his intellectual activity. Not until the Cinquecento are the bonds uniting science and art into one homogeneous organ of knowledge loosened; not until then does the idea of the autonomy of art begin to imply that art is also independent of the world of science and learning. There are periods when art is turned in the direction of science, just as there are periods when science is turned in the direction of art. In the early Renaissance the truth of art is made dependent on scientific criteria, whilst in the later Renaissance and in the baroque scientific thinking is in many cases shaped in accordance with artistic principles. The perspective in painting of the Quattrocento is a scientific conception, whereas the Universum of Kepler and Galileo is a fundamentally aesthetic vision. Dilthey is right when he speaks of the "artistic imagination" in the scientific research of the Renaissance,[32] but one could speak with equal justification of the "scientific imagination" in the artistic creation of the early Renaissance.

The prestige of the scholar and the scientist in the Quattrocento was not attained again until the nineteenth century. In both epochs all efforts were concentrated on promoting the expansion of industry and trade by new ways and means, by new scientific methods and technical inventions. This partly explains the primacy of science and the reputation of the scientist in both the fifteenth and the nineteenth centuries. What Adolf Hildebrand and Bernard Berenson understand by "form" in the plastic arts[33] is, like Alberti's and Piero della Francesca's concept of perspective, more a theoretical than an aesthetic conception. Both categories are signposts in the world of sense experience, means towards the elucidation of spatial relationships, instruments of optical knowledge. The aesthetic philosophy of the nineteenth century can no more hide the theoretical character of its foundations than can the Renaissance the predominantly scientific nature of its interest in the external world. In the spatial values of Hildebrand, the geometrism of Cézanne, the physiological interests of the impressionists, the psychological interests of the whole of modern novel and drama, wherever we turn, we perceive a striving to find one's way about in the world of empirical reality, to explain the world as presented to us by nature, to multiply, to introduce order into and to work up into a rational system the data of sense experience. For the nineteenth century, art is an instrument of knowledge of the external world, a form of living experience, and of the analysis and interpretation of man. But this naturalism directed towards objective knowledge has its origin precisely in the fifteenth century; it was then that art underwent its first course of scientific training, and even today it is still living to some extent on the capital invested at that time. Mathematics and geometry, optics and mechanics, the theory of light and colour, anatomy and physiology were its tools, and the nature of space, the structure of the human body, movement and proportion, studies of drapery and experiments with colours were the problems with which it was concerned. That, for all its scholarliness, the fidelity to nature of the Quattrocento was merely a fiction is best seen from that means of expression, which may be regarded as the most concise epitome of Renaissance art: the central perspective used in the reproduction of space. Perspective was in itself no invention of the Renaissance.[34] Even classical antiquity was familiar with foreshortening and reduced the size of individual objects according to their distance from the spectator; but it was not acquainted with the representation of space based on uniform perspective and directed to one optical point, neither was it able or eager to represent the different objects and the space-intervals between them continuatively. The space in its pictorial representations was a compositum made up of disparate parts, not a uniform continuum—in the words of Panovsky, it was an "aggregate space," not a "systematic space." Only since the Renaissance has painting been based on the assumption that the space in which things exists is an infinite, continuous and homogeneous element, and that we usually see things uniformly, that is to say, with a single and motionless eye.[35] But what we actually perceive is a limited, discontinuous and heterogeneously compacted space. Our impression of space is distorted and blurred at the edges in reality, its content is divided into more or less independent groups and pieces, and, since our physiologically conditioned field of vision is spheroid, we see, to some extent, curves instead of straight lines. The picture of space based on planimetric perspective such as Renaissance art presents us with, characterized by the equal clarity and the consistent shaping of all parts, the common vanishing point of the parallels and the uniform module of distance measurement, the picture which L. B. Alberti defined as the transverse section of the optical pyramid, is a daring abstraction. Central perspective produces a mathematically accurate but psycho-physiologically impossible representation of space. This completely rationalized conception could appear to be the adequate reproduction of the actual optical impression only to such a thoroughly scientific period as the centuries between the Renaissance and the end of the nineteenth century. Uniformity and consistency were in fact the highest criteria of truth during the whole of this period. It is only in recent times that we have again become aware of the fact that we see reality not in the form of a consistently organized and unified space, but rather in scattered groups from different visual centres, and that, as our eye moves from one group to another, we add together the total panorama of a more extensive complex from partial views of the whole, just as Lorenzetti did in his great mural paintings in Siena. At any rate, the discontinuous representation of space in these frescoes makes a more convincing impression today than the pictures drawn according to the rules of central perspective by the masters of the Quattrocento.[36]

The versatility of talent, and especially the union of art and science in one person, has been felt to be particularly characteristic of the Renaissance. But the fact that artists were masters of several different techniques, that Giotto, Orcagna, Brunelleschi, Benedetto da Majano, Leonardo da Vinci, were architects, sculptors and painters, Pisanello, Antonio Pollajuolo, Verrocchio, sculptors, painters, goldsmiths and medallists, that, in spite of advancing specialization, Raphael was still both a painter and an architect, and Michelangelo a sculptor, painter and architect at the same time, is connected more with the craft-like character of the visual arts than with the Renaissance ideal of versatility. Encyclopaedic learning and practical versatility are in fact medieval ideals; the Quattrocento takes them over along with the tradition of craftsmanship and abandons them to the same extent as it abandons the spirit of craftsmanship. In the later Renaissance we more and more seldom meet artists practising different kinds of art at the same time. But with the victory of the humanistic conception of culture, the idea of the *uomo universale,* an intellectual tendency opposed to specialization, comes to the fore again and leads to the cult of a type of versatility which is more akin to the dilettante than the craftsman. At the end of the Quattrocento both tendencies vie with each other. On the one side, the universalism of the humanistic ideal, suited to meet the requirements of the upper classes, reigns supreme. Under its influence the artist tries to supplement his manual skill with knowledge of an intellectual and cultural kind. On the other side, the principle of the division of labour and specialization is triumphant and gradually attains supreme power even in the field of art. Cardano already points out that to be occupied with several different things at the same time undermines the reputation of a cultured man. As opposed to the tendency to specialize, reference must be made above all to the remarkable fact that of the leading architects of the High Renaissance only Antonio da Sangallo had prepared himself for the career; Bramante was originally a painter, Raphael and Peruzzi continued to combine painting with architecture, and Michelangelo is and remains above all a sculptor. The fact that the architectural profession was taken up comparatively so late in life and that many of the masters received a predominantly theoretical training for it shows, on the one hand, how quickly practical education had been superseded by intellectual and academic education, and, on the other, how architecture becomes to some extent the pastime of an amateur. At all times the grand seigneur has in fact been fond of acting not merely as a patron but also as a dilettante architect.

Ghiberti needed several decades to complete the doors of the Baptistry and Luca della Robbia also spent nearly ten years on his Cantoria for the Cathedral in Florence. On the other hand, Ghirlandajo's method of working is already characterized by the *fa presto* technique of the genius, and Vasari sees a direct token of genuine artistic talent in ease and speed of production.[37] Both elements, dilettantism and virtuosity, contradictory as they are in themselves, are united in the humanist, who has been rightly described as the "virtuoso of the intellectual life," but one might describe him equally well as the unspoilt and eternally youthful dilettante. Both elements are contained in the ideal of personality which the humanists are concerned to realize; but in their paradoxical union there is expressed the problematical nature of the intellectual life led by the humanists with its roots in the concept of the literary profession itself, of which they are the first representatives—the concept of a professional class which claims to be perfectly independent but is in fact tied in many ways. The Italian writers of the fourteenth century still came very largely from the higher classes of society; they were members of the urban aristocracy or the sons of well-to-do bourgeois. Cavalcanti and Cino da Pistoja were of noble extraction, Petrarch was a notary's son, Brunetto Latini was himself a notary, Villani and Sacchetti were prosperous merchants, Boccaccio and Sercambi the sons of rich merchants. These writers had hardly anything in common with the medieval minstrels.[38] But the humanists belong neither to a class-determined, nor to a culturally and professionally uniform social category, they include clerics and laymen, rich and poor, high officials and minor notaries, merchants and schoolmasters, lawyers and scholars.[39] The representatives of the lower classes come, however, to form an ever-increasing proportion of their total numbers. The most famous, most influential of all of them is the son of a shoemaker. They are all town-born and bred—this is, at any rate, one characteristic which they share; many of them are the children of poor parents, some of them child prodigies, who, intended for a promising and highly attractive career, find themselves in unusual circumstances from the very start. Exaggerated ambitions aroused early in life, years of exacting study, often involving economic hardship, of struggle in tutorial and secretarial work, the search for position and fame, friendships with the great, jealousy-ridden animosities, cheap successes and undeserved failures, overwhelming honours and admiration, on the one hand, and vagabondage on the other—all these experiences could not fail to have an influence and inflict great moral injury on them. The social conditions of the age offered opportunities to a man of letters and threatened him with dangers which were apt to poison the spirit of a gifted young man from the outset.

The precondition of the rise of humanism as a, theoretically, free literary profession was the existence of a comparatively broad propertied class, able to provide a ready-made literary public. It is true that from the very beginning the most important centres of the humanist movement were the courts and state chancelleries, but most of its supporters were well-to-do merchants and other elements who had acquired money and influence through the rise of capitalism. The works of medieval literature were still intended only for a very limited circle, consisting usually of people already well known to the writers; the humanists are the first authors to address themselves to a broader and to some extent unknown public. Something in the nature of a free literary market and a public opinion conditioned and influenced by literature has only existed since their time. Their speeches and pamphlets are the first forms of modern journalism; their letters, which circulated amongst a relatively wide public, were the newspapers of their day.[40] Aretino is the "first journalist" and, at the same time, the first blackmailing journalist. The freedom to which he owes his existence first became possible in an age in which the writer was no longer absolutely dependent on a single patron or a strictly limited circle of patrons, but had so many potential customers for his products that he no longer needed to be on good terms with all of them. But, after all, it was only a comparatively small educated class on whom the humanists could rely for their public, and, compared with the modern man of letters, they still led a parasitical life, unless they had private means and were, therefore, independent from the very start. They were usually dependent on the favour of the courts and the patronage of influential citizens, whom they normally served as secretaries or private tutors. They drew salaries from the state, pensions and benefices instead of the old board and lodging and donations—their rather costly maintenance was regarded by the new élite as one of the inevitable expenses in the up-keep of an elegant household. Instead of a court singer or fool, a private historian or professional panegyrist, the gentleman of private means now kept a humanist in the house, but the services he performed, though the forms it took were somewhat sublimated, were in fact very much the same. On the other hand, more was expected of him than the mere performance of these services. For, just as the upper bourgeoisie had formerly allied itself with the hereditary aristocracy, it now wanted to enter into relation-ship with the intellectual aristocracy. Through the first great alliance it acquired a share in the privileges of noble birth, through the second it was to become intellectually ennobled.

Labouring under the misapprehension that they were intellectu-ally free, the humanists were bound to feel their dependence on the ruling class humiliating. Patronage, that age-old and unproblematical institution, which was one of the things a poet of the Middle Ages took for granted, became a problem and a danger for the humanists. The relationship of the intelligentsia to property and wealth assumed increasingly complicated forms. To begin with, the humanists shared the stoical view of the wander-ing scholars and mendicant friars and regarded wealth in itself as valueless. As long as they were merely students, teachers and literati, they did not feel themselves called upon to change this opinion, but when they came into closer touch with the propertied class, an insoluble conflict arose between their former views and their new way of life.[41] It did not occur at all to the Greek sophist, the Roman rhetor, or the medieval cleric to move outside his fundamentally contemplative position in life, which engaged him in nothing more practical than educational work, and to compete with the ruling classes. The humanists are the first intellectuals to claim the privileges of property and rank, and intellectual arrogance, likewise a hitherto un-known phenomenon, is the psychological weapon of self-defence with which they react against their lack of success. The humanists are first en-couraged and promoted in their ambitious strivings by the upper classes but are nevertheless finally held down. From the very outset, there is mu-tual suspicion between the arrogant cultured class, fighting against all external ties, and the matter-of-fact, fundamentally unintellectual business class.[42] For just as the dangers of the Sophistic way of thinking had been felt acutely in the age of Plato, so now, too, the upper class is, for all its sympathy for the humanist movement, full of unconcealable suspicion against the humanists, who do in fact constitute a destructive element on account of their rootlessness.

The latent conflict between the intellectual and the economic upper class is nowhere openly engaged as yet, least of all by the artists, who, with their less developed social consciousness, react more slowly than their humanistic masters. But the problem, even if it is unadmitted and unexpressed, is present all the time and in all places, and the whole intelligentsia, both literary and artistic, is threatened by the danger of developing either into an uprooted, "unbourgeois" and envious class of bohemians or into a conservative, passive, cringing class of academics. The humanists escape from this alternative into their ivory tower, and finally succumb to both the dangers which they had intended to avoid. They are followed in this by the whole modern aesthetic movement, which, like them, becomes uprooted and passive at the same time, serving the interests of conservatism without being able to adapt itself to the order which it supports. By independence the humanist understands the lack of ties; his social disinterestedness is really an alienation from society; and his escape from the present is irresponsibility. He abstains from all political activity, in order not to tie himself down, but by his passivity he only confirms the holders of power. This is the real "trahison des clercs," the betrayal of intellectual values by the intelligentsia, not the politicization of the spirit, for which it has been blamed in recent times.[43] The humanist loses touch with reality, he becomes a romantic who calls his estrangement from the world aloofness, his social indifference intellectual freedom, his bohemian way of thinking moral sovereignty. "The meaning of life for him is"—as an expert on the Renaissance has put it—"to write a choice prose style, to shape exquisite stanzas, to translate from Greek into Latin. . . . What is essential to his mind is not that the Gauls should have been conquered, but that commentaries have been written about their having been conquered . . . the beauty of the deed yields to the beauty of the style. . . ."[44] The artists of the Renaissance are by no means so alienated from their contemporaries as the humanists, but their intellectual existence is already undermined, and they no longer succeed in finding the adjustment which enabled them to adapt themselves to the structure of medieval society. They stand at the crossroads between activism and aestheticism. Or have they already made their choice? At any rate, they have lost the connection between artistic forms and extra-artistic purposes, a simply and absolutely unproblematical reality taken for granted by the Middle Ages.

The humanists are, however, not merely non-political aesthetes, idle speechifyers and romantic escapists, but also enthusiastic world-reformers, fanatical pioneers of progress and, above all, tireless pedagogues, rejoicing in the future. The painters and sculptors of the Renaissance owe them not only their abstract aestheticism, but also the idea of the artist as an intellectual hero and the conception of art as the educator of humanity. They were the first to make art an ingredient of intellectual and moral culture.

2/

THE DIVINITY
OF THE PAINTER

"If the painter wishes to see beauties to fall in love with, he is master of producing them; and if he wishes to see monstrous things to terrify, or clownish and ridiculous things, or things that are truly moving, he is lord and god thereof. . . . The deity that resides in the science of the painter causes the mind of the painter to transform itself into a similitude of the divine mind, since it proceeds with free power to generate the diverse essences of various animals, plants, fruits, landscapes, plains, ruins of mountains, tremendous fearful lakes that inspire terror in those who look upon them, and likewise pleasant, gentle, and delightful places, variegated meadows moved in gentle waves by gentle motions of the winds, looking back at the winds that fly from them . . ."

—from Leonardo's *Treatise on Painting*,
folios 13 and 68

The Nature of His "Classic" Art

by Heinrich Wölfflin

F ALL RENAISSANCE ARTISTS, Leonardo was the one who most enjoyed the world. All phenomena captivated him—physical life and human emotions, the forms of plants and animals, the sight of the crystal-clear stream with the pebbles in its bed. To him, the one-sidedness of the mere figure-painter was incomprehensible.

> Do you not see how many and how varied are the actions which are performed by men alone? Do you not see how many different kinds of animals there are, and also of trees and plants and flowers? What variety of hilly and level places, of springs, rivers, cities, public and private buildings; of instruments fitted for man's use; of divers costumes, ornaments and arts?[1]

He is a born aristocrat among painters, sensitive to delicacy, with a feeling for fine hands, for the charm of transparent stuffs, for smooth skin, and above all, he loves beautiful, soft, rippling hair. In Verrocchio's *Baptism* he painted a few tufts of grasses, and one sees at once that they were painted by him, for no one else had quite this feeling for the natural grace of growing things. The strong and the soft are equally his province. If he paints a battle, he surpasses all others in the expression of unchained passions and tumultuous movement, yet he can catch the most tender emotion and fix the most fleeting expression. In single "character" heads he shows himself the most uncompromising of realists, and then suddenly he flings all that aside and loses himself in visions of ideal faces of almost

From *Classic Art* by Heinrich Wölfflin, tr. by Peter and Linda Murray from the eighth German ed. (New York: Phaidon Publishers, 1952).

unearthly beauty, dreaming of sweet, soft smiles, which seem reflections of an inner radiance. He discovered the painterly charm of the surfaces of things and yet he can think as a physicist and an anatomist. Qualities which seem mutually exclusive are combined in him: the tireless observation and collection of data of the student, and the most subtle artistic perception. As a painter, he is never content to accept things merely by their outward appearance: he throws himself into investigating, with the same passionate interest, inner structure and the factors governing the life of every created thing. He was the first artist to make a systematic study of proportion in men and animals and to investigate the mechanics of movements like walking, lifting, climbing, pulling, and it was he, too, who made the most comprehensive physiognomical studies and thought out a coherent system for the expression of emotions.

For him, the painter is like a clear eye which surveys the world and takes all visible things for its domain. Suddenly the world revealed itself in all its inexhaustible riches and Leonardo seems to have felt himself united by a great love to all living things. Vasari tells a story which reveals this: he was sometimes seen in the market-place, buying caged birds that he might give them back their freedom. This incident seems to have impressed the Florentines.

In so universal an art there are no major and minor problems; the ultimate subtleties of light and shade are not more interesting than the most elementary task—the rendering of a three-dimensional object in apparent solidity on a flat surface—and the artist who, more than any other, made the human face a mirror of the soul can still say, "Relief is the principal aim and the soul of painting." Leonardo was so sensitive to so many more aspects of things that he was forced to seek new technical methods. He became an experimenter who could scarcely satisfy himself. He is said to have allowed the *Mona Lisa* to leave his studio before he considered it to be finished. Technically, she is a mystery, but even where the medium is obvious, as in the simple silver-point drawings, he is no less astounding. He is perhaps the first to use line with expressive sensibility and there are almost no parallels for the way in which his contours are made up of touches of varying firmness. He models with simple, parallel, even strokes; it is as if he needed only to stroke the surface to bring out the roundness of the form. Never have simpler means been used to greater effect, and the parallel lines, like those which occur in older Italian engravings, give an inestimable unity of effect to the drawings.[2]

We have but few completed works by Leonardo. He was untiring in observation and insatiable in his search for knowledge, he continually set himself fresh problems, yet it seems as if he wished to solve them only for himself. He could never bring himself to a definite conclusion or to finish off a picture, and the problems which he set himself were so far-reaching that he may well have felt that his solutions were only provisional.

1. THE LAST SUPPER

After Raphael's *Sistine Madonna*, Leonardo's *Last Supper* is the most popular picture in the whole of Italian art. It is so simple and expressive that it impresses itself upon everyone. Christ is at the centre of a long table, with the Disciples disposed equally on either side of Him. He has said, "One of you shall betray me," and the unexpected words have thrown the gathering into an uproar. He alone remains calm, His eyes downcast, and in His silence lies the repeated, "Verily I say unto you, that one of you shall betray me." One feels that there is no other possible way of depicting the event, and yet *everything* in Leonardo's picture is new, and the very simplicity is a triumph of the highest art. If we look around for Quattrocento prototypes, we find a good example in Ghirlandaio's *Last Supper* in Ognissanti, dated 1480 and, therefore, about fifteen years earlier. This picture, one of the master's best works, retains the typical older elements of the composition, the scheme which was handed down to Leonardo: the table with projecting ends, Judas isolated on the near side, the other twelve in a row on the far side, with St. John asleep beside the Lord, one arm on the table. Christ's right hand is raised, and He speaks, but the announcement of treachery must already have been made, for the Disciples are grief-stricken. Some protest their innocence, and Peter challenges Judas.

To begin with, Leonardo has broken with tradition in two ways. He takes Judas from his isolated position and places him in the same row as the others, and then he emancipates himself from the traditional motive of St. John lying on the Lord's breast—where he is usually shown asleep—a pose which is bound to become awkward when combined with the "modern" seated position at table. In this way, he obtains greater unity in the scene, and the Disciples can be split into two symmetrical groups on either side of the Saviour; in this he is governed by the need for an architectonic arrangement. He goes still further, and forms smaller groups—two groups of three on each side, left and right—and thus Christ becomes the dominating central figure, unlike any of the others. Ghirlandaio's picture is a gathering without centre, with more or less independent half-length figures set one beside another, confined between the two great horizontals of table and wall, with its cornice hard above their heads. Unfortunately, a console supporting the roof projects in the centre of the wall. What does Ghirlandaio do? Without allowing it to embarrass him, he calmly moves his Christ to one side. Leonardo, to whom the emphasis on the central figure was of cardinal importance, would never have tolerated such a console. On the contrary, he uses the background to help him towards his goal, and it is through no coincidence that Christ sits framed in the light opening of the door at the back. Next, he breaks away from the limitations of the two horizontal lines; naturally, he retains the table, but above it the silhouettes of the groups must be allowed free play, so that quite new emotional effects are created. The perspective of the room, the shape and decoration of the walls are harnessed to the effect of the figures, everything is subordinated to their plasticity and scale—hence the depth of the room, and the dividing up of the walls by single hangings. The overlapping forms increase the plastic illusion and the repeated verticals accentuate the diverging movements. It is noticeable that these surfaces and lines are all small so that they cannot seriously compete with the figures, while a painter of the older generation, such as Ghirlandaio, sets a scale, with his great arches in the background, which is bound to make the figures look small.[3]

As we saw, Leonardo retained only one great line, the indispensable one of the table, yet even here there is something new. I do not mean the omission of the projecting ends—he is not the first to do that; the innovation lies in having the courage to depict a physical impossibility in order to obtain a heightened effect. The table is far too small. If the covers are counted it is clear that all the people there could not have sat down. Leonardo wishes to avoid the effect of the Disciples lost behind a long table, and the impression made by the figures is so strong that no one notices the lack of space. Only thus was it possible to arrange the figures in closed groups and yet keep them in contact with the principal figure. And what groups, what gestures these are! The words of Our Lord have struck like a thunderbolt and a storm of emotion has broken out: the Apostles comport themselves, not without dignity, but like men who are about to be deprived of their most treasured possession. An immense fund of new expression is added to art, and although Leonardo does not lose touch with his predecessors, it is the unheard-of intensity of expression which makes his figures appear to have no parallels. When such forces are brought into play, it is obvious that many of the subordinate interests of earlier art must be omitted. Ghirlandaio had to deal with a public which would examine every detail with attention, which had to be regaled with rare plants, birds and other animals, and he paid particular attention to the setting of the table, even counting out so many cherries to each of the company. Leonardo contents himself with the essentials. He may reasonably expect that the dramatic content of the picture will distract the spectator from such minor curiosities. Later, others carried this simplification even further.

This is not the place to describe the motives of each figure in detail, but something must be said of the economy which governed the distribution of the roles. The end figures are calm: two profiles enclosing the whole scene, and both quite vertical. Their tranquillity extends to the second members of the groups, and then the movement begins, increasing within the groups at either side of Christ, whose left-hand neighbour throws his arms wide apart "as if he saw the earth opening at his feet," and at His right hand, quite close to Him, Judas draws sharply back.[4] The sharpest contrasts are juxtaposed: Judas sits in the same group as St. John.

The contrasted arrangement of the groups, as well as the relationship subsisting between them—on the one side, the connecting links approach the front plane, on the other they are developed in depth— involve the kind of analysis which will continually occupy the student, and all the more so, as the calculations underlying them are concealed by the apparent simplicity of the arrangement. Indeed, they are of only secondary importance, compared to the one great effect reserved for the main figure. In the centre of all the tumult, Christ is quite still, His hands spread listlessly out as one who has said all there is to say. Unlike the older pictures, He is not represented as speaking, He does not even look up, but the silence is more eloquent than any words. It is the fearful silence which leaves no room for hope. In the face and gesture of Christ there is a calmness and greatness which may be called aristocratic, in so far as aristocratic has the meaning of noble; a word which cannot be applied to any painter of the Quattrocento. It would almost seem that Leonardo had made his studies from a different type of humanity, did we not know that he created the type himself. He has here drawn on the best in his own nature, and in any case, this air of greatness was to become the common property of the Italians of the sixteenth century. From Holbein onwards, what trouble the Germans took to acquire the magic of such a bearing! Yet, it must be insisted, that which makes the figure of Christ appear so different from all earlier representations is not to be explained solely by His face and gesture, but, even more essentially, by His role within the composition as a whole. In the earlier masters, the unity of the scene is lacking: the Apostles converse among themselves while Christ is speaking, and it is not always clear whether the scene depicted is the announcement of treachery or the Institution of the Eucharist. In any case, it was quite beyond the horizon of Quattrocento thought to make the silence following speech the motive of the principal figure. Leonardo was the first to venture this, and, by doing so, he reaps the infinite advantage that he can sustain the keynote for as long as he wishes: the original impulse to the emotional excitement continues to echo, and the action is at once momentary, eternal and complete.

Only Raphael understood Leonardo in this. There is a *Last Supper* from his School, engraved by Marcantonio,[5] where Christ is depicted at a psychologically similar moment, staring, motionless, into space, His eyes wide open and looking out of the picture, His head a pure vertical, and the only one in the picture which is seen from the front.

Andrea del Sarto falls below this level, in a composition (Florence, S. Salvi), which has some fine passages of painting, when he chose the moment at which the traitor is made known by the dipping of the sop, while Christ turns to St. John and consolingly takes his hand—a charming idea, but one which destroys the domination of the principal figure and the unity of feeling. Maybe Andrea said to himself that it was no use competing with Leonardo.

Other artists introduced trivialities, thinking to contribute something new. In Baroccio's large *Institution of the Eucharist* (Urbino), while the Lord is speaking, some of the Disciples call to the landlord to fetch more wine, as though they were going to drink a toast.

Finally, there is an observation to be made about the relationship between Leonardo's picture and the room where it is painted. It is well known that it decorates the end wall of a long, narrow refectory, which is lit from one side only, and Leonardo took the actual source of light as the source for his picture, which was not an unusual idea. The light comes from high up on the left, so that the opposite wall in the picture is only partly illuminated and the variety of tones between light and dark is so considerable that, by comparison, Ghirlandaio seems all one tone and flat. The brightly lit tablecloth stands out and the play of light on the heads gives them a strongly plastic effect against the dark wall, and there is still another effect gained by this use of the actual source of light: Judas, who has been taken out of his usual isolation and set among the other Disciples, still remains an isolated figure, for he is the only one to sit with his back completely turned to the light, so that his face, therefore, is entirely in shadow. This simple and effective means of characterization was, perhaps, recollected by the young Rubens when he painted his *Last Supper*, now in the Brera.

2. THE MONA LISA

In the Quattrocento, occasional attempts had already been made to go beyond the mere representation of the sitter in portraits; more was wanted than that sum of features which gives the likeness, more than the permanent forms of the head, which give the character. Something was sought for which should mirror the mood of the hour, and record the passage across the face of momentary emotions. Some of Desiderio's busts of girls have just this quality: they smile, and the smile is not a stereotyped one, but the genuine reflection of a happy moment. Everyone knows these young Florentine women with joyous mouths and brows arched over eyes which, even in marble, seem to sparkle. There is a smile, too, on the face of the *Mona Lisa*, but only a very faint smile, in the corners of the mouth and almost imperceptibly trembling across the features. Like a breath of wind rippling the water, the soft planes of the face are moved, and the light and shadow play across it in whispered dialogue, to which we never tire of listening. Poliziano says somewhere, "She flashed with a sweet, fond smile."[6] I doubt if the conception and expression recur in the Cinquecento itself, when smiling no longer was in vogue, or, rather, only the subdued smile that we see in Sebastiano del Piombo's *Dorothea*.

The brown eyes look out from under the narrow lids, not Quattrocento eyes with a forthright sparkle, but a veiled glance. The lower lids are almost horizontal—reminding one of the Gothic form of eye where the same motive is used to give a moist and liquid effect—and all the part below the eyes speaks of great sensibility, of fine nerves beneath the skin.

The absence of eyebrows is striking. The curved surface of the eye-sockets runs, without transition, into the exceedingly high forehead, but this is not an individual peculiarity, for a passage in the "Cortegiano" tells us that it was fashionable for women to pluck their eyebrows.[7] A wide extent of forehead was also accounted a beauty, so that the hairs above the forehead were also sacrificed, which explains the enormous foreheads of the busts of girls by Mino and Desiderio, where the joy in modelling the white surfaces created with such tender feeling by the chisel on the white marble, outweighed all other considerations, so that the natural divisions were eliminated and the zone of the forehead extended upwards beyond reason. The *Mona Lisa* is, in this respect, an example of Quattrocento taste, tor the fashion changed immediately afterwards and the line of the forehead was again lowered, and now one realizes how much better it is when eyebrows define the form. The copy of the *Mona Lisa* in Madrid has had eyebrows deliberately added.

The hair, chestnut-brown like the eyes, falls in soft waves down her cheeks, as does the loose veil which is laid over the head.

The lady sits in an armchair, and one is surprised to find so rigid and vertical a carriage of the head accompanied by such softness of execution. Obviously she bears herself according to the fashion, for an upright carriage implied distinction, as may be seen in Ghirlandaio's frescoes of the Tornabuoni ladies, bolt upright on their visits. Later, the fashion changed and the newer ideas on the subject are directly reflected in the poses of the portraits.[8]

Apart from this, the picture is not lacking in movement. For the first time, Leonardo adopted the half-length instead of the bust size, with its abrupt cutting of the body. He posed the model sitting sideways, with the upper part of the body half turned and the face seen almost directly from the front, adding the movement of the arms, one lying along the arm of the chair, the other coming forward in foreshortening with one hand laid over the other. It was not merely for decorative purposes that Leonardo added the hands, for their placid gesture adds greatly to the characterization and one feels the delicacy of touch of these sensitive fingers. In this, Verrocchio anticipated Leonardo, if, indeed, the celebrated bust in the Bargello is by him and not due to the young Leonardo himself.

The costume is simple, almost prim—to an artist of the Cinquecento the line of the bodice must have seemed hard. The pleated gown is green, of the green which was afterwards used by Luini, and the yellow-brown sleeves are not, as in earlier fashions, short and narrow, but reach to the wrist and are crumpled into a multitude of transverse folds so that they make an effective accompaniment to the smoothly rounded forms of the hands and the delicate fingers, untrammelled by rings; the neck, too, is unadorned.

The background is a landscape, as in some older pictures, but it does not come right up to the figure, since there is a low parapet between them and the view into the landscape is confined between columns. One must look closely to appreciate this motive, which had important consequences, since, except for their bases, the columns appear only as narrow strips. The later style did not rest content with such slight indications.[9]

The landscape itself stretches away into the distance, above the eye-level of the sitter, and it is of an unusual kind—fantastic, jagged labyrinths of mountains with lakes and streams scattered between them. What is strangest is their dream-like aspect suggested by their indeterminate execution. They are of a different order of reality from the figure and this is no caprice on the part of the artist, but a means of increasing the apparent solidity of the figure. It is an exposition of some of Leonardo's theories concerning the appearance of distant objects which he also set out in his Treatise,[10] and its success is such, that, in the Salon Carré of the Louvre where the *Mona Lisa* hangs, all the neighbouring pictures, even those of the seventeenth century, look flat. The landscape is painted in shades of brown, green-blue and blue-green passing into the blue of the sky; these are exactly the colours used by Perugino in his little *Apollo and Marsyas*, also in the Louvre.

Leonardo said that modelling was the soul of painting. If anywhere, it is in front of the *Mona Lisa* that one begins to discern the significance of these words. The delicate undulations of the surfaces become a personal experience, almost as if one had glided over them with a spirit-hand. The aim is not simplicity but complexity, and anyone who has contemplated it for a long time can confirm that it needs to be studied from close up, for it loses much of its peculiar effect if seen from a distance. This is even more true of photographs of it, which, therefore, are unsuitable as a wall-decoration. In this, it is basically different from the later portraits of the Cinquecento, and in a certain sense it marks the conclusion of a movement rooted in the fifteenth century, and is the apogee of that refined style to which the sculptors, in particular, devoted all their efforts. The next generation of Florentines did not go any further with this, and it was only in Lombardy that these delicate threads continued to be spun.[11]

3. THE VIRGIN AND CHILD WITH ST. ANNE

Compared with the *Mona Lisa,* Leonardo's other picture in the Louvre, the *Virgin and Child with St. Anne,* attracts less appreciation from the public. The picture is probably not entirely the work of Leonardo's own hand and has suffered in its colour, while the qualities of draughtsmanship which it contains are but little prized by modern eyes, and indeed, scarcely understood. Yet the cartoon alone, in its day (1501), aroused tremendous excitement in Florence and caused a general pilgrimage to the convent of the Annunziata, where Leonardo's latest miracle could be seen.[12] The theme might well have proved arid enough; one recollects the inflexible way in which older masters arranged the three figures—one sitting on the lap of the other and all three turned to face the spectator—

and yet here this dry one-on-top-of-the-other arrangement is transformed into a group of the greatest subtlety and the lifeless framework is imbued with animated movement. Mary sits sideways on her mother's lap; smiling, she bends forward and grasps the Child with both hands while He, at her feet, tries to bestride a lamb. He looks up enquiringly, still holding firmly on to the head of the unfortunate crouching animal, which tries to shrink away although the Child already has one leg over its back. Smiling, the youthful-looking grandmother watches the merry game.

The problems of grouping in the *Last Supper* are further developed here. The composition is infinitely thought-provoking, saying much in little space; all the figures have contrasting movements and the opposing directions of the main forms are resolved into a compact, closed mass which can demonstrably be contained with an equilateral triangle. All this is the fruit of strivings, perceptible as early as the *Madonna of the Rocks,* to subordinate the whole composition to simple geometric forms; but how diffuse the earlier work looks beside the compressed riches of the *St. Anne*! It was not love of the artificial, the over-wrought, which led Leonardo to attempt more and more movement within an ever-diminishing space, for the strength of the effect is increased in proportion. The difficulty lay in preserving the clarity and calm of the total effect, and that was the rock on which his feebler imitators foundered. Leonardo attained complete lucidity and his principal motive—the bending forward of the Virgin—is of enchanting beauty and warmth, with all the minor beauties, which so often led the Quattrocento astray, subordinated to it with an unsurpassed mastery of expression. Consider the way in which the lines of shoulder and head, light on dark, stand out in relief, yet retain their wonderful softness. How calm, yet how full of movement! The restraint of St. Anne provides a most telling contrast, and the group is closed below, in the happiest way, by the Child glancing upwards, and His lamb.

A small picture by Raphael, in Madrid, reflects the impression made by this composition. As a young man in Florence, he attempted a similar problem, substituting St. Joseph for St. Anne, but with much less success. The lamb alone is very wooden, for Raphael was never successful as an animal painter, while Leonardo could succeed in anything he undertook. But a more formidable competitor than Raphael now entered the lists against Leonardo—Michelangelo.

The *St. Anne* contains none of the grasses, flowers and reflecting pools of water of the *Madonna of the Rocks*; the lifesize figures are everything. But what is more important than their actual size is their scale, the proportion of the picture-surface which they occupy. They fill the canvas more effectually than do the figures in the earlier works, or, to put it another way, the picture surface is smaller in proportion to its contents. This is the scale of proportion which became typical of the Cinquecento.[13]

4. THE BATTLE OF ANGHIARI

It is not possible to say much about this battle-piece, which was commissioned for the Great Council Chamber of Florence, since the composition no longer exists even as a cartoon, but only in the incomplete copy by a later hand; yet it cannot be passed over, since the problems raised by it are too interesting.

Leonardo studied horses very deeply—more, perhaps, than any other artist of the Cinquecento—and his interest arose from his love for the animal.[14] He was occupied for years in Milan with an equestrian statue of Duke Francesco Sforza, never cast, but for which a complete model once existed, the destruction of which is to be reckoned among the greatest losses of art. It seems to have been originally conceived as a demonstration of movement surpassing Verrocchio's *Colleoni* monument, and thus he arrived at a group of a galloping horse with a prostrate foe beneath its hoofs; the same idea as that which had already occurred to Antonio Pollaiuolo.[15] Occasionally the misgiving is expressed that Leonardo's figure might have become too much of a painter's conception, but if this has any justification it can only be with reference to sketches for this design, for the motive of the leaping horse cannot be regarded as definitive, since, in the course of the work, a development towards greater unity and simplicity took place, similar to that observable in the sketches for the *Last Supper,* and Leonardo ended up with the horse simply walking, the earlier projects for a sharp contrast of direction between the heads of horse and rider being quite significantly modified. Only the backward bend of the arm with the marshal's baton remained unaltered, since Leonardo wished to enrich the silhouette and fill up the empty right-hand space behind the rider's back.[16] The only source of information left to us concerning the large battle-piece in the Florentine Council Chamber, in which Leonardo sought to turn his Milanese studies to account, is the drawing in the Louvre, ascribed to Rubens,[17] from which Edelingk engraved a well known and excellent plate. It is scarcely likely that the drawing gives everything that was in the picture, but in general it corresponds with Vasari's description.

Leonardo intended to show the Florentines, once for all, how to draw horses; for his principal motive he chose a cavalry action during the battle—the fight for the standard—with four horses and four riders in impassioned violence and the closest physical contact. The problem of composing a group with the utmost plasticity is taken here to a pitch which verges almost on the boundary of the unclear.[18] The northern engraver emphasized the pictorial, painterly aspect of the composition, so that a central dark mass is surrounded by lighter ones; an arrangement which we may well believe is Leonardo's in principle.

At that time, the specifically "modern" task was the composition of interlocked masses and one is surprised at not coming across more battle-pieces. The School of Raphael is the only place where a major work of this kind was produced, and the *Battle of Constantine* represents the general Western conception of the classical battle-piece; in it, an advance was made from the merely episodic to the representation of a real mass action, yet although this celebrated work offers far more than Leonardo did, it is so afflicted by its imperceptive lack of clarity that one sees, already, the loss of visual sensibility and the approach of decadence. Raphael certainly had nothing to do with this composition.

Leonardo left no School in Florence. Everyone learned from him, but the impression he made was superseded by that of Michelangelo. Clearly, Leonardo developed towards a conception of figures on the grand scale and, in the end, the figure became all-in-all for him. Yet Florence would have worn a different aspect had it been more Leonardesque, and the traces of Leonardo which survive in Andrea del Sarto or in Franciabigio and Bugiardini do not really signify very much. A direct continuation of his art, or, at any rate, of one side of it, is to be found only in Lombardy, but the Lombards, though gifted as painters, are utterly deficient in the architectonic sense. They never grasped the structure of the *Last Supper,* and Leonardo's grouping and involved movement offered solutions to problems outside their range. The more spirited made of movement something wild and confused, the others are of a tiresome uniformity. In Lombardy, it was the feminine side of Leonardo's art which was most influential, the passive emotions and the soft, almost smoke-like modelling of youthful bodies, particularly of feminine forms. Leonardo was extremely sensitive to the beauty of the female body; one could even say that he was the first to realise the soft texture of the skin. His Florentine contemporaries also painted female nudes, but it was just this charm that they lacked. Even those among them who were the most painterly in feeling, such as Piero di Cosimo, were primarily interested in form rather than in the quality of the surface. With the awakening of a more subtle sense of touch, manifested in the type of modelling used by Leonardo, the female body acquired a new artistic significance, and we could deduce from these psychological premises that Leonardo must have devoted much study to this theme, even if we did not happen to know that such pictures by him did once exist.

The most important seems to have been a *Leda,* which we know only from copies, principally in the form of a beautiful nude in slight movement, standing with her knees pressed together and caressing, rather than repulsing, the swan. This figure, with twisted torso, tilted head, arm reaching across the body, and one shoulder lowered, exerted a very considerable influence. (The best known version is in the Galleria Borghese, Rome, and was at one time ascribed to Sodoma.)[19]

The female nude thus became a common theme among Leonardo's Lombard followers, but as they had but little feeling for movement as something affecting the whole body, it is scarcely surprising that they abandoned whole-length figures and contented themselves with half-length schemes. Even a subject like *Susannah in the Bath,* where one might reasonably expect to find a thorough study of the plasticity of a figure, is circumscribed within this arid formula (picture by Luini in the Galleria Borromeo, Milan). As a general type of this style, the unpretentious half-length figure of *Abundance* by Giampietrino is here reproduced (Pl. 10).[20]

Leonardo as Verrocchio's Coworker

by W. R. Valentiner

HILE RAPHAEL QUITE frequently signed his works, and Michelangelo jealously guarded his artistic property against other artists, it was not in keeping with Leonardo's nature to trouble himself to preserve the authorship of the wealth of ideas which poured out from him. Not only was he amiable by nature, communicative and ready to be of help: the formative arts were but a part of his all-embracing knowledge, perhaps not even, in his own mind, assuming the first importance, to judge from the well-known letter to the duke of Milan where, in enumerating his talents, he names his ability as a painter and sculptor only at the end of the long list. More than with other masters was his artistic work a play—this is shown above all in his drawings—a recreative play in the intervals between fatiguing application to technical or philosophical problems or tasks in the field of natural science. But when he turned to the greater themes of painting or sculpture, he was interested above everything else in the solution of a fundamental problem; when he had succeeded in solving it to his own satisfaction, perhaps only theoretically, he liked to leave the execution of it to others; and what happened further with the work of art, seems to have troubled him but little, much less did it occur to him to sign it. He was so independent and had so little vanity that in the execution of his work the identity of the patron had not the slightest influence with him. He might let princes or popes wait for their commissions, while perhaps the order of a poor friend of art so

From *Art Bulletin,* Copyright 1930, Vol. 12, pp. 43–89; New York. Reprinted by permission of the editor, H. W. Janson.

absorbed him that he worked over it tirelessly day and night. We are reminded of the anecdote of Vasari, which is not without an inner probability: A peasant on the estate of Leonardo's father brought a shield to him one day with the request to have it painted by an artist. Ser Piero da Vinci gave it to his son Leonardo, who took unbelievable pains with it. He planed the shield down, covered it over with stucco, and then gathered together all kinds of beasts and insects, which he used as models. When the shield was finished and his father saw it, he was startled and amazed at the astonishing realism of the representation; he gave the owner of the shield a cheap substitute and kept Leonardo's shield, which he sold later for one hundred ducats to a dealer, who in turn sold it to the duke of Milan for three hundred ducats. On the other hand, Isabella d'Este exerted herself in vain again and again to secure a work by Leonardo, and when he was in Rome, it was not long before he angered the pope by making him wait too long for the execution of an order which it seems did not happen to appeal to him at the moment.

His carelessness in communicating his knowledge doubtless explains the possibility of Leonardo's long association with Verrocchio at a time when he had already entered the painter's guild as an independent member—a student relationship completely impossible with Michelangelo, and with Raphael, after he had left the atelier of his teacher, unthinkable. To be sure, we must also assume that the gifted young master could carry out his ideas in Verrocchio's workshop unhindered and that they were used freely and even found grateful acceptance with the older master. Evidently the teacher and pupil understood each other so well that the expression of their ideas often completely fused and the boundary line between their work is to-day scarcely to be drawn with certainty. The influence was doubtless mutual; for Verrocchio, himself a personality far surpassing the average, was just in his best years when Leonardo came to him, and many of his greatest tasks still lay before him.

Through this generosity in sharing his ideas the problem of the art of Leonardo is rendered considerably more difficult for the investigator. We now know that a large part of his artistic productions of the later period, from his first stay in Milan on, is contained in the extensive work of the pupils who carried out his ideas, and it has been shown in our own day with considerable success, especially by W. Suida,[1] how the original compositions of Leonardo can be reconstructed out of his pupils' work. But we know also that a vast part of the work and the ideas of the master in his earlier Florentine period is contained in the work of his fellow artists and above all in that of his teacher, Verrocchio.

But where is the line to be drawn? At each step which we make in this so often trod and still uncharted territory of Leonardo investigation, we see opposed to each other the most varied possibilities, brought about by the widely diverging ideas of the numerous scholars. Even if we look around us at the first early work of Leonardo, the ground totters under our feet and it may happen with us as with Faust's attempt at the translation of the Bible, when he was baffled by the first sentence: "Here already I am at a standstill." We know that Leonardo started painting very early, else he would not have been taken into the painters' guild at the age of twenty. We are better informed about these years of the Florentine paintings than about any other period; we know an especially large number of paintings from the Verrocchio workshop and we may also assume from the fame which Leonardo enjoyed in his own lifetime that not very many of his works have been lost; and yet the first absolutely certain painting of the artist is one preserved only in the ground painting, which he did in his thirtieth year, the Adoration of the Kings in the Uffizi. About everything which the master created in painting or sculpture before this the opinions of scholars still differ from each other.

It seems, however, that as far as the question of the paintings is concerned, the sceptics will be defeated by those among the investigators (like A. Venturi, Bode, Suida, and Aldo de Rinaldis) who attribute to Leonardo the major part of certain outstanding works done in Verrocchio's workshop, who believe in his coöperation in Verrocchio's Baptism of Christ, and give to him the female portrait in the Liechtenstein Gallery, the Annunciation in the Uffizi, and even, wholly or partly, the Madonna with the vase of flowers in the Munich Pinakothek.[2] Most radical among the sceptics stands the Norwegian Jens Thiis,[3] who bases his work primarily upon Berenson, but, it seems to me, exaggerates the latter's opinions in an unfavorable way; he assumes, as does Sirén, an indefinite Verrocchio pupil as the creator of those early works attributed to Leonardo or gives them to imitators, even the Benois Madonna in Petersburg, whose authenticity no one now doubts and which in the meantime has found acknowledgement by Berenson.[4] Sirén, in a careful, well-thought-out theory, assumes the coöperation of Leonardo in the Baptism of Christ and in the Annunciation in the Uffizi and attributes the portrait in the Liechtenstein Gallery, the Munich Madonna, and part of the Annunciation to the same unknown pupil of Verrocchio, while the Italian scholar Aldo de Rinaldis gives to the young Leonardo the Liechtenstein portrait, attributes to him with reservation the Annunciation in the Uffizi, and ignores the Munich Madonna. In the most recently published works E. Hildebrandt regards the

Liechtenstein portrait as a work of Leonardo, and accepts at least Leonardo's collaboration in the other paintings, while R. van Marle joins forces with the older scholars and pronounces the Vienna portrait as well as the Florentine Annunciation to be the work of Verrocchio, and the Munich Madonna, on the other hand, a work by Lorenzo di Credi.[5]

The question of the sculptures which might be attributed to Leonardo has been treated in general less thoroughly and, as it seems to me, with less competence.[6] Still we may say that the Verrocchio sculpture scholars from Müntz and Bode to Mackowsky and Miss Cruttwell agree in the opinion that the great advance shown in the sculpture of this master in the 70's and 80's of the fifteenth century cannot be otherwise explained than by the strong influence of the younger master upon the teacher; and the collaboration of Leonardo in at least one of his marble works, the female bust in the Bargello, is almost universally accepted (Mackowsky, Bode, Suida, Hildebrandt).

Still another result has, I believe, come about from the Leonardo investigation of the last decades—much as individual opinions differ from each other: that one should not separate too much the hands of pupil, fellow pupil and teacher in their entirety, attributing works as a whole now to Verrocchio, now to Lorenzo di Credi, and now to the young Leonardo, but should rather consider the possibility of certain parts of a composition having been executed by the teacher and others by one or another of the pupils. This seems more likely to have been the method employed in such an atelier as that of Verrocchio. We know that Leonardo executed one of the angels in Verrocchio's Baptism of Christ; it is attested by Vasari and Albertini and seldom disputed by the critic. It is then very likely that the young Leonardo was also employed in other paintings in the Verrocchio workshop. But it is just as probable that when in similar fashion Verrocchio called upon his most gifted pupil to collaborate with him in a work of sculpture, he did not give him the whole work to execute but more likely one or another figure in it. We shall return to an example of this kind in the terra cotta relief of the Resurrection from the Villa Careggi (Pl. 35). We know besides that there existed an extensive division of work in Verrocchio's atelier and that now one and now another part of a work of sculpture or painting would be turned over to the pupils gifted in painting as well as in sculpture.[7] Berenson has rightly pointed out that Lorenzo di Credi drew an angel for the plastic execution of the Forteguerri monument in Pistoja. We may assume that Francesco di Simone was also active in the execution of the work in marble—not to mention the sculptors who later finished the monument—while the first preliminary design certainly originated with Verrocchio.[8] The share which this Francesco took, especially in the works of marble from Verrocchio's workshop, for example the reliefs of the Tornabuoni monument and some of the Madonna reliefs, may be estimated with considerable probability.[9] For the more spacious altarpieces in the territory of painting, the same suppositions are of still more weight. While in smaller works the execution of at least the painting would from practical considerations be left to one and the same artist, the minute preparations which the execution of a large altarpiece involved and the frequently occurring interruptions in the work of the busy artists employed in the Verrocchio workshop, often made necessary the collaboration of several of the fellow workers. That the altar in the Cathedral of Pistoja, for which Verrocchio received the commission, was executed by him alone has been accepted by scarcely anyone; Bode and Berenson practically give its execution to Lorenzo di Credi. That Leonardo also probably had a share in it, we shall attempt to show here.

Finally, we must accustom ourselves to the thought that the drawings of Verrocchio and of the pupils in the atelier of the master passed from hand to hand and were used first by one and then by another. We shall see presently that in all probability Leonardo used drawings of Verrocchio in his compositions, and it is not at all out of the question that Leonardo's drawings were also used even by his teacher. That they were soon enough used by his fellow pupils, such as Lorenzo di Credi, perhaps also by Perugino, is known well enough. We cannot marvel sufficiently over how quickly Leonardo's ideas, which he expressed in his drawings, traveled, not only through Italy but into foreign countries. We see the Flemish Quentin Massys scarcely ten years after the creation of the original, producing a painting after a drawing by Leonardo, and a still shorter time elapsed before Fernando de Llanos introduced into the painting of Spain motives which he had copied in Leonardo's atelier from the master.[10] All of which goes to prove the greatest liberality of Leonardo in parting with his spiritual possessions.

We must therefore, in the case of Leonardo, whose temperament disposed him to activity on several works at one time, reckon with a more extensive participation in the execution of the sculpture as well as the paintings of Verrocchio's workshop during Leonardo's activity there than in the case of his fellow pupils. With the greater development of style criticism to-day it should be possible to appraise this collaboration more precisely than it was at the time of the first fundamental Leonardo investigations by Müntz, J. P. Richter, and Müller-Walde.

Let us briefly bring before our minds the few dates of Leonardo's youthful development so far as they have been handed down to us by documentary evidence. Born in Vinci in 1452 as the illegitimate child of the notary Ser Piero, Leonardo came to Florence, according to Vasari, "as a boy" (he says in one place *"giovanotto,"* in another *"fanciullo"*) to be an apprentice to Verrocchio. In what year that was cannot be specified with certainty.[11] The opinions of scholars vary between 1462 (Gronau), 1465 or 1466 (R. van Marle), 1466 (Müller-Walde, Thiis, Hildebrandt), 1467 (Müntz), "some time before 1468" (Suida), and 1469 or 1470 (A. Venturi, A. de Rinaldis). A. Venturi assumes that Ser Piero first took his son with him to Florence when he himself, as is documentarily evidenced, moved to Florence in the year 1469. According to this Leonardo would have come to Verrocchio as an apprentice not before his eighteenth year. Not only does this contradict Vasari's statement, it was a usual custom to send young artists to be apprenticed to a master at as early an age as thirteen or fourteen;[12] all the more may we expect this in the case of Leonardo, if he developed as early as one may from all accounts assume. It is also not probable that he would already have been taken into the painters' guild in 1472, if he had been an apprentice for only two years. To be sure, Leonardo is mentioned as living with his father in Florence in 1469. However, his reception into an atelier does not necessarily infer that he lived with his teacher. Leaving out of the question one of the landscape drawings dated 1473, which attests but little to Leonardo's style, we do not find another documentary mention until 1476.[13] In this year he is mentioned twice as living with Verrocchio. Again there is a pause until 1478. In the beginning of this year he received a commission from the city council, the first independent one of which we hear. He was to paint an altarpiece for the chapel of St. Bernard in the Palazzo Pubblico and received his first payment in March of that year. The work remained uncompleted, however, and a few years later was executed by Filippino Lippi.

A note on a drawing by the artist points to two smaller commissions at the end of this year, 1478, two Madonna pictures very likely begun in November. One assumes, with probability, that the memorandum refers to the Benois Madonna in the Hermitage and to the Madonna with the Cat, known only through preliminary studies. A drawing can be dated to the end of the next year, 1479, which represents the murderer of Giuliano de' Medici being hanged and which shows exact specifications that make it seem possible that the artist expected the commission to paint for the city the portrait of the murderer on the wall of the Bargello as a warning example to the people, although the order had already been given a year before to Botticelli, who had possibly executed it without having actually seen the murderer, who had escaped.

But we can identify with certainty only one commission, of March, 1481, with an existing work by the artist: the uncompleted Worship of the Magi which he was to have executed for the Cloister of S. Donato di Scopeto. It may be that the work was interrupted by the master's moving to Milan, which probably took place in the year 1482.[14] However, Leonardo is not mentioned in the documents in Milan earlier than April, 1483.

It is not entirely certain when Leonardo left the workshop of Verrocchio. At any rate, in the year 1481 he no longer lived with his teacher, but in his own dwelling. We would gather from the fact that several independent commissions of the artist are mentioned in the year 1478, that he was scarcely any longer active as painter for Verrocchio. But nothing contradicts the assumption that the closest friendship existed between the two until Leonardo's departure from Florence; and that Leonardo also worked together with Verrocchio later on as a sculptor, an activity which was a predominant one with Verrocchio in his later years, is very probable from the close relation of Verrocchio's work to the style of Leonardo in these years. If this is so, it explains the remarkable silence of the documents concerning any kind of activity of Leonardo as a sculptor in his Florentine period. That this activity must have been a significant one, is confirmed by that letter to Lodovico il Moro in which Leonardo emphasizes his experience in the execution of works in terra cotta, marble, and bronze, and also that he could execute an equestrian statue in bronze.

Even though we cannot determine definitely the date of the beginning and the end of Leonardo's activity in Verrocchio's workshop, this much is certain, that the younger artist was active together with his teacher at least eight years, at most sixteen years, with greatest likelihood about ten years—from 1468 to 1478—and at any rate for at least six years after he became a free master. That out of this long period, so important in the development of the artist, no more should be preserved from Leonardo's hand than an angel in Verrocchio's Baptism of Christ, as some of the extremely sceptical investigators assume (even his cowork in Verrocchio's composition is occasionally disputed) is not very probable. It is also scarcely accidental that from 1478 on, when the artist was independent, the number of ascertained paintings and especially drawings begins suddenly to increase. There are preserved to us a number of studies for the mentioned Madonnas of 1478–1479, as well as for a Nativity of a little later time, which lead up to the numerous preliminary studies for the Adoration of the Kings of 1481. From these drawings we conclude not only that the artist worked lightly and quickly, but also that he was extraordinarily diligent in the preparation of his compositions and changed them completely over and over again before he accepted them as ripe for possible execution. That this rich creative activity did not set in only with his twenty-sixth or twenty-seventh year is naturally to be assumed; we may presume that it expressed itself with similar vitality, if with less originality, in the ten or at any rate six years earlier in the workshop of Verrocchio. It is therefore quite probable that the artist had a share in one way or another in the best works which issued from the atelier of his teacher from 1470 to 1478. Only we may not suppose that Leonardo's style already expressed itself *purely* in works of this kind—first because the workshop routine permitted the cowork of other artists, and again because in spite of all the early development of his talent, he seems to have shared with other great masters a gradual evolution of his personality.

Now there has been noticed among the paintings of the Verrocchio workshop from the period of about 1472 to 1478 a peculiarity of those compositions like the Annunciation in the Uffizi, the female portrait of the Liechtenstein Gallery, and, in a certain sense, also the Madonna with the Carnation in the Munich Pinakothek in that they possess in spite of certain weaknesses a remarkable treatment of light, and details of an astonishing fascination of form. Although these paintings have been frequently rejected as Leonardo's work, they make their appearance time and again in the discussions, and we believe, rightly. And when it is pointed out that these early works are too insignificant for the great master, it should be emphasized that scarcely one of the greatest masters of the South or North—we mention only Donatello and Raphael among the Italians, Rembrandt and Rubens among the Netherlanders—came into the world full armed as did Athena from the head of Zeus. On the contrary, the better we become acquainted with the youthful works of the great masters, all the clearer becomes the amazing development from remarkably awkward beginnings within the course of a few years. The distance from Donatello's clumsy statuettes on the Porta della Mandorla of the Florentine cathedral to the bronze David, or that from Raphael's altarpiece of S. Tolentino to the Madonna del Granduca is still greater than that between the Munich Madonna with the Carnation and the Adoration of the Kings in the Uffizi. That this masterwork from the end of Leonardo's Florentine period was not the beginning but rather the end of a long development is shown by the rediscovery of the Benois Madonna, which was created only two years before the Adoration of the Kings, and which in some respects is so awkward that it found acceptance with scholars as a work of the master only after the greatest opposition.

But what is true of the early works of other great masters is also true of Leonardo's, that, if put in the right order, they show a coherent, logical, and rapidly moving development, such as can be expected only of a most talented artist, and that, besides, they were from the very beginning far superior to those of his fellow workers. In Leonardo's case this is especially true when compared with Lorenzo di Credi,[15] to whom one is time and again inclined to attribute some of the works which come into discussion as early works of Leonardo. In this one assumes that Credi was a better artist in his early years than in his later period, quite evidently without reason; for why should such an insipid artist, in whom we can trace no development at all from his twenty-fifth year to the end of his life, have had such an interesting youth? This is all the less probable because such a definitely early work as the Madonna with the Child and St. John in Dresden shows him to be a by no means important artist or even one with ideals other than those of his later years. With this agrees also the documentary memorandum that he received from Verrocchio in 1480 a *yearly* salary of twelve gulden, while for the altarpiece of 1478 Leonardo had already received a first payment of twenty-five gulden and Verrocchio sixty gulden for the altarpiece of Pistoja. In his activity as a painter we cannot therefore expect much from Lorenzo di Credi previous to 1480—he was at that time twenty years old—although he may have distinguished himself later in the Verrocchio workshop as a designer and sculptor, for which Verrocchio seems to have held him in especial esteem.

From these general observations we turn to individual problems, first in the field of painting, then in that of sculpture, so far as they enter the discussion of Leonardo's early period.

I

Bode has rightly pointed out the connection between the small Annunciation in the Louvre (Pl. 12), which is generally regarded as a work by Leonardo, and the drawing of the female portrait in left profile in the Uffizi (Pl. 16). Indeed it is scarcely to be doubted that the master used this study for the head of Mary. Bode logically assumes the drawing to be by Leonardo's hand. Sirén, on the other hand, finds relations between the *en face* head of Mary in the Annunciation in the Uffizi and the Uffizi drawing, and recognizes the same model in both; he assumes the drawing to be by the same hand as the corresponding part of the Uffizi panel—the hand of his Verrocchio pupil A. It seems certain to me that the drawing betrays the style of Verrocchio rather than that of Leonardo (Berenson designates it as a copy after Verrocchio); it belongs to that group of Verrocchio's drawings of beautiful heads of women which were praised by Vasari and which, as he remarked, were imitated by Leonardo, sheets which are among the most beautiful expressions in the field of the graphic arts of the early Renaissance in Florence. In the sharp, pointed line treatment of the radiating strands of hair, they are characteristic of Verrocchio's style at the period of the Baptism of Christ, as a comparison of the treatment of the hair of Christ and the Baptist in this painting shows.[16] It seems to be the mature technique of an older, highly accomplished painter-sculptor rather than that of a youth, as Leonardo was at that time.

We are confronted with the curious fact, already suggested in our introduction, that Leonardo as a twenty-five year old artist—the little Annunciation is generally dated in the period around 1476–1478—still used drawings by Verrocchio for one of his compositions.

Now there is found to be a similar relation between painting and preliminary drawings in the case of the Madonna with the Carnation in Munich (Pl. 11). W. Suida has consistently attributed the splendid drawing of a head of a Madonna in the Louvre (Pl. 13), which he decisively connects with the painting, to the master who executed the latter, in which he, with A. Venturi, Bode, and others, recognizes the hand of Leonardo. But the attribution of the drawing to Verrocchio, which has been expressed in other quarters,[17] seems to me to be right, and, from the foregoing, still not contradictory to the attribution of the painting to Leonardo.

There are two more drawings belonging to Verrocchio which are connected with the Munich painting. One of them is the beautiful head of a girl in black crayon in the British Museum (Pl. 14), which stands almost as close to the head of Mary in the painting as the Louvre drawing. The other is the often-mentioned silver-point drawing in Dresden (Pl. 15), which with still greater probability was used for the painting of the Madonna in Munich. For the same reasons that Bode attributed the profile head in the Uffizi to Leonardo, he also assigns these two sheets, in the British Museum and at Dresden, to him. This seems to me upon various grounds impossible. Both drawings are done right-handed. But as anyone who has gone at all deeply into the study of Leonardo's drawings can easily notice, there are among the certain drawings of the master's not a single one which is right-handed,[18] as Morelli and Berenson have already established. It also appears highly improbable that an artist whose writing[19] and method of drawing were adapted in the cleverest manner to left-handedness, should have possessed equal facility with his right hand. Moreover, Leonardo was born left-handed, as was attested by his contemporaries Fra Luca Pacioli and Fra Sabba Castiglione, and his early drawings are, in fact, so far as I can determine, drawn without exception with the left hand. Apart from this, neither of the two drawings, especially the London sheet, agrees sufficiently with Leonardo's early drawings to take them away from Verrocchio. The Dresden drawing is frequently attributed to Lorenzo di Credi; it seems to me, however, that Thiis has hit the truth when he shows it to be superior to Credi and gives it to Verrocchio. For this speaks also its repeated use in Verrocchio's workshop, a distinction which fell to the lot of scarcely a drawing of the at that time still quite young Credi, as well as the fact that the other drawings—those used for the Munich Madonna composition—originated with Verrocchio.

If we attribute the Munich Madonna to Leonardo, he has evidently made copious use of the material of his teacher, while at the same time adding plenty of personal characteristics of his own, especially in the treatment of the folds, in the modeling of the Child's body, in the formation of the landscape, and not least in the technique, which, in fact, in the strong admixture of oil, which results in a peculiar curdling of the surface, agrees with that of the Liechtenstein portrait and the Madonna in the Grotto. The motive of the window openings at each side of the Madonna is also frequently used later by Leonardo, and not anywhere employed by Verrocchio, and is explained by Leonardo's tendency to use fine nuances of light and shadow. He liked to place the head of the principal figure in half shadow against a dark ground and to create as contrast by means of an aperture a strong light effect. Thus we see the bright window at the side of the Benois Madonna and this was also intended in the Madonna with the Cat, as a drawing in the British Museum[20] proves. Thus he opened the dark rocks at either side of the St. Jerome in the picture in the Vatican and again in the Madonna in the Grotto, and in the Litta Madonna in the Hermitage he returned to the two window openings as in the Munich Madonna. Like all great masters, Leonardo remained peculiarly consistent in the employment of certain motives throughout all periods of his art.

A more incidental motive is the repetition of the pearl-fastened carnelian of the Madonna's breast ornament, to which Bode and Suida have called attention. It is met with again in the Benois Madonna and the Madonna of the Rocks and in the little painting in the Dreifuss collection in Paris, which is closely related to Leonardo, and in the altarpiece in Pistoja. Aside from the copy by Lorenzo di Credi in his altarpiece in Naples, after the Madonna in Pistoja, it is found only in Verrocchio's terra cotta relief in the Bargello, and turns out to be one of the properties in the Verrocchio workshop.

II

To come back to the Dresden drawing, not only are opinions divided as to the question of its authorship, according to which it is attributed now to Lorenzo di Credi, now Verrocchio, and now Leonardo, but also the question of its employment in the executed paintings. Not only has it been pronounced a study for the Munich Madonna as well as for the Madonna of the Dreifuss collection, but also a study for the altarpiece in Pistoja and again for the Madonna of Credi's altarpiece in Naples. To begin with the last opinion, recently expressed by E. Hildebrandt, it is certainly not conclusive; for the Naples painting is a part copy after the one in Pistoja and it is not to be assumed that Lorenzo di Credi made a fresh study from nature, as the Dresden sheet obviously is, when a finished execution was already in existence to be copied. The same is true of the opinion expressed by Thiis, that the drawing served as a preliminary study for the Madonna in Pistoja (Pl. 17). At the left of the drawing there are still visible two studies of the head of the Christ Child (Pl. 15). These heads have the same outline as the Child in the picture in the Dreifuss collection[21] and are very closely related to the one in the Munich painting, while in the altarpiece in Pistoja and in the one in Naples the Child is turned in the other direction. It cannot, therefore, be doubted that the study was used first for the Madonna of the Dreifuss collection and for the one in Munich. But the Munich Madonna agrees so exactly with the one in Pistoja, especially in the position of the hands, that it is not reasonable to suppose that the one picture came into existence without the knowledge of the other. From the fact that the study from nature in Dresden agrees more closely with the Munich composition than with that in Pistoja, the Munich example must be the first and that in Pistoja the later, simplified version. This agrees also with other stylistic characteristics, from which is to be assumed that the Munich painting was created before the one in Pistoja. This may have been, according to the assumption of Bode and Suida, between 1472 and 1475. We know of the altarpiece in Pistoja (Pl. 17), that the commission was secured by Verrocchio, and that it was to be executed as a memorial to Bishop Donato de' Medici, who died in 1474. It is very probable that the commission was secured in 1475 or 1476. We learn from a later document, of the year 1485, that the altar was six years previous to this—that is in 1478–1479—"almost completed," but that on account of the cancellation of the final payment, it was not finished and delivered.[22] That Lorenzo di Credi could not have executed the painting in its principal parts is, aside from the question of the superior quality of certain parts of the execution, improbable on account of his youthful age at the time (1476–1478). But he may well have finished it in the year 1485, when Verrocchio was in Venice. That his feeble style is to be somehow recognized in the painting, accords with the judgment of all scholars (Berenson, Bode, van Marle, Sirén, Thiis); and it explains the tradition which begins with Vasari, that Credi was the creator of the altarpiece. To be sure, there is another tradition opposed to this, which prevailed in Pistoja in the beginning of the seventeenth century, according to which the painting was executed by Leonardo. Although not so much store can be laid in such a late tradition, yet in this case it may contain a grain of truth.

Now if we consider the Munich painting as a work of the young Leonardo, done about 1472–1475, it does not appear very probable that his master—if Verrocchio were the sole creator of the altarpiece of Pistoja— would have taken over a few years later almost exactly the in some respects still awkward composition of his pupil. But the borrowing of the motive is easily explained if Verrocchio, after first laying out the painting, in which the attitude of the Madonna was not yet decided in its details, left the greater part of the execution to his pupil. The position of the Madonna lies exactly on the borderline between the composition in Munich (and that of the Dreifuss collection) and the later Benois Madonna. The upper part of the body, the left hand, and the costume, even to the familiar breast ornament, agree with the one; the pose of the Child, Who sits on one of the mother's knees, with His left arm stretched across His body and one of His feet drawn up, agrees with the other. If the position of the legs of the Child is shown in a contrary fashion in the Benois Madonna, we still observe that in the not much later composition of the Madonna with the Cat, which can be seen in the drawing in the British Museum,[23] there is again the same position of the legs as that of the Child in the altarpiece in Pistoja.

To be sure, Lorenzo di Credi has also occasionally imitated this attitude of the Child, for example in the altarpiece in the Louvre, but with less significance in the contraposition of the limb masses and with a strangely empty expression of the mostly incorrectly drawn face. How much the Child of the Madonna in Pistoja agrees with Leonardo's conception even in the drawing of the toes and the separating muscles between foot and leg, is shown by a comparison with the study of children in the familiar pen drawing in Windsor (Pl. 19).

On the other hand, there will be found also a substantial difference between this conception of the Madonna who with almost shy expression balances the playfully moving Child upon her lap, and that of Verrocchio, in whose Madonna compositions the figure of the Madonna, formed as it were out of bronze, with spread-out yet firmly grasping hand, holds the sturdy Child upon her lap or lets Him stand close to her (paintings in the Berlin Gallery and in the Metropolitan Museum). Moreover, with Verrocchio the head of the Child is always covered with a thick circlet of bronze locks, while we encounter here the almost bald head of Leonardo's early period, which Lorenzo di Credi imitated.

With regard to the two saints, in the one on the right in particular, the S. Zeno, the Verrocchiesque character has been rightly pointed out, although we are strongly reminded, in the details of the execution, especially in the folds of the surplice which fall upon the ground, of Leonardo's early style: the pointed, triangular folds placed opposite each other are closely related to those of Leonardo's angel in the Baptism of Christ in the Uffizi and to those of both figures in the little Annunciation in the Louvre (Pl. 12).

Berenson has rightly concluded the drawing in the Louvre (Pl. 21) to be a preliminary study for the John the Baptist[24] and has attributed it to Lorenzo di Credi. It is more than anything else a drapery and head study: the position of the Baptist was already given; therefore the feet and arms are only indicated. It is to be assumed that another study preceded this one. It is in my opinion no other than Leonardo's familiar drawing of the youthful nude John in Windsor (Pl. 20), which Müntz first published as a Christ in Hades and which was described by him and others as a late work in connection with the late composition in the Louvre. By Berenson it is, however, rightly considered as an early work; with remarkable intuition he has even dated it to a definite year, 1476, just at the time when the work on the altarpiece of Pistoja was begun in Verrocchio's workshop.[25] But it seems that no one has yet pointed out its connection with this composition, although the position of the feet, and the lines of the entire body, if one disposes of the drapery, agree with the John the Baptist in the altarpiece. Every one knows that Leonardo usually sketched nude bodies for the clothed figures of his compositions, as the sketches for the Adoration of the Kings and the Last Supper prove; and beardlessness in the sketches of figures which he represented with beards in the executed compositions is also frequently encountered. In this regard also Lorenzo di Credi's study in the Louvre showing a beardless head forms a transition to the executed figure in the altarpiece of Pistoja. That Leonardo had already presumably carefully executed the flesh parts of the altarpiece, above all the feet of the saint, as Credi's study lets us assume, appears to me to be shown by the extremely characteristic shape of the toes, thighs, and knees, with their masterly understanding of anatomy. Let us compare for a moment the wide flat feet and the knees of Leonardo's anatomical drawing in the Academy in Venice (Pl. 18), which was first published in Fra Giocondo's *Vitruvius* (1511), but which must have been created much earlier as it still bears quite Verrocchiesque features, especially in the head. Also Leonardo's famous drapery study in the Louvre (Pl. 22), which was copied by Lorenzo di Credi (Lugt collection), may well have been a preliminary study for the sitting Madonna of the Pistoja altarpiece. Naturally Leonardo did not follow closely his own study in the executed composition, as did the less inventive Ghirlandajo when he copied it almost exactly in his altarpiece of 1484 in the Uffizi.[26]

The beauty and variety of the landscape background in the altarpiece of Pistoja, which differs so essentially from the schematic landscape forms of Lorenzo di Credi, have often been rightly stressed. But just as little would we be able to believe Verrocchio capable of the ingenious scenery, which betrays a true pleasure in the study from nature of the Tuscan landscape.

The landscape in his paintings is, to be sure, fashioned with more austerity than is Credi's landscape, but it is in another sense vague and cold and without particular significance, and entirely subordinated to the plasticity of the figures, in which Verrocchio the sculptor was interested above everything else. It certainly meant no more to him than it did to Botticelli, who was criticized by Leonardo in his *Treatise on Painting* on account of his lack of interest in landscape forms. One of the essential differences between the art of Verrocchio and that of Leonardo is the great love of the younger master for landscape art; no one has yet denied that where unusual individual landscape forms are to be found in works from the Verrocchio atelier, the influence of Leonardo has made itself felt.[27] Not only does the background in the painting in Pistoja show the pointed mountain contours—once with the river between the mountains—which are familiar to us from Leonardo's compositions from the Munich Madonna to the Mona Lisa; the trees around the throne also and the plants in the vases show an individual representation of forms, such as we would expect Leonardo, above all others in the Verrocchio workshop, to have been capable of.[28]

Still another accessory in the painting seems to point to Leonardo: the execution of the Asia Minor carpet with the long tassels which fall over the parapet in the foreground of the picture. Every student of these carpets knows that they never had this long fringe and that they were never so represented by other artists of the period (Raffaellino del Garbo, Holbein, etc.). It seems to me to be a characteristic caprice of Leonardo to use these tassels as a termination at the edge of the picture and to represent them with a love in the portrayal of the knotted forms and of the effect of light and shadow on the individual threads, that would scarcely have occurred to any other painter of that period.

If, then, we regard Verrocchio as the master who laid out the composition in its essential parts—the openings on either side of the throne especially (which remind us of the background of the silver relief of the Opera del Duomo) permit the assumption of his authorship—we yet believe that Leonardo took a substantial part in its execution (above all in the Madonna and Child, the John the Baptist, and the landscape). The whole picture was finally—unfortunately for the impression of the whole—finished by Lorenzo di Credi about 1485.

It appears to me very probable that the predella with the Annunciation in the Louvre, which was once attributed to Lorenzo di Credi, but later on came to be accepted as a youthful work of Leonardo's, was painted by Leonardo for the altarpiece in Pistoja. Until now it has not been possible to name a single altarpiece for which it might have been destined, if we assume its creation to have been about 1476–1478. For as Bode has rightly pointed out, it does not agree either in time or style with the Adoration of the Kings of 1481, as Seidlitz thinks possible.[29] If one imagines the predella in the center below the altarpiece of Pistoja, he will see how well it suits this place; in the case of the angel and of the Virgin the folds of the garments spread out radially on the floor in a manner quite similar to those of the enthroned Madonna and the St. Zenobius in the main panel above. The costume of the angel below in the predella with the sleeve rolled up at the elbow and the slits and puffs of the underarm is the same as in the enthroned Madonna, and although this was the costume of the period, it is encountered with Leonardo elsewhere only in the Annunciation in the Uffizi and the Benois Madonna, for he soon afterwards foresook the idea of clothing his holy figures in contemporary costumes.

The point of vision of the predella seems to indicate that it was placed in the center; and that such a representation of the Annunciation in the center underneath the enthroned Madonna was in keeping with the age, is evidenced by the altar of Cosimo Rosselli in S. Spirito in Florence (Pl. 27), which was created not much later (1482). Perhaps we may succeed in finding the other two parts of the predella which belongs to the altarpiece in Pistoja; presumably they portray legends from the lives of the two saints in the large panel above, or representations of the Nativity and the Adoration of the Kings; they may be looked for among the works of Lorenzo di Credi, who as the finisher of the altarpiece possibly executed them.

Finally it must be pointed out in this connection that a memorandum on the drawing by Leonardo in the Uffizi which is dated 1478 mentions Pistoja.[30] From this it has been occasionally assumed that the artist stayed in Pistoja around this time, which would agree with the assumption of his activity on the altarpiece of the cathedral about 1476–1477.

III

Before we proceed to Leonardo's participation in another large altarpiece, the one commissioned by the city of Florence for the Chapel of St. Bernard in the Palazzo Pubblico, let us make a few preliminary remarks regarding the reliability of the source from which the mention of this activity is taken.

Among the sources from which we have secured our information regarding Leonardo, scarcely one has proved to be so valuable as the biography in the Codex of the Anonimo Gaddiano, written in the 40's of the sixteenth century.[31] Though less detailed than Vasari's, of which it is quite independent, it has proved to be—in the instances in which it differs from Vasari's—unusually accurate and dependable, and most of the accounts are confirmed by documentary evidence. To these belong the statements regarding the contents of Leonardo's will; the account of his stay in Florence in the year 1508, and his relations with Giovanni Francesco Rustici; the important notice of his stay with Cesare Borgia;[32] the more detailed accounts of Leonardo's pupils, for instance the Spaniard Fernando and his collaboration in the execution of the Battle of Anghiari; and finally the patronage of Lorenzo de' Medici during Leonardo's first Florentine period and his recommendation to the court of Milan, to which he was sent by Lorenzo together with Atalante Migliorotti. All of these accounts are missing in Vasari or are incorrectly reported, for example, the date of Leonardo's removal to Milan, which the Anonimo gives with evident exactness.

While documentary confirmation of the majority of these statements has long been known, the remarks of the Anonimo regarding the interest of Lorenzo de' Medici in the young Leonardo, which is not mentioned by Vasari, had been given scarcely any credence, until in recent times a sort of confirmation has been found for this also in Leonardo's manuscripts. It is only a short remark, which Leonardo wrote down in later life, but it is significant enough. He says: *"Li Medici mi crearono e distrussono."* ("The Medici have created me and destroyed me.")[33]

We can reconstruct the reason for his indignation at the time he made this remark, which as all agree was written about 1515. Both of the sons of Lorenzo de' Medici had treated him unfairly. The lack of consideration he had received at the hands of Giovanni, Lorenzo's eldest son, Pope Leo X, is well known. The other case refers to Giuliano, Lorenzo's youngest son. In the famous description which Antonio de Beatis, secretary to the cardinal of Aragon, gives of his visit to Leonardo at Amboise on August 10, 1517, he speaks of three paintings which Leonardo showed him and which, with the greatest probability, have always been identified as those which after Leonardo's death came into the possession of King Francis I and then to the Louvre: the Mona Lisa, St. John the Baptist, and the Madonna and St. Anne. The Mona Lisa is described as *"un quadro di certa dona fiorentina facta di naturale ad istantia del quondam mag'co Juliano de Medici."* Suida says the connection with Giuliano de' Medici seems extremely puzzling, but A. de Rinaldis[34] thinks it not impossible that the Mona Lisa had been painted in Florence about 1505 as an order from Giuliano de' Medici, "who was so much occupied with mathematics and women," and that Giuliano might have given it back to Leonardo in Rome when he got married in order to avoid the jealousy of his wife, Filaberta of Savoy. This hypothesis seems still more plausible when we remember that in Leonardo's manuscripts we read the following passage, certainly written at Rome: "At daybreak on the 9th of January, 1515, Giuliano de' Medici il Magnifico left Rome for Florence, where his marriage was to take place, and on the same day the King of France died."[35] In regard to this, J. P. Richter, the best interpreter of Leonardo's manuscripts, remarks, "Two benefactors lost to him in one day! This is doubtless the poignant meaning contained in this curt sentence." We understand the significance of this passage better since we know that with the departure of Giuliano, Leonardo's hope of receiving what he deserved for the picture was gone forever. Very likely Giuliano left the picture on which Leonardo had worked for years with him and never paid for it. This would also explain why Leonardo took the painting with him to France, since in case the picture had been ordered by the husband of La Gioconda, it would likely have stayed in Italy.

Since Leonardo speaks of himself as "created" by the Medici, he must have been much indebted to them in his youth, and we do well to assume the statement of the Anonimo to be correct. He writes: *"Stette da giovane col magnifico Lorenzo de' Medici, et dandoli provisione per se il faceva lavorare nel giardino sulla piaza di San Marcho di Firenze, et da lui haveva 30 anni, che dal detto Magnifico Lorenzo fu mandato el duca di Milano a presentarli insieme con Atalante Migliorotti una lira, che unico era in sonare tale extrumento."* [36] ("As a youth he lived with Lorenzo de' Medici, who gave him commissions; he allowed him to work in the garden at the Piazza San Marco; when he was thirty years old he was sent by this Lorenzo il Magnifico, together with Atalante Migliorotti, to the duke of Milan, to present him with a lyre which he knew how to play with distinction.")

Since the account of the Anonimo is an historical source of the first order, there is no reason to assume that this statement should not be as accurate in details as his other accounts. The observation which Thiis[37] makes in this connection, "There is no information as to any other relation between Leonardo and Lorenzo 'il Magnifico'; it would seem rather as if Leonardo for some reason or other was not sufficiently appreciated by the great art patron of Florence, and perhaps this was one of the reasons for his leaving the town of his birth at the age of thirty," stands in direct contradiction to this account. Could there have been anything more honorable for the artist than to be sent by the ruler of Florence as an emissary to the duke of Milan in company with a celebrated musician, with the princely gift of a precious lute? And if we do not know the commissions which according to the Anonimo were given to the artist by Lorenzo, is it not comprehensible enough, considering the small number of documents relating to Leonardo's early period which we possess; might it not be due to our faulty interpretation of these few existing documents?

The drawing of the murderer of Giuliano de' Medici, which Leonardo executed in 1479, is perhaps connected with a commission of Lorenzo's or of the city—which at this time was synonymous. If Leonardo assisted in the altarpiece of Pistoja, he worked on a monument dedicated to a Medici and in whose erection Lorenzo was at least indirectly not without a part. We return later to the terra cotta relief from the Villa Careggi, which can certainly be traced to a commission either of Piero's or possibly Lorenzo's, and in which we believe Leonardo to have participated. And we may certainly also assume that Leonardo owed to Lorenzo de' Medici that first public commission from the city for the altar for the Chapel of St. Bernard. And this for the following reason: Two weeks before Leonardo received the commission, it had been given to Piero Pollaiuolo. If it was suddenly withdrawn from him, only a powerful personality could have had a share in it. That this was no other than Lorenzo de' Medici, we may assume from the fact that it can be demonstrated that two months later the same Piero Pollaiuolo had withdrawn from him another commission which he had already received and which was now given to the atelier of Verrocchio. As much as Lorenzo seems to have esteemed Antonio Pollaiuolo, it is obvious that he had no predilection for the art or the personality of his brother Piero. In the bestowal of the commission for the Forteguerri tomb, after the models of Piero Pollaiuolo and Verrocchio had been considered, the Pistojans had decided in favor of the former, principally because it was cheaper. Fearful of Lorenzo de' Medici, they considered it advisable to hear his opinion; they therefore sent both models to Florence. But Lorenzo was of a different opinion than the Council of Pistoja; he decided in favor of Verrocchio, and the Pistojans revoked their decision and gave the commission to Verrocchio (March 17, 1478).[38]

From the position of authority which Lorenzo de' Medici occupied in the city of Florence shortly before the Pazzi conspiracy (April 26), it is next to impossible that a commission for a chapel of the Palazzo Pubblico could have been bestowed without his orders. But his preference was evidently given at this time to the atelier of Verrocchio, to which Leonardo belonged. This atelier, whose head was, so to speak, Lorenzo's court artist, had not only executed the sculptures of the Villa Careggi, the bronze putto with the dolphin now in the court of the Palazzo Vecchio, and the bronze David, but also, a few years before, the decorative works for the joust of Giuliano de' Medici (January 28, 1475), in which it is possible that Leonardo also had already had a part.

Now the Anonimo Gaddiano, whom we have found so excellently orientated, reports: "*Comincio a dipignere una tavola nel detto palazzo* [Palazzo Pubblico] *la quale di poi in sul suo disegno fu finita per Filippo di Fra Filippo.*"[39] ("He began to paint an altarpiece in this Palazzo Pubblico which was later finished, after his design, by Filippino Lippi.") And again he writes in the biography of Filippino Lippi: "*Dipinse nella sala minore del consiglio del palazzo de Signori la tavola dove è una Nostra Donna con altre figure la quale haveva cominciata a dipignere Leonardo da Vinci; et detto Filippo la finì in sul disegno di Leonardo.*"[40]

Vasari knows nothing of this participation of Leonardo's in an altarpiece completed by Filippino, but, as in the other instances, documents have shown the Anonimo to be right. In spite of this, no significance has been attached to these statements in the Leonardo literature. It is either explained that Filippino has handled an entirely new motive—assuming that the commission of the city originally called for the Appearance of the Madonna to St. Bernard—or, as Venturi recently remarked, that in the executed altarpiece of Filippino's, not a trace can be discovered of Leonardo's alleged cartoon. So far as the first objection is concerned, the representation, to be sure, which Bernardo Daddi had painted in 1355 and which was to be painted anew, was an appearance of the Madonna to St. Bernard; but in the contract with Leonardo[41] nothing at all was said of the subject, but only a new conception of the altar painting requested; besides this, it may be clearly concluded from the wording of the second account of the Anonimo, that the composition which was executed by Filippino was the enthroned Madonna, which he completed from Leonardo's design. Thus Filippino Lippi was not the one to undertake the change of subject, if a literal revival of the trecento motive was actually the original intention, which has not yet been proved.

According to the documents, Leonardo received the commission for the altarpiece from the priors of the city of Florence on January 10,[42] and that he began the execution eagerly we may assume from the fact that on March 16 he received a first payment of 25 gulden. To whom other than to Lorenzo de' Medici was he indebted for so high a valuation of his art? Even Botticelli received for his altarpiece of the year 1483 only 35 gulden in all. We may gather from this that the ever-prudent priors had not paid out this sum to Leonardo, if he had not worked on the altarpiece itself and needed the paints for it. It may be then that the question of the preliminary work which Filippino later found, does not concern itself with a cartoon but with an under-painting, as in the case of the later Adoration of the Kings.

In order that the altarpiece might be completed, the signory, as is well known, turned to Domenico Ghirlandajo on May 20, 1483—only, then, after Leonardo had finally moved to Milan—and as Ghirlandajo could not be secured in the following year, to Filippino Lippi, who completed his painting (Pl. 23) in a remarkably short time—by February, 1485. Thus the documentary record entirely agrees with the statements of the Anonimo, and we have every reason to ask whether nothing more is to be discovered in Filippino's altarpiece in the Uffizi of the composition and the spirit of Leonardo.

Indeed, a comparison of the altarpiece in Pistoja and the painting executed by Filippino suffices to discover relations in the composition as a whole and in the position of the individual figures. To be sure, Filippino has stamped all the figures with the impress of his types, and in his drawing of the narrow faces and long slender fingers, in the color scheme

as well as in the transparent, iridescent nimbuses, he has retained the decided style which he had developed almost from his first work. Still, I
believe, we can sense through the superficial painting of Filippino the imposing composition of Leonardo, which shows itself to be the exact continuation of the altarpiece of Pistoja. The attitude of the Madonna is
similar to that in the early work both in the manner in which she holds
her head and in the position of the hands. The Child sits in both instances
upon the Madonna's right knee and turns toward the saint who stands on
the left; but in Filippino's altarpiece a closer relation to the saint has been
brought about, and in place of the gesture of blessing, Christ turns the
pages of a prayer book; but the position of the feet, especially that of the
toes, has remained almost unchanged. The position of the arms of John
the Baptist and St. Zeno is also essentially the same, except that here Filippino has used impressions of Botticelli also, particularly in the figure of
the Baptist who is to be found similarly conceived in the indeed scarcely
earlier large altarpiece of Botticelli's of 1485; and the St. Zeno has assumed
a more dramatic and devout attitude, which might well be in keeping with
the greater advance of Leonardo's art. The folded arms of the saints and
the astonished gesture of St. Bernard are motives which accord with the
conception of the youthful Leonardo and are to be found in a similar
fashion in his early works. But more Leonardesque than anything else
appears to me to be the upper part of the composition. This motive of the
free flying angels with a coat of arms and intertwined ribbons, which is
not to be found earlier in this form, but which is frequently copied later
on, surpasses in boldness of invention and drawing the power of a twenty-
five-year-old painter of the type of Filippino. Even Botticelli in his later
compositions, and obviously Raphael and Fra Bartolommeo, used the idea,
and if Filippino later employed the same motive frequently and, above all,
shows the same fondness for ornamental ribbon work, it only proves how
strong the impressions were which he received in his youth from Leonardo.[43]

In the case of the interlaced ribbons about the coat-of-arms, we
are already reminded of Leonardo's Milan works, with which Filippino
at that time can scarcely have been acquainted; they prove again that nearly
all the motives which Leonardo employed later are already contained in
his youthful works. But the hovering angels above an ecclesiastical composition occupied the mind of the master just at the time that he designed
the altarpiece of the Uffizi, which is proved by the drawings executed about
1478: first the sketches of the Bonnat collection and of the Academy in
Venice (Pls. 24, 25) with the representation of the Nativity, a composition
which is generally dated before that of the Adoration of the Kings; and

then the wonderful sheet of the Malcolm collection, British Museum (Pl. 26), likewise a certain drawing of the Florentine period, in which Berenson rightly still sees suggestions of Verrocchio, and which is also reminiscent of the remarkable combination of coat-of-arms and ribbons in the Uffizi composition. That this profile drawing of the flying angels and the form of the angels also, reminds us of the angels of the terra cotta relief of the Villa Careggi, likewise speaks, as we shall see, for an origin about the year 1478.

But more important than these details is the progress in the whole composition of the altarpiece in the Uffizi, which signifies a first breaking through the flat style of the quattrocento in the direction of the plastic compositions of the cinquecento. Compared with the altarpiece in Pistoja, but compared also with the contemporary paintings of other artists, even Botticelli, the composition suddenly shows a powerful effect of depth. We illustrate herewith side by side the altarpiece of Botticelli's of 1483 (Pl. 28) and that of the unimportant Cosimo Rosselli of 1482 (Pl. 27), which represents an adequate average performance of Florentine painting of this time, and are astonished to see how flat and quattrocentesque even Botticelli's work looks beside the altarpiece of St. Bernard.

In Botticelli's composition the saints stand before the throne almost upon the same plane; the Madonna, the Child, and the angels behind are formed so large that they seem to belong to nearly the same relief plane of the foreground. The architecture also, although in its perspective artistically deepened, is just at the point where it recedes, again drawn into the first plane by the curtains which are held by the angels. On the other hand, we see in Filippino's altarpiece an entirely new principle of artistic deepening of space as well as of the figures, which are placed in a half circle toward the depth in close relationship to each other, while the architecture in sharp, sudden accents emphasizes the depth within a narrow compass toward the niche. This deepening of space is still further emphasized by the *chiaroscuro* of the whole as well as by the modeling of the single figures.

Now Filippino was, to be sure, a very gifted and precocious artist, but no one will consider him the genius who broke through the concepts of the quattrocento in an entirely new sense. This genius was admittedly Leonardo, and the decisive work in this respect is generally held to be his Adoration of the Kings of 1481, although it is frequently rightly pointed out that already the position of Leonardo's angel in Verrocchio's Baptism of Christ overcomes the principle of flatness. The altarpiece of St. Bernard stands as to date between these two creations, and we believe that its composition is just as decisive an achievement in the development of painting as that was.

The Adoration of the Kings marks a great advance in so far as

Leonardo here created the conception of depth in cinquecentesque sense *without* surrounding architecture—the architectural details are relegated to the background—solely by the skillful grouping of the figures in free landscape. But before this was done he had to give to the traditional form of the altarpiece in architectonic frame a new style. The commission which he received in the beginning of the year 1478 for the altarpiece of St. Bernard was not only the first independent commission; it was at the same time an order of the city—and one may well suppose that Leonardo would have produced something completely new and unheard of. In the altarpiece of Pistoja he was bound to Verrocchio's scheme, but here he had free rein, and with the consistency peculiar to genius developed the new principle out of the traditional form which he had learned from his teacher.

As proof that Leonardo was indeed in 1478 so far advanced in deepening the space of his compositions, we reproduce a little-known drawing of the Hamburg Kunsthalle (Pl. 38),[44] which from the style we can place with certainty in this period, and which shows the principle of compact figures with enframing architecture in a more simplified form than the altarpiece in the Uffizi. The forming of the niche with the projecting architectonic masses in strong foreshortening well permits its comparison with the architecture of this great altarpiece, and both of the figures, although in an entirely other motive, are still so artistically grouped that we obtain a similar feeling for compact massing toward the depth as in the large altarpiece.

IV

That part of the biography by the Anonimo Gaddiano which refers to Lorenzo de' Medici befriending the young Leonardo and giving him work in his garden near the Piazza di San Marco, has formerly been scarcely taken into consideration. But if the information given by this biographer is to take on the significance which we believe it should, we must look for a confirmation of these statements.

Now we know through Vasari what peculiar significance this garden had. He writes in the life of Michelangelo: "At this time the sculptor Bertoldo had a position in the garden of Lorenzo de' Medici near the Piazza di San Marco; not so much as custodian and overseer of the many beautiful antique works of art which Lorenzo had gathered together at great cost and installed there, but because Lorenzo intended to create a school of prominent painters and sculptors, for which he had selected Bertoldo, a pupil of Donatello, as principal and director; all the more as he was old and could no longer work. . . ." The period of which Vasari speaks is the end of the 80's, when Michelangelo entered this school of sculpture in 1489 to make such rapid progress that Lorenzo took him into his own house in 1490, where he remained for two years, until the death of the sovereign.[45] Bertoldo was at that time, indeed, already old; he died in 1491 in Lorenzo's Villa Poggio a Cajano as one of his closest friends.[46]

But at the time when Leonardo was educating himself, Bertoldo was at the height of his career. In the 70's were created his best known medals, which according to Bode were executed mostly for Lorenzo de' Medici, beginning with the medal of Emperor Frederik III (1469), that of the Venetian senator Francesco Diedo (1475), that of Mathias Corvinus (1476–1480), Filippo de' Medici, archbishop of Pisa (about 1478), Sultan Mahomed II (1480), and above all the famous double medal of the Pazzi conspiracy of April, 1478. But at that time was also executed the artist's masterpiece, already mentioned by Vasari, the bronze relief of a cavalry battle (now in the Bargello, Pl. 30), which as Bode has proved, reproduces the composition of a half-destroyed antique sarcophagus now in the Campo Santo in Pisa, completed in his own manner. Lorenzo, in whose companionship Bertoldo was often found, frequently visited in Pisa after the reëstablishment of the university (1472) and the restoration of the Campo Santo, and doubtless gave the impulse to the reproduction and completion of the antique sarcophagus. In the inventory of Lorenzo's legacy of 1492 Bertoldo's bronze relief above the fireplace in one of the rooms of the Palazzo Medici is mentioned.

Whoever was familiar, therefore, with the composition of the relief in its details, must either have studied it in Bertoldo's atelier or in the Palazzo Medici. Indeed, we believe we may assume an exact knowledge of the relief by Leonardo.[47]

To be sure, the employment of related motives leads us to a later, the second Florentine, period, when he executed the cartoon for the Battle of Anghiari, yet, as we have already pointed out more than once, it is characteristic of him, as of all great masters, that his fundamental ideas were outlined for him from youth on. And thus it has been quite often shown that the idea of the cavalry battle appears as early as about 1480 in drawings and in the Adoration of the Kings. We believe that the impressions which Leonardo received from Bertoldo (who at the end of the quattrocento was the best sculptor of moving horses not only in relief but also in bronze statuettes)[48] together with his inborn predilection for the study of horses, gave the impulse to his representations of this kind in painting and sculpture.

There is no pre-Leonardesque composition which shows such similarity in the groups of fighting horsemen, with the defeated lying under the horses, represented in the Battle of Anghiari, as does Bertoldo's relief (Pl. 30). And if we read in his *Trattato della pittura* how much his mind was affected by the motive of the cavalry battle, we may assume that he was influenced by a strong impression of his youth.

But also with regard to details, we find sufficient analogies with his studies of horsemen from earlier as well as later periods. The frequently found motive of a horse, especially, which while galloping to the left tosses its head far back to the right side (Pl. 31), is first encountered in Bertoldo's relief. One should not object that Leonardo's studies are obviously enough studies from nature. It is so difficult to observe such complicated attitudes of a galloping horse in the actuality that in such cases the artist had especially to rely upon his imagination; and it is quite possible that Leonardo supplemented his imagination by the impressions which he found in the completed relief.

Among the plaquettes and medals which Bode attributes to Bertoldo there is one which bears a strikingly Leonardesque character, the plaquette which—used as pommel of the hilt—is to be found in several replicas in Berlin and in the Gustave Dreifuss collection at Paris and which represents Bellerophon killing the Chimera (Pl. 32). The same representation appears on the reverse of a medal of which, however, only one specimen has been preserved, which shows on the obverse Federigo of Urbino. G. F. Hill, the excellent connoisseur of Renaissance medals, recognizes in it the medal which, according to Vasari, was executed by Francesco di Giorgio and portrays Federigo.[49] The representation on the observe, which Bode attributes to Bertoldo, must therefore also have been done by this great Sienese painter, sculptor, and architect, who was for a time in the service of the duke of Urbino. The modeling of the male nude agrees so well with that of the nude figures on the so-called Discordia, the stucco relief in the Victoria and Albert Museum, that the medal, according to Hill, Schubring, and others, must be attributed to the master of this relief, in whom we recognize Francesco di Giorgio.

This relief, which has been treated often enough in art literature and which is attributed now to Verrocchio, now to Bertoldo or Pollaiuolo, and was defended until the last by Bode as a work of Leonardo's, does not need to be discussed again here.[50] It suffices to establish the fact that the opinion first expressed by P. Schubring, who recognizes in the relief the hand of Francesco di Giorgio and who attributes to him correctly also the bronze relief in the University of Perugia and that in the Chiesa del Carmine in Venice, has found general acceptance.

In spite of this fact, I believe that Bode had a right intuition, inasmuch as connections may indeed be established between the art of Francesco di Giorgio and that of Verrocchio's workshop, and with Leonardo. We know that Francesco di Giorgio met Leonardo in Milan in 1490; he was appointed by Lodovico il Moro, probably at Leonardo's instigation, to go to Milan to report upon the construction of the cathedral and betook himself in June of this year in the company of Leonardo to Pavia to study there also the cathedral, which was in the process of building. We may assume at any rate that during this prolonged association of the two masters an intimate exchange of ideas must have taken place. But we may also assume that Francesco di Giorgio was known in Florence for a longer period since he entered into the competition instituted by Lorenzo de' Medici for the façade of the cathedral in Florence.[51]

We might indeed assume that Francesco di Giorgio had already had connections with the Verrocchio workshop in the 70's, when he went frequently from Siena to Urbino. In spite of the fact that he had a highly individual style of his own, it is scarcely a mere coincidence that his bronze reliefs could be regarded for a long time as works of Verrocchio's and Leonardo's and that they were created just at a time when we find the Verrocchio workshop betraying similar tendencies. It is quite probable that Francesco di Giorgio who, as it seems, began to work in bronze not earlier than the beginning or middle of the 70's—after he was active, especially as a painter, with Nerroccio—had connections with the most prominent atelier for this technique in Florence, that of Verrocchio,[52] or perhaps even developed his technique here. We can date three of his bronze works about 1475-1478: viz., the plaque with the Lamentation in Venice, which comes from the palace of Urbino and represents Duke Federigo as the donor together with his son, the young Guidobaldo; probably belonging with it, the plaque with the Scourging, now in Perugia; and the medal of Federigo with the representation of the Chimera on its reverse. These works were presumably executed in Urbino shortly after the artist's arrival in 1478; but it is also possible that·they were created before that time in Florence, as is assumed by Bode for the sake of his Leonardo theory, and by A. Venturi, who previously attributed them to Bertoldo. These critics point out that the young Guidobaldo, who was born in 1472, does not look more than three years old[53] and that Federigo da Urbino had owned since 1472 a palace in Florence which had been assigned to him by the city. But if Francesco di Giorgio lived in Florence it must have been before the middle of 1478; for soon after the Pazzi conspiracy a war broke out—in August, 1478—between Florence and the cities of Siena and Urbino which were allied with Naples, and Francesco di Giorgio, called to Urbino by Federigo, had to supervise the military preparations and fortifications against Florence; this, however, did not hinder either one again taking up his relations with Florence soon after the suspension of hostilities.

We believe we are able to mention still a fourth bronze work as having been done by Francesco di Giorgio about this time: a medal portraying on the obverse Alfonso II, Duke of Calabria, and on the reverse celebrating this commander-in-chief of the troops allied against Florence as the victor of the battle of Poggibonsi. This medal was attributed to Bertoldo by Bode, but Hill rightly remarks that it is improbable that a Florentine would have made a medal celebrating the defeat of his city, the more so since the style of the execution is much more picturesque, which is also admitted by Bode. Now we know that Francesco di Giorgio executed for Alfonso II a representation of the battle of Poggibonsi in commemoration of the victory of the Neapolitans over the Florentines, and Schubring[54] assumes that the representation in question was a military sketch or a geographical battle picture. One easily assumes that by the representation mentioned in the documents was meant the medal, on whose reverse the hills around Poggibonsi are represented, or that the medal was created simultaneously with the painting. The picturesque style of the portrait as well as the representation of the profile in which the drawing of the mouth especially reminds us of that on Federigo's medal, and the allegorical scene on the reverse agree very well with the conception of Francesco di Giorgio, as we gather from his bronze reliefs; and the individual postures of the figures on the reverse recur in a very similar fashion on the relief of the Discordia.[55]

Now it is certainly not a mere coincidence that just in the bronze works created by Francesco di Giorgio about 1478 we encounter tendencies which correspond to those of Leonardo's during these years, particularly the predilection for the representation of a momentary movement accentuated to the utmost, such as is expressed by flying angel forms or galloping horsemen. Never before this do we meet in relief work such a daring reproduction of highly agitated angelic figures who swing themselves in the air in artistic foreshortening as seen in the relief of the Lamentation by Francesco di Giorgio. Not without reason have they reminded Bode of the above-mentioned drawings of Leonardo (Pls. 24–26), to which must be added the charming sheet with dancing girls in flying drapery in the Academy in Venice. No other strove so hard as Leonardo for the emancipation of the reproduction of movement and it is quite remarkable that this emancipation also appears with Francesco di Giorgio just at this time, while the movement of his figures in previous works is just as constrained as with Pollaiuolo, if not more so. For this reason we may assume Leonardo's influence upon his art, although at this time Francesco was already nearly forty years old.

In the case of the representation of the Battle with the Chimera, we might indeed almost assume that he made use of a drawing of Leonardo's, so closely does it resemble in details Leonardo's artistic interest in the reproduction of prancing horses (Pls. 33, 34). Such a use of a drawing would be by no means incompatible with the spirit of that period, much less if Francesco di Giorgio and Leonardo were friends, since, as we have seen, no one was more generous in parting with his ideas than Leonardo.

The representation of a struggle between dragons and a horse-man sitting on a violently prancing steed, already occupied Leonardo in early drawings, and later we frequently encounter motives of galloping horsemen who charge the enemy with couched lance, on which occasion the horse opens its mouth so wide that the teeth and the upper jaw become visible (Pl. 33), decidedly an unusual motive, which recurs on the plaquette of Francesco di Giorgio's, but is nowhere else met with in his works. A representation of an open mouth of a lion, which may be compared with that of the Chimera on the plaquette mentioned before, is also to be found on one of the sheets with studies of horses' heads with wide-open mouths (Pl. 33).[56]

After this digression concerning the relations of Leonardo to Bertoldo and Francesco di Giorgio, we return to Leonardo's art and ask ourselves where we can best follow his own ideas in the field of sculpture during his activity in Verrocchio's workshop at this time.

V

One of the most important monuments manifesting the collaboration of Verrocchio and Leonardo appears to me to be the terra cotta relief with the Resurrection (Pl. 35), in the Villa Careggi, near Florence, which in my opinion was created about 1478. Following the example of Gamba, who first published it[57] it is, however, usually referred to as an early work of Verrocchio; and, as frequently happens in such cases, an opinion once expressed is indiscriminately adhered to by all the following authors.

Miss Cruttwell has observed[58] that the relief must have come into existence at a later time than Verrocchio's Baptism of Christ "from the superior excellent and freedom of execution, the flexibility of the figures and the assurance and even audacity of the treatment." But the Baptism of Christ is now generally dated about the middle of the 70's or even 1475–1480. It is therefore no longer permissible to date the relief from the last years of Cosimo il Vecchio, before 1464, less so since it seems scarcely probable that Verrocchio should have already worked for Cosimo, the patron of Donatello, while Donatello was still living (he died in 1466). Verrocchio's activity for the Medici is attested by the documents not earlier than under Piero (1464–1469), for whom he created the slab for the tomb of his father, Cosimo, in S. Lorenzo after Cosimo's death; it is a comparatively unpretentious and unadorned work, which was followed—not earlier than 1472—by the larger commission given by Lorenzo de' Medici for the execution of Piero's tomb, likewise in S. Lorenzo. The Lavabo in the vestry of the same church was probably executed for Piero also; it is a purely decorative piece like the tomb for Piero. We hear through the documents about two other commissions from the signory—both evidently received through the intervention of the Medici: that for the bronze globe (palla) on the cupola of the cathedral and that for the large bronze chandelier[59] for the Palazzo Vecchio (both executed in 1468 and 1469).

It was not earlier than the first half and about the middle of the 70's that Verrocchio was commissioned with the first sculptured figures by Lorenzo de' Medici: the bronze David in the Bargello and the bronze putto in the Palazzo Vecchio. Until then the Medici made use of the skill of Verrocchio almost exclusively for decorative works. It is for this reason also that one may assume that the relief of the Resurrection was created at about the same time as these sculptural bronze works done for the Villa Careggi. Finally, the fact that the relief contains Leonardesque features proves that it can scarcely have been executed before the time when Leonardo was working with Verrocchio.

If the relief did not come later on into the Palazzo Vecchio, to which Lorenzo assigned both of the bronze figures, the reason for it obviously was that it was built, as Conte Gamba observed, into a wall as a tympanum of the entrance wall of the chapel which Michelozzo had erected for Cosimo: it fits exactly in size and volume into this place, where later on in the seventeenth century an opening was made for a window. The relief was taken out on this occasion and put aside, until at the end of the nineteenth century it was rediscovered broken behind a wall of the villa by the owner, Mr. Carlo Segré.

With great likelihood it may be identified as the work which is quoted as no. 5 *"per una storia di rilievo chon più figure"* in the list of the works done by Verrocchio for the Medici and which after the expulsion of the Medici was presented to the city council by Verrocchio's brother Tommaso.[60] It also finds mention in the inventory of Lorenzo de' Medici's collection of works of art of the year 1492 under the inaccurate description, however, which is characteristic of the inventories of that period: *"Una tavola d'altare con cornice dorata, dipintovi dentro un sepolcro con nostro Signore sconfitto di croce, con cinque figure."*

The relief, which is not easily accessible and of which only a single photograph has become known (used for Miss Cruttwell's book and for Bode's *Denkmäler*) is the largest terra cotta relief by Verrocchio in existence; it was executed with the utmost care and afterwards finely painted and gilded over (of which substantial traces are still preserved) as would be expected from the importance of the customer, Lorenzo de' Medici, for whom it was created.

Masterly and often praised is the sleeping youth in the foreground ("the mental and physical relaxation of a sleeper has never been better rendered," says Miss Cruttwell), but the bearded, helmeted sleeper behind at the right and the guard who is just arising in the left corner are also excellently characterized in their postures. In the composition as a whole Bode is reminded of the Forteguerri tomb, the design for which Verrocchio executed, as we have seen, at the end of the year 1477. Regarding the figure of Christ, most scholars call attention to its similarity to that in the Baptism of Christ; but the figure on the relief (Pl. 44) is considerably more graceful and its head reminds us of the preliminary studies of Leonardo for the Last Supper which, as is well known already make their appearance during his Florentine period.

The nearness in time to the painting of the Baptism of Christ, in which Leonardo executed one of the angels, makes it appear possible that in this relief also the young artist lent a hand in assisting his much-occupied master. Two of the foreground figures especially remind us of Leonardo and their modeling seems almost to surpass the power of his teacher: the guard crouching in the right foreground and the terrified, screaming soldier behind at the left. Miss Cruttwell characterizes the first one well with the following words: "In the half-naked figure on the other side, there is a suggestion of the enchained Titans of Michelangelo." That Leonardo's figures when executed in sculpture also possessed a cinquecentesque fullness and strength of limb which make us think at once of Michelangelo as the greatest representative of cinquecento sculpture, can be demonstrated by the bronze groups of John the Baptist and the Pharisees on the baptistry in Florence, which were created by Leonardo's pupil Rustici with the assistance of the master.[61] In this group the muscular limbs of the figures point to the termination of a style development whose beginning is to be observed in the powerful figure in the relief of the Villa Careggi and was not peculiar to Michelangelo alone.

If by reason of this figure Miss Cruttwell remarks that the relief is "a curious link between the art of the Quattrocento and that of the Cinquecento, and a remarkable instance of Verrocchio's progressive and innovating tendencies," we might attribute these progressive tendencies rather to Leonardo than to Verrocchio, who was older by just those fifteen years which often signify the partition between two generations.

We have a further proof of how Leonardesque this corner figure of the terra cotta relief is in the drawing by Leonardo in the Hamburg Kunsthalle (Pl. 38), which, however, represents an entirely different motive (Phyllis and Aristotle) but reproduces almost the identical complicated position of the masculine figure. With such an unusual position one can scarcely assume an accidental agreement between the figure of the drawing and the plastic form, with the left foot drawn up in an identical manner and the right arm resting above it; thus when Leonardo created the drawing he must have exactly remembered the figure of the relief; and it is natural to assume that both compositions were created almost simultaneously because we have here modifications of the same position problems and not a slavish copy. The spread-out thumb and arched hand which is shown in the drawing in the left hand of Aristotle and in the relief in the right hand of the guard (Pl. 39) is, by the way, characteristic of both the young Leonardo and Verrocchio, and is shown for example in the Amor of the beautiful drawing of the resting Venus in the Uffizi which is attributed now to Verrocchio,[62] now to Leonardo.[63]

Still more than with the right corner figure of the Careggi relief, may we assume the probability of Leonardo's collaboration in the screaming soldier behind at the left (Pl. 40). The unusual treatment of the forms has also impressed Miss Cruttwell. She writes: "The savage half-animal face of the soldier, yawning like a roused tiger, is Leonardesque in its energy—offering in its modernness a bizarre contrast to the conventional treatment of the theme." One may well assume that this critic would have also arrived at the supposition of Leonardo's collaboration if she had not dated the relief too early. Indeed, it seems to me that the expression of the face as well as the technical treatment surpasses Verrocchio.

It is of course true that Verrocchio was from the beginning

an artist of intense feeling and of keen observation, but ponderous and a stranger to all representations of passionate and rapid movement. That he felt deeply is shown, among other examples, in the expressive relief of the Lamentation in the Berlin Museum, but the slowness of his temperament is evidenced by the detailed, overladen handling of the masses of his draperies; and wherever agitated, advancing figures appear, especially in his paintings, the movement is frozen, as it were, or the minuteness of the details hinders the expression of the fleeting motion. Never has he dared to portray crying figures with wide-open mouths.

Leonardo, on the other hand, especially liked to occupy himself with just this problem. In looking through his compositions and drawings for this, it is astonishing to find how frequently he portrayed animals and human beings with open mouths. The quickness of his perception, the pleasure he took in reproducing momentary movement, made this a congenial motive and one which, as is well known, he used repeatedly in the representation of the cavalry fight of the Battle of Anghiari (Pl. 42), and of which he also speaks in his *Trattato della Pittura* in the instructions to painters for the reproduction of fighting scenes: "The bowed lips (in the faces of the defeated) show the upper teeth and the teeth are parted as by cries and shrieks of pain . . . Others you must depict crying loud with wide-open mouth and in flight. . . ."

As the same problems run through Leonardo's art during his entire life—we have already shown this in other connections—we find in comparatively early drawings this interest in the representation of open jaws in the portrayal of dragons, lions, and horses. Upon a sheet with caricatures which probably originated within the first Florentine period, there also appears a grotesque form with wide-open mouth in the middle of the composition (Pl. 41).

In the reproduction of this strange motive with the pencil, the brush, or the plastically molding hand, Leonardo arrived at the same observation which later Dutch painters of the seventeenth century such as Frans Hals, or modern artists made: that quick movement can only be portrayed by means of a swift, impressionistic technique. It is for this reason that the execution of the shrieking figure in the terra cotta relief, in its hasty, pictorial treatment differs materially from the more draftsmanlike and harder modeling of the other figures, which show Verrocchio's manner.

Leonardesque appear to me also the angels, especially the one at the right, with his Greek profile and his backward-floating hair. Verrocchio and most of his contemporaries among the sculptors depict the heads of flying angels for the most part turned half toward the front; to be sure, Luca della Robbia, to whom the artist of the Careggi relief is related in the composition as a whole, also shows three of the angels in profile, but not with the backward-sloping forehead and the backward-blowing shock of hair which we frequently find in Leonardo's drawings, for example the allegorical representation of the Malcolm collection, in the British Museum (Pl. 26).

Finally, the position of the left corner figure, whose head is broken off, also shows, at least indirectly, a connection with Leonardo's art. In a painting of the Resurrection by Fernando de Llanos in the Cathedral of Seville (Pl. 48) we meet the same unusual position, in which the guard kneels with one leg on the ground, while the other is already drawn up as for a standing position. This Llanos was Leonardo's pupil in Florence in the summer of 1505 and worked in 1509 on this altar in Seville, in which it can be shown that he copied single figures and groups from Leonardo's works such as the Adoration of the Kings of 1481, the cartoon of the Battle of Anghiari, etc.[64] W. Suida has pointed out in this connection that the figure which stoops behind the shield in his Resurrection is taken from the Battle of Anghiari. It is therefore easily believable that he also borrowed the above-mentioned figure from Leonardo.[65] If that is actually the case, we may assume that about 1505, when he was Leonardo's assistant, the composition of the Careggi relief was considered in Leonardo's atelier as his artistic property, since de Llanos appears to have borrowed from no other master for his paintings.

As we have remarked, the composition of the relief of the Villa Careggi is strikingly related to that by Luca della Robbia in the Cathedral of Florence, which antedated it by a generation (the one by Luca was created about 1445, Pl. 36). The general arrangement is quite similar in the two reliefs: five soldiers lie similarly disposed about the grave; the principal space in the foreground is occupied by one of the sleepers stretched out lengthwise toward the right; Christ stands upon a small cloud above the sarcophagus with the same position of the arms and a related disposition of drapery; even the cover of the sarcophagus is correspondingly placed, and the laurel tree at the left and the palm at the right are strikingly alike.

The stylistic differences are, however, very material. Not only are the separate figures much more strongly individualized with Verrocchio; the whole composition is much more freely and dramatically constructed. Christ is more lightly suspended, is higher and more remote than in Luca della Robbia's composition; the ground around him is left more empty, and only two instead of four angels are distributed upon the plane.

The three planes of relief—the furthermost upon which the angels appear, the one in the middle with the figure of Christ, and the one in the foreground with the guards grouped together—are much more strongly accented than with Luca; this is especially noticeable in the foremost plane, with the towering guards. Thus a feeling is created of a greater breadth of the plane and of a stronger plastic effect, which is in accordance with the style of the late quattrocento and the early cinquecento.

The relations between Luca della Robbia, who died only in 1482, and Verrocchio seem to have been of a friendly nature. We know that Luca once borrowed bronze from Verrocchio for the completion of his doors in the cathedral.

But stylistic points of contact between him and Verrocchio cannot be established as in the case of the Verrocchio workshop and Andrea della Robbia. There is a replica[66] of a relief from the Verrocchio workshop of the Madonna with standing Child, glazed in the workshop of Andrea, whose stucco reproduction in an English private collection (Pl. 46) has been attributed by Theodore Cook and A. Venturi—but certainly without grounds—to the young Leonardo.[67]

While at the beginning Andrea della Robbia attached himself entirely to Luca's style, about the middle of the 70's a distinct change took place with him in the direction of the types of the Verrocchio workshop. In the 60's the Madonnas and the children still have the smooth-lying hair and the somewhat elongated shaped faces of Luca's; the reliefs of children on the Foundlings' Hospital, created about 1463–1466, still have nothing which reminds us somehow of Verrocchio's boys with their features terminating in baroque lines and with their curly-locked heads.

But about 1475–1478 we encounter a series of portrait-like heads on medallions (Kaiser-Friedrich Museum, Liechtenstein Gallery, Metropolitan Museum), some angel statuettes (Victoria and Albert Museum) and a St. Michael (Braunschweig)[68] in which the fine, sweet, and regular features are surrounded by an abundance of beautiful locks, exactly as in Verrocchio's David. It seems to me that there is no question that this change, which until now has not been observed, can be traced to the influence of Verrocchio and especially to Leonardo, whose inventive genius contributed these elements. The resemblance, for instance, between the type of Verrocchio's David and that of the boy's head in the Liechtenstein Gallery appear to me striking. We are reminded in this connection that Vasari mentions that there existed heads of smiling boys and women in terra cotta and stucco from Leonardo's youth, and we may assume that the reflections of these types play in many of the heads of Andrea della Robbia, who absorbed inspiration from every side and who also glazed the works of other sculptors in his atelier.[69]

Leonardo had an admiration for the art of the della Robbias, at least for their technique, as we gather from his *Trattato della Pittura* where, of contemporary artists, with the exception of Botticelli, he mentions only the della Robbias. He refers to their art occasionally in treating the question of the superiority of painting to sculpture as proof that painting by means of glazing the colors upon a terra cotta foundation can give a durability as of sculpture: "They practise this art," he continues, "in different places in France and Italy, especially in Florence in the family of the della Robbias, where they have invented a method of executing works regardless of size in glazed terra cotta painting."

That artistic connections existed between Andrea della Robbia and the workshop of Verrocchio, a master of the same age, is conceivable. But it would have been extremely remarkable if a stylistic relationship had existed between the art of Luca della Robbia, who represented the spirit of the first half of the quattrocento and that of Verrocchio and the young Leonardo who represented a new and entirely different kind of period. The borrowing of the composition of Luca's cathedral relief for the relief of the Villa Careggi can only then have been of a fortuitous nature. We would probably not be wrong in assuming that the reason for it lay in a wish of the patron and not in an intention of the artist.

But why should Lorenzo de' Medici, who gave the order for the Careggi relief, recommend a sort of imitation of Luca's composition? Why did he choose as model for the reproduction on the main wall of his house chapel just the relief over the entrance to the old sacristy in the cathedral, and not perhaps Luca's equally beautiful relief of the Ascension over the entrance of the new sacristy? Perhaps we can account for it, at least conjecturally.

During the murderous assault upon the Medici on April 26, 1478, Giuliano fell at the high altar of the cathedral, Lorenzo saving himself by flight into the old sacristy. Over the entrance, affording protection as it were to him who crossed the threshold, is affixed Luca's relief of the Resurrection. It may be, therefore, that Lorenzo commissioned Verrocchio to execute for his house chapel as a symbol of gratitude for his escape, a relief with the same representation as that connected with Luca's composition.

We also know that Lorenzo de' Medici wished to keep alive the horrors of the Pazzi conspiracy and his escape by means of celebrations and through artistic commissions. For this reason Bertoldo's double medal was created with the portraits of Lorenzo and Giuliano de' Medici and the representation of the happenings of that dreadful April day at the high altar of the cathedral. At any rate, the dating of the execution of the relief in the summer of 1478 would accord with the stylistic indications.

To prove our assumption plausible, we review the following activity of Verrocchio and Leonardo for the year 1478. On the tenth of January Leonardo received the commission for the altar of the chapel of St. Bernard in the Palazzo Pubblico. He immediately set to work, and received a first payment on March 16 upon the completion of the underpainting. On March 17, or a few days later, Verrocchio received the big commission for the Forteguerri tomb for the cathedral in Pistoja. Leonardo's collaboration in this work does not seem probable since he was otherwise engaged. But an interruption of his work on the Bernard altarpiece must have very soon occurred. The reason was probably the Pazzi conspiracy on April 26, which as may be easily understood, temporarily placed in question a work for which the order had been given by the city council. According to our assumption, the activity on the Resurrection relief of the Villa Careggi would have set in during the summer, which would also explain Verrocchio's neglect of the work on the Forteguerri tomb. Leonardo's drawing with Aristotle and Phyllis may have been created soon after the completion of the relief, which is followed by the preliminary studies for the Madonna with the Cat and the Madonna Benois. The last months of this year (November?) accord with the memorandum of Leonardo: ". . . *bre 1478 incominciai le 2 Vergini Marie.*" ("I began in . . . ber 1478 the two Madonna pictures.") From this we may determine that his occupation with the composition of the Madonna with the Cat and the Madonna Benois interested him more at the end of the year than the continuation of the great altarpiece for the Bernard chapel.

Now with regard to the remaining sculptures of Verrocchio which were created during the period of Leonardo's sojourn in his workshop, there can be scarcely any doubt that the younger master in one way or another directly, or indirectly through his spiritual influence, participated in the execution of Verrocchio's three famous bronze works of the 70's: the Putto with the Dolphin,[70] the David, and the group with the doubting Thomas. This has often been stated and has been made plausible by Leonardo's contemporary drawings.[71] But with the hitherto known material one will probably never succeed in establishing Leonardo's share in full detail.

It seems possible to specify the collaboration of Leonardo in the silver relief with the representation of the beheading of the Baptist, for which the directors of the cathedral gave the commission to Verrocchio on July 24, 1477. Verrocchio was paid for the model on August 2 of this year, and for the executing of the work he received the payment upon its completion in 1480; the execution thus falls at a time when Leonardo was very probably still associated with Verrocchio.

The relation to Leonardo of the two quarreling soldiers at the right side of the relief has rightly been pointed out time and again.[72] We know more than one drawing of Leonardo's which would indicate his preoccupation with these two figures: the famous profile drawing of a warrior in the British Museum (Malcolm collection) is connected with the head of the right-hand soldier, as Berenson was the first to notice; the cuirass of this soldier is, as has been noted, reproduced on a sheet in Windsor; and the profile of the left-hand soldier recurs almost exactly in a red chalk study which Leonardo later used for the Judas in the Last Supper. We may thus assume Leonardo's collaboration in these corner figures of the relief if anywhere.

But that, finally, Leonardo also had a share in the execution of the Colleoni is in the course of the Leonardo investigation becoming ever more probable. How would it have been possible for Leonardo, who from his youth on was more interested in the portrayal of horses in art than any other master of the Renaissance, and made his predilection known through innumerable drawings, to have maintained a passive attitude while Verrocchio busied himself with the plan for the equestrian statue? Leonardo was at that time still in Florence and certainly still most closely connected with Verrocchio's workshop, when Verrocchio in accordance with the resolution of the signory in Venice set himself to work on July 30, 1479, and had advanced the figure of the horse so far that it could be transported from Florence to Venice in July, 1481. We see the clearest connection with the model in one of the advancing horses in the background of Leonardo's Adoration of the Kings which was created in the summer of 1481. Malaguzzi-Valeri has even pointed to drawings of separate parts of the horse with measurements by Leonardo's hand, that can be conceived scarcely otherwise than as preparatory studies for the model of the Colleoni. If we observe further how Leonardesque the type of the Colleoni itself is, as was first pointed out by Mackowsky, how much more really in keeping this ideal type is with the mentality of Leonardo than with that of Verrocchio, we will welcome with particular satisfaction Malaguzzi-Valeri's hint of the possibility of the solution of the dating question so far as it has until now presented difficulties. The objection has frequently been made to the theory of Leonardo's collaboration on the Colleoni, that at the time it was completed he had long been in Milan. On the other hand, Mala-guzzi-Valeri's observes rightly that when Verrocchio resumed the work on the Colleoni statue about 1485—he had destroyed the first model of the horse in 1481 out of wrath over the resolution of the signory not to give him the execution of the rider also—Leonardo is just in this year not mentioned in Milan. Thus nothing would stand in the way of the suppo-sition of Leonardo's sojourn in Venice at this time and a further collabora-tion in Verrocchio's workshop in this city.

Finally, we may also assume that Leonardo had not commended himself in that letter to the Duke of Milan as being in a position to ex-ecute an equestrian statue, and that he had not been given the commission, if his collaboration on the Colleoni in the workshop of Verrocchio had not been known.

With this activity of the master's in the field of sculpture, also, during the last year in Florence, we now comprehend the reason for his not continuing the work on the great altarpiece for the Bernard chapel of the Palazzo Pubblico, while for the interruption of the work on the altarpiece of the Adoration of the Kings a sufficient reason is given in the removal of the artist to Milan.

11. Leonardo, *Madonna and Child*. Munich, Alte Pinakothek.
Photo: Bruckmann-Art Reference Bureau.

12. Leonardo, *Annunciation*. Paris, Louvre.
Photo: Agraci-Art Reference Bureau.

13. Verrocchio, *Head of a Madonna.*
Drawing. Paris, Louvre.

14. Verrocchio, *Girl's Face.* Drawing. London, British Museum.
Photo: Art Reference Bureau.

15. Verrocchio, (now attributed
    to Lorenzo di Credi), *Por-*
    trait of a Woman. Dresden,
    Kupferstichkabinett. *Photo:*
    Art Reference Bureau.

16. Verrocchio, *Head of a Woman*. Drawing. Florence, Uffizi.
    Photo: Alinari-Art Reference Bureau.

17. Lorenzo di Credi (?), *Madonna and Child with Sts. John and Zenobius.*
Altarpiece. Pistoia, Cathedral.   *Photo: Brogi-Art Reference Bureau.*

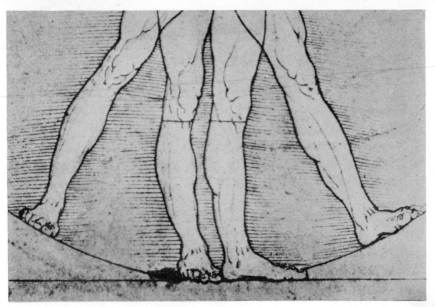

18. Leonardo, *Canon of Proportions,* detail.
Venice, Academy of Fine Arts.

19. Leonardo, *Child with Cat.* Drawing.
Windsor Castle, Royal Library, No. 12564.

20. Leonardo, *Study for a Youthful St. John
the Baptist*. Silverpoint drawing.
Windsor Castle, Royal Library, No. 12572.

21. Lorenzo di Credi, *Study for St. John
the Baptist*. Paris, Louvre.
Photo: Art Reference Bureau.

22. Leonardo, *Drapery Study for a Seated Figure*. Paris, Louvre. *Photo: Art Reference Bureau.*

23. Leonardo and Filippino Lippi (?), *Madonna and Saints*. Florence, Uffizi.

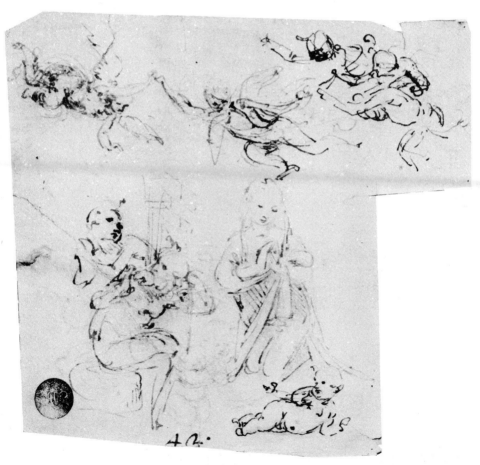

24. Leonardo, *Madonna Adoring Infant Christ and Other Figures*. Venice, Academy.   *Photo: Osvaldo Böhm, Venice.*

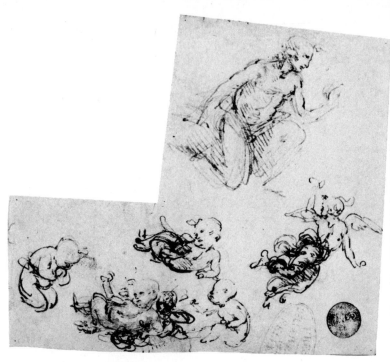

25. Leonardo, *Kneeling Youth and Putti*. Venice, Academy of Fine Arts.
Photo: Osvaldo Böhm, Venice.

26. Leonardo, *An Angel Placing a Shield*
on a Trophy and Separate Studies of
the Angel. London, British Museum.
Photo: Art Reference Bureau.

27. Cosimo Rosselli, *Madonna and Saints.* Florence, S. Spirito.
Photo: Brogi-Art Reference Bureau.

28. Sandro Botticelli, *Madonna and Saints*. Florence, Uffizi.
Photo: Alinari-Art Reference Bureau.

29. Leonardo, *Horse and Rider*.
London, Collection Norman R. Colville.

30. Bertoldo di Giovanni, *Battle*, detail. Bronze relief.
Florence, Museo Nazionale.
Photo: Alinari-Art Reference Bureau.

31a and b. Leonardo, *Horses*. Windsor Castle, Royal Library, Nos. 12336, 12334.

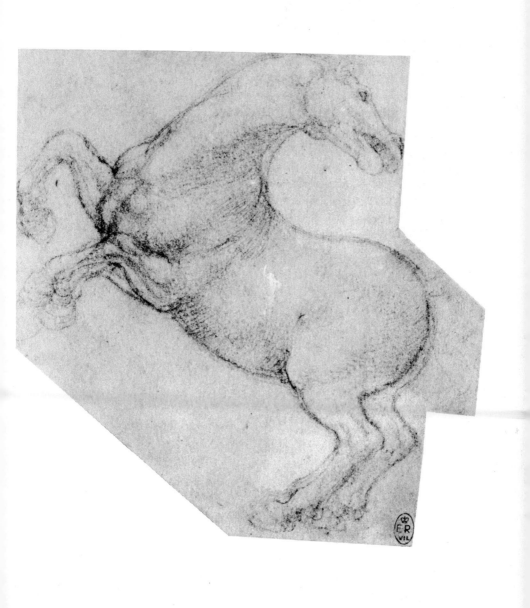

32. Francesco di Giorgio, *Bellerophon Killing the Chimera*.
Plaquette. Berlin, Museum.

33. Leonardo, *Studies of Horses' Heads and a Rearing Horse*.
Windsor Castle, Royal Library, No. 12326.

34. Leonardo, *Studies of Horsemen for Battle of Anghiari.*
London, British Museum.   *Photo: Anderson-Art Reference Bureau.*

An Attempt at Revaluation

by *Bernard Berenson*

I

s A BOY I felt a repulsion for Leonardo's "Last Supper." The faces were uncanny, their expressions forced, their agitation alarmed me. They were the faces of people whose existence made the world less pleasant and certainly less safe. It was quite enough, for at that time I was not aware that, apart from the faces, a painting had any interest. Yet the figures, too, seem to have affected me, for I remember feeling that they were too big and that there were too many of them in the room.

Forty years have gone by since those first reactions towards a famous masterpiece, and they have offered me opportunities enough for coming to terms with it. For hours and hours I have sat gazing at it, with concentrated attention, receptive, eager to let it hypnotize me if it could. For as many other hours I have studied it as a scholar and as a critic. I have tried to find in it all that the adepts thought that they had seen, all that the rhetoricians persuaded me that they had felt; and I dare say I, too, ended in speaking with tongues.

If I did, it was to help my unbelief, for neither subtlest argument nor whirling dervish enthusiasm quite converted me. "Yes, of course," I would say, "the rhythm of the composition is truly wonderful, the articulation of the groups masterly, the action of the hands most effective. The details, too, even to the tapestries on the wall, are exquisitely rendered. But what a pack of vehement, gesticulating, noisy foreigners they are,

From *The Study and Criticism of Italian Art* by Bernard Berenson (London: G. Bell and Sons, Ltd., 1916).

with faces far from pleasant, some positively criminal, some conspirators, and others having no business to be there. No! I will have none of them. They are not company for me."

But I never dared say it out loud.

My next meeting with Leonardo took place in the Louvre, but it was years later, and I was no longer the child reacting to a sensation as a bell to its knocker, but a youthful aspirant for artificial paradises, full of elaborately prepared anticipations, determined to feel and understand whatever had thrilled and transported others. I would not be left behind or shut out. So I gave myself long exposures before the works of the Florentine genius, and particularly before his supreme creation, as I was taught to regard it, the "Mona Lisa." Standing on the slippery floor of the Salon Carré, breathing its lifeless air, with the nasty smell of fresh paint in my nostrils, occasionally stealing a moment's rest on the high stool of an absent copyist, I would spend the hours of long summer days trying to match what I really was seeing and feeling with the famous passage of Walter Pater, that, like so many of my contemporaries, I had learned by heart.

I wonder even now how far I succeeded, for brought up almost exclusively on words, I easily yielded to incantations and talismanic phrases. They put me into states of body and mind not very different from those produced by hypnotic suggestion, and I should have stayed under the spell, if only I had been kept away from the object. But the presence of the object disturbed coma and prevented acquiescence. Its appeals grew and grew until finally it dared come into conflict with the powers of a shaman so potent even as Walter Pater. My eyes were unglamoured and I began to look. What an enchanted adept died in me when I ceased listening and reading and began to see and taste!

What I really saw in the figure of "Mona Lisa" was the estranging image of a woman beyond the reach of my sympathies or the ken of my interests, distastefully unlike the women I had hitherto known or dreamt of, a foreigner with a look I could not fathom, watchful, sly, secure, with a smile of anticipated satisfaction and a pervading air of hostile superiority. And against this testimony of my instincts nothing could prevail. I argued with myself many scores of times that the landscape was mysterious and fascinating, that the conscious art of the painter was marvellous, for it was at once bold and large in conception and delicate and subtle in execution. Then the mass of the figure was imposing yet simple, the modelling persuasive, the existence convincing. I learned to revel in these qualities, to enjoy analysing them, and to dwell lovingly upon each point. I was soothed by the collectedness and fullness of her pose, delighted with the simple yet unobvious device by which her sloping shoulder is given a monumental breadth, and amused by the wary intricacies in the hair and folds. And besides, were not four centuries unanimous in repeating that "Mona Lisa" was one of the very greatest, if not absolutely the greatest achievement of artistic genius?

So I hoped that my doubts would die of inanition, and that my resentment, convinced of rebellious plebeianism, would burn itself out of sheer shame. But neither happened, although in the meantime I too had become a prophet and joined my voice to the secular chorus of praise.

One evening of a summer day in the high Alps the first rumour reached me of "Mona Lisa's" disappearance from the Louvre. It was so incredible that I thought it could only be a practical joke perpetrated by the satellites of a shrill wit who had expressed a whimsical animosity toward a new frame into which the picture had recently been put. To my own amazement I nevertheless found myself saying softly: "If only it were true!" And when the news was confirmed, I heaved a sigh of relief. I could not help it. The disappearance of such a masterpiece gave me no feelings of regret, but on the contrary a sense of a long-desired emancipation. Then I realized that the efforts of many years to suppress my instinctive feelings about "Mona Lisa" had been in vain. She had simply become an incubus, and I was glad to be rid of her.

But I did not dare even then. Who was I to lift up my feeble voice against the organ resonances of the centuries?

"Mona Lisa," however, was not the only masterpiece of the Tuscan Empedocles that I had come to the Louvre to worship. The high altar was hers, but next came the "Madonna with St. Anne," and here too I adored but failed to understand, until I understood and ceased to adore. Behind the post-hypnotic suggestions I was endeavouring to follow out, something in me rebelled against the arrangement and the expression. The Blessed Virgin, the Child, the landscape I joyously consented to, but St. Anne—she alarmed me with her airs of a great lady and look of indulgent omniscience. Besides, I was distressed in body and mind to see what she was doing. Seated on no visible or inferable support she in turn on her left knee alone sustained the restless weight of a daughter as heavy as herself. The silhouette, moreover, was unavoidably confused, and, but for the grace of incorruptible European sense, might easily have initiated patterns ending in the dizzy fantasies of South Indian sculpture.

The "St. John" occupied the altar opposite in the imaginary

shrine to Leonardo erected by my masters. I no longer recall what spiritual rewards I was to expect if I inclined my heart and understanding to worship here too. But though I was too innocent to suspect the reason, I felt far from comfortable in the presence of this apparition looming tenebrously out of the murky darkness. The face leered at me with an exaggeration of all that had repelled me in the "Mona Lisa" and in the "St. Anne." And I could not conceive why this fleshy female should pretend to be the virile, sun-dried Baptist, half starved in the wilderness. And why did it smirk and point up and touch its breasts? Inspired by my good angel, I concluded that I was too young to fathom such mysteries, and so I gave this picture no further attention until I became a Morellian and decided that it could not be by Leonardo. Then for a score of years and more, something like a Freudian complex forbade my looking or thinking of the picture. At present I fear I must charge Leonardo with the crime. Possibly he did not paint it entirely with his own hand, for it must be conceded that no other of the few famous works of the master has so little beauty of line or colour or touch. But that only takes away extenuating circumstances that better quality would have furnished.

To follow out the post-hypnotic suggestion of my mesmerizers completely, I had to worship at two altars more, one dedicated to the "Virgin of the Rocks," and the other to the "Belle Ferronière." It took no too arduous spiritual combat to perform either act. I should have been glad if in the altarpiece the draperies, instead of attracting attention to themselves, served better to explain the Madonna's relation to the ground; I should have preferred a colouring less gray and dun, but I needed no enchantment to feel the humanity and mystery of the rest. The problem of the composition offended me not at all then, and indeed very little now, for it is not thrust upon one, and had Leonardo never sacrificed more to academic interests, it is likely I should have had no occasion to be making these confessions.

My whole heart went out to the portrait of the girl known as "La Belle Ferronière." I was on my own level again, in my own world, in the presence of this fascinating but yet simple countenance with its look of fresh wonder. Here too was colour that made me happy, supple modelling of quiet planes, and a contour as self-imposed as of a Laurana bust. For these reasons, however, the Morellian in me—only a secondary personality I venture to plead—began before long to doubt whether it could be Leonardo's. I assimilated it to Boltraffio because it was more like his imitations of its own self (as I perceived later) than to anybody else's type. I passed through a shameful moment when I resented this beautiful thing because I could not name its author. Happily I soon recovered my senses and returned to my early love. I fear, however, that in discussing Leonardo we cannot safely count her as his. But whose in all the world if not his, and if his, in no matter how limited a sense, in what moment of his career could he have created her?

So much for the objects of worship in the imaginary temple to Leonardo conjured up in my mind and firmly fixed there by the wise men whose incantations had enthralled me. At the same time, or soon after, I made acquaintance with three other works by the master for which somehow no niches had been prepared in my mental shrine. Two of them may have seemed relatively unimportant, namely, the "Annunciation" of the Louvre, and the "St. Jerome" of the Vatican. But the neglect of the third I cannot explain on artistic grounds, for ever since I made the acquaintance of this work, the Uffizi "Epiphany,"[1] I have had an increasing sense of its being, unfinished and blurred though it is, the most spontaneous, most comprehensive, and most satisfactory of all Leonardo's paintings. Its neglect must have been due to the fact that my inspiration had come from the stagnant pools of Academicism whose waters had not been troubled since the times that disregarded all that was not *contrapposto, chiaroscuro* and eloquence. It is true that these masters of mine, who, in their notions of the artists whom the intervening centuries always held in honour, remained victims of the dreary formulas of the class room, were the same who, when they got away from their horse-hair furniture and stippled prints, appreciated so poignantly a genius like Botticelli, although numerous generations begot of petty precept and mechanic prescription had never heard of him. Yet when it came to Leonardo, these victims of Academic teaching undervalued a masterpiece like the "Epiphany," because it was so little what they expected of that genius, being scattered and offering few opportunities for striking *contrapposto,* and concentrated *chiaroscuro,* and as few for grandiloquence.

I never felt called upon to take an attitude toward other paintings ascribed to Leonardo, for I did not accept them. There remains, however, the "Leda." Although the original is lost, copies tell us what she must have been like. She must have been twin to the blasphemous "St. John," as fleshy and as round, as contorted for purposes of *contrapposto,* and as murky with overwrought *chiaroscuro.* Given the ideal intention clearly manifested in proportions and expression, both she and her giant swan would have shocked me by their naturalism and over-display of abdominal rotundities.

But all these doubts, questionings, and spiritual combats might have remained confined to my breast—a breast once so subject to incantations and still filled with a *pietas* tending to make me loyal to the ancient gods. But one unhappy day I was called upon to see the "Benois Madonna," a picture that had turned up in Russia some few years ago, and has since been acquired by the Hermitage.

I found myself confronted by a young woman with a bald forehead and puffed cheek, a toothless smile, blear eyes, and furrowed throat. The uncanny, anile apparition plays with a child who looks like a hollow mask fixed on inflated body and limbs. The hands are wretched, the folds purposeless and fussy, the colour like whey. And yet I had to acknowledge that this painful affair was the work of Leonardo da Vinci.

It was hard, but the effort freed me, and the indignation I felt gave me the resolution to proclaim my freedom.

II

Of course there remains something to be said in defence, in extenuation and in explanation; and at the end there may appear a Leonardo quite different from the sorcerer held up by an uncritical admiration.

But first I feel called upon to meet the objection sure to be raised against one like myself, supposed to subordinate illustration to decoration, for being at the trouble to attack Leonardo's fame as an illustrator.

To begin with, and as a matter of fact, it has never been my intention to advocate the view that illustration and expression were of no consequence. In my "Florentine Painters," published more than twenty years ago, I laid as much stress upon "spiritual significance" as I did upon "movement" and "tactile values." But the last term was new, mysterious, and promising, and thus ended by attracting all the attention, the more so that I had taken the human interest and ethical appeal in works of art for granted, as calling for no definition or discussion, and had felt free to devote my zeal to the part of the theory whose strangeness demanded exposition and defence. Moreover, I insisted in that small volume and in others which followed, that a painting made up almost entirely of illustrative elements could never count as a great work of art, while on the contrary, a great work of art might be as devoid of intentional illustration, as unconscious nature itself. This also could not but encourage the view that in my opinion the subject did not matter, and that its meaning was no concern of ours.

I venture therefore to say a few words about "Illustration." It will be remembered that I have comprised under that term more than used to be given to it, letting it stand for all value in a work of art beyond what is due to the immediate sensation of colour and the ideated sensations of tactile values, movement, and space composition. These values I have called "decoration," and in a sense it is true that spiritual significance is outside its purpose. We are, however, so centred, so socialized and so attuned that it is difficult if not impossible to avoid finding a meaning even where none was intended, and to cherish this meaning more perhaps than the object it sprang from. *Le sens n'est qu'un parasite qui pousse quand-même sur le trombone de la sonorité.* We may call this inevitable parasite "the over-meaning," for it is probably over and beyond what the artist himself had in mind, and certainly beyond what he could hope to convey with precision.

For the over-meaning is due to the fact that be what may the immediate instrument of the artist, his ultimate instrument is the human heart. And the heart is of a mechanism so subtle, so varied and so uncertain as to baffle any precise calculation of its working and to put it beyond the reach of accurate control. We know how inconstant, how capricious, how many-minded and irrational it is, and how when it does reason its reasoning is unknown to reason. (*Vide* universal literature *passim.*) It will respond easily and reliably only to the most primitive cries, those rising from the animal appetites and passions. Indeed, culture may be regarded as an effort to delay and to blunt these pre-human responses, and to use energy saved by preventing precipitation on that plane to lift us to a higher one. But once on that higher plane, the poor heart is left to itself, and it is so difficult to foretell how it will react that the amount of agreement we have come to with regard to matters beyond immediate animal need is sheerly miraculous. By what hidden ways, for instance, have people of a certain degree of civilization the world over come to identify given complexes of lines and shadows as the unfailing symbols of definite states of body and mind? Why should one look and bearing be recognized everywhere as intended to uplift us to the skies, and another as to degrade us to the gutter? But although we have arrived at a certain uniformity of reaction towards these appearances and thus to agree upon their meaning, it holds only for the extreme ends of the gamut of emotional resonance. Between flutter almost infinite shades of expression, the interpretation of which grows more and more doubtful as we approach the mean. Thus we all recognize the expression of horror and indignation on the face of an apostle in Leonardo's "Last Supper," and we see the lust of battle on the faces in the "Fight for the Standard" ("Battle of Anghiari"), but how many of us not following out the post-hypnotic suggestion of the rhetoricians would agree upon what is behind Mona Lisa's look? Its over-meanings are not only as many as there are spectators, but more still, for it will appeal differently to the same spectator at different periods of his life and in different moods.

If the artist has no control of the over-meanings except of the most elementary kind, it would surely be wise of him to avoid those intricate and uncertain expressions which lay themselves out to manifold contradictory interpretations, and to confine himself to the simplest looks and attitudes. All others, far from setting up an immediate reaction of the kind to produce a sense of greater capacity and smoother working of our faculties, as the work of art should, are puzzling, bewildering, and even baffling as problems proposed by science justly may be. For scientific activity, it should never be forgotten, finds its scope in the unravelling of puzzles, in the taming of what is bewildering, in the overcoming of what is baffling. Quite the opposite is artistic experience—it can for the spectator scarcely be called an activity—for it is intransitive and it aims neither at conquest nor capture, but at ecstasy. It comes to one not as a conscious reward of deliberate working toward an end, in the way that revelations come to thinkers and all other gifted men of science, but as an immediate, instantaneous and unearned act of grace, absolutely complete, and therefore, while it lasts, unchanging. For the artistic moment, as we may designate this ecstasy, is unaware of what preceded it, although it almost certainly was a long and severe training, and takes no thought of what will follow, although it probably will be a closer approach to perfection. But to consciousness the aesthetic moment is completely isolated, not to be modified and not to be qualified.

If that be so, it follows that, whatever merits "Mona Lisa" may have as pure decoration, although it is scarcely these that have perpetuated her fame, as illustration she is not really satisfactory. Looking at her leads to questioning, to perplexity, and even to doubt of one's intelligence, which does not interfere with our being fascinated by her, but does effectually prevent the mystic union between the work of art and ourselves, which is of the very essence of the aesthetic moment. That it is the fault of conflicting over-meanings I can scarcely doubt, for now we all know Chinese heads from Long-men, Hindoo heads from Borobodur, Khmer heads from Angkor, and heads from hundreds of other Buddhist sites, far more self-contained, far more inward, and far more subtle, which neverthe-less, because of the untroubled clearness of the meaning, charm us into that ecstasy of union with the object contemplated which art should produce.

A portrait like "Mona Lisa"—a portrait of a person regarding whom we either do not have or do not desire to obtain other information—has, however, this advantage, that at least it cannot conflict with a character or event, or legend, or myth already fully formed in our minds. Educated people visualize, no matter how gropingly and vaguely, the heroes and the actions of story, and cherish a definite, if crude, expecta-tion of how they are to be represented. The illustrator who does not come up to this expectation is thrown aside as unworthy, the one who opposes it is hated. Indeed, in my own generation, for all but a few, that was nearly the whole of art. I understand that this is no longer so, and art now con-sists of criss-cross dabs of dirty colour. Νήπιοι ουκ ἴσασιν.

A soul-less dauber may get so absorbed in the mere technique of a painting as to remain unconscious of its meaning. But for the rest of us there is no way of ignoring the human appeal of a picture. We may throw it out of our minds, but it comes back through our hearts; and defiantly as we may pretend that it does not matter, its claims are the first to demand satisfaction. The most pressing of these claims is that the meaning suggested to us by the representation before us shall not contra-dict or oppose the spirit of the ostensible subject as conceived by ourselves. I naturally speak of those few among us who have autonomous artistic selves; for art, being for most people the eminent domain of "prestige values," is the chosen paradise of humbug. It is there where kings stalk naked because they are supposed to wear raiment visible to the good and true only. It is there, too, where everybody is a Polonius who sees whatever the effrontery of a Hamlet bids him. There is therefore no such school of sincerity as the *examen de conscience* of aesthetic experience, for no other self-questionings make such demand upon our truthfulness, our sense, our judgement.

Yet even in art there are limits to credulity and submissiveness. We may, with Ruskin, see all sorts of depths in the candid puerilities of a Carpaccio, and all sorts of portents in the discoloured brushwork of a Tintoretto. We may even submit to the passes made over us by Pater using the "Mona Lisa" as a sort of magician's wand; we put up with apathetic and youthful St. Sebastians: but we cannot but revolt when asked to find delight in a work of art manifestly at war with its ostensible subject, as is impudently the case with Leonardo's "St. John."

The figure of the Precursor is one of the most clearly outlined, most definitely characterized, and most inalterable in Christian history. There is no better subject for Unanimism. His mention evokes in all of us the same ascetic, haggard image of obsessed proselytism. To satisfy this expectation, Leonardo gives us, not something non-committal, as Piero della Francesca or Antonello da Messina might have given, with an existence of its own overpowering enough to vanquish and replace a disappointment, but a well-fleshed epicene creature, with an equivocal leer, pointing upward with an operatic twist as if to invite us to look up, not to Christ first appearing upon the world, but to Bacchus clattering along with all his rout. No qualities of decoration, even if far superior to those found here, could ask for justice after such a blasphemy.

The case of the "Last Supper" is not quite so unimaginable. A Southerner at home among the ample movements, eloquent gestures, and vehement speech of an Italian market-place might find nothing amiss in Leonardo's presentation. But to us Northerners the sounds and sights of a Neapolitan crowd are deafening and fatiguing, if not positively repellant. And matters are not much improved by placing the figures in a way to bring into full relief their heroic proportions, the sinister or even criminal faces of some of them, and the purposeless grandiloquence of others. It only adds to our alarm and distress. We Northerners expect a quieter, gentler, more subdued humanity of Our Lord and His Apostles on the occasion of their last supper; and, although we are ready to tolerate conventions of type, scale, and environment up to a point, these must not flatly contradict either our notion of probability or sense of seemliness. I am too repelled by the illustrative side of Leonardo's "Last Supper" to be able to do full justice to the design as decoration, although it is possible that, if as decoration it was great enough, I could partly overcome my repulsion. Probably it is not great enough, but of that I may have another word to say later on.

It is scarcely necessary to discuss the other pictures that I have inveighed against; but we may remark, in passing, that for us of to-day, despite the shambles, stenches, and malpractices to which apparently a certain school of anthropology, inspired by *la nostalgie de la boue,* would reduce primitive Hellenic civilization, Greek mythology, woven as it is into our earliest and sweetest impersonal concepts, remains the realm of ideal shapes and symbolical actions. Distasteful therefore is every literal rendering and naturalistic interpretation of a mythological subject, and Leonardo's "Leda" is at once too heroic in size and too post-nuptial in forms, while the swan is far too big and real. Correggio's rendering of the myth is there to prove with what idyllic playfulness it can be treated, and with what absence of uncomfortable suggestions.

III

Although the question has already been half answered in the course of the foregoing pages, it will perhaps be more satisfactory at this point to meet it squarely. The question is how to account for the admiration lavished upon these pictures that I have been depreciating. One could impatiently reply "that it was all an affair of mesmerism, hypnotism, and suggestion." No doubt, but why did not the adepts select other pictures and other masters for their mystifications: why Leonardo in general and these paintings in particular?

To give adequate answers to these questions will be difficult until some such book is written on Leonardo in the Nineteenth Century as Italian scholars have given us on Virgil and Ovid in the Middle Ages, for there was a parallel in the fate of their reputations. In the absense of such a treatise, I venture to outline my own makeshift explanation.

It will be remembered that, in Mediaeval Italy, the Roman poets were changed into wizards who defied the laws of nature almost as flagrantly as if they were thaumaturgic saints. The last century was too enlightened to turn anyone into a sorcerer and miracle worker, and, besides, the public concerned was not of the ignorant but of the cultured classes. Education, however, does not destroy the mythmaking faculty; it causes it to transfer its activities to fields less obviously impossible. And the man of letters who would smile at the vulgar herd, with its worship of material signs and wonders, will, in his imperious need of adoring idols, insist on deifying genius and magnifying its works. Once the artist had touched the skies with his sublime forehead, his creations were beyond blame and beyond praise. They were not to be analysed, no attempt was to be made to understand them; they were not even to be appreciated. They were there to bow to, to cense, and to pray to, for ever. As I recall the writings on art and literature that inspired my youth, it was very like a sacred dance.

The apotheosis of the artist, with which class especially we are concerned, is fairly recent. There were no complete instances of it in antiquity, which reserved this honour for the founder, the promoter, and the ruler, and scarcely ever for what we now, with a quite modern concept, regard as the man of genius—never whole-heartedly at least. The myths of Prometheus and Daedelus are to the point, for they are sermons in story against the pride of the intellect. Homer may seem an exception, but as he was directly inspired by the Muse, he ranked, although so high, yet only as her favourite.

To account completely for the worship of genius that sprang up a hundred years ago would probably be equivalent to accounting for the whole Romantic Movement. Much was due, no doubt, to the longing felt, sooner or later, by most people for identifying themselves with somebody or something beyond their own ordinary selves and workaday lives. Some of it followed upon the more than epic, more than legendary careers of Napoleonic times. Some, possibly to disappointment in military heroes, and a revulsion from their activities. It had been demonstrated that the world was as potter's clay in the hands of genius. If this world ended by drying and crumbling before it could be shaped to the heart's desire, the greater the need for a still more plastic realm of being where failure was less likely, and, at all events, less patent. For the Restoration brought back a number of things, but never the Rococo beatitudes about the golden mean.

Many people thereupon found satisfaction for their need of enthusiasm and adoration in the plastic realm of religion, but others in the still more plastic realm of art, and the worship the first dedicated to the Saints, these bestowed upon the great Artists. And for the first time in history the artist, from the artisan, craftsman, mechanic that he had been hitherto, was transfigured into a demi-god. He was endowed with qualities which raised him above the miseries of want and care, above the tyranny of habit and above material ambition. Like all other gods he was unconditioned. He was free to take any shape, and even to alter his nature. He could with his fiat create and destroy. The world was only an emanation of his being. Whatsoever he did was necessarily perfect, and whatsoever his divine hand had touched had the sacredness of a relic. Kings had no higher and more pressing task than to entertain him.

But be what may the reasons for the worship of the artist that seized the Western world a hundred years ago, no artificer of the past lent himself so well to apotheosis as Leonardo. Attainments and achievements of such quality in so many different provinces of art and science had never before been united in one man; and this man happened to be quite conscious and well aware of his worth. He was thus the first artist of modern times to consider himself raised far above the mechanic station occupied by his fellows. And he seems to have behaved in a way calculated to make his contemporaries take him at his own valuation. He dressed with originality and distinction, bore himself impressively. Surrounded, so to speak, by censor-swinging acolytes, he acted the part of hierophant and modern Empedocles, and was not far from being a precursor of Paracelsus. The remembrance, tinged with mystery, of these claims to sovereign consideration added to unmistakable and manifold genius, made him, as it were, the arch-type of the artist as well as the first and worthiest object of the new cult.

This transfigured Leonardo naturally shared in all the attributes of deity. He was unconditioned; he obeyed no law; there was no necessary sequence to his conduct; all that he did was perfect; and everything he left behind him was a relic if not a fetish.

It followed that as an artist there was nothing he might not have done. If it was too unlike the average aspect of his works, it was a sign of his having been lifted high above the laws of habit and the drag of mental inertia. If the painting was hideous, the god was poking fun at nature, showing how he could surpass her in ugliness as well as in beauty. And indeed it would be hard to get to the end of the pictures that people not so long ago cherished and adored as Leonardo's. I have found among them not only paintings from every region of Italy, from Spain, from France, from the Netherlands and the Rhinelands, but even from the Tyrol and Styria, and they have been of dates ranging from fifteen to seventeen hundred.

Yet, as might be expected, it was the work of his more immediate pupils and followers that attracted most worshippers, because their authenticity after all was more penetratingly convincing than that of a Madonna painted on copper in the style of a remote descendant of Rubens. With rare exceptions, Luini's hand-painted chromos with their cosmetic smiles, Giampedrino's nut-brown inanities, Oggiono's pinched, sweetish faces, Predis' schematic miniatures enlarged to the size of life, Boltraffio's compass-outlined countenances were adored as Leonardo's. How little artistic appreciation and judgement were engaged we may deduce from the fact that Walter Pater, the most delicate, the most subtle, and the most exquisite of all rhetoricians, was enraptured with the stupid *pasticcio* of a "Medusa," and reproduced, presumably as the quintessence of Leonardo, a Milanese drawing of dubious expression and mediocre quality, on the title page of his "Renaissance"—the only illustration occurring in his works.

Conceive an image of Leonardo composed out of all these elements, and you will be assisted to understand the nature of the worship offered him in the liturgy composed by the fathers and hymnologists of his church. But well as it may account for the origin of the liturgy, it fails to explain just why the few pictures described in the first section of this essay, the "Mona Lisa," the "St. Anne," the "Baptist," the "Last Supper" and the "Leda," occupy the chiefest altars.

The truth is that these idols had stood on the altars of the humble primitive structure, scarcely a church but rather a "meeting-house" where disciples united to discuss, to appreciate, to praise, if not to worship. Their Leonardo was not yet a god. He was only a great inventor who made two discoveries, *chiaroscuro* and *contrapposto,* destined to transform the arts of design. It was as illustrations and triumphs of the new science and the new method that the pictures in question were first admired and prized.

In other words, the original interest in Leonardo was almost purely Academic. Although, like every innovator, he had many precursors, he was the first to perfect and to teach, to systematize and to practice a new science. He furnished models and examples of notation by means of light and shade chiefly, and of action attained by twisting the human body around its own axis. Like most other innovations these were double-edged. They enlarged the possibilities of expression, and made it possible at least to depict a face as agitated as in life, or looking a part as if on the stage. Reserve was no longer imposed by the imperfections of the instrument, and every one was now able to give full utterance to his precious soul. Man has never yet been known to decline an invention that puts greater facility and more power into his hands, no matter what the consequences. Inventors even in our day, when they are common enough, get appreciation and rewards somewhat out of scale with those apportioned to less utilitarian talents. Primitive man probably regarded them as gods, and Mediaeval and even Renaissance man as wizards.

In the arts of design as practiced for thousands of years, invention has almost always aimed at finding instruments or receipts for quality. The striving is not necessarily useless, for, assuming that this is a rational universe, everything that exists must have a cause, and this cause must have worked through means ideally intelligible. But thus far we not only have failed to discover a mechanism that can be relied on to produce artistic quality, but we can scarcely conceive of using anything so complicated, so elaborate and so subtle as such a mechanism would have to be.

Nearly all the contrivances invented hitherto have served merely to conquer material difficulties of representation, and thereby to mask the absence of quality. What Leonardo did was to enable poorly endowed artists to satisfy an eye which seldom sees beyond its utilitarian needs. There is a challenge to the intellect in line from which chiaroscuro is free. Quality quite apart, a fault in drawing will strike thousands where a fault in light and shade will offend scarcely one. The latter process has therefore every advantage, if the aim be to produce an illusion, and for the self-same reason it can be formulated and mechanized up to a point. On the other hand the practice of functional line admits of no aids for the blind, no crutches for the unsteady, no short cuts and no substitutes for talent and hard work. The ungifted and ambitious find an enemy only less invincible in the exquisite surface of true, clear colour mated to functional line, and they would soon be brought to acknowledge defeat if *chiaroscuro* did not help them to blur, smudge, veil and hide. If the Western world lost for centuries its sense of colour, and could in our day, when the worst was over, believe that the negative and timid Whistler or the positive and crude Cézanne were great colourists, it was due chiefly to the practice of *chiaroscuro*.

Contrapposto, the turning of the body on its own axis, Leonardo's other invention, was not quite so fatal as the first, because it was less concerned with specific quality than with general design and illustration. But besides leading to the most jejune and tasteless affectations all over Europe, lasting to within two or three generations from our own, it had the more immediate effect of killing Florentine Art. No Tuscan painter or sculptor born after Leonardo's death produced a single work with the faintest claim to general interest. Happily its bad effects are now over, while *chiaroscuro* is still destroying many who might be artists, and helping to fame many others, the sight of whose painting is a miseducation. But when it was new, *contrapposto* must have seemed a contrivance as simple as it was effective in the hands of the unfortunates who had no cultivable instincts regarding the posture of the human figure.

If Leonardo was admired through the centuries, it was not because he was a supreme artist, but, paradoxical as it may sound, because he introduced inventions which seemed to make the teaching and practice of art easier, and it followed that those of his works which best exemplified *chiaroscuro* and *contrapposto* were the most constantly referred to, and the most highly esteemed.

And it was these self-same late works which for centuries had been admired chiefly, if not solely, for professional and even pedagogic reasons, that the Romantic rhetoricians, when they deified Leonardo as the sovereign genius, took over without question as the sacred objects of their worship. So they found themselves in the position of having to furnish reasons of their own for treating as masterpieces works selected by a different and more prosaic order of ideas. They might have been put to it if they had undertaken proof and demonstration. Priest-like they composed instead a hypnotizing and mesmerizing ritual. It kept us enthralled for two or three generations, and even now I am more than half horrified at this attempt of mine to shake off the spell.

For the sake of historical completeness, I must refer to one interest that, attaining great popularity toward the end of the XVIIIth century, contributed to the Romantic interpretations of Leonardo's paintings in general, and of "Mona Lisa" in particular. That interest, however, had nothing specifically artistic about it, nor indeed was it much more than phrenology and kindred futilities of that and more recent times. It was the interest in physiognomy fostered and preached by Lavater, and encouraged for a while by Goethe. No doubt it was largely responsible for a great many of the more elaborate utterances about the enigmatic and impenetrable depth of the "Mona Lisa."

IV

In the attempt to give the illustrative elements their proper place and due value in the work of art, and in the effort to suggest that the traditional admiration lavished upon Leonardo's most famous masterpieces had a professional and Academic rather than a literary and poetic origin, I have made statements which could easily lead the reader to anticipate the explanation I now venture to offer as to why these works, despite the praise of the schools and the adulation of the sophists, are not, to humanists like ourselves, quite satisfactory. The explanation is simply this, that in the paintings which arouse my resentment the aesthetic moment has been sacrificed to other interests.

The aesthetic moment has already been defined in the course of this essay as that peculiar condition of ecstasy which art should aim to produce. Whatever interferes with this rapture, no matter how worthy in itself, is a nuisance, and whatever succeeds in preventing it, as effectively prevents the coming into existence of the perfect masterpiece. It follows that besides much else which does not concern us at present, all questions of ways and means, essential though they be to the craftsman, must be carefully hidden away from the spectator. Hence the adage as old as Greece and Rome that the art of arts is to leave no trace of how art has been achieved.

But what can be more opposed to this than an interest so

exorbitant in technical processes that it draws most of the spectator's spontaneous attention to itself! It is indeed being given the stone of science when one has been promised the bread of beauty. I know it is what the artist himself is apt to study and to prize in the work of art. *He* is quite right, for it is his business to learn how to create, and triumphal displays of mastery are his best schools and academies; but what have *we* got to do with all this, we who are not artists nor going to be artists, but aesthetic mystics craving to identify ourselves with the object of our contemplation!

The aesthetic moment in the "Mona Lisa" has been sacrificed to effects of *chiaroscuro* more subtly worked out, more insistently logical than any perhaps that had yet been achieved. It is possible that a further sacrifice was made to produce the enigmatical, impenetrable expression. On the other hand, it is conceivable that this expression itself was only a by-product of a technical preoccupation. Leonardo may have been thinking only of a mask, features, projections, dimples, and ripples which happen to have a parasitic human value, although for him they were merely tasks he had set himself in *chiaroscuro*. I suspect that, whatever the theory of his compendious series of scholastic recipes known and worshipped as the "Treatise on Painting," in practice he got so absorbed in problems of *contrapposto* and *chiaroscuro* as to forget spiritual significance. It is at least difficult to credit him with any clear and specific illustrative purpose when we find the same head and bust with but slight variations of expression, figuring now as the Baptist, now as St. Anne, and again as Leda. Being human countenances posed in a certain way, they cannot help conveying a certain meaning, but there is no sufficient reason for assuming that they owed their existence to another impulse than did, for example, Monet's haystacks. Those are no more studies in *plein air* than these in light and shade and posture; and it is only because the face is so immeasurably more familiar to us than a stack of hay, that we find more variety in the first than in the last. It is my impression that, like Uccello, like Baldovinetti, like Verrocchio even, the absorption in the science of his craft ruined the artist. His was a greater gift, and the ruin is not so lamentably obvious as in the closest parallel among his immediate precursors, Baldovinetti; but there is scarcely less of a contrast between his spontaneous genius, as manifested in drawings, and the quality of most of his highly elaborated paintings than there is between the exquisite works full of grace and loveliness of the youthful Baldovinetti, and the tasteless dulness of the same artist turned scientist.

I need not attempt to describe or define the quality and characteristics of Leonardo's drawings. The universal delight in them is scarcely to be questioned, and they certainly do not sin by being too painstaking and over-laboured. If they have a fault, it is, in fact, that they are at times too free and easy, and tend to be a little slack and calligraphic. With rare exceptions, which include some of the heads for the "Last Supper," their author seems to have regarded drawing no less than writing as but a means of note-taking, and left both unspoiled. Both his sketches and his prose, however, have a style of such simplicity, and candour, and unpretentiousness that one cannot but suspect that in temperament Leonardo was as natural as he was gifted, and that, to start with, he was endowed with a singularly happy sense of what is direct, swift, graceful, unstudied, and unaffected. Perhaps if his genius could have developed in a community less lashed by the furies of intellectualism, Leonardo would have avoided and escaped his errors, and would not have ended as the worst of corrupters, and the foremost forerunner of the Tenebrists and other pretenders of the later Cinquecento.

Unfortunately his passion for science, for schematization, for doing things by an Academic rule carefully pigeon-holed in a huge columbarium of other precepts and maxims, and, above all, his fascinated absorption in *chiaroscuro* and *contrapposto,* made him, as even a brief comparison between some of his paintings and the sketches and studies that served for them will attest, lose not only the sense of adequate illustration, and human significance, but his native gift of persuasive, natural, unforced action and composition as well.

To begin with the earliest, it is doubtful whether we possess any jotting done with an eye to the Hermitage "Madonna," but in the Uffizi and the British Museum we have a number of pen sketches made in preparation for other Madonnas of the same time, and in the Louvre we have the large design for one nearly identical in intention, pose, and action.[2] While all are singularly free and swift, natural and graceful, the Louvre "Madonna" stands out from amongst them as something which could be scarcely less premeditated, less laboured, or more like a flash of mind miraculously fixed upon paper. Nothing European hand has done is more worthy of the dematerialized art of the Far East; while—to be concise and comprehensive—nothing an Italian ever did was more pettily Dutch than the Hermitage "Madonna." We find the same striving for the utmost definition, the same fussiness over light and shade and minute distracting detail as in those *magots,* as Louis Quatorze justly called them. We see how, with every painstaking thought and laboured touch, something vanished of the noble daring and fearless freedom which inspired such a sketch as the Louvre "Madonna," until at last there was left only the manifest intention of displaying science, skill, and dexterity.

The autograph studies for the "Last Supper" are either slight pen jottings not to the present purpose, or chalk drawings far more elaborated. They are not yet so worked up as to rival in tastelessness with one or two overdone children's heads at Oxford from Michelangelo's worst years, but they have lost enough in freshness and sparkle to have created doubts regarding the authenticity of some of them. The fundamental faults, however, of this most famous of European paintings lie far deeper. On the illustrative side they consist, as I said early in this essay, in what is, for us Northerners at least, a vice of interpretation; on the decorative side, for all the genius displayed in the articulation of the grouping and the perfect accord of the rhythm, there are unconquerable difficulties in the nature of the subject. For certain subjects are unfit for serious treatment in the figure arts, and this happens to be one of them. It can be dealt with only as pure illustration by candid souls like Fra Angelico and Sassetta, who do not draw attention to the insoluble problems of the design. Leonardo's intellectual pride, on the contrary, was attracted by them, and the result is a composition consisting entirely of figures ending at the waist line, of torsoes with heads and arms but no abdomen and no legs. And in sober truth I come nearest to enjoying them as great art when I visualize them as museum fragments skilfully put together from the wreck of some noble pediment. But then I must think away many of the heads and hands.

We possess no sketches for the head of the "Mona Lisa," but a number of profiles from various periods of Leonardo's career, some nearly contemporary with her. Perhaps the most admirable are the one at Windsor of a young woman wearing a coiffe on the back of her head, and the probable portrait of Isabella d'Este in the Louvre. Both are of a naturalness and limpid simplicity not surpassed even by that highest achievement of earlier Florentine portraiture, the Poldi Profile. We cannot but conclude that it took an effort as gigantic as it was unfortunate for the author of these spontaneous creations to turn into the constructor of the "Mona Lisa."

Enchanting drawings of a beautiful girl stooping naked among the tall reeds to pluck flowers, while she fondles a swan, have everything to recommend them, both as human value and pictorial theme. Besides being positively attractive, and singularly free from unpleasant suggestions, the flow of all the curves, the rhythm of the nude, the bird, and the foliage have a beauty no less than lyrical. Yet all this had to give place to a monumentally sculptural conception odiously unsuitable as an idea and carried through with all the unsparing insistence of a pitiless chiaroscuro. There is, even in Florentine art, no more repulsive instance of confusion between the kindred but distinct arts of sculpture and painting than this half-realistic, half-heroic female of gigantic size courted by a swan no less huge.

But the most convincing instance of Leonardo's surrender of his native genius to professional problems and academic ideals is offered by the two versions of the "Virgin with St. Anne," the black chalk cartoon in London, and the painting in Paris. The first has perfect naturalness of look and posture, and a simple impressiveness of design, with nothing far-fetched and dear-bought. There is something truly Greek about the gracious humanity of the ideals here embodied, and it is no less Greek as decoration. I can still subscribe to what I said about it more than fifteen years ago: "One can scarcely find draped figures contrived in a more plastic way without going back centuries to those female figures which once were clustered together on the gable of the Parthenon." There was, however, no room in this cartoon for the exhibition of skill in conquering difficulties of composition. It required scarcely any subtleties of *chiaroscuro,* still less of *contrapposto,* and is not even pyramidal. So Leonardo discarded it, and contrived with logic absolute the Louvre design—a pyramidal design which, had it been completed, would have enjoyed a superabundance of *chiaroscuro.* Even in its present unfinished state, it revels in every kind of affected and acrobatic *contrapposto*—as artificial and masterly and wonderful as the most admired of forensic Latin periods.

The contrast between the cartoon and the painting is the more damaging as the former is already completely thought out in conception, and almost fully elaborated in essential execution, and thus escapes the possible retort that the difference is due to the advantage all slight sketches have over fully finished works. For in a sketch we expect the essentials only of pose and action, and trust the expression will be supplied in the achieved design. It stimulates us to the life-enhancing exercise of our own faculties by inviting us, as it were, to associate ourselves with the artist in completing his task. How true were Leonardo's instincts, and how faulty his theories, may be inferred from the fact that in his drawings, where there was little call to surrender native gifts to intellectualistic ambition, there reigns the greatest spontaneity and freedom. Among his autograph sketches, one at all highly finished is rare, and one unpleasantly laboured does not exist.

V

Florentine art tended to be over-intellectual, and of that tendency Leonardo was the fullest exponent. For in him it not only grew so conscious and so explicit as to get formulated into a series of axioms, problems and doctrines, but no other artist grew so indifferent to everything but their illustration and solution. Even Michelangelo, who is wrongly made responsible for the worst ravages of the theory of *contrapposto,* was not such a ruthless adept of it. In the one instance where he was going to abandon himself to its fascination as completely as Leonardo did in his "St. John," disgust got the better of him, and, after altering the posture somewhat, he let others complete the "Christ" of the Minerva. Besides, it never would have occurred to him to accumulate conflicting effects. In painting, he regarded fresco as the only manly art, and fresco admits no subtleties of *sfumato*. (It is significant, by the way, that Leonardo is not known to have painted in fresco.) Nor do we find trace of *sfumato* effects in Michelangelo's one finished panel picture. Leonardo's ideal, nearly realized in his "Baptist," must, on the contrary, have been to convey by means of *chiaroscuro* the impression, not of a coloured picture, but of one of those highly polished, dark brown, counterpoised bronzes associated with the names of Baccio Bandinelli and Gian Bologna. For *contrapposto* and *chiaroscuro,* in so far as they belong to art in any other sense than do studio properties and lay figures, or, for that matter, canvas and brushes, can contribute to the same end only when attention is drawn to neither; for the first can be properly employed by the sculptor alone, and the second by the painter, seeing that the one tends to the heroically monumental and the other to the freely pictorial.

Now it is this tactlessness, this recklessness, this blinkered way of pursuing an idea or formula or doctrine to its logical bitter end, never realizing the conflict with another idea, never seeing the absurdities, if not ferocities, it ultimately leads to, that we object to in intellectualism. With intellectual art in itself we have no quarrel, for it is the supremest form of art, the one from which all the others draw their inspiration, and without which there would be none deserving the name. Indeed, it was only when at last after myriads of years of manual and visual effort made by nameless precursors, the Greek mind, more immediately preceded by feeble Egyptian and Babylonian attempts, applied itself consciously and deliberately to problems of proportion, posture, rhythm, and composition, that the impulse to represent and counterfeit and adorn ceased to be mere handicraft, and became a clarified system of design worthy to be called art. For only then was it able to transcend the haphazard of the actual and to present us with an ideal, yet convincingly possible, humanity and humanized world. But at its best moments—those moments so brief, yet of everlasting consequence—Greek art never gave way to intellectualism, that is to say, it never allowed itself to lose sight of the aesthetic end by a too great absorption in the scientific means. On the contrary, it not only carefully kept these out of sight, but unhesitatingly sacrificed them to that high tact and happy compromise without which art is no more to be attained than life is to be lived. Still less would Greek art before Pergamon have abandoned itself to the logic of any one principle, no matter how necessary and fruitful the principle itself might be when used as an ingredient. But logic has been the ruin of most of the more ambitious and more intellectual art movements of the last eight centuries, from Gothic architecture to Cubist painting. For all we know, logic may reign supreme in a mechanical universe, but it enjoys a far less general obedience in the world of men, a world chiefly of rival desires, ideals, and dreams rather than of law. In this world every one and everything brings his or its own logic, and any system carried far enough is certain to cross another, if not to end in a blind alley or absurdity. Life is impoverished, not enriched by the fanatical adherence to one desire, one ideal, one dream fostered and permitted to hypnotize and mesmerize us into action. Few of the worst horrors of history are due to other causes, and it alone is responsible for the most monstrous horror of all which is being enacted now.

What is true of life is as true of art, which, regarded comprehensively, is its guide. Its ultimate aim is ecstasy, and any diversion that prevents our reaching that state is bad. There is no theory, no principle, no method that cannot be misused in this way, not even the highest, and most essential. Leonardo, for his part, misused two instruments whose loss, as a matter of fact, art would scarcely feel. In his most famous works they lie about like builder's and carpenter's, painter's and upholsterer's tools in what should be an ideal house. Wherefore I no longer rank these works with the masterpieces of the world's art. And I must confess that it makes me sceptical about the man himself, for a man who could be so carried away by misplaced interests savours more of the crank than the genius. Perhaps Leonardo was only the greatest of cranks.

I have tried, not a little frightened at my own temerity, to expose and bring down nearly all the famous idols of Leonardo's art, the "Mona Lisa," the "Last Supper," etc. If my words meet with any response in the minds of my readers, we may agree to inquire what, in fact, remains of Leonardo as an artist.

But first a word as to my temerity. The step just taken was, it seems to me, bound to follow upon the effort of Morellianism. Morellianism, surgical, pitiless, iconoclastic even as it seemed, was yet inspired by the Romantic ideal of genius and founded on the axiom that the greatest artist from cradle to grave never derogated from his greatness, and on its converse that whatever the great artist did was necessarily faultless. It was in defence of this that we Morellians fought for authenticity with the uncompromising zeal of Legitimists. It was, indeed, a brave fight and worthy, although it fortified the snob collector's blind confidence in mere names, and led him to accumulate unpalatable but authentic daubs by Rembrandt and other prolific geniuses. But the very method of establishing authenticity by tests so delicate, so subtle, and so complicated has led us on, little by little, to conclusions the exact opposite of the axiom with which we started out. Strict connoisseurship has taken the further and more painful step of recognizing that there are poor things among the autographs of the great artists, and that not every Bellini or Botticelli, Raphael or Rubens, Velasquez or Van Dyck is a flawless masterpiece.

To return to Leonardo and the question of what we feel remains of him as an artist, that, too, has already been more than half told in the course of this essay.

We may be bold enough to divide him up into two artists, so to speak, the Quattrocento, and the Cinquecento Leonardo. Of the second I believe I already have said enough. At the worst his works will remain masterpieces of great importance in the history and dialectic of painting. That they are bound to retain their pedimental prominence at the apex of the world's aesthetic achievement I doubt. There will be no return of this sort either to him, or to his Bolognese descendants, or to any other of the dethroned idols of our European past. Many people assume that admiration is merely a matter of fashion, and that we get tired and crave for novelty. No doubt novelty is a mighty goddess, not unlike Kali in some respects. But we are not now where we were a century ago. Then it was a choice between the few schools, the few epochs, known to our tiny West European civilization. Since then, beginning with the truly godlike creations of Greek art, the art of all the rest of the world has been thrown open to us. Even now we are only beginning to make acquaintance with it all, and it will take generations before we understand it. By the time that this has happened, it will tax the aesthetic energy of cultivated society as a whole to grasp the masterpieces alone. The individual when bored with one kind will never have to go to a lower for want of one equally great. His *sacra fames rerum novarum,* his greed for novelty, will be able to vent itself without ever coming to an end of the best, although of course one cannot guarantee that he, too, may not occasionally be attacked by *la nostalgie de la boue,* and rummage among refuse.

Why indeed should this cultivated society of the future return to the "Mona Lisa"? There is nothing in her expression that is not far more satisfactorily rendered in Buddhist art. There is nothing in the landscape that is not even more evocative and more magical in Ma Yuan, in Li-Long-Men, in Hsia Kwei and a score of other Chinese and Japanese painters. There is less reason still why it should return to the "Last Supper," or the "St. Anne," or the "Baptist."

There remains the Quattrocento Leonardo, the author of all the drawings of whatever period, and some paintings. As a draughtsman his touch has a singular lightness and grace; my aesthetic life would be the poorer without it. It has given me real joy, and has helped to feed the secret springs of my being. And yet Leonardo can scarcely be ranked with the mightiest draughtsmen. Indeed, the word "mighty," so suitable to a Rembrandt or Dürer, or Michelangelo, sounds almost as out of place in connection with Leonardo as, let us say, with Watteau, the exquisite and lovable.

The Quattrocento paintings are not altogether easy to sum up just at present. The Hermitage "Madonna" obliges me to reconsider the canon of Leonardo's works. The man who could do a thing as bad as that may have done others, but the present estimate must be based upon two works only, the "Adoration of the Magi" and the "Virgin of the Rocks," although the second is no longer an achievement of the unspoiled Quattrocento. For me Leonardo is most himself, because most like his drawings throughout his career, in the happily unfinished "Adoration." Had he completed it, he might have ruined it as he did the Hermitage "Madonna." I can believe that his best instincts prevented this act, for study has led me to conclude that when an artist was perfectly happy in his task he seldom failed to achieve it. But this unfinished "Adoration" is truly a great masterpiece, and perhaps the Quattrocento produced nothing greater. Does this work alone suffice, however, to place its creator, where he has been placed hitherto, above all his contemporaries and predecessors? Was he really so much more the artist than the painter of the "Primavera," of the "Birth of Venus," and a score of other great designs? I cannot see that he is. I can see no reason why, leaving all other considerations out of the question, and judging him by his artistic achievement alone, the Quattrocento Leonardo should be placed above Botticelli. Happy for him if he falls no lower.

The Illusion of the Real

by Herbert Read

HE SEARCHING QUESTION we must ask is whether any new dimension of consciousness was attained by these artists [Piero della Francesca, Alberti, and Leonardo] and, if so, in what way did it differ from the Greek sense of beauty, or from the paleolithic sense of vitality. That the fifteenth century witnessed a great advance in the sciences of mathematics and geometry is no doubt true; but we are concerned with sensibility and not with theoretical knowledge, and it may well be doubted whether the consciousness of space as such—space in the scientific or representational sense—advanced at all between the twelfth and the fifteenth centuries. The architects of the Middle Ages were extremely learned men, scholastics in their own field, as Panofsky has pointed out,[1] and we have only to look at the notebooks of Villard de Honnecourt, which may be dated about 1235, to realize that it was not for lack of an elementary knowledge of optics or geometry that painting before the fifteenth century failed to apply a coherent system of perspective to the representation of reality.[2] There must have been an assumption, unformulated perhaps, that a science that was very necessary for the construction of buildings had no necessary connection with art. At any rate, the medieval artists saw no connection between this particular science and the expressive arts of painting and sculpture. "High Gothic design," to quote Panofsky,

> remains inexorably linear; and High Gothic space, though already continuous, remains inexorably finite ... The action ... unfolds in a

From *Icon and Idea* by Herbert Read (Cambridge, Mass.: Harvard University Press, 1955). Reprinted by permission of the publisher.

direction parallel to the representational plane, passing across our field of vision rather than advancing or receding within it. We see a world of forms communing with each other within their space but not, as yet, a world of forms communing with the spectator within a space in which he shares. . . . In short, High Gothic art, its world constructed without reference to the visual processes of the beholder and even without reference to his very existence, is still unalterably nonperspective. And now we can almost predict that "modern" space was to come into being when the High Gothic sense of volume and coherence, nurtured by sculpture and architecture, began to act upon the illusionistic tradition that had lingered on in Byzantine and Byzantinizing painting; in other words, in the Italian Trecento.[3]

There seems little doubt, therefore, that space consciousness, whether composite and finite in the Greek and Roman sense, or continuous and infinite in the modern sense, was slowly developed from the practice of artists. The struggle to represent realistically, to create an illusion of reality, caused the artist to disengage, from his vague field of sensation, first the voluminousness of physical entities like human beings, then the relative position of such entities in groups, and finally a felt and substantial space, welling up between such entities and binding them together in a space, which is also the space within which the spectator is situated. Space as such, conceptual, infinite, was a consequential induction from the concrete spaces first realized by the artist. But a fatal possibility then existed: to make space creation the sole criterion of art.

The kind of painting that developed from the time of Masaccio onwards was constructive in the sense that it applied an architectonic science to the representation of man and of Nature. The claim made by Alberti—we may take him as representative—was that a knowledge of the laws of optics would enable the painter to be more effective in producing his purely aesthetic, sensuous effects. That is what the Van Eycks and Masaccio had been doing—using perspective, not schematically or scientifically, but as an effective compositional device, as a perfect rendering of the "good" Gestalt. Alberti specifically disclaims any intention of making art a science of representation. He says: if the result does not please the eye, it will be of no interest to the painter. His favorite word is "concinnitas," and this implies an agreement of the parts of a composition with the whole of it that can be grasped only intuitively. Sensibility is the final criterion.[4]

That was to be forgotten, but before we deal with the fatal dissociation of sensibility that followed in the sixteenth century, let us note a subtle variation of sensibility in relation to perspective. It was possible to treat perspective—the perspectival image—as a thing-in-itself; not merely as a symbol, as Panofsky has shown in another brilliant essay,[5] but as an emotional factor, as a thing of beauty inspiring ecstasy. For this purpose there was no need for the perspective to be exact: it could be exaggerated— there could be more than one system of perspective in a single picture; but these receding lines of vision, these diminishing figures, the harmonic graduation of every element represented—the whole perspectival complex— worked on the senses, much as Gothic vaulting had worked on the senses, and the results, in a painter like Jacopo Bellini or Piero della Francesca, were wonderfully moving—the most exquisite variation on space consciousness ever achieved by the miniature and two-dimensional craft of the painter.

But only an artist of Bellini's or Piero's intelligence and sensibility could maintain such a delicate equilibrium. To keep the artistic consciousness uncorrupt would have meant keeping the *sensation* of perspective distinct from the *idea* of perspective, and that proved too difficult. "Our art," Bernard Berenson has observed, "has a fatal tendency to become science, and we hardly possess a masterpiece which does not bear the marks of having been a battlefield for divided interests." The decisive battlefield was to be the mind and art of Leonardo da Vinci.

To see in Leonardo anything less than a supreme genius would have an air of paradox and impertinence. But it is a tragic fact—indeed, the fact of tragedy—that a man can be at the same time great and disastrous: it is the destiny typified in Faust, exemplified in Napoleon. We cannot deny to Leonardo a purity of consciousness in which feeling—his feeling for the personality of the particular woman he used for a model in the Uffizi *Annunciation,* for example—remains suspended as in a kind of crystalline equilibrium, in poetic innocence. If science intervened, it was only to serve as an instrument which the painter unconsciously grasped. But in those lost or never completed monumental transcripts of reality, of which the Anghiari battlepiece was the type, the science is all too evident, and the immediate sensibility, present in the preparatory sketches, is lost in the conscious effort of composition.

This great but divided nature is revealed in all its tragic grandeur in the notebooks, the last testament of classical art. They show with a detail and careless abandon that have never been exceeded the workings of a great mind. There, side by side, we find feelings and sensations recorded in all their poetic actuality, and these same feelings and sensations converted to idea, coldly analysed and dissected, materia physica, what Donne, in a phrase which Charles Eliot Norton loved to repeat, called

> Those unconcerning things, matters of fact.

Here, from the notebooks, is an experience, a thing seen, held in the pure consciousness, as sensation:

> Amid the whirling currents of the winds were seen a great number of companies of birds coming from distant lands, and these appeared in such a way as to be almost indistinguishable, for in their wheeling movements at one time all the birds of one company were seen edgewise, that is showing as little as possible of their bodies, and at another time showing the whole measure of their breadth, that is full in face; and at the time of their first appearance they took the form of an indistinguishable cloud, and then the second and third bands became by degrees more clearly defined as they approached nearer to the eye of the beholder.
>
> And the nearest of the above-mentioned bands dropped down low with a slanting movement, and settled upon the dead bodies, which were borne along by the waves of this great deluge, and fed upon them, and so continued until such time as the buoyancy of the inflated dead bodies came to fail, and with slow descent they sank gradually down to the bottom of the waters.[6]

This is pure observation, such indeed as a scientist would make. But the analytical reason has not yet intervened with its *why* and *how,* and therefore the vision, realized in words, is conveyed in all its integrity to the reader, and a direct emotional response takes place. The same faculties would be engaged in giving a plastic representation to the same scene in paint. But when Leonardo, in another place, begins to instruct the painter in methods for making such a representation, he lays down precepts which were to corrupt the artistic consciousness of Europe for the next three centuries. "Holding up the mirror to Nature" is the substance of it all, and this is what Leonardo actually recommended:

> When you wish to see whether the general effect of your picture corresponds with that of the object represented after nature, take a mirror and set it so that it reflects the actual thing, and then compare the reflection with your picture, and consider carefully whether the subject of the two images is in conformity with both, studying especially the mirror. The mirror ought to be taken as a guide—that is, the flat mirror—for within its surface substances have many points of resemblance to a picture; namely, that you see the picture made upon one plane showing things which appear in relief, and the

mirror upon one plane does the same. The picture is one single surface, and the mirror is the same. The picture is intangible, inasmuch as what appears round and detached cannot be enclosed within the hands, and the mirror is the same. The mirror and the picture present the images of things surrounded by shadow and light, and each alike seems to project considerably from the plane of its surface. And since you know that the mirror presents detached things to you by means of outlines and shadows and lights, and since you have, moreover, amongst your colours more powerful shadows and lights than those of the mirror, it is certain that if you but know well how to compose your picture, it will also seem a natural thing seen in a great mirror.[7]

The mirror might have been made an image of the pure consciousness, but only metaphorically speaking. This literal application of the mirror represents a corruption of consciousness because consciousness is not thus mechanically inclusive. Even the eye, as experimental psychology has proved,[8] does not receive the kind of image that is reflected by a flat mirror—various distortions arise when an effort is made to represent the peripheral objects in a field of vision in relation to the point of focus. A mirror reflection corresponds to the laws of perspective, but in vision objects "regress" (in different degrees in different people), and what is actually seen is not a perspective representation but a phenomenal shape that approximates to it. But the real objection to Leonardo's precept springs from the fact that consciousness is never simply visual: it is a total sensational experience in which are combined sensorimotor responses of a complex range—not merely conditioned reflexes to color, for example, but also associated tactile sensations. Some of Leonardo's precepts are recommendations to the painter to observe his own sensational reflexes, so that he is not deceived into copying conventional types; but the majority of his precepts are in effect nothing but formulas for such conventional types: the fixation of emotional clichés. Here is an example from the notebooks:

> A man who is in despair you should make turning his knife against himself, and rending his garments with his hands, and one of his hands should be in the act of tearing open his wound. Make him with his feet apart, his legs somewhat bent, and the whole body likewise bending to the ground, and with his hair torn and streaming.[9]

A whole repertory of such histrionic attitudes, for most of which Leonardo was responsible, passed into the academies which began to rise up all over Europe in the seventeenth century, and not till Constable, Delacroix, Manet, and Degas revolted against such artificiality was the artistic consciousness again purified. Even then it took the best part of a century for consciousness to recover its complete integrity.

Leonardo was fully conscious of the dangers of a theoretical approach to art, and again and again warns the novice not to place theoretical precepts above the observation of nature. But conscious as he was that "the supreme misfortune is when theory outstrips performance," he nevertheless insists on the conscious, analytical approach in art. He did not discount the imagination; but

> you should apply yourself first of all to drawing, in order to present to the eye in visible form the purpose and invention created originally in your imagination; then proceed to take from it or add to it until you satisfy yourself; then have men arranged as models draped or nude in the way in which you have disposed them in your work; and make the proportions and size in accordance with perspective, *so that no part of the work remains that is not so counselled by reason and by the effects in nature.*[10]

He is preoccupied throughout his notebooks with the science of perspective, which he calls "the bridle and rudder of painting."

> Those who are enamoured of practice without science are like a pilot who goes into a ship without rudder or compass and never has any certainty where he is going.
>
> Practice should always be based upon a sound knowledge of theory, of which perspective is the guide and gateway, and without it nothing can be done well in any kind of painting.[11]

Leonardo realized that perspective is an ambiguous term— recognized, indeed, a distinction between "natural" perspective and "accidental" perspective,[12] the former being scientifically geometrical, the latter "that which is created by art," an adaptation of theoretical perspective to the flat surface on which this perspective is represented in a painting. But the whole purpose of his precepts is to recommend the artist to check the accidental perspective of art by the natural perspective of science, and there is no sign anywhere in the notebooks that he regarded perspective as in any sense "symbolical"—that is to say, as a technique to be used for the expression of subjective feeling. The phenomenal world is the only reality, and art is the representation of this phenomenal world in all its actuality— "the eye is the universal judge of all objects." That the heart might wish to represent things differently from the way the eye sees them never seems to have occurred to Leonardo—unless that realization came to him when he wrote, at the foot of a "page of mathematical and architectural drawings, and others anatomical of the generative functions," *I have wasted my hours*.[13] And there is a note in the Forster MS that is still more tragical: "If liberty is dear to you, may you never discover that my face is love's prison."[14]

I will attempt to summarize the main conclusion of this somewhat rambling chapter. Out of a conceptual notion of "real" space had arisen an illusion of the real itself, of a positive and measurable reality. An external world was posited, solid and substantial in its continuum of space, and the artist was expected to represent this external reality by practical methods that could be acquired in academies of art. A prodigious skill was developed in Western Europe, the main object of which was no longer to create symbols for feeling or intuition, but rather to construct an illusion of space through which objects could be seen in perspectival coherence. The objects could, of course, be arranged to tell a story, but the story must then be judged by a moral criterion—the criterion so forcibly advocated by Tolstoy in *What is Art?* But more often reality was its own justification—the reality of the landscape or the still-life, sufficient in its own there-ness. This simulacrum attained, with no emotional satisfaction, pathos or sentiment is then introduced: feeling is indulged, not defined. But the purpose of art is not to expend feeling, or excite feeling, but rather to give feeling *form*, to find its "objective correlative," so that we may recognize it for what it is, for what it signifies in our discourse. Art is always the instrument of consciousness, as apprehension, realization, materialization.

The metaphor of the mirror was to be replaced, during the Romantic period, by other metaphors of a more appropriate kind—Coleridge's fountain, Hazlitt's lamp[15]—but no metaphors are really adequate for the artistic process. Art itself is a metaphoric activity, finding (rather than seeking) new symbols to signify new areas of sensibility. The post-Renaissance period should be regarded as one in which an infinite refinement of accepted symbols took place, and, as a parallel or consequent development, there was an infinite refinement of imagination and thought. But a time came when all that could be done had been done: refinement ended in sophistication, and little remained but repetition and return. But out of this very weariness and fantasy a new consciousness was to be born—the consciousness of the unconscious. A further attempt was made to circumvent all ideals, whether of God or of Man, and to present not the illusion of the real but the reality of consciousness itself—subjective reality.

3/

TO SEE MIRACULOUS
THINGS

"...Drawn by my eager wish, desirous of seeing
the great confusion of the various strange forms
created by ingenious nature, I wandered for some
time among the shadowed cliffs, and came to the
entrance of a great cavern. I remained before it
for a while, stupefied, and ignorant of the existence of such a thing, with my back bent and my
left hand resting on my knee, and shading my
eyes with my right, with lids lowered and closed,
and often bending this way and that to see
whether I could discern anything within; but this
was denied me by the great darkness inside. And
after I stayed a while, suddenly there arose in me
two things, fear and desire—fear because of the
menacing dark cave, and desire to see whether
there were any miraculous thing within."

—from Leonardo's Manuscript in the
British Museum, folio 155b

The Beginnings of
Modern Science

by Alexander Koyré

 E SHALL EXAMINE the history of the exact sciences during the Renaissance under three headings—mathematics, astronomy, and physics or mechanics—even though the term "exact" cannot be properly applied to them, except in anticipation of future developments.

Needless to say, this division is highly artificial. The history of astronomy cannot be studied apart from that of mathematics—or even of physics. Nevertheless, our approach has the advantage of emphasizing the inherent logic of historical processes that would otherwise seem quite haphazard.

In fact, many of the external influences which historians have called turning-points in the history of science are completely illusory. Thus the appearance of the cannon did not cause the emergence of the new dynamics—it was precisely the behaviour of cannonballs that Leonardo da Vinci, Tartaglia and Benedetti were unable to explain. The needs of navigators, of ecclesiastical calendar computers and of astrologers ought to have led to the correction of existing astronomical tables, but they did not; nor did they persuade Copernicus to change the traditional order of the celestial spheres and to place the sun at their centre. Commercial needs and the rise of banking certainly helped to spread elementary mathematical knowledge, but they cannot explain the spectacular advances made by early

From *The Beginnings of Modern Science* (1450–1800), ed. by Rene Taten, tr. by Arnold Pomerans (New York: Basic Books, Inc., 1964). Reprinted by permission of the publisher.

16th-century Italian algebraists, nor their systematic attempts to "symbolize" arithmetical and algebraic operations.

However, though the series of events constituting the evolution of mathematics, astronomy and physics cannot be explained in isolation —it is always vain to "explain" an invention or a discovery—they can at least be made intelligible. The history of scientific thought cannot content itself with less or demand more.

THE REVIVAL OF MATHEMATICAL STUDIES

Fifteenth-century mathematicians devoted most of their energies to the discovery and study of medieval, Arabic and, later, of Greek texts, and to the widest possible dissemination of their newly-acquired knowledge.

Two events, in particular, helped to hasten this development: the fall of Constantinople, which drove a host of scholars with their Byzantine manuscripts into Italy; and the invention of printing. However, the first printed books were little concerned with mathematics, and many works written in the middle of the 15th century (for example, those of Nicholas of Cusa, Peurbach and Regiomontanus) were not printed until very much later. Those of Chuquet and Piero della Francesca were not printed at all, but in 1472 Sacrobosco's *Sphaera* was published at Ferrara and at about the same time Peurbach's *Theoricae novae planetarum* appeared in Nuremberg. While Ptolemy's *Quadripartitum* was printed in Venice as early as 1484 and 1493, no Latin edition of the *Almagest* was printed before 1515 (Venice) and no Greek edition until 1538 (Basle). Euclid's *Elements* (in the Campanus edition) was published in 1482 at Venice and in 1491 at Vicenza. Medieval mathematicians were not forgotten, for though the works of Leonardo of Pisa were not published before the 19th, nor those of Levi Ben Gerson before the 20th century, some of the writings of Thomas Bradwardine, of Jordanus Nemorarius and even of Nicole Oresme appeared much earlier. Jordanus' *Arithmetic* was printed in 1496, 1503, 1507, 1510 and 1514; Bradwardine's *Arithmetic* in 1495, 1498, 1502, 1503, *etc.* Bradwardine's *Geometry* in 1495, 1516 and 1530; and Oresme's *De latitudine formarum* in 1483 and 1496. At the same time, there appeared the first popular textbook: an anonymous arithmetic published in Treviso in 1478. There followed a host of Italian and German works of a similar kind.

· · ·

LEONARDO AND MATHEMATICS

The work of Leonardo da Vinci, like that of his friend Luca Pacioli, spanned the 15th and 16th centuries. A universal genius without equal, the greatest of great amateurs, as J. Coolidge has called him, Leonardo da Vinci left his mark on all branches of science: geometry, mechanics, geology, geography, biology, anatomy, botany and optics. Nothing escaped his inexhaustible curiosity and nothing remained unchanged after his intervention.

Leonardo da Vinci (15th April 1452–2nd May 1519) was not the product of a university or of Italian humanism. Though Pierre Duhem, in his famous *Études sur Léonard de Vinci, ceux qu'il a lus et ceux qui l'ont lu* (Paris, 1909–13), depicted him as a great scholar imbued with the tradition of medieval science and instrumental in handing it on to his 16th- and 17th-century successors, modern historians have rejected this interpretation almost unanimously. For them, as for his contemporaries, Leonardo was an *uomo senze lettere,* an unlettered man, lacking a classical education and with no Latin and no Greek. He was a self-taught scholar, albeit one of genius.

This historians—and Leonardo's contemporaries—are both right and wrong. They are wrong to underplay the lessons which the young Leonardo must have learnt from Andrea del Verrocchio, in whose workshop he served as an apprentice and to whom he owes his scientific background. Great workshops like Verrocchio's, where not only painters but bronze-casters, stonemasons, draughtsmen, architects, builders and civil and military engineers were taught their respective trades, were far more akin to modern technical colleges than to painters' studios. Clearly the practice of all these "arts"—including painting, which involved familiarity with perspective—called for a great deal of scientific and mathematical preparation.

Historians are right to insist on the predominantly practical nature of Leonardo's training, for it is in this way that his concrete approach and vocabulary are best explained. At heart, Leonardo was a constructor of engines rather than a theorist. Thus, his geometry was generally that of the engineer, and his answers were practical solutions, rough and ready, capable of being implemented with existing instruments, and not elegant abstractions. For him, as for many of his contemporaries, science meant action rather than contemplation.

A good example of his pragmatic approach is his method of inscribing regular polygons in a circle as a means of squaring it. Inscribing polygons with 3, 6, 8 and 24 sides is an easy matter, and Leonardo performed it with a fixed compass. (Such constructions, which had been studied by Pappos and particularly by Abū'l Wafā, became very popular in Italy during the 16th century.) The inscription of heptagons and pentagons, however, is much more difficult, and Leonardo had to make do with approximate solutions. He rectified and squared the circle by rolling it along a straight line. This solution indicates a complete misunderstanding of the theoretical problem involved, but is fully justified in engineering practice.

Undoubtedly it was from Luca Pacioli, whose *Summa* he was one of the first to read and with whom he later contracted a firm friendship, that Leonardo gained most of his mathematical knowledge. But he was also indebted to Albert of Saxony, Jordanus Nemorarius, whom he frequently quotes, and to Nicholas of Cusa. It seems most unlikely that he studied Archimedes at first hand, but there is little doubt that he knew of his writings through Eutocios and Valla, with whose *De expetendis et fugiendis rebus* he was certainly familiar.

It seems odd that Leonardo never studied algebra. Perhaps he found it too difficult or too abstract. By contrast, he was a born geometer and his extraordinary practical gifts in this field more than made up for his theoretical shortcomings. His interesting musings on the fundamental concepts of geometry reflect a strong Aristotelian and Cusanian influence.

Leonardo was not afraid to introduce infinitesimal concepts (limiting values) into his work. To determine the centre of gravity of a semicircle, for instance, he assumed that it could be divided into "so many pyramids [triangles] that the concavity of their base would become almost imperceptible, almost a straight line." In general, however, Leonardo's methods were simpler, more straightforward and more elementary. It was no doubt intuition which led him to his most remarkable discovery: the determination of the centre of gravity of a pyramid. It seems that, applying to solids the same arguments that held for plane figures, he was able to find the centre of gravity of the tetrahedron—at the point of intersection of its "axes" (the straight lines joining any angular point to the centre of gravity of the opposite face). He then discovered that the straight lines joining the centres of the opposite faces of a tetrahedron also intersect in its centre of gravity; finally, he generalized this into the theorem that the centre of gravity of any pyramid is found on its axis, at a distance of one quarter of the axis from the base.

Though Leonardo's studies on the transformation of one solid into another "without diminution or increase of matter" were inspired by

Nicholas of Cusa's *De transmutationibus geometricis* (1450), he solved Cusanus' problems (the transformation of a number of cubes into a single cube, and the transformation of a cube into a right prism, and conversely) by Valla's method of mean proportionals. Leonardo also studied original transformations, *e.g.* the transformation of a cube into a pyramid.

Leonardo was fascinated by the lunes of Hippocrates. Apart from mentioning them frequently in his *Notebooks,* he began a special treatise on them, the *De ludo geometrico,* which, like all his other works was left uncompleted. His interest in them is best explained by his appreciation of their aesthetic properties and by the ease with which they could be combined in all sorts of ways with other geometrical figures. As he went along, he discovered a number of their very simple properties, previously unknown in the West. Thus he established that the sum of the lunes constructed on the sides of a right-angled triangle is equal to the area of the triangle itself.

Let us finally mention the highly ingenious mechanical solution (by means of a special compass) of a problem in optics, known as Alhazen's problem, which was not to find a geometric solution for another 150 years (Huygens). Leonardo's solution involved a very profound knowledge of the properties of conic sections, and such knowledge was exceptional in his day.

. . .

ASTRONOMY

THE COSMOLOGY OF NICHOLAS OF CUSA

An important chapter in the history of cosmology was written when Nicholas of Cusa challenged the classical conception of a closed and hierarchical universe. As against this cosmology, which had held sway for almost two thousand years, he introduced a universe "of which the centre is everywhere and the circumference nowhere." Rejecting the view that the celestial spheres revolve about the earth as their centre, he was also forced to reject the distinction in the universe between "sublunary" and "celestial" regions. The universe is indivisible and the earth is but one of many celestial bodies, as noble as any other. Like them, it radiates light and has its proper motion.

In his *De docta ignorantia* (1440), Nicholas of Cusa attacked the "presumptuous science" of the astronomers and philosophers with unprecedented boldness, denying the existence of privileged directions and places in the universe; "above" and "below" had ceased to be anything but relative terms. An observer placed on the sun or a planet would invariably see the earth revolving about and above him, and hence believe he was at the centre of its motion. Motion itself is not absolute, but varies from one apparently immobile reference system to the next.

The destruction of the classical cosmos was a prerequisite of the scientific revolution of the 17th century—hence the great historical importance of the *De docta ignorantia*. Small wonder that Cusa's contemporaries and successors—except Leonardo da Vinci—opposed it with all their might. Not until Giordano Bruno did Cusa's great work begin to exert any appreciable influence on astronomy, for it was only then that Cusa's unlimited universe finally became the infinite universe of modern thought. In fact, since Cusa denied the existence of fixed points and of perfectly uniform motions, and hence the periodicity of celestial events, 15th- and 16th-century observational astronomy would have become paralysed had astronomers adopted his views without any qualifications. Cusanus himself seems to have gone back on them when he wrote in his *De venatione sapientiae* (1462):

> God has endowed every body with its own nature, orbit and place, and has set the earth in the middle of all, decreeing that it be heavy and deviate neither upwards nor sideways.

Even so, he left the earth free to rotate on its own axis. In an earlier note in his own handwriting, written on the last sheet of an astronomical treatise issued at Nuremberg in 1444, Cusanus had claimed that the starry sphere revolves from east to west in twelve hours, while the earth revolves in the same direction in twice that time. Hence it travels round the poles of the world, "as Pythagoras says," once in a day and a night, "but the eighth sphere revolves twice, and the sun a little less than twice, in a day."

In other words, to an observer on the earth, this would produce the same effect as if the earth were immobile while the starry sphere revolved once in twenty-four hours. The annual motion of the sun is the result of its lagging slightly behind the other stars.

From these brief remarks it will have become clear that Nicholas of Cusa cannot be considered a direct precursor of Copernicus.

· · ·

LEONARDO AND ASTRONOMY

Though Leonardo da Vinci was not an astronomer, and though he did not make those astronomical discoveries which some over-enthusiastic historians have attributed to him, he was one of the first, if not the first, Western writers to have realized that moonlight is reflected light. Again, though he did not invent the telescope, as has sometimes been claimed, he made a very important discovery (unrecognized in his day) by which he became the precursor of Galileo: he appreciated the sub-jective nature of the halo of the fixed stars and consequently of their ap-parent dimensions.

Leonardo's cosmological views, though never fully elaborated, fell between those of Cusanus and Copernicus. Despite the famous phrase in the *Notebooks, Il sole non si muove* (the sun does not move), it seems unlikely that Leonardo subscribed to the heliocentric doctrine. On the other hand, it is clear that, following Nicholas of Cusa, he abandoned the geocentric view and, by the double step of likening the moon to the earth and the earth to the moon, he inferred the terrestrial character of the moon and the celestial character of the earth. In effect, he said that the moon consists of the same elements as the earth, namely earth, air and water. He also claimed that because it resembles the moon, the earth must enjoy the dignity (*noblesse*) of a star.

> The earth is not in the centre of the universe [the influence of Cusanus is unmistakable] but is in fact in the centre of the elements which accompany it and are united to it. And if one were to be upon the moon, then to the extent to which it together with the sun is above us, so far below it would our earth appear, with the element of water performing the same office as the moon does for us.

Moreover, it seems most likely that Leonardo thought of the earth as spinning on its axis, and that he defended this view against classical objections. This is borne out by a reference to the motion of "a heavy body falling through the air while under the action of a circumvolutory motion with a period of twenty-four hours."

. . .

. . . The analogy drawn by Cusanus between a "spirit of life" animating a non-living body and the *impetus* activating a body in motion shows clearly how much of a traditionalist he really was. To him, *impetus* was a purely transitory phenomenon that opposed the natural tendency of the body. Nevertheless, the ideas propounded in the *De ludo globi* had a great influence on Leonardo da Vinci and Copernicus, and hence played an appreciable role in the history of dynamics.

. . .

PHYSICS

Leonardo da Vinci's contribution to physics was indubitably the most original of the period. While there is no doubt that many discoveries (for instance the discovery of the principle of inertia and of the law of falling bodies) have been wrongly attributed to him by Venturi, Libri, Pierre Duhem and, more recently, by V. Somenzi, there is no doubt that Leonardo's work was far more important than the views of such hypercritical scholars as Olschki and Dugas would suggest.

FROM TECHNIQUE TO SCIENCE

Leonardo da Vinci was a man of unrivalled technological genius. His transformation of mere technique into technology was foreshadowed by his famous remark that experiment is vastly superior to speculation and book-learning, and is the true basis of all scientific theories. Thus, he was able to describe mechanics as the paradise of mathematics, in which the latter comes into its own and turns empirical art into applied science. This transformation was hastened by his many drawings and plans of engines which were never presented in the form of pictures, as in 15th- and 16th-century technical albums, but as geometrical scale-drawings. One might say that, though Leonardo's geometry was often the geometry of the engineer, his engineering technique was invariably that of the geometer.

Despite his praise of theory, Leonardo did not publish a single theoretical work, or if he did, no such work has come down to us.

What we have, instead, is a mass of fragments of uncertain date, repeating, completing and often contradicting one another. Their study, though greatly improved by Guido Ucelli's admirable edition of the *Scritti della mecanica* (Milan, 1940), remains extremely difficult because of their fragmentary nature, their inaccurate terminology and their vague formulation. Hence, Leonardo's contribution to mechanics must not be sought in his general formulae and definitions, but rather in his analysis of concrete or semi-concrete cases. Leonardo da Vinci's strength lay in his exceptionally acute perception of concrete reality, and not in his powers of abstraction.

"VIRTUAL VELOCITIES" AND SIMPLE MACHINES

Leonardo's mechanics were based on Aristotle—or rather on the apocryphal *Problems of Mechanics*—to which he added a number of amendments, notably his own doctrine of *impetus*.

Leonardo used the basic principle of Aristotle's statics—which we might call the "principle of virtual velocities"—to explain the behaviour of simple machines: pulleys, tackles, levers, balances, *etc*. In addition, he used the principle of virtual displacements, the discovery of which has been wrongly attributed to him. He would sometimes speak of both principles in the same breath, no doubt because he believed them to be identical. In fact, the difference between them was first appreciated by Descartes.

Leonardo was an expert on the workings of simple machines. He considered the lever and the balance as the rational models of mechanical relationships, all of which were said to be based on mechanical equilibrium.

He found that the pull of a weight placed on the end of a lever decreases as the lever is tilted from the horizontal, and that it is proportional to the distance of the weight from the vertical drawn through the fulcrum. Hence, in a balance with bent arms, it is not the length of the *real* arms which matters but that of the *potential* arms. Like all his predecessors, Leonardo was keenly interested in the problem of the inclined plane. Studying the equilibrium of two heavy bodies connected by a thread and placed on two intersecting planes, he showed that the two bodies are in equilibrium when their weights are proportional to the "obliquity" of the planes, a term which he unfortunately failed to define. However, a drawing in *Manuscript H*[1] shows that the relative weight of a body placed on an inclined plane is inversely proportional to the gradient of the plane.

Though Leonardo's studies of the tension of threads were not very profound, it was through them that he was led to the parallelogram of forces. This discovery would have been of tremendous importance had he been able to generalize the solution. But once again his brilliant intuition was not joined to a correspondingly great gift for theoretical abstraction.

LEONARDO'S DYNAMICS

Leonardo made his greatest contribution to science in dynamics, though over-enthusiastic historians have exaggerated its importance more even than that of his contribution to statics.

As Pierre Duhem has shown, Leonardo's dynamics were, in fact, based on the *impetus* doctrine, and his concrete formulations were clearly influenced by Albert of Saxony and by Nicholas of Cusa. From Albert he took his method of calculating the ratio of the motive force to the internal or external resistance, and from Cusanus the notion of compound *impetus*. Leonardo considered *impetus* as a "virtue created by motion" and "impressed by the motor on the moving body." Though *impetus* can be produced in various ways, in every case a force bestows upon the moving body a derived force similar to itself. *"Impetus is the impression of motion which is transmitted from the motor to the moving body."*

The motion of a projectile can be resolved into three phases. In the first, the motion is purely violent—the projectile moves in a straight line; in the second, the motion is part violent and part natural, *i.e.* the violence of the throw is counteracted by the projectile's natural tendency to fall back under the action of its own weight, and the projectile describes an arc; in the third phase, where nature's laws are restored, the projectile drops in a straight line towards the centre of the earth.

In the case of a hemisphere rolling along a plane, Leonardo agreed with Cusanus and eliminated the rectilinear part of the trajectory. Had he extended his remarkable realization that a trajectory can be completely described by mixed motion to the case of projectiles, Leonardo would have forestalled Tartaglia by some 50 years. As it was, he failed to do so, though he admitted the possibility of completely curved motion in the case of water jets, and though, on one occasion, he even abandoned the fundamental theory of the rectilinear character of violent motion altogether, contending that:

> Everything movable thrown with fury through the air continues the motion of its mover; if, therefore, the latter move it in a circle and release it in the course of this motion, its movement will be curved.

ACCELERATION AND AIR RESISTANCE

Leonardo adopted the Aristotelian principle that the velocity of a moving body is proportional to the motive force and inversely proportional to the resistance the moving body meets. "If a power move a certain weight a certain distance, it will move double that weight through half the distance." Aristotle's principle can also be applied to the excess of the "power" over the resistance rather than to their ratio, and it is this method which Leonardo generally used. He argued that the reaction of the ambient air has two opposite effects: on the one hand it helps the acceleration of the descent by setting up a direct wave in front of the falling body, thus reducing the resistance in its path and, by means of a reflex wave, surrounding the body and pushing it from behind; on the other hand, it resists the motion though, since its density is uneven, the air resistance is not uniform. Hence it follows that the motion of a falling body is neither uniform nor even uniformly accelerated; uniform acceleration is effected by a compensatory mechanism which Leonardo discusses at length, confusing the respective roles of time and distance. In fact, this confusion was characteristic of Leonardo's day.

IMPACT, ACTION AND REACTION

Though Leonardo discovered neither the law of falling bodies nor the principle of inertia, he came very close to the discovery of Newton's third principle, that an action is always opposed by an equal reaction. Thus, in his studies of percussion, he stated that "everything striking against a resisting object leaps back from this object with equal force," and it was on this principle that he based his analysis of impact phenomena. Though a century ahead of his time in this respect, Leonardo failed to formulate the new conception of motion which his approach implied. Percussion was to him a special case of violent motion, opposed to natural forces and causes. It is produced whenever a body in rapid motion meets a resisting object. A heavy body hitting a plane is hit, in turn, by an equal force and deflected at an angle equal to the angle of percussion. The reflected motion is governed both by the simple force of the *impetus* (which controls the incident motion) and by the simple "percussive" force. Analysis shows that the reflected motion is composed of two motions according to the principle of the parallelogram of velocities. Hence the two motions, or the two motor forces, can coexist in one and the same moving body without impeding each other. From this view it was but a short step to the principle of the conservation of momentum.

Leonardo denied that *impetus* is lost in percussion, and claimed that the conservation of *impetus* or of motive force governed the impact of elastic bodies, a view which has obvious similarities with that of Descartes. However, Leonardo's conservation of *impetus* was not absolute, for he held that the resulting motion was restricted to a limited distance.

The conservation of motor force, and the equality of action and reaction in percussion formed the basic theory of Leonardo's analysis of different cases of percussion. Despite certain errors of calculation, his solutions were astonishingly accurate, which is the more surprising since he distinguished between the impacts of elastic and "soft" bodies.

He argued that impact leads not only to the formation of two equal and opposite forces, but also to the total or partial transfer of "force" from the percussing body to the object of the percussion. This transfer may appear as the exchange of "reciprocal forces," or else as the sharing out of the total force available between the agent and the object.

The mechanics of the 16th century has nothing to offer that is comparable with the level of Leonardo's analytic thought, and such heights were not reached again until the advent of Jan Marcus Marci von Kronland a hundred years later.

. . .

ANATOMICAL KNOWLEDGE

Seventeenth-century biologists knew a great deal about human anatomy, and they applied that knowledge to their studies of vertebrates. Many of them dissected domestic or captive animals and described their internal structure. However, this work followed no general plan, and what comparisons were made were made incidentally. True, as early as 1555 Belon had indicated the homology of the principal bones of birds and man, and Leonardo da Vinci had established a clear correspondence between the human leg and foot and the hind leg of the horse, but no one else (except Aldrovandi, who simply reproduced Belon's diagram) had followed their example.

Art and Science

by George Sarton

LEONARDO DA VINCI beautifully illustrates the best aspects of the Renaissance.[1] In earlier chapters I was obliged to deal with some of its less attractive features, and it is pleasant to end with one of the immortals. Leonardo is as alive today as he ever was.

Since the growth of knowledge is the core of progress, the history of science ought to be the core of general history. Yet the main problems of life cannot be solved by men of science alone, or by artists and humanists; we need the cooperation of them all. Science is always indispensable but never sufficient. We are hungry for beauty, and where charity is lacking nothing else is of any avail.

Two illustrious figures who typify the Renaissance man's feeling for both art and science are the Florentine Leonardo da Vinci and his younger contemporary, Albrecht Dürer of Nuremberg. They never met, nor did they influence each other, but they were children of the same age, and the scientific problems they encountered were similar. Dürer devoted more time to art, Leonardo to science. Leonardo was the better scientist and the deeper philosopher.

Since most of the people who have studied Leonardo's work are men of letters or art critics, it is necessary to explain that the historian of science cannot use their methods without danger. An eloquent sentence, of which there are so many in his manuscripts, may testify to his literary genius. A single incomplete sketch may reveal the great artist. But we

From *Six Wings* by George Sarton (Bloomington, Ind.: Indiana University Press, 1957). Copyright © 1957 by Indiana University Press. Reprinted by permission of the publisher.

cannot draw large conclusions from a single remark on a scientific topic, unless the idea is developed and confirmed. For example, we cannot call Leonardo a predecessor of Copernicus merely on the ground that he once wrote, "The sun does not move." [2] What exactly did he mean? There is no way of knowing. A man of science must prove, or at least explain clearly, what he has in mind. The illustrious Sigmund Freud has ventured to reconstruct Leonardo's secret psychology on the basis of a single fragment in which Leonardo alludes to a dream of his childhood. [3] Such reasoning is completely unscientific, but Freud's fame has given his book on Leonardo an undeserved prestige.

On the other hand, Leonardo's scientific genius is far more difficult to evaluate than that of other men of science whose works were published in their own lifetimes. There are three reasons for this. First, it is not always possible to know what he meant, and his notes were never revised for publication. Second, Leonardo was a child of the Renaissance, and almost every one of his ideas has mediaeval roots. [4] Moreover, the tradition that he gathered was not a literary tradition but rather an oral and manual one.

Leonardo was born on April 24, 1452 (New Style) [5] at Borgo di Vinci, in the foothills above Florence; he belonged on the paternal side to a well-known family but was born out of wedlock. His parents married soon after his birth, but they did not marry each other. His father founded a new family in which Leonardo was not wanted. If he had been well born, his father would probably have provided for his education and sent him eventually to the University of Florence, where he would have been crammed with Latin and scholastic learning. Instead, it was thought in the family circle that apprenticeship to a skilled craft would be good enough for him, and he was sent to the *bottega* (or studio) of Andrea del Verrocchio (1435–88). This was a blessing in disguise, for instead of an academic education that lacked contact with reality, he received the best kind of training for a boy of his temperament and genius. His father's choice of Verrocchio was an extremely happy one, and we cannot help being grateful to him for having entrusted the upbringing of young Leonardo to a man who was then one of the leading artists and craftsmen of Florence.

In Verrocchio's studio Leonardo was given a chance of learning many crafts, of discussing every question of the day, and of solving real and tangible problems such as life and art suggest at every turn. Verrocchio was not only a very great artist; he was a thinker, an ingenious craftsman—in a word, Leonardo's prototype. Leonardo was about 12 or 13 years of age when he was apprenticed to Verrocchio and he spent about twelve years in the studio of the Via del Agnolo; these were the formative years of his life. We may say that Leonardo received his whole education from Verrocchio and the many other artists[6] who came every day to the studio. We may even assume that without Verrocchio the miracle of Leonardo would not have occurred. Verrocchio was Leonardo's St. John the Baptist.

It is not my purpose to speak of Leonardo as a man of letters. His literary works consist of an enormous mass of fragments (notes and drawings) that has come to us in the greatest disorder. Some of his thoughts are so deep that one is reminded of Pascal's *Pensées,* but Leonardo's notes are fragments from many very different books, all mixed together; and to this hodgepodge are added incongruous and capricious notes, dreams, and hallucinations.

Another curiosity that has puzzled the critics and will always continue to puzzle them is the fact that the notes are written in mirror writing: in order to read them one must hold them up to a mirror. Why is this? My guess is that Leonardo was left-handed[7] and that when he began to write without anybody's supervision, he wrote naturally in reverse as left-handed children often do. Then he realized the advantage of such writing for the sake of secrecy and continued to use it. There is no doubt that his mirror writing was fluent and easy; it is sometimes very hard to decipher it even with the help of a mirror.

Very few of the fragments are dated or datable. One of our greatest difficulties is that Leonardo often contradicted himself on fundamental issues and it is impossible to know which was his final opinion.

The most pathetic document concerning him is the draft of a letter that he wrote in 1482–83 to the duke of Milan, Lodovico Sforza, to offer his services. He enumerates all his merits as inventor and military engineer; it is only at the very end that he mentions his artistic abilities. At this time he was 30 years old, and some of his less gifted friends were already established and famous.[8] All his life he was the victim of his ambiguous genius. As André Gide put it: "Avec du talent on fait ce qu'on veut, quand on a du génie on fait ce qu'on peut."

The "duce" of Milan accepted his services and, what is better, he seems to have left Leonardo plenty of freedom, for this first Milanese period (1483–99) was fertile in every one of his chosen fields (painting, anatomy, mathematics, technology). After the duke's defeat[9] and the capture of Milan Leonardo's life became that of an exile, a refugee, passing restlessly from one city to another. The best of these errant years (*il tempo della vita errante,* 1499–1512) were again spent in Milan, this time under French rule. In this, his second Milanese period, he continued his efforts to canalize streams, studied geometry with Luca Pacioli[10] and anatomy with Marc Antonio della Torre.[11] In 1512, however, Milan was reconquered by the Italians and Leonardo was obliged to move out (I imagine he was compromised as a collaborator). He obtained the patronage of Giuliano de' Medici[12] and went to Rome in 1513, accompanied by his young friend, Francesco Melzi. They spent two years at the Belvedere in the Vatican, but the proximity of Michelangelo, whom he disliked,[13] and of the German Giovanni degli Specchi,[14] who was a deceiver, irritated him and drove him away. He finally accepted the hospitality of François I in Cloux, near Amboise.[15] Leonardo and Francesco traveled to Cloux in 1515; they brought with them three paintings, St. Anne with the Holy Virgin and Child, St. John the Baptist, and the portrait of a woman (probably Mona Lisa, La Gioconda),[16] also all his notes and anatomical drawings, which he bequeathed to Francesco Melzi.[17] He died in Cloux on May 2, 1519.

To return to his scientific work, two aspects of it began very early, in Verrocchio's *bottega:* the "science of painting" and mechanics. Leonardo's idea that there can be a "science of painting" may be an illusion, but after all, why should one not speak of painting science just as one does of medical science? In both cases scientific facts or theories are applied to an art, the art of painting or of healing. The science of painting included, in the first place, linear perspective, which was exciting Florentine artists, Filippo Brunelleschi, Leon Battista Alberti, Paolo Uccello, Piero delle Francesca, Andrea del Verrocchio, and Leonardo; and second, the far subtler matter of aerial perspective, which for centuries had been mixed up with optics, meteorology, the theory of colors and shades, and many other things. The Chinese had made penetrating observations on this subject at least as early as the sixth century,[18] and Leonardo was the first to rediscover some of them in the West.

Leonardo was a born mechanician as well as a painter; his mechanical tendencies were fostered in Verrocchio's studio. Verrocchio was a sculptor, a painter, and a goldsmith; his best known work is the equestrian statue of Bartolommeo Colleoni in Venice, perhaps the greatest monument of its kind in the world.[19] The erection of such a monument involved the solution of many mechanical problems. During the years of his adolescence Leonardo was constantly speculating about various machines that would make it easier to satisfy the needs of peace and of war. The only available source of continuous power was hydraulic;

it was necessary to dig canals, which were the best means of moving heavy materials, and to build water-mills on running rivers.

Leonardo's quaderni are full of mechanical projects, drawn in such complete and precise detail that they sometimes look like blueprints; in fact, it has been possible to reconstruct some of the machines that he invented. But had he invented them? That is not certain; there were many inventors in the fifteenth century, and even in the fourteenth.[20] Most of them were illiterate, and in many cases secrecy was their only protection.

From hydraulics Leonardo passed to aerodynamics, and he made a good many observations, detailed and accurate, concerning the flight of birds. His projects were comparable not to those of Daedalus and Icarus, but rather to those of engineers of the last century who tried to solve the problem of human flight before motors had been invented. Leonardo asked himself very reasonably, "Why should man not be able to do what the birds do?" and reasoned that to imitate them we should, first of all, find out exactly how they do it. The observations he made on that subject were not equaled until the nineteenth century.[21] How do birds soar, how do they fly with or against the wind, how do they direct their flight and reach their goal? He observed the adjustment of wings and their flexing, the various kinds of feathers, the movement of the tails, and how these means are used for going up and down, gliding, soaring, balancing, and alighting without breaking their legs. In short, Leonardo did everything that could be done in his time. It would be wrong to call him a forerunner of Copernicus or Harvey, but he fully deserves to be considered one of the pioneers of aviation.

It would be very misleading to imagine that Leonardo resembled a present-day inventor, whose aim is more often than not to make money. He was a practical man, but he was also a philosopher, so much in love with his ideas that he lost interest in their realization. As we all know, when an inventor suddenly has a great idea, that is not the end of the matter but the beginning; the most difficult task is still to come. He has to work out innumerable details, ascertain industrial and commercial possibilities, and adjust his plans to reality. Leonardo, having no patience and no talent for that sort of thing, could not be a successful inventor. He was a little like those men who love to flirt with women, but withdraw if their advances are too welcome. They do not want to be involved. He was a philosopher rather than an engineer, more interested in principles than in their application. Unfortunately the principles of mechanics were as yet by no means clear. Leonardo continued old traditions that can be traced back to Aristotle and Archimedes, but were extremely irregular, capricious, and secret. Did he know the ancient and mediaeval writings on mechanics? It is very improbable. He mentions Archimedes half a dozen times, and he mentions also Biagio Pelacani and Albert of Saxony. This does not prove much. All these writings were in Latin, and Leonardo's knowledge of Latin was empirical and rudimentary. Being an Italian, he could get the gist of a Latin sentence, but he could not have read a Latin book. He was almost illiterate, read very little and quoted less.

In spite of what has been claimed to the contrary, he was not a mathematician; he loved mathematics in the Platonic style but knew only the elements, and those not too well. He was a mechanician by instinct and tried all his life to understand the phenomena of statics and dynamics; he even tried to understand the rules of hydraulics and aerodynamics, but in vain. He could write: "Mechanics is the paradise of mathematics because it gives us the fruits of that science." [22] That was a poetic saying, an admirable intuition, but the fruits were still very far from maturity. It was impossible to solve the fundamental problems, because they could not yet be formulated. Leonardo continued bravely the mediaeval incubation; the birth could not take place until the time of Simon Stevin and Galileo, and mechanics began to mature only toward the end of the seventeenth century with Huygens and Newton.

In the marvelous field of mechanics Leonardo, genius though he was, could only grope his way like a blind man. In another field, however, it was possible to obtain valuable results at once. This was anatomy. Here again he was continuing mediaeval traditions, for it is wrong to believe that dissections were forbidden throughout the Middle Ages. There were distinguished anatomists like Mondino de' Luzzi and Guido da Vigevano. Human dissections, however, were rare and badly organized; the obstacles came from scholasticism rather than from religion. The experimental spirit was hardly awakened, and what is worse, the art of observing with precision and without prejudices was almost unknown. Physicians were dominated by Galen and Avicenna to such an unbelievable extent that they were unable to see with their own eyes. It was here that Leonardo's genius revealed itself, though even in this case the revelation was incomplete and miscarried.

One can say that modern anatomy was founded by two men, Italian and Flemish: Leonardo and, a little later, Andreas Vesalius of Brussels. There is an essential difference between them, however; Leonardo dissected some thirty bodies and left an abundance of notes and drawings, but he never composed an anatomical treatise. Vesalius, however, published in 1543 a great work, *De humani corporis fabrica,* which is truly the basis of modern anatomy. Leonardo's notes and drawings remained almost unknown until our century; Vesalius' book deeply influenced all the anatomists who followed him. One must conclude that Vesalius alone is the founder.

Nevertheless, although Leonardo's immediate influence was negligible, his anatomical work was astounding. Vesalius was a physician and a professor of anatomy, who might have been expected to perform dissections. Yet Leonardo, an artist and a mechanician, performed many and did them as well as Vesalius, though not as methodically.

The dissections that students perform today in the anatomical laboratories of our medical schools are very easy; running water, refrigeration, and antiseptics have greatly lessened the unpleasantness of such work. None of these conveniences was available to Leonardo, and the fulfillment of his self-imposed task required tremendous will power.[23] Moreover, while Vesalius was assisted by a professional artist, John Stephen of Calcar, Leonardo was obliged at various stages of his horrible task to interrupt it and begin immediately another kind of work of extreme delicacy, drawing as accurately as possible what he saw. Some of his anatomical drawings have never been equaled.

Leonardo's curiosity went far beyond that of other painters and sculptors, who were obliged to have some knowledge of artistic anatomy, that is to say, the layout of superficial muscles. The Florentine artists, who were draftsmen rather than colorists, studied that kind of anatomy with enthusiasm. That tradition, begun by Donatello, was carried to extremes by Antonio Pollaiuolo and brought back to moderation by Verrocchio and Leonardo. The sculptor's model or the painter's sketch must be sufficiently precise and sensitive to indicate the presence of muscles. The spectator must be able to divine their presence without being too conscious of them.

Artistic anatomy has been dominated from the beginnings of art by mathematical and mystical considerations. The love of symmetry and of numbers has led artists of all times to discover arithmetical relations between the sizes of different parts of the body and to establish a canon of human beauty. Such preoccupations existed in ancient Egypt, India, and Greece.[24] Leonardo and his younger contemporary, Albrecht Dürer, were no strangers to them.

Leonardo was interested not only in the beauty of the human body; he was searching for beauty in the three kingdoms of nature. He left behind many sketches of animals, plants, shells, and rocks. Some of his investigations would be classified today in the fields of physical geography, mineralogy, and geology. His drawings make us think of those of Ruskin, whose curiosity in both art and science was equally keen and complex. He was one of the first to give a rational explanation of fossils; the shells found imbedded in mountain rocks were the remains of creatures that had lived in the seas or on beaches and had been lifted up later on. He was one of the first men in the West to explore the high Alps not only as an artist but also as a man of science. The peoples of Europe were generally afraid of mountains, which they fancied were inhabited by goblins, gnomes, and devils. Christianity had not succeeded in dissipating or even in diminishing those superstitions, while Buddhism had encouraged opposite ones. The Buddhists of China and Japan have always associated high peaks with divine power and their most popular temples have been built upon the slopes or the tops of mountains. From this point of view, Leonardo was an Oriental. His thoughts on art and nature would ravish Indian, Chinese, or Japanese readers. His instinctive Orientalism was caused to a large extent by his lack of Western superstitions and inhibitions. His nonconformism was that of a truly great man; it was not deliberate, but spontaneous and natural.

His thought was much more scientific, more rational, than that of the great majority of his contemporaries, but he was not completely free from prejudice. Such freedom is hardly possible in our own time; it was absolutely impossible in his. Men of genius have a freer mind and a clearer vision than other men, but there is a limit to their clear-sightedness and to their emancipation. Leonardo's mind was shackled by two kinds of prejudice, which may be named Platonic and Galenic.

The first was represented mainly by the idea of microcosm and macrocosm, first explained in the *Timaios* of Plato and widely transmitted by the Neoplatonists and the Qabbalists. The microcosm of our body is a much reduced copy of the macrocosm of the universe: our bones are like the rocky skeleton of the earth; there is in us a lake of blood comparable to the seas; the rhythm of our breathing and of the pulse is like that of the tides, the "circulation" of blood is like that of water; the fur of animals, our hair, and the feathers of birds are like grass and leaves; rumbling in the bowels is like an earthquake, and so on. Those comparisons, which could be extended indefinitely, were commonplace in his time, at least among intellectuals.

It is not necessary to assume that Leonardo read either the *Timaios* or any one of the many books derived from it, for such ideas were in the air; he had heard them referred to or discussed in Verrocchio's *bottega* and elsewhere. Analogies as vague and grandiose as those of the microcosm and macrocosm would easily seduce the imagination of poets and artists.

During the Renaissance Platonic prejudices colored every thought; the prejudice that I call Galenic was less common. The motion of the blood, revealed by the pulse, was explained by Galen[25] not as a real circulation (possible only in a closed trajectory) but as a rhythmical back-and-forth movement. Even so, in order to justify his explanation, he was obliged to assume that the blood penetrating the right ventricle passes through the wall (*septum cordis*) and thus reaches the left part of the heart. How did it pass through the *septum,* which seems watertight? Through invisible holes. Leonardo was so hopelessly obfuscated by this Galenic invention that he was able not only to see these invisible holes but to draw them.[26] It would be hard to find a better example of the limitations even of genius. Leonardo's was a free mind and a great genius, yet he had been bamboozled by Plato's magic and Galen's authority to the extent of seeing things that did not exist and even of showing them to other people.

One ends by asking oneself—and I must do so at the risk of vexing my readers—whether Leonardo was really one of the great scientific creators.

His love of science and his zeal need not be argued; it is certain that his activities were those of a man of science as well as those of an artist, but is it possible to ascribe to him a single discovery, except such as are contained implicitly in his drawings?

In order to receive credit for a discovery it is not enough to make it. One must explain it; one must prove very clearly that one has understood it; one must be ready to defend it. One might say that a discovery is not completed until it has been justified in public.[27] An original idea that crosses a man's brain like lightning is as necessary as the seed of a plant, and just as insufficient if the seed does not germinate.

Leonardo's ideas were like seeds that failed to mature. They remained buried in his notes and drawings. He sometimes thought of writing books on anatomy, painting, and perhaps other subjects, but he never did so. Fra Luca Pacioli wrote to Duke Lodovico Sforza on February 9, 1498 that Leonardo had completed "a treatise on painting and on the motions of the human body," and Giorgio Vasari declared in 1550 that a Milanese painter had shown him a manuscript of Leonardo's which he intended to publish in Rome.[28] It is improbable that these manuscripts ever existed, at least in a form ready for publication, but it is possible that Leonardo's disciple, Francesco Melzi, who inherited his archives, may have composed an anthology of extracts (or commissioned someone else to compose it). There is in the Vatican Library a collection of 944 extracts from Leonardo's notes (*Codex Urbinas 1270,* XVIth century) which is the indirect source of the *Trattato della Pittura* dedicated to Queen Christina of Sweden and published in Paris in 1651, two centuries after Leonardo's birth. As to the anatomical treatise, it did not even achieve such indirect, tardy, and posthumous publication.

In short, Leonardo never published his ideas; he did not even take the trouble to put them in order for publication. This failure may have been partly due to his lack of literary education, for which his genius was never able to compensate. His defects were very different from those of the majority of his contemporaries. Their books are chock full of quotations to the point of incomprehensibility. Leonardo's notes contain hardly any quotations, and his references to "authorities" are rare and vague; for example, he refers nine times to Aristotle, six times to Vitruvius, five times to Archimedes, as many times to Ptolemy and Pliny, twice to Avicenna's anatomy.[29]

The most elaborate part of Leonardo's scientific work is that on anatomy, yet this exerted little, if any, influence. The only anatomist with whom he worked and consulted was Marc Antonio della Torre (1481–1511), who was thirty years younger than he, died very young, and left no traces.[30]

As long as Leonardo was alive, few people had a chance of seeing his anatomical drawings. I can name only Antonio de Beatis, secretary to Louis, cardinal of Aragon, who admired them in Cloux. Vasari and Gian Paolo Lomazzo saw them later in Melzi's hands, but they were not competent to appreciate their scientific value. One might say that the evolution of anatomy would have been the same if Leonardo had not existed.

Leonardo was one of the greatest men of science in history, but the world which admired him as an artist did not discover the man of science until many centuries after his death. He remained unknown by his own fault, for he did nothing to publish his discoveries; in most cases, indeed, he did not even bother to complete them.

This lack of perseverance has hurt the artist almost as much as the man of science. He has left us only a few paintings (less than ten) and some of them are not quite finished. The equestrian statue which would have rivaled Verrocchio's Colleoni was not cast.[31] The Last Supper which he painted in the refectory of Santa Maria delle

Grazie in Milan has faded until it is but a pale image of what it was. He spoiled other paintings by technical experiments or capriciously abandoned them. Nevertheless, he influenced many younger painters,[32] while he failed to influence contemporary scientists.

Nothing is more curious and perplexing, however, than the caprices of the mechanical inventor. Leonardo invented or reinvented a whole series of machines, yet he overlooked two of the greatest inventions not only of his time but of all time: printing and engraving. He could not have been unaware of their existence, for printed books, woodcuts, and copper engravings had become fairly common before the end of his life;[33] one could buy them in many shops in Florence, Milan, and elsewhere. Leonardo must have handled printed books, but he did not refer to them.[34] He made drawings for the *Divina proportione* of Luca Pacioli (Venice: Paganinus, 1509), and it may be that he engraved them himself. He must have seen woodcuts and engravings, but I found only a single phrase in his abundant writings which may possibly refer to them, "il modo di ristemparlo."[35] Did he despise such inventions, as did some Florentine snobs?

A man as intelligent as he was should have understood at once that these two inventions were of incalculable value, not only because they permitted the indefinite multiplication of copies with little effort, but chiefly because they made possible the production of copies that were identical and standard. This was important in every field, but especially in science. It made possible, for example, the publication of mathematical books and astronomical tables that could be used with confidence (errors could be definitely corrected in a later edition). Engraving permitted the addition to the text of accurate illustrations that enormously increased its practical value. How did it happen that Leonardo ignored and rejected all this? Evidently he had some blind spots, in spite of his genius.

We are always reminded of his two weaknesses, lack of formal instruction in his youth, and lack of material ambition. He was and remained all his life *un uomo senza lettere*. Some of our greatest men were illiterate; genius can exist without education and the best education in the world will not give genius to the man who lacks it. It is probable that Leonardo paid but little attention to books, and if so, why should he have bothered about printing?

The abundance of his notes should not mislead us; they were not those of a man of letters but rather those of a man of science and a philosopher. He sometimes wrote brilliant sentences, but this was due to his power of thought rather than to power of expression. Besides, he never went beyond the composition of sentences or paragraphs; he may have thought of writing books, but he never made the necessary effort. Such repugnance to writing is not rare among real artists, technicians, and even men of science. The latter are ready to take infinite pains in their investigations, but they often have trouble in writing up their reports and sometimes they postpone that unwelcome task indefinitely.

Leonardo could have written a book if he had wanted to, but he never wanted to badly enough. It is the same with his paintings; he could easily have painted many more, but he never had enough energy. Yet the very few paintings that he managed to complete suffice to immortalize him.

He is the best example of a rare and precious type: the man who does not give the full measure of his genius. Most talented people do the opposite. They try to give us more than their measure, that is, they bluff us. They begin to write a book before they know their subject, and learn as they go along. On the other hand, there are men of science and learning who never cease to accumulate notes and never find time to organize them and put them in good form. Leonardo belonged to the second group, but not because of defects in his nature. This was noticed by that devil of Aretino, Pietro,[36] in a spark of decency: "I tell you that Leonardo was equal to the very greatest, but his genius was of such a high quality that he could never be pleased with what he had done."

We should not forget that he lived in an age that was as revolutionary as ours but far more cruel. It was the age of despotic rulers like Lodovico Sforza and Cesare Borgia (the "Prince" of Machiavelli) and of violent enthusiasts, like Savonarola. Leonardo preserved his equanimity and his wisdom. He was an artist, a poet, a contemplator, a dreamer. On account of such "weaknesses" he became greater, closer to perfection, than if he had been more capable and "efficient." If a man is good and wise, why should he be efficient into the bargain?

The best way to explain this, the deepest and most moving aspect of his personality, is to compare him with another artist of his own time, Albrecht Dürer[37] of Nuremberg. As artists they were both supreme, each in his own way, but it is certain (to me at least) that Leonardo was the greater man. While Leonardo was a dreamer, paralyzed by his genius, Dürer was a practical, capable, and "efficient" man. If a man made a contract with Dürer for a portrait, he would be sure to get it at the agreed time together with the bill; if he made such a contract with Leonardo, he might get it or he might not. Administrators generally prefer the more docile and dependable type, and from their point of view they are right. It is not surprising that Dürer achieved material success and that Leonardo did not.

The comparison between these two men is valid because they were interested, roughly speaking, in the same things; the difference between them was that Leonardo accumulated notes and perplexities, while Dürer's thoughts, though less deep, were more fertile. Dürer would not bother much about a subject unless he had a practical purpose, such as the writing of a book. He not only prepared his books as any bookmaker would, but he printed them. We have three treatises written and illustrated by him. The first, *Unterweysung der Messung mit dem Zirckel und Richtscheyt,* contains instructions for measuring with compass and ruler (1525); the second, *Etliche Underricht zu Befestigung,* is devoted to fortifications (1527); the third, *Vier Bücher von menschlicher Proportion,* to the proportions of the human body (posthumously published in the year of his death, 1528).[38]

The fact that Dürer was concerned with artistic anatomy and not with deeper anatomy is significant. Dürer was always practical and earthbound; Leonardo was the opposite. While Leonardo disdained typography and engraving, Dürer understood immediately the commercial possibilities of both arts. Instead of producing a single drawing, a woodcut or copperplate enabled him to publish at once a hundred copies or more. Moreover, he was quick to realize that it was no more difficult, but far more profitable, to publish whole albums of engravings, such as the Passion of Our Lord or the Life of Our Lady. He established himself as printer, engraver, and bookseller. Each of his three books bears the note (in German), "Printed in Nuremberg by Albrecht Dürer, the Painter." At the commercial fairs of Frankfurt and Nuremberg Dürer had his own shop and display. When he traveled in the Low Countries in 1520–21 he brought with him a large number of his engravings, which were easy to pack and profitable to sell; he distributed free copies to important people, princes, bishops, or governors, whose good will he wished to capture, and he sold many more. We are well informed about his business dealings, because he kept careful accounts of all his receipts and expenditures. Another typical trait: Dürer signed all his works and often added the date.

Leonardo did not bother about such matters. He was as indifferent to chronology as the Hindus and for the same reason, for he considered all things *sub specie aeternitatis.*

Dürer was a businessman,[39] a man of substance living in his own comfortable house; he was capable of taking some interest in scientific questions, but he was not a man of science. Leonardo, on the contrary, was a pure artist, a disinterested inventor, a man of science, a cogitator, a Bohemian; he was decidedly not a businessman or an administrator. He was anxious to obtain not money, or power, or comfort, but beauty and truth. He wanted to understand God, nature, art, himself, and other men. I admire them both but I love Leonardo.

Few people are able to understand this, because their ideals are confused and upside down. They like to speak of spiritual values but they always give top priority to material values. They speak of beauty and art but comfort comes first. They speak of peace but make war almost unavoidable. They pray on Sunday but their motto is: Business first, business and power, conformity to social conventions, etc. Most men are social hypocrites. Leonardo was not.

Leonardo was a rebel, one of the worst or the best kind, one who does not even bother to state his disagreement and disapproval but pursues his own mission.

Leonardo's self-portrait, made by him toward the end of his life,[40] shows a tired face. Leonardo was then less than 67 years old, but he had suffered much because of the world's cruelties and his own anxieties. His outstanding merit is to have shown by his own example that the pursuit of beauty and the pursuit of truth are not incompatible. He is the patron of all those men, few in number, who love art and science with equal fervor.

Leonardo was a defender of reason, an enemy of superstition, but an idealist. There was in him an original and deep conviction that the only things that really matter are spiritual. The supreme discipline is that of love. As he put it, "The love of anything is the fruit of our knowledge of it, and grows as our knowledge becomes more certain." [41]

One might add, and no doubt he did so, that without love there can be no real knowledge.

35. Verrocchio (and Leonardo?), *Resurrection of Jesus.*
Terracotta relief. Florence, Museo Nazionale.

36. Luca della Robbia, *The Resurrection of the Redeemer.*
Glazed terracotta relief. Florence, Cathedral.
Photo: Alinari-Art Reference Bureau.

37. Leonardo, *Madonna and Child with a Cat*. Florence, Uffizi.
Photo: Alinari-Art Reference Bureau.

38. Leonardo, *Aristotle and Phyllis*. Hamburg, Kunsthalle.

39. Verrocchio (and Leonardo?), *Resurrection of Jesus*, detail. Florence, Museo Nazionale. *Photo: Brogi-Art Reference Bureau.*

40. Verrocchio (and Leonardo?), *Resurrection of Jesus,* detail.
Florence, Museo Nazionale.　　*Photo: Brogi-Art Reference Bureau.*

41. Leonardo, *Five Grotesque Heads*. Windsor Castle, Royal Library, No. 12495r.

42. Leonardo, *Head of Warrior with Turban*. Oxford, Ashmolean Museum.
   Photo: Anderson-Art Reference Bureau.

43. Leonardo, *Study of the Head of a Man
   Shouting and of a Profile*.
   Budapest, Museum of Fine Arts.
   Photo: Art Reference Bureau.

44. and 45.
Verrocchio (and Leonardo?),
Resurrection of Jesus,
details. Florence, Museo Nazionale.
Photos: Brogi-Art Reference Bureau.

. After Verrocchio, *Madonna with Child.*
Stucco relief. London, private collection.

47. After Verrocchio, *Madonna with Child.*
Stucco relief. Florence, private collection.

48. Fernando de Llanos. *Resurrection*. Seville, Cathedral.

49. Portrait of Cesare Borgia. (Coin?)

50. Leonardo, *Studies of the Head of Cesare Borgia*. Turin, Royal Library.
Photo: Anderson-Art Reference Bureau.

1. Portrait of Cesare Borgia.
Engraving in Paolo Giovio's *Elegi*.

52. Leonardo, *St. John the Baptist.*
Paris, Louvre.
Photo: Alinari-Art Reference Bureau.

53. Leonardo, *Virgin of the
Rocks.* Paris, Louvre.
*Photo: Alinari-Art
Reference Bureau.*

54. Leonardo (?), *La Belle Ferronière*. Paris, Louvre.
Photo: Alinari-Art Reference Bureau.

55. Leonardo, *St. Jerome*. Rome, The Vatican.
Photo: Anderson-Art Reference Bureau.

56. Leonardo, *Adoration of the Magi*. Florence, Uffizi.
Photo: Alinari-Art Reference Bureau.

57. Leonardo, *Benois Madonna*. Leningrad, Hermitage.

58. Leonardo, *Portrait of Isabella d'Este*.
Paris, Louvre.

59. Leonardo, *Virgin and Child with St. Anne and Infant St. John.*
Black chalk cartoon. London, Royal Academy of Arts.
Photo: Alinari-Art Reference Bureau.

Man Without Letters

by Giorgio de Santillana

S I LISTENED one day to George Sarton, our beloved G.O.M. of the History of Science, castigating passionately Leonardo for his Platonism (for Platonism and Progress are, undeniably, antagonistic, and Progress is what Sarton cared for), I wondered if any more unjust accusation had ever been levelled at Leonardo, strange and even perverse as he undoubtedly was.

Whence this passionate argument, in which I probably outran the limits of careful measure:

Alexander Koyré has shown us Galileo the platonist, and we are entirely in agreement. Galileo was a platonist, not only in his manner of explaining the concrete by means of the abstract, but also in the Socratic method of his *Dialogue,* and especially in his tendency, here and there avowed, toward panmathematicism. But nevertheless there is the fact that Galileo was thought to be a platonist by order and obedience, so to speak; for the mathematical sciences were under the aegis of Plato, and Galileo's friends and followers were platonists—much better platonists, actually, than he ever was. There is no doubt at all that the entire group of the Accademia dei Lincei was platonistic before it was anti-aristotelian, and in a vividly militant manner. With Ciampoli, the young prelate who heroically sacrificed his career in order to allow the *Dialogue* to be printed, one glimpses platonistic insights that border on heresy.

Galileo, then, had good reason to belong to the "sect," as it was

From *Léonardo de Vinci et l'expérience scientifique au seizième siècle* (Paris: Presses Universitaires de France, 1953), tr. by Starr and Jim Atkinson. Printed by permission of the author.

called; but more significant is it that he insisted on holding explicit reservations about platonism as a philosophy. For, as Koyré has very ably proved, he was first and above all an archimedean. It is Archimedes who was his master in the new science, and Democritus as well; Plato is merely his guarantor, so to speak, in the world of philosophy. What is most "platonistic" in Galileo is his pythagoreanism.

But, it might be said, is not Archimedes, again, in the spirit of Plato? I wonder. There is a whole pious tradition, created by Plutarch and other orthodox thinkers, which is to be discounted. Archimedes himself was, perhaps, somewhat in Galileo's position. Among the great Greek scientists after Plato, there is actually a visible tension between an accepted philosophy and the necessities of their craft, which impel them toward physics, technology, indeed very raw operationalism. In the work of Ptolemy, which has been rather fully preserved for us, this struggle is explicit. It is inevitable, and as old as time. Daedalus could not, I daresay, be as much of a "platonist" as Pythagoras (if you don't mind my inverting the times) because he had to manage the Research and Development Center for the National Defense of the Cretan Empire.

Well, there you are: Leonardo is much more of a Daedalus than a Pythagoras. If we pause a moment over this idea, we shall see that, despite his technical advancement, his counterparts were not Heron of Alexandria and Polycletus, but rather those half-fabulous, Palamedean figures, the first great artist-craftsmen, the *technitai:* Rhoecos and Theodoros of Samos, Harpalos, Hicetas, and Eupalinos. I am well aware that this is not a new idea; it was present in the mind of Valéry when he wrote the dialogue *Eupalinos* and the *Introduction à la méthode de Léonardo de Vinci.* But since I am trying to establish reference points as an historian, I cannot but be happy to find myself at his side. I am well aware, also, that I am making mythic comparisons. But Leonardo is, precisely, an irreducibly mythic personality. That is what he was to his contemporaries; he escaped their understanding in spite of their attention to his work. No one, outside of Shakespeare and possibly Rembrandt, is more mythic than he.

When we come closer to the historical person, the impression persists. At that time, metaphysical platonism was in sway among artists: consider Paolo Uccello, Piero della Francesca—his direct predecessor— Leon Battista Alberti, Botticelli. Leonardo remains outside of all that: Leonardo, the "man without letters," the solitary man of incomprehensible fantasies, he of whom Michelangelo scornfully said that he had found no one to work his bellows for him.

Similarly, he is far less a platonist than his teacher of mathematics, Luca Pacioli, whose *Divina Proportione* he nevertheless helped to edit.

And yet, it will be said, what about the Divine Proportion, and his studies concerning the symmetries of the human body? But these things were in the air; they came out of Vitruvius, and were common parlance. Ictinus, too, had been thinking of them twenty centuries before, when he built the Parthenon; and he could not have borrowed them from the yet-unborn Plato. One might, in that case, think instead of the influence of the Pythagorean Philolaus, whom modern criticism insists upon reducing to the status of a character in some dialogue—for it is well understood among the Right People that there could not have been any truly philosophic ideas before the Academy and the Academicians giving regular courses in it (for the first time). But that is another story.

The platonists firmly believed in the mystery of numbers, whereas Leonardo develops a rather special notion of mathematics, one closer to the spirit of his old practical teacher, Benedetto dell'Abaco, than to that of Copernicus. The mathematical instrument that he indefatigably pursued was, for him, really an instrument: a means of construction, a way—as Valéry would put it—of making himself an equerry of his own ideas. It is not the contemplation of a suprasensible world, but the study of the geometrical skeleton of the real one.

His style reveals to us the same distance. Had I the time to do so, I could show through stylistic analysis that Leonardo has nothing in common with the robed and lettered brood of his time, or even with Leon Battista Alberti. His language is, essentially, spoken Tuscan, such as it continues among the peasants of his region, with its rich pungency, its simplicity, its artlessly graceful turns of phrase, its countless anacolutha. Obviously he knows how to organize it, but then that develops from Machiavelli. It is his friend Machiavelli who is the closest to him as far as style is concerned—Machiavelli, whom elsewhere I have tried to show to be a born physicist, a *physiologos* lost among the social sciences—and also the tough-minded Guicciardini, as he is in the *Ricordi;* in various other places, in some of Leonardo's flights of lyricism, there is a hint of Ariosto, another man of no great learning.

That is the intellectual pedigree.

But then, it will be said, all that famous reading, all those authors cited in the Notes, all those influences reconstructed by Duhem and many others? Well, that is the point.

I simply ask that one page of manuscript be looked at with an open mind. We are immediately struck by the neat, practiced handwriting, sure and rapid; the handwriting of a notary's son, whose graphic formation fits in so well with the drawings. But when we read, the spelling proves to be a pure chaos, one that far exceeds the irregularities of the day.

The words are severed and broken, and also amalgamated. Leonardo writes exactly as the peasants of his century wrote, and as they still write today. The spelling is that of the servant-girl or the recruit. The phonetization is the same. They, too, cut and combine, in the effort of spelling out syllable after syllable, thus breaking the cadence of the spoken word. Leonardo writes rapidly and knows how to retain the cadence, but he remains bound up by his little world's way of writing. He uses archaic verbal forms which have disappeared from contemporary literature: thus *laldare* for *lodare, altore* for *autore.* Doubtless he must have spoken in the same way. If Dante shaped the "illustrious vernacular," one might almost say that Leonardo clung to expressing himself in High Demotic, creating the language of learned ignorance. "Savage is he who saves himself." He will never write in the style of *messieurs de la ville,* as Rousseau would say. This is a rejection that extends to their concepts, their logic, and their values.

This man without letters is not illiterate, but as a mistrustful, suspicious, and captious artist-peasant, he examines letters from without. He takes and he leaves. Thus in Pico della Mirandola and his Florentine elders he finds a whole subtle pythagoreanism which might seem to be cut out for him. His friend Botticelli will let himself be taken up with it; Leonardo rejects it categorically, all the while taking his idea of man from Pico—or perhaps rediscovering it there. His own pythagorean ideas will be taken from Ovid: the plurality of worlds, the community of the living, vegetarianism. This is the doctrine of the *Hieros Logos,* the true and the ancient doctrine, which he has identified as if by instinct.

It seems to me that the merit of Duhem lies in his having shown, by reconstructing the sources and the intellectual atmosphere which Leonardo certainly knew and made use of, to what extent all of this was actually a foil for his own thought. Assuredly, he read a great deal; he relied even more upon conversation, which so often becomes a spoken, two-way dream.

Long ago Séailles observed that it is the name of Archimedes which most often recurs in Leonardo's notes. Certainly Leonardo frequently sought out the master's texts, and from this Martin Johnson has drawn the conclusion that the best part of Leonardo's science is patterned upon Archimedes.

However, there is little enough in common between the thought of the historical Archimedes and that of Leonardo. And, since I have mentioned Machiavelli's name, I might attempt an analogy. No one has reflected more passionately than Machiavelli upon the sources of Roman grandeur; yet Machiavelli's early Romans, such as he saw them through Livy, are a myth. They are the unattainable summits blocking off the horizon of his historical vision. This did not preclude his deriving out of that vision a theory of the social man, stamped with the clearest scientific spirit. Leonardo is in rather the same position with respect to the "superhuman" Archimedes. Machiavelli attributes Plutarchian attitudes to the Romans; to Archimedes, Leonardo attributes fantastic machines like his *architrònito,* the "steam cannon." One might almost say that the same mythic distance exists between Archimedes and Leonardo, as between Leonardo and Paul Valéry.

The men who have inspired us are not always those we know the best. I am reminded of Diderot, who was always appealing for authority to the ideas of Francis Bacon. Herbert Dieckmann, who knows Diderot as few others do, has recently shown that this man, so enormously well informed, had never read Bacon. Diderot cites only a few sentences of his, always the same ones, and cites them inappropriately. When it came to writing the "Bacon" article for the *Encyclopédie,* he had to resort to one of those little *abbés* who had read everything.

We see those *abbés* again with Leonardo. He notes: "Tell Brother Giovanni to show you *De Ponderibus."* Brother Giovanni would explain it to him.

What, then, had he read—really read—from the past? First of all, obviously, the poets. He was perfectly at home with Dante, the poet of his city. Pulci's *Morgante Maggiore* had a great influence on him. Only too well did he know that strange potpourri by Cecco d'Ascoli, the *Acerba.* As for the rest, he drew it from the Pocket Encyclopedias or Popular Sciences of his time: Ristoro d'Arezzo, the *Quadriregio,* Valturius. Only after he was forty did he approach the study of Latin, and then it was Ovid, that treasure-trove of medieval fantasy, whom he absorbed. He got an inkling of the Stoics, and through them of heraclitean intuition. He knew some things from Horace, and studied Pliny and Vitruvius. But we need only look at his word-lists and his pathetic little grammar exercises during that period to see how foreign a tongue Latin was to him. He draws up study lists of Latin words which he has extracted from his Valturius, to etch them into his memory; and we realize that he is thinking for the first time about their connection with the words that he knows. At the outset, he actually takes the trouble to learn the literary Italian of his day, which he had known only at a distance. His Latin remains shaky and rudimentary; he gets lost in its syntax and confuses subject and object in his exercises. This man will never be able to puzzle out a text without the help of a friend. As for Greek, whatever Giovio may say about it, he knew not a word.

What he did do was listen. Books and those who knew books were, for him, a quarry where he sought materials. It is only thus that he treated certain results of Archimedes, or the abridgment of Heron of Alexandria published by Giorgio Valla. He took notes on conversations and ideas heard at random. Thus that famous jotting "The sun does not move" seems surely to be an opinion he picked up somewhere, perhaps listening to people talking about Philolaus, for it has no correspondence at all to the rest of his thought.

This is why he hates summaries. He would have the facts, the results, not the frameworks. He seeks these everywhere in conversations, and thus finds himself having unwittingly absorbed massive doses of Aristotle, which will slow down his thought.

One might go on. But in the end, we are brought back to Springer's old judgment about his art, a judgment that seems to have been confirmed by modern criticism:

> The role of ancient art in Leonardo's thought is insignificant, and in his painting it is nil.

What if he did study Vitruvius and the Canon of Proportions? What if he did draw, diligently, classical monuments and mythological motifs? If he did exhort the student to imitate the ancient rather than the modern?—all that remains commonplace, the language of the day. Once he produces, it is something else again.

A strange man, who by his own opinion put himself in a line with Giotto and Masaccio, as masters of the return to nature; while for us he is the first painter to break away from nature and move toward expression. It is true that by "nature" he meant something other than what we mean. And this leads us to the threshold of his scientific thought.

Leonardo, the first of the moderns—"that Italian brother of Faust," as Michelet so rightly said. One imagines him leafing through *De Ponderibus,* Buridan, Albert of Saxony and his anonymous master,[1] and even Themon, "Son of the Jew," consulting his friends, laboriously deciphering, here and there, wherever his instinct told him that he would gain something by it. With respect, to be sure. Sometimes with too much respect.[2]

One single example. Leonardo is meditating upon the flight of birds. He writes (I am quoting from memory):

> And since all movement tends to conserve itself, and in the same direction; or rather, since the *impetus* conserves itself for a time, while exhausting itself . . .

There you have it: the law of inertia was already on the tip of his pen, it was coming to him from that area of nature which might best reveal it to him—but just then he remembers his reading. And also he knows —he believes—that nothing is conserved.

Galileo, who did go through university, who labored over the huge folios of his Pisan professors and the works of his predecessors, will have to spend thirty years of enormous effort to shake off acquired theories (including his own), and to reach the point that Leonardo touched by instinct. Touched: for this man cannot, will not, plumb the abstract to draw out the concrete.

Let us return to the instinct, the labor of the imagination upon a darkly foreign soil. Then . . .

Then, my mind returns to those other Leonardos, those Greeks of the little-known years between the twelfth and fifth centuries B.C., scouting around in the towns of Asia Minor or in that strange international port of Ugarit, having texts and processes of calculation explained to them. "We must see . . ." they were saying; "There are things here. . . ." But actually, they were already seeking something completely different. They were being given devices, but they were searching for science.

An arbitrary comparison, it will be said; the *jeu d'esprit* of an historian of science. But listen:

> The shaking of earth pressing upon earth moves a small distance from the point of impact; water, struck by water, makes circles which go far away; the voice goes farther in the air, and even farther goes the spirit in the universe; but since it too is finite, it would not be able to extend to the infinite.

How contemptuous can a man be of what was taught by all the platonists, neoplatonists, peripatetics, paraperipatetics, and other advocates of the Idea or the Logos; how must he scorn dualism, be ignorant of, or indifferent to, the supernatural; how must he categorically reject all their knowledge down to the very idea they have of knowledge—to write such a passage?

Notice that this is in keeping with the sum total of his thought. Thus he denies the possibility of spirits, for the following reason: in every part of space there is one element or another, and so there is no place anywhere for spirits.

A mechanist? No. Rather, a monist; and it is here that we might suspect him of stoic leanings, for when he is about to define force, he speaks of it as if it were a "spiritual" thing. But it is immediately clear that the "spirit" in force is an *impetus,* which is dissipated like other living forces, "rolling toward its dispersion while it diversifies itself through causes."

If we wish to talk of force before physics, this is not a bad way of talking about it. It is, rather, the successors of Leonardo who remain entangled in this notion, using an idea originating in a vitalistic analogy and trying to give it an abstract status which, in the long run, could only turn out to be metaphysical.

Leonardo does not get tangled up this way in deductions, because he avoids promoting a discovery to the rank of abstraction. This is what keeps him from establishing a science. But *a* science is, precisely, what he does not wish to establish.

Let me use this subject to give an example of how influences and precedents are discovered. There is no doubt that Nicholas of Cusa influenced Leonardo. The cosmological themes of this remarkable mind are discernible in Leonardo's cosmology; his advocacy of "learned ignorance" was certainly an encouragement; the idea of the synthesis of contraries is perceptible in Leonardo's art, and may come, in part, from him.

This is not enough for Duhem: he wants to show that the definition of force, too, comes from the Cardinal of Cusa who, as an orthodox platonist, speaks of mechanical force as having a spiritual origin in that which moves of itself—that is, the soul. This is the very definition found in the *Phaedrus.* And in fact, remarks Duhem, Leonardo speaks of force as though it originated from spiritual movement: "This spiritual movement, flowing through the limbs of animals, swells their muscles," Hence, etc.

Speak of preconceptions. It takes quite a lot of good will to see orthodox platonism in that. A force thus described is truly physical. And from other passages, we know that Leonardo uses that word "spiritual" as an honorific tag to designate something that resists analysis. Force is *tutta in sè tutta*—almost as we would speak of a photon.

Rather, we see clearly throughout the rest of Leonardo's thought that the word "spiritual" is *defined* by the notion of force. His entire universe is, so to speak, biological, but within it, life is nothing but a form of organization which can mobilize forces, a sort of momentary focus of universal energies constantly in precarious strife with universal dissolution. It is in this, perhaps, that he is the most profoundly modern. For him everything is harmony, rhythm, momentary combination, dispersion; Leonardo's demon, like Maxwell's, is perpetually dying of the very act of creating difference and information, hence life. Its myth is fundamentally that of our present-day physics—the myth of Balzac's *Peau de Chagrin*.

And I shall go further: I shall venture to say that he did not adopt the theory of *impetus* because he read it somewhere else; rather, because his "force" gets dispersed and transformed, he will go to the Parisian scholastics, hoping that they will clarify that idea. His extremely direct intuition of inertia comes up against his rejection of the one sufficient abstraction. It would not suffice for his physics, which is much more complex than that of Descartes. For it is precisely Leonardo's physics which is at cross purposes with his mechanics.

This engineer will not be deceived; he knows that everything cannot be reduced to mechanics, at the cost of ending up with the absurdity of the man-machine. At the same time, he remains a physicist, more of a physicist than Descartes, for he avoids the dodge of the *res cogitans;* also, he is more modern, more Leibnizian if I may call it that, simply because he remains obstinately close to the real.

What, then, is he like?

Leonardo is not at all epicurean, and accepts nothing of the sect. Yet his theory of vision is plainly democritean. Vision is not an active function, as had been taken for granted by almost everybody; it is the reception of images, *eidola,* which peel off bodies; for "at daybreak, the air is peopled with countless images, which are attracted to the eye as to a magnet." The source of this idea is his theory that geometrical space contains all forms, which is the very source of the presocratic idea, for the theory of *eidola* appears historically before Democritus, in the early pythagoreans. Let us read on:

> The spirit passes instantaneously from west to east; it is even more rapid than vision, and all the great incorporeal things approximate the spirit in velocity.

This has a very old ring to it, like the words of Dante's Ulysses. And what shall we say of an aphorism like this one:

> Wrongly do men inveigh against experience, and reproach it bitterly for deceiving them. Let them leave it in peace, and turn against their own ignorance, which lets us be carried away by vain and senseless desires to such a point that we expect of experience what it cannot give us.
>
> Wrongly do men cry out against innocent experience, too often accusing it of trickery and of false demonstrations.

He tries twice, this thinker in "fragments." And it is there already, almost word for word, in a text of Democritus that he did not know. It has the latter's simplicity, his gait, his style, his cadence, his phrasing. And it is most different from the style of the stoic maxims, which he knows and quotes elsewhere.

Actually it is almost impossible to distinguish Leonardo's moral wisdom—in his maxims as well as in his fables—from that of Democritus which is nevertheless so personal. And one cannot say that Leonardo knew it; for it has almost nothing in common with that of Epicurus, so much better known. Democritus' moral texts have been identified only in our own day, by Diels.

What, too, shall we say of this fragment, which might be attributed to Archytas of Tarentum, at the latest:

> Flax is consecrated to death and to human corruption: to death, through snares and nets, with which birds, fish, and animals are trapped; to corruption, through the funerary shroud in which the dead are wrapped, for in this garment do they suffer corruption.
>
> Moreover, this flax parts from its stem only when it begins to soften and rot; and it is appropriate that we use it to make crowns and ornaments for funeral processions.

If we should begin to wonder whether our imagination is in the process of playing tricks upon us, we would have only to look to Michelangelo for reassurance: to Michelangelo, Leonardo's compatriot and contemporary, that other artist-peasant, whose language was so vigorous and so pungent. In all of Michelangelo's prose, even the most direct, there is absolutely nothing of the presocratic cadence; he is a Tuscan of his own century.

Let us pause at one of Leonardo's strange reflections, which the young Parmenides, too, must certainly have made:

> My opponent says that void and non-being are one and the same

thing; but void is in space, and non-being is outside of space; space is divisible, and non-being is not.

Surely here is the initial idea of Eleatic non-being, of which Leonardo rightly says that in it everything is contradiction, that it cannot be thought of in any fashion because it is not anywhere:

> In the presence of nature, it [non-being] finds its associates among things that are impossible.

And yet, when he moves on to other things—to contemplating the total presence of all possible forms and lines in space—he adds:

> Among all great things, Nothingness is the greatest. It remains within time, and devours all that is or shall be; but it possesses nothing of the indivisible present, and it does not extend to the essence of anything.

"It remains within time. . . ." That is why, appended Parmenides:

> What men call becoming and perishing, being or being not, change of place and alteration of gleaming colors, are nothing but names.

The essence is elsewhere: in this we see asserted the idea of the truth of the world as an eternal present, as the body of geometrical space.

Let us go on further.

In his studies of marine fossils found in the mountains, Leonardo returns to the path cleared by Anaximander—a path since abandoned, and one which will remain an object of derision for Voltaire and Buffon. And if the posture of his mind so closely repeats that of the Milesian physicist, it is because they possessed fundamental images in common: the primordial vortex, the separation of the elements, the evolution of the world in the shifting contrast of opposites, the Ionian ἐπικράτεια, so different from the categorical contraries of aristotelianism. And this comes to its conclusion in fire, which again is not the Fire Finale of the stoics, but an actual process:

> The fertile earth, following the law of growth, will eventually lose the water hidden in her breast, and this water, passing through the cold and rarefied air, will be forced to end in the element of fire. Then the surface of the earth will be burned, and that will be the end of all terrestrial nature.

Let us note that this process is merely the natural continuation of that conceived as its origin by Anaximander; it is the third phase, after which the metastable unity that assures life for a time will be broken.

It is thus—I quote—that operate

> the hope and the desire to return to one's country, to go back
> to the original chaos, as with the moth going toward the flame, or
> the man always impatiently awaiting the next season and the next
> year, always finding that the anticipated things are too slow to
> come; and who does not realize that he is aspiring to his own
> annihilation. But in its quintessence, the desire is the spirit of the
> elements which, finding themselves imprisoned in the life of the
> human body, continually aspire to return to their source. And
> know that this aspiration is the quintessence of nature, and that
> man is a model of the world.

It is clear; a model in this sense. This is in no way Pico della
Mirandola's microcosm with its magical correspondences, its sympathies,
its ἴυγγες.

Nor is it stoic. One need only consider the prodigious series
of drawings about the Deluge, with the world's return to the primordial
vortex. And nothing, absolutely nothing of all the Christian or semi-
Christian platonism (any more than of the a-Christian averroism, it might
be added). Obviously ideas are not born out of nothing. But at times the
"something" is even smaller than the Gospel's mustard seed. Leonardo's
whole theory about geological evolution probably springs from Ovid—
Ovid again—in a passage that well-read men used to treat as one more of
those fantasies:

> . . . Vidi factam ex aequore terram
> Et procul a pelago conchae jacuere marinae

Ovid attributes it to Pythagoras, although it actually comes
from Anaximander. It makes no difference. For Leonardo, who was studying stratifications and who was already headed in that direction, it is
enough, just as a few words of Aëtius were enough for Copernicus to set
out on his way.

Leonardo's level of thought enabled him to find Anaximander
even elsewhere. And it is remarkable to see this cosmologist—this universal
man who seeks the "paradise of the mathematical sciences"—refuse to find
it where these sciences are most clearly asserted: in the heavens, where
the pythagorean Copernicus will find it at once. He rejects or is unaware
of geometric cosmology as a whole; he does not want to "save the appearances": he feels that they do not need saving. Our friend Klibansky, in
order to soften the vehemence of Sarton's attack against Leonardo's
platonism, has suggested that even for such as did not follow Plato's

doctrine, there were many common sayings of Plato which had irresistibly entered their consciousness. Well, here is one of Plato's common sayings that did not stick.

The cosmology of Leonardo's day is half-platonist and half-materialistic. Leonardo is neither one nor the other. And here we have him seeking other reasons—which ones?

In the "F" manuscript of the *Codex Atlanticus*, which fortunately is preserved in its original structure, there is the complete plan for a treatise *On the World and the Waters*, which starts with a wholly unmathematical cosmology, and the place of the earth among the celestial bodies; then passes to the effect of the waters upon the earth over the course of time, in order to culminate in hydraulics. Here we clearly see outlined that idea of water, the central and living element, the amniotic fluid, as it were, of the universe, in which the heavenly bodies—themselves, like the moon, covered with oceans—seem to float.

It is a strange theory in defence of which Leonardo feels obligated to take Epicurus as well as Plato to task (for he has no more love for the one than for the other), a theory in which the orbits are not circles, nor any other pure geometrical form: a purely presocratic, even a prepythagorean, theory. It is easy to recognize that *physis* of the ancients, which we understand so poorly. This *physis* is Thales' water, but also Anaximander's Boundless, a generative fluid which, we are told, was conceived in imitation of the *gonimon* and which does not lend itself to any of our reductive attempts. A theory seemingly originating in the mists of time and yet, a purely physical *physis,* a truly Ionian universe. Leonardo, like his ancient colleagues, wants to speak—Aristotle says—"as a *physiologos.*"

I had long sensed this affinity with the Ionians, and I discovered that such an idea had previously come up in the sixteenth century. Edgar Wind describes a contemporary Milanese painting representing Heraclitus and Democritus. The man who cries and the man who laughs —a current contrast indeed. But it seems Heraclitus has Leonardo's features, and Democritus, representing someone unknown, has the look of a younger disciple. That was a good guess since Leonardo's notions embrace both men, and in a more profound sense than could be imagined by those humanists who had at their disposal only a half-dozen clichés concerning these presocratics. In Leonardo there is the vision of force "living its own death, dying its own life"; there is the hidden harmony of opposites; there is also the serenity and the tireless scientific curiosity of Democritus. Above all—and this has only been apparent since the philologists have assembled the texts—there are the same frame of reference, the same solutions, the same level of attention—and the same strange shiftings of attention that sometimes baffle us.

Unfortunately, only when a man is accustomed to both the Greek of the presocratics and the Italian of Leonardo, does the stylistic resemblance become striking. It is an experience that is not easily communicated. Everything is there: the same stylistic harshness, the choice of words, the turns of speech and foreshortenings, the brusque endings, the ingenuousness, and that prose, inherited from the logographers, which used to make the fourth century say that the "ancients" strung their sentences together instead of organizing them. There is also thought closing itself off in aphorism, and those very odd transitions from the particular to the general, those exhibitions of a logic which, although it remains hidden from us, is logical all the same. "If only," he sighs, "real things were to be found in books...."

And he does not mean facts, for there are books that give these —Pliny, for example. A difficult notion, and we can easily see that even his own Italian lets him down in these circumstances. What he wanted to say is something Greek could attain at a single stroke with its peculiar *ex parte objecti* constructions, such as λέγειν τὰ ὄντα. Surely what he wanted to express is the state of mind of a Xenophanes, whom he did not know:

καὶ εἴ τις τὰ μάλιστα τύχοι τετελεσμένον εἰπών

If it sometimes chanced that someone said what is really accomplished ...

To say the accomplished, the final statement—actually, τετελεσμένον, is not easy to translate. Perhaps we should say: "If only the things they told us were truly and utterly so."

This is not a lawyer's, nor even a mathematician's expression; rather it is that of an artist—and one who does not think at that point of being an artist.

Transmission? Only the slightest bit. One might think of Diogenes Laertius, translated by Traversari in 1450. Such as he is, "the greatest imbecile in antiquity" might have been greatly valuable to Leonardo; even through his poor epitomes, Leonardo might have re-encountered his thought among the early Ionians. Leonardo mentions Diogenes, but did he really read him? He mentions Anaxagoras, alone, and quotes from him; it is one sentence which must have been repeated to him. Otherwise he would surely quote others, and since he does so nowhere, then perhaps that is the measure of his learned information.

Therefore it is more of an encounter or a rediscovery. One might speak about parallel mental constellations, or subterranean waters enduring under the surface of history. There undoubtedly is a primitive —in the best sense of the word—idea here, rediscovering the same reasons. As Leonardo would say, there are infinite reasons in history which were never in books. There are all kinds of invisible transmissions; all kinds of pickups and amplifications along wave-lengths that have almost faded out.

Above all, there is this. As Nietzsche said, every mold for our thought was created in Greece during the earliest centuries. We naturally return to these molds in times of crisis when we sense that developments have gotten out of hand. There is nothing surprising about Bayle's return to them—a third attempt—and this with full awareness of what is involved: the digging of the advance trenches for a new rationalism. With Leonardo, who has only a few elusive inklings, it is more surprising. But that is precisely the point: he has to rediscover a mold along the lines of those previous ones; a mold vaster in scope than those of his day, greater in potentialities that are more implicit, more dormant, if I may venture to say so. He must find a level where objective, analytical, and aesthetic thought are not yet dissociated, where each supports the other; for his mind is creative in each of these spheres, and he cannot think without using all three modes of thought.

This idea of an aesthetically justified science is certainly not peculiar to him. The idea is present in platonism, and still exists in modern science three centuries after Leonardo—particularly in the principle of least action, which is not a discovery of Maupertuis or Voltaire's Dr. Akakia, since it was formulated on several occasions, and insistently, by Leonardo and others—the principle Euler still persists in considering heuristic and of eminent domain.

So the idea, in its most abstract form, is not foreign to us. But with Leonardo it is not at all abstract—nor was it so with those living before abstraction. By means of a few allusions which his successors will dismiss, Leonardo discovers a φύσις αὐτάρκης, a universe in which everything is immanent physical clarity, where nothing is fixed or transcendental, where everything is force, life, and movement (an idea, by the way, which will be basic and seminal for Galileo): a universe ruled by a rigorous necessity and an impassive justice, where the hidden harmony and coincidence of opposites subsumes good and evil in an ambivalent duality—a cosmos in which everything is beauty, a beauty which has never known itself.

It is this universe that Leonardo feels is fitting for a scientific artist, an artist of the "exact fantasy," as he calls it.

To the platonists who define art as an inferior and twice-removed copy of Ideas, Leonardo answers sharply: "Painting is a philosophy and a legitimate science of nature." For it is therein that what in the universe is unconscious of itself emerges. That is where truth breaks through. Provided, however, that this truth has been constructed in depth, through the knowledge of all of nature's effects that contribute to the creation of the image.

A man who thinks in such a way is not seeking a method; surely it is useless to reproach him on this account, as if he were an unsuccessful Descartes.

As with the presocratics, he has to attempt his own διάκοσμος; he has to be able to say, "That is the way things are."

He will hardly be able to be an orthodox believer, either. And actually Leonardo's feelings about the Visible Church are lukewarm, nor does he bother to hide them.

Leonardo's biographers have made a concerted effort—extending to the official celebrations of his fifth centennial held recently in Rome —to make him out to be orthodox, as Galileo has been made out to be a perverse conspirator. Perhaps they think like the founder of cities in St. John Perse's *Anabase* (again I quote from memory):

> If somewhere there be a hidden prophet, convalescent deep in a cowshed, my advice is that he be killed. If not, there will be revolt.

Says Leonardo (and we wonder what lies behind it):

> I painted God as a child, you imprisoned me. Now that I am painting him as a man, you will do worse.

Leonardo, like Baudelaire, is a little too much the prophet in the cowshed.

Nevertheless, here is what Vasari was writing in 1550, before his pious and sanctimonious 1568 revision:

> He used to philosophize about natural things and their properties; he never ceased to observe the sky, the course of the stars and the intrinsic qualities of living things; such heretical ideas came to him that he drew near to no religion; he held it in greater esteem to be a philosopher than a Christian.

Need we quote such revealing words as "All our knowledge begins in the senses"; or else these bold pronouncements:

Therefore, reader, observe what we can believe out of the things our ancients have told us, considering that they wanted to define what the soul and life are, things which are not subject to proof; whereas experience continually shows us things about which so many centuries knew nothing, or else it corrects our false beliefs.

Here again is the opening out of the ancient mind with respect to its myths. "We have been taught many false things," said Xenophanes, "but men find better ones with seeking."

Leonardo's originality was all the greater since the recent past is rich with conclusive systems, dogmatic assertions, and subtle controversies. He notes:

For it actually happens that wherever reason is absent, shouting takes its place, something that never happens when things are certain. We shall therefore say that wherever there is much clamor, there is no true knowledge, because truth has one single term which, once it is made known, silences controversy forever.

Obviously all this is modern too. It might be mistaken for Galileo; but let us not forget that Galileo dared openly to say those things only after he had brought to light in the texts, behind the aristotelian screen, "an older and better school," which reinforced his opinions. With Galileo, there is conscious continuity; with Leonardo, instinctive continuity. We shall never know for sure what Giordano Bruno might have been thinking before revealing the secrets of "Pythagoras and Solomon." We know what Leonardo was thinking, without having discovered either one or the other: Leonardo, in turn, is the man who will be able to enlighten us about Galileo's original attitudes. For he knows none of the compromises of the "educated man."

In post-romantic criticism, there was sometimes talk of a real "anti-humanist program" on Leonardo's part. That pushes the thesis to absurdity. Leonardo would very much have liked to have the resources of humanism, and it hurts him that he cannot "cite the authorities." But just as he rejected the platonic *noesis,* without thereby scorning hellenistic philosophy, so what he rejects in humanism is the verbal solution of all physics and metaphysics.

Of all the creative minds in the Renaissance, he is the only one to reject *in toto* the universal consensus of the *docta pietas,* in which humanism, religion, philosophy, and even the more or less diversified heterodoxies, found a comfortable niche. And that is done not through indifference or materialism, but through a considered and ardent affirmation: the affirmation of a cosmology that is entirely *other*.

Where shall we find this cosmology? In his notes, almost everywhere—but not necessarily in words. It is very much to Berenson's credit, in his studies of Florentine drawing, to have pointed out that Leonardo has a deep distrust for the competency of words, and that for him drawing is the form that can carry the most content, even in the region of thought we normally term "abstract."

It is difficult, really, to see the enormous multiplicity of Leonardo's drawings, especially compared with the very small number of finished works, as mere technical exercises and preparatory sketches. Johnson has clearly shown that what we are looking at is the very act of reflection; as Valéry would say, these notebooks are the entire journey of the mind.

Leonardo certainly knows this.

O speculator upon things, do not boast of knowing the things that Nature attends to by herself, according to her order; but be delighted with knowing the end of those things that your mind conceives.

A strange and ambiguous sentence, which could just as easily presage Vico's historicism with its *conversio veri et facti,* as modern scientific nominalism at its most extreme. But then, what a contradiction it would be with the rest of Leonardo's notions!

Let us consult the text:

Di quelle cose che son disegnate dalla mente tua.

Watch out. Ravaisson-Mollien, and later MacCurdy, read *disegnate* as "conceives." But Leonardo is not a modern, and he has no pre-Kantian inspirations. He says, "*drawn,* or *designed,* by your mind"—an entirely different matter. This text is a marginal note, very much in place, on a page devoted to the technique for fusing metals. Therefore it is "the drawings of your mind," but consequently in the sense of the *homo artifex.* And it would also be fair, in Leonardo's sense, to understand "which your mind *perceives,*" because perception and drawing are the same thing for him.

But let us note that he said, "knowing the *end* of those things your mind perceives"; it is clear that he is not thinking merely of the man who knows how to fulfill his craft. This is a metaphysical idea, addressed to the "speculator upon things." The point of departure is an exhortation to be a Daedalus rather than an Aristotle; but in a flash of intuition, since this note is as direct as a drawing, he says that there is a level of reality where the artist creates a universe of discourse that goes beyond man, yet is linked to him.

One may, then, think of those lines, the most argued-about of all, by the enigmatic Parmenides:

καὶ σύ ταῦτα μαθήσεαι, ὥς τα δοκούντα
χρῆν δοκίμως εἶναι διὰ παντός πάντα περῶντα.

It is the promise of his deity: "You shall also see how sensory data can furnish a coherent totality for him who is making a general survey of things."

A very direct sense, which was unfalteringly seen by Wilamowitz—and which generations of commentators have attempted to skirt by the sheer force of unnatural contortions.

Such a universe is open to the mind. It is a universe of perceptions, and in it perception becomes, in some sense, normative. The forms are "true."

For Leonardo, delight is the role of the young animal, the smile of creation; he never tires of contemplating it in his children, in his snorting colts, or in his kittens, playing or licking themselves—the kittens he puts everywhere in his sacred subjects, to the great dismay of his pious patrons.

Further on, there are action, grandeur, horror, forces hurling themselves toward death, the carefully compared ferocity of those heads of horses, men, and lions, caught in the attack. There is effort, tension, monstrosity. There is ugliness and unconscious suffering; above all, there is conscious suffering, everywhere. A brief annotation:

> The more feeling there is, the more suffering.
> Great agony.

In all of this, there is a very beautiful order. There is a logic, the supreme knowledge of the prime mover, elsewhere called "force, divine or other," which was able to allot to all those powers the quality of their effects in the necessary proportion. The universe has no frustration; it operates to its full power, it knows how to express itself. And everywhere the law is, "All power comes of a breaking of balance."

> Lightness is born of weight, and weight of lightness. While paying for the blessing of their creation, their life increases in the same measure their movement does; at the same instant, too, each destroys the other in the mutual atonement of their death.

Anaximander would speak this way; yet it is not Anaximander, but Leonardo, who is speaking.

What is man in all this? On this point Leonardo's ideas are nearly the same as Pico's. Man for him is one of nature's greatest variables. He is the center of many possibilities. Angel, animal, and still other things besides, for nature is full of an infinite number of reasons "which never were in experience."

Yet also—and in this he is much more melancholy than Pico— man is a discouragingly unstable variable, one that does not move along a curve prearranged by destiny—for man is his own creator. His themes are supplied from without; it is his job to filter them and to create out of them a being consistent with himself—and this idea, too, came once to Democritus. But here nature is something more than blind necessity: it is the interplay of forms and chance.

To consider a deviation in man which causes him to resemble a wolf is like seeing a manifestation of the same force that will make a rock appear to us in the form of a whale, or that of a whale that has turned rock, "an arrogant form that once used to sow terror among the living," and which the variations of sea and time have transformed into a bleak foundation of other rocks.

A saying from Chateaubriand comes to mind—quite orthodox, as usual:

> Man himself is only a crumbled edifice, the wreckage of sin and death—everything in him is mere ruins.

Leonardo would put it differently. He would say: man is creation's terrible failure. This has to be made good immediately, since it is impossible to go on from there.

Let us take a look at his *Prophecies,* which are agreed to be trifling witticisms. Actually they are a list of unnatural things that to us seem natural. *Industrious peoples shall be seen whom brutes deluge to steal their wealth*—these are the bees. *Countless innocents shall be seen slaughtered before their mothers' eyes*—these are young goats. Still clearer:

> On earth creatures shall be seen who are constantly killing one another. Their wickedness shall be limitless; their violence shall destroy the world's vast forests; and even after they have been sated, they shall in no wise suspend their desire to spread carnage, tribulations, and banishment among all living beings. Their over-reaching pride shall impel them to lift themselves toward heaven.
>
> Nothing shall remain on the earth, or under the earth, or in the waters, that shall not be hunted down and slain, and what is in

one country, dragged away into another; and their bodies shall become the tomb and the thoroughfare for all the living things they have ruined. O Earth, what restrains you from opening up and from engulfing them as one, into the deep fissures of your chasms, so that the face of heaven no longer beholds so cruel and abominable a monster!

This relates closely to those drawings of the final period, invoking catastrophe—a genuine figurative expression of an abstract idea.

Perhaps that is the last word of the enigma, just as in the "Last Supper," as carefully constructed as *The Divine Comedy,* the central theme is man betrayed by humanity.

For man is a marvel, and yet in a nature where everything is good because it is logical, men alone are cruel and senseless.

With Leonardo there is pure contemplation, fantasy; there is also the sudden shiver of awareness, the στυγερόν, the icy Styx. "We are all murderers."

From that point, we have the flight toward possibility, all possibilities: those countless machines, and those machines to make machines —the revival of the medieval dream of Alexander, conquering kingdoms in the air and in the sea—the redemption of man through creation and intelligence.

Michelangelo, that great hater of Leonardo who constantly accused him of finishing nothing, unwittingly grasped the idea. Michelangelo asks his pardon, as it were, after his death, invoking Leonardo's assistance to finish his own work:

> . . . onde a me non finita verrà meno
> s'or non gli dà la fabbrica divina
> aiuto a farlo, ch'al mondo era solo.

And surely Michelangelo was the man to understand him. Leonardo remains the loneliest man who ever lived.

On the Relation Between Leonardo's Science and His Art

by Kenneth Clark

IT IS USUAL to treat Leonardo as a scientist and Leonardo as a a painter in separate studies. And no doubt the difficulties in following his mechanical and scientific investigations make this a prudent course. Nevertheless, it is not completely satisfactory, because in the end the history of art cannot be properly understood without some reference to the history of science. In both we are studying the symbols by which man affirms his mental scheme, and these symbols, be they pictorial or mathematical, a fable or a formula, will reflect the same changes. They are very little influenced by accidents. Discoveries may appear to be accidental, but in fact each epoch gets the discoveries it needs. Aristarchus discovered that the earth moves round the sun, but the idea lay dormant till Copernicus; Poggio found the works of Tacitus in the Medici library, read them and put them quietly back on the shelves. They would have destroyed the humanist's mental picture of Antiquity. If the Laocoon had been unearthed 200 years earlier we may be certain that it would have been buried again. So with Leonardo, the discoveries and anticipations which he made in the art of painting, some of which could not be absorbed till a far later date and some of which are becoming comprehensible only now, must be looked at in relation to what our ancestors would have called his natural philosophy. One cannot be understood without the other.

We must admit, however, that whereas the study of Leonardo's art is, for the most part, exhilarating and enthralling, the study of Leo-

From *History Today*, 1952; Vol. 2: 301–313; London. Reprinted by permission of the editor and author.

naɪdo's thought is disheartening and difficult. There are three reasons for this which anyone may be glad to have set down. The first is that his manuscripts are not, as was once supposed, made up chiefly of original observations, but are to a very large extent commonplace books in which he copied down what he had read. Even Richter, from whose admirable volumes[1] Leonardo's writings are chiefly known, did not (or would not) recognize this, and actually says that he was not a great reader. An instance of this wilful disregard of Leonardo's sources is still to be found in the new edition of Richter's *Literary Works*. Leonardo had written "Cosa mortal passa e non *dura*," which is a line from Petrarch. The reading is clear and unmistakable. Richter transcribed it "Cosa mortal passa e non *d'arte*," which, although neither an original thought nor an idiomatic Italian sentence, was actually taken by the Vincian society as its motto. The degree to which Leonardo's MSS. are made up of quotations was first made clear by a scholar named Solmi, who published in his *Fonti dei Manoscritti di Leonardo da Vinci* several hundred of his sources. Since then a great many more have been identified. Now, there is nothing dishonourable in this discovery. In 1480 most of the writings which Leonardo would wish to read existed only in manuscript; and even those which had been printed were often hard to come by. It was usual, in the *quattrocento,* for scholars to make copies of whole books which interested them, and the habit of compiling vast commonplace books of information lasted up to the eighteenth century. The notebooks of John Evelyn in Christ Church library are one example among many. But of course this discovery does make the study of Leonardo's thought very much more difficult, because unless we have a complete grasp of the state of knowledge, in the Renaissance, we can never be certain when Leonardo is making an original observation. The same is true of technology. Of the hundreds of machines scattered through Leonardo's notebooks, which are inventions, and which are simply drawings of things seen? Here I am afraid we must resign ourselves to never knowing the truth. Nothing is more baffling than the history of technology, partly because before the age of patent law, every guild and every city tried to keep its mechanical devices a secret, and partly because people do not preserve out-of-date machinery. It happens that Leonardo was almost the first man to draw machinery who was a great enough artist for his drawings to be preserved.[2] Personally I believe that most of these drawings are based on existing machines, but that Leonardo liked to extend and elaborate them, often beyond the technical resources of the day. I think it doubtful if he discovered any new mechanical principles. But even if this is an overstatement, it remains almost impossible to say how many of the "inventions" in Leonardo's notebooks can in any sense be called his own.

This would not be important if he had put other people's ideas in a new and significant order, but (and this is our second difficulty) the disorder of the notebooks is absolute. This disorder is partly due to the fact that Leonardo lived at an interlunar period in the history of thought. The logical system of scholasticism, which compelled all facts into the service of God, had broken down under the weight of its own elaboration. The new rationalism of the seventeenth century, with its faith in the laws of nature, had yet to be evolved. Leonardo hated generalizations because he saw them as leading directly to the kind of metaphysical speculations which, at that date, had lost their value for the human spirit. "It is true," he says, "that impatience, the mother of stupidity, praises brevity, as if such persons would not need a lifetime to acquire a complete knowledge of one single subject, such as the human body; and yet they want to comprehend the mind of God in which the universe is included, weighing it minutely and mincing it into infinte parts, as if they had to dissect it." This is a remarkable anticipation of the scientific attitude, and, in consequence, some writers on Leonardo have referred to the disorder of the notebooks as if it had some positive value. Any order, they say, would have implied some preconceived idea, prejudicial to the purity of the facts. M. Valéry's famous introduction to the Method of Leonardo is based on a slightly more subtle version of the same argument: he says that Leonardo's sense of order was so all-embracing that the facts were equally valid however they were related to one another. *"Il a un sens extraordinaire de la symétrie qui lui fait problème de tout."* There is a grain of truth in this; but by itself, as an explanation of Leonardo's disorderliness, it will not do. We cannot say of the painter of the *Last Supper* that he lacked the synthetic faculty; but the fact remains that he had a real aversion from arranging his observations. He says more than once that he has not done so for lack of time, but this is unconvincing, because he will record the same observations and proofs, in almost identical language, dozens of times. Clearly, this gave him great satisfaction; and it helped to put off the evil day when he should have to do something with the mass of material he had collected. There must be many researchers in our Universities who sympathize with him.

The third cause of bewilderment in Leonardo's manuscripts is one which scholars brought up in the rational-scientific traditions of the last century almost always shirked; one which would, indeed, have in-validated their whole picture of him: Leonardo's mind passed without warning, and almost without consciousness, from fact to fantasy, from experience to imagination. A symptom of this is the impracticability which remains one of the most paradoxical things about him. The most scientifi-cally minded artist of the Renaissance painted his two great wall paintings with so little science that they almost immediately disintegrated. The in-ventor of elaborate machinery had so little technical skill that he was unable to cast in bronze the horse for the Sforza monument, and the Duke had to send to Florence for one or two masters more apt for the work. We have no record of how Leonardo's bombards and ballistas, tanks and battering rams, to which he attached such importance, stood the test of war. It is true that he was employed by that eminently practical man (in small things) Cesare Borgia. But then his powers of persuasion were ir-resistible. After his return to Florence in 1503 he persuaded the Florentine Government—probably the most hard-headed body in Europe—to accept his design for diverting the Arno so that it should no longer enter the sea by Pisa, but in Florentine territory. Some of his maps for this still survive, and some drawings of men digging, but no trace of the canals; and in fact his scheme was wholly beyond the technical powers of the time. It is typical of Leonardo's mind that his notes on the subject are, up to a point, quite factual; but that when he comes to the real difficulty, a range of hills, he says simply, "At Serravalle I shall cut through"; without the slightest indication how.

Now, although Leonardo scholars have not really faced the im-plications of these sudden swervings into fantasy, they have not been able to ignore them altogether, as they play a great part in his notebooks, both in his writings and in his illustrative drawings. I may illustrate this by one small symbolic example. Leonardo was fond of drawing artesian screws and other spiral devices. On a sheet of doodles in the *Codice Atlantico* he has drawn such a spiral for its own sake, and he has endowed it with a kind of monstrous life, so that it changes, like Aaron's rod, into a serpent. And above it he has written "Body born of the power of projection of Leonardo Vinci, disciple of experience." [3]

This interweaving of fact and fantasy in Leonardo's mind is partly due to a medieval element which is frequently perceptible in his paintings; and students of the middle ages have grown accustomed to the way in which the most powerful intellects accepted as evidence in a rational scheme fantasies which would not deceive a modern child. But

Leonardo was not only the heir of a myth-accepting system of thought; he was an imaginative artist, haunted by certain visions which his inward eye had rendered as real to him as any observation. If he passes freely from reason to imagination, he passes as freely back from imagination to reason. This is the origin of his famous advice to a painter to study "stains on walls or the embers of a fire wherein he may find divine landscapes, battles, figures in violent action or even the expressions of faces. These the painter will be able to reduce to their proper form"; and Leonardo adds, "be sure you know the structure of all that you then wish to depict."

I quote this familiar passage, because it leads to the first clue I can offer to anyone attempting the study of the notebooks. They are the work of a great artist. Leonardo's interest in science grew so intense that we forget that up to the age of thirty-five we know him solely as a painter and as one of the greatest draughtsmen that have ever lived. It is often said that Leonardo drew so well because he knew about things; it is truer to say that he knew about things because he drew so well. This at any rate is consistent with a chronological approach to the manuscripts. And here I offer a second clue to the study of Leonardo's mind. It should be studied chronologically. This method disposes of some of the difficulties which I have said that the notebooks might present. For example, the fact that so much is copied from other writers simply reflects Leonardo's powers of self-education. Brought up in the country, and destined at an early age to the craft of painting, he must have been taught in his childhood what used to be called "the three Rs"; of which in Florence the last, arithmetic, was given particular importance. He would not have learnt Latin; and in fact we know that he taught himself Latin in about the year 1494, and copied into two of his notebooks, those known as MS. H and the Trivulzian, the greater part of Niccolo Perotti's Latin Grammar and Luigi Pulci's Vocabulary. When we consider how few learned writings were, at that date, available in the vulgar tongue, we realize what a turning-point this was in his intellectual development.

The first of Leonardo's writings which can properly be called scientific are of a slightly earlier date—between 1485 and 1490—and, as might be expected, they are part of an attempt to give a scientific basis to the art of painting. In this Leonardo was following an established practice of the early Renaissance. Plato had established four liberal arts—arithmetic, geometry, astronomy, music—which were the basis of all true knowledge. This number was afterwards increased to seven by the addition of grammar, logic and rhetoric; and in the middle ages this list was the subject of various glosses and expansions. But none of these included painting among the liberal arts. This had much distressed the painters of the Renaissance, partly from reasons of prestige, and partly because they were convinced by Plato's arguments, and thought that some mathematical or harmonic basis really was necessary if painting were to be a branch of true knowledge: hence the purely mathematical approach of early books on Art such as Alberti's *della Pittura,* and Piero della Francesca's *Prospettiva Pingendi.* Leonardo also wished to raise the status of painting from a manual to an intellectual art. A large part of his *Treatise on Painting* is devoted to this end, especially the comparison of the arts, the so-called *Paragone;* and it was therefore an historical necessity that his study of the science of painting should be built on mathematics. "Let no one who is not a mathematician read my works": this and similar warnings occur throughout the notebooks, and are borne out by the numerous diagrams in Leonardo's earliest dated manuscript, that known as MS. B in the library of the Institut de France. Most of these treat of light and shadow. He also wrote a treatise of perspective, now lost. We know of it from references in Vasari, and Benvenuto Cellini bought a copy while in the service of Francis I. The loss is most unfortunate because we can tell from Cellini's description and from some of Leonardo's notes in other manuscripts that he had greatly enlarged the theory of perspective. These matters are too technical to be of general interest, but I mention them in order to emphasize a point of great importance: that Leonardo began his study of phenomena with an all-controlling belief in mathematics. This was partly because mathematics were certain—"In them," he says, "one does not argue if twice three makes more or less than six: all argument is reduced to eternal science, and they can be enjoyed in a peace which the lying sciences of the mind cannot attain"—and partly because mathematics were the source of harmony. Leonardo although usually considered an Aristotelian, accepted with eagerness the Platonic faith in proportion. In the *Treatise on Painting,* for example, he speaks of the senses being satisfied by a harmonic relationship of the parts which compose the whole; and in MS. K (49) he writes, "Proportion is not only to be found in number and measure, but also in sounds, weights, times and places, and in every power that exists." It is such a sentence as this which justifies the statement of Gabriel Séailles,[4] in that admirable book from which M. Valéry drew so much of his material, that for Leonardo the universe was a mathematical reality overlaid by appearances.

But although Leonardo accepted for a time this framework of

mathematical reality, he was not sufficiently platonic to believe that appearances were unreal. If challenged he might have said that their reality was complimentary to that of mathematics. In fact his instinct as a painter, no less than his natural curiosity, led him to value appearances far more highly. I said just now, to the men of the Renaissance painting was a branch of knowledge. Leonardo says, "If you despise painting, which is the sole means of reproducing all the known works of nature, you despise an invention which, with subtle and philosophic speculation, considers all the qualities of forms: seas, plants, animals, grasses, flowers, all of which are encircled in light and shadow." He goes farther and claims that by his creative power the mind of the painter is transformed into the likeness of the mind of God. And this is only achieved by intimate understanding of all that he creates. He must consider *all* the qualities of forms—animal, vegetable or mineral. And so Leonardo takes up the study of biology, botany and geology.

He begins with man. Anatomy had been studied by the Florentine artists since the early fifteenth century. Antonio Pollaiuolo, who had a great influence on the style of Leonardo's drawings, was certainly a skilled anatomist. But from the start Leonardo exceeds the demands of art-school anatomy. For example, his inquiring mind must investigate the inner structure of a skull. The drawings of a bisected skull in a sketchbook dated 1489, of the same period as the studies of light striking a sphere, are amongst the most delicate and perceptive he ever did. Ten years later he was studying anatomy as an end in itself, and by 1504 he was examining the problem of generation. It is the first example of a change from the mechanical to the organic which was to be the main direction of his mind during the next twelve years. At about the same date he begins to study comparative anatomy. In his pre-scientific period he had made some drawings of a bear, and after its death had dissected its feet, clearly with a view to comparison with the human foot: but there are no notes on the subject. In 1504 he investigates the subject far more thoroughly. On a sheet at Windsor which also contains a sketch for the *Battle of Anghiari,* he compares the legs of a horse and a man, a comparison which is carried farther in one of his pocket-books, MS. H. This method of comparison and analogy, which may properly be called scientific, was to be used more and more by Leonardo in his other investigations. I may add that Leonardo never entirely lost sight of his original aims in anatomy. He intended to write a systematic treatise on anatomy, and notes in 1510 that it will be finished in the Spring of that year. This note occurs in a MS. which was, perhaps, to form part of the work; and both in pose and treatment of the muscles it anticipates the standard anatomical figures, the so-called *écorchés* which figured so prominently in academies of art up to the present century. But the art-school anatomies in this book are done in an unusually dull and lifeless style, as if he were discharging a tiresome duty. There is far more interest in the almost contemporary drawings illustrating his notes on the vital human organs, the heart, lungs, etc. Here we are brought back to the curious limitation of Leonardo's mind which I mentioned earlier. Although these drawings seem to show that he had observed the circulation of the blood as a fact, he never states it as a principle. Still less does he propound a theory of evolution, although from his notes on comparative anatomy it seems to be in his mind. As his experience enlarged he became more and more opposed to general statements of any kind, and this dislike of formulation (if it was a conscious dislike, and not some curious incapacity) is alone responsible for the fact that Leonardo is not one of the central figures in the history of science.

So the progress from mechanism to organism begins with anatomy. But man is a part of nature, and Leonardo's keen sense of analogy suggested that a similar organization, with similar laws of growth, existed in the vegetable and even the mineral world. The old medieval doctrine of the microcosm and macrocosm must be proved by observation. Once again he observes with the eye of an artist. His pocket-books are full of notes on the structure of trees and plants. Accompanying these sketches are clear-sighted observations of the colour of leaves, of reflected light and transparency. They might be the notes of an Impressionist and in fact are very similar to observations in the sketch-books of Constable. The same book, MS. G., contains notes on what Leonardo called *la prospettiva di colore,* the modification of colour by atmosphere, a subject which he also studied during his expeditions in the mountains. And there are notes on the colour of smoke and mist, which remind us of Goethe. Only his dislike of formulas prevented him from anticipating Goethe's theory of translucency. His interest in the play of light, in accordance with the general drift of his mind, developed from state to motion. In contrast with the static diagrams of the 1480's later studies show him trying to analyse the sparkle of light on the waves. The drawings of plants done at the date of the *Leda*[5] certainly had a dual intention. To some extent they were preparatory to the picture, to some extent accurate botanical studies complete with details of seed pods and notes of similar genus, etc. Or was this, after all, only one intention? Was this scientific knowledge of a seed pod necessary if the plants in the *Leda* were to have their full significance as symbols of vegetable vitality, of the unsubduable demand for rebirth. Leonardo's notes often indicate that his scientific observations continued to be linked with his intentions as a painter, long after they seem to us to have diverged on their own.

Where botany is concerned it is hard to say that his researches carried his art any farther. The flowers in the *Vierge aux Rochers*[6] (Pl. 53) are surely accurate enough for any painter, even for one who felt the need to know more than he showed. In geology, on the other hand, I believe that Leonardo's investigations resulted in a real advance, both artistically and scientifically. He had inherited the tradition of fantastic rocks dating back to Hellenistic painting, and since we look first at those objects in nature which have received the blessing of art, these were the subject of his first geological observations. The rocks in the *Vierge aux Rochers* show a little more knowledge than those of his contemporaries, but they are much less closely observed than the flowers, where he had behind him the long tradition of Gothic naturalism. But during the 1490's, the great period of Leonardo's mental expansion, he begins to take a more scientific interest in landscape, and sees rock forms as part of the whole earth's structure. This is what he shows us in the beautiful drawing at Windsor of a storm breaking over the foothills of the Alps, which records an observation, but one chosen for its effect on the emotions. By very slight changes it could become the background of the *Mona Lisa*.

In the background of the *St. Anne* this balance between the scientific and the fantastic is developed. Leonardo has made more studies of rock formation, and he has spent much time in the mountains, studying the bones of the earth with the same concentrated attention that he gave to the bones of man. And at this point, he formed a concept which was to have a profound effect on his mind. It is hinted at in a passage in the manuscript known as the Leicester Codex, which contains, to my mind, the finest of all Leonardo's speculations. "Nothing originates," he says, "in a spot where there is no sentient, vegetable, and rational life; feathers grow upon birds and are changed every year; hairs grow upon animals and are changed every year. . . . The grass grows in the fields, and the leaves on the trees, and every year they are, in great part, renewed. So that we might say that the earth has a spirit of growth; that its flesh is the soil, its bones the arrangement and connection of the rocks of which the mountains are composed, its cartilage the tufa, and its blood the springs of water. The pool of blood which lies round the heart is the ocean, and its breathing, and the increase and decrease of the blood in the pulses, is represented in the earth by the flow and ebb of the sea." So the earth, like man, and plants, and light—the solid earth—is in a state of continual change. Corroborating and extending this concept were the shells and fossils which Leonardo had observed when investigating the structure of mountains. How had they got there? The answers to this question, which occupy many pages of the Leicester Codex, show Leonardo's mental processes at their best. We see the value of his tiresome obstinacy, his determination never to take anything on trust. He will not for a moment admit the idea of special creation, and he advances decisive arguments against the accepted idea, that shells had been carried to the tops of mountains by the Flood. Readers of Gosse's *Father and Son* will recognize that in this he was in advance of an eminent naturalist of the nineteenth century. In the end he concludes that the whole earth is constantly being worn away, and remade by the action of water. What blood is to the body, water is to the earth, *l'acqua e il vetturale della natura*. He had returned to the conclusion of Heraclitus, that everything is in a state of flux. But this is no longer an inspired guess (for such I take it are most of the generalizations of pre-Socratic philosophy), but the result of a thousand painstaking observations. The inescapable conclusion of Leonardo Vinci, *dissciepolo della sperientia*.

These discoveries were made about the year 1510 when Leonardo was living in Milan. It was a period of intense activity, when, beside the scientific researches I have just alluded to, he was engaged on a number of works of art, some official, like the monument to Marshal Trivulzio, some intensely personal, like the *Virgin and St. Anne* and the *St. John* in the Louvre. Such activity did not admit of hesitation or distraction. The urge to discover and record the facts had lost none of its force. He was still driven on to clothe with flesh the mathematical and harmonic structure in which, twenty years earlier, he had so firmly believed. But in 1512 outside events disturbed him. An alliance of Spaniards, Papal Mercenaries and Venetians drove the French out of Milan, and the city, which had been gradually losing its veneer of civilization, became completely disorganized. Leonardo retired to the villa of his friend, Francesco Melzi, and a year later, like every other artist in Italy, made his way to the Rome of Leo X. The Pope gave him rooms in the Belvedere of the Vatican, and treated him with honour. But he could not settle to work. Vasari records the Pope's exclamation of despair, *"Oime, costui non e per far nulla."* "Alas, this fellow will never do anything because he begins by thinking of the end of a work before the beginning." Vasari also recalls scientific jokes with which he occupied his time—animals of paste which flew, and a lizard dressed up to look like a dragon; and this statement is borne out by many sheets of scribbles dating from this epoch, containing puzzles and similar trifling. We are told that he executed for Giuliano de' Medici a book of geometrical games, and may presume that it contained figures similar to those in plate 66, which have about as much to do with geometry as a crossword puzzle has to do with literature. What had happened? Partly, no doubt, the new atmosphere did not suit him. The solitary old exquisite who had lived for so long according to his fancy, remote from the world, found himself quartered among half the leading artists of Italy, crowding, criticizing, jockeying for position. But I think that something far more fundamental had taken place. To put it crudely, he had got out of his depth. The facts which he had collected to clothe his mathematical framework had grown too numerous and too complex; and they had led him to a conclusion for which his mathematics were inadequate: that the basis of all phenomena was change and movement. No wonder he despaired of ever putting his researches in order. From the Uffizi *Adoration* onwards he had shown a dislike of finishing things. And now the knowledge that he could never put the work of his lifetime into a final form gave him an agonizing sense of frustration. *Di mi se mai fu fatta alcuna cosa*—tell me if anything was ever done. These were the first words to flow from his pen at any vacant moment. *Di mi se mai, di mi se mai,* again and again, dozens of times, we find it on sheets of drawings, among scribbles or mathematical jottings, or beside the most painstaking calculations. It is the *leit motif* of his old age. A drawing at Windsor, which dates from these years, seems to symbolize his state of mind. It shows an old bearded man seated in profile, his head on his hand, gazing into the distance, with an air of profound melancholy. His nutcracker nose and sharply turned down mouth remind us of the old men in Leonardo's unconscious scribbles, but his curling beard and large deep-set eye recall the likenesses of Leonardo himself. Even if this is not strictly a self-portrait we may call it a self-caricature, using the word to mean a simplified expression of essential character. Opposite him on the sheet are studies of swirling water and a note comparing its movement to that of plaited hair; and although these studies were not intended to have any connection with the old man, for the sheet was originally folded over, they are like the projection of his thoughts.

For of all Leonardo's interests the most continuous and obsessive was the movement of water. At various times in his life he had been able to turn this obsession to semi-practical ends by applying himself to problems of canalization and irrigation. But the quantity of his notes on the subject—it forms one of the largest and most disheartening sections of his written work—and the quality of his drawings show a passion with no relation to practical life. Some of his studies of swirling water are amongst the most direct expressions of his sense of form, springing from the same mysterious source as his love of knots and tendrils. A sheet at Windsor shows water taking the form of both hair and flowers, racing along in twisted strands, and pouring from a sluice so that it makes dozens of little whirlpools, like a cluster of ferns with long curling tendrils. His superhuman quickness of eye has allowed him to delineate forms of movement since confirmed by spark photography, and we must take these drawings of water as genuinely scientific. But as he gazed half-hypnotized at the ruthless continuum of watery movement, Leonardo began to transpose his observations into the realm of the imagination, and to associate them with an idea of cataclysmic destruction which had always haunted him. The result is a series of drawings at Windsor which, even now, are less famous than they deserve to be.

Each epoch of taste finds in a great artist's output certain symbolic works, through which, for the time, he is popularly known. Leonardo, in the late eighteenth century, was known through his caricatures and grotesques; in the late nineteenth century through the *Mona Lisa's* smile. To the present age those visions of catastrophe, in which a huge cloud fills the sky like a menacing flower, and sends down ribbons of destruction on to the peaceful landscape, may seem the most poignant and relevant of all his works. In Leonardo's conscious mind they were probably connected with certain writings and sermons foretelling the end of the world, which were common in the years before the Reformation. But to anyone who has followed the development of his spirit they have a deeper and more personal significance. Leonardo has taken that branch of scientific investigation to which he had given the most concentrated thought and in which his eye had been most continuously engaged, and has used it, as Michelangelo came to use his knowledge of the human body, to express his sense of tragedy. And what was this tragedy? It was the failure of human knowledge in the face of the forces of nature; and for Leonardo the symbol of this failure was precisely that flux, that continuum to which all his researches had led him.

We can see now that this failure was relative. Leonardo had gone too far ahead of his times. He had made a discovery which should have been buried or put back on the shelves. He had been the disciple of experience in an age before experience could be absorbed. It was possible *in his art* to anticipate the theories and spatial movements of the next 100 years. But it was not possible *in his thought* to do the work which was to occupy the philosophical, mathematical and scientific genius of the seventeenth century, and was to culminate in Newton's discovery of the calculus. Here, once more, was a framework into which Leonardo's observations could have fitted. But in 1516, when he accepted Francis I's invitation to settle in France, these triumphs of the human mind were far out of sight; and Leonardo was glad to retire like an old magician, into a kind of hermetical seclusion.

4/
THE PSYCHOLOGY
OF THE ENIGMA

"O Leonardo, why do you labor so?"
—Leonardo's marginal note in the
Codex Atlanticus, folio 71a

*"...This is the way of knowing the performer of
so many wonderful works, and this is the way of
loving so great an inventor! For in truth great
love is born of great knowledge of the thing
loved: and if you did not know it, you could
not love it, or could love it but little. And if you
love it for the good you expect to get from it,
and not for its sublime virtue, you are acting like
a dog that wags his tail and fawns before someone who can give him a bone. But if the virtue
of that man were known, he would love him
much more, if that virtue served his designs."*

—Leonardo on the tireless study of nature, in
The Treatise on Painting, folio 77

On Freud's Study of Leonardo

by Brian Farrell

I

T IS GENERALLY agreed that Leonardo da Vinci is a complex and puzzling individual. When we contemplate his life and work we find ourselves struggling to understand him and to dispel the enigma he presents. In this essay, Freud offers us his own attempt to understand Leonardo.

When we are ordinarily puzzled by someone, for example, our new neighbour next door, what puzzles us are the apparent inconsistencies in his life and general conduct. Thus, our new neighbour might say he is very interested in gardening, but he lets his large garden go to ruin; when his luggage came it was seen to contain various pieces of sporting equipment, but he appears to play no sport and hardly goes out at all. We would probably be puzzled by items of this sort. But when we discover that his wife has only just died, that gardening and sport were joint activities of theirs, and that he is still too distressed by her death to take up the normal round again, we then feel we have solved the puzzle—that we now understand him. We succeed therefore in understanding our neighbour when we can produce an explanatory narrative about him which (*a*) removes the apparent inconsistencies and presents a coherent picture of him instead; and (*b*) is true.

Now we are puzzled about Leonardo, at least in part, for the very same reasons that we are perplexed about our neighbour. His life and work present us with glaring inconsistencies. Possessed of prodigious talents in many directions, his actual achievements seem to fall far short of his real capabilities—his inability to finish a piece of work, for instance, was notorious. His painting and drawing is full of feeling but hardly ever in his written records does he exhibit any feeling for any human being whatever. Moreover, his artistic work as a whole presents a mysterious picture to the student. In the words of Sir Kenneth Clark he is "the Hamlet of art history," [1] and his whole life leaves us uncertain whether he is an artist distracted by his scientific interests or a scientist who also happened to be an artist. In this essay Freud offers us the fruits of his own attempt to understand Leonardo. He tries therefore to give us an explanatory narrative in which the inconsistencies of Leonardo's life and work are removed and the whole exhibited as a coherent story. However, it is not unlikely that Freud's essay will strike many ordinary laymen as an odd and fantastic exercise. Hence it is worth noting and remembering how it does resemble the sort of explanatory narratives we offer about people who puzzle us in ordinary life.

But, of course, there is a critical difference between Freud's essay and the narrative we offered about our new neighbour. In seeking to understand and explain our neighbour, we make use of the psychology of ordinary life—of common sense. Thus we remove the inconsistency between our neighbour's professed interest in gardening and his actual neglect of his garden by showing that the latter is an expected outcome of his bereavement and present very depressed state. However, in attempting to explain Leonardo, Freud does not restrict himself to the psychology of common sense. On the contrary, what Freud is specifically concerned to do is to try to understand him by means of the very technical concepts and generalizations of psycho-analytic theory. In addition to making use of the psychology of common sense wherever necessary, Freud applies to the data we have about Leonardo the technical apparatus of psycho-analytic theory—as far as he and others had developed it at the time. It is this feature that makes Freud's essay quite different logically from a common sense narrative about a person. What is more, it is this feature that also logically distinguishes Freud's essay from the attempts usually made to understand Leonardo by art critics, historians of art, and specialists of this type; for these specialists also rely for the most part on a psychology of common sense to resolve the enigma of Leonardo. No doubt, it is a sophisticated and subtle common sense—somewhat removed from the simple-minded notions and generalizations sufficient to understand our new neighbour. But it nevertheless remains, largely or wholly, a psychology of common sense.

Now when the ordinary person, or the art critic, or the historian of science or art turns to this essay by Freud, he is likely to be interested, puzzled, and disconcerted. He will be interested because he will feel that Freud's narrative is illuminating, that because of it he now understands things about Leonardo that he did not understand before, and so on. But he will also be disconcerted and puzzled because he will not know what to make of it all. How much credence should he attach to Freud's story? What reasons are there to believe that it is true? These doubts about the essay are quite natural and understandable. As we have seen, what distinguishes Freud's essay about Leonardo from the usual run of narratives is that it uses the technical concepts and generalizations of psycho-analytic theory. If these concepts and generalizations had the logical character of, say, the concepts and generalizations of mechanics or the kinetic theory of gases or the theory of genetics, then they would be generally accepted and there would be no problem. All we should have to be sure about was that Freud had applied the concepts and generalizations of psycho-analysis correctly to the particular instance of Leonardo. If the consensus of the scientific world was that Freud had applied them correctly to the data of Leonardo's life and work, the ordinary man and art critic could then rely on this consensus and agree that Freud *had* explained the puzzling phenomena presented by Leonardo. He might be surprised by Freud's explanatory narrative; but then surprise is characteristic of scientific explanation. He might not even grasp it himself, but again failure by laymen to grasp an explanation is frequent in science. What there would be no room for would be any doubts and perplexities about Freud's account itself. But, of course, we all know that the concepts and generalizations of psycho-analysis have a logical character that makes them very different from the concepts and generalizations of mechanics or genetics. Because of these differences there is at present no consensus in the scientific world about the concepts and generalizations of psycho-analysis. Some thinkers, indeed, even maintain that psycho-analysis is not a scientific enterprise at all. So the ordinary person or the student of art is unable to fall back on a consensus of scientific opinion about psycho-analysis, and therefore about this essay by Freud. The scientific world gives him no guidance on the question. When he reads the essay he finds in it a technical psychology whose validity he cannot personally assess. He finds that this psychology is being applied to a particular historical figure, and that he is unable to determine for himself how legitimate the application is. Naturally, therefore, he is bewildered by Freud's essay. Naturally, he wonders how much credence to attach to it. Is Freud's story about Leonardo just a typical piece of psycho-analytic phantasy? Or is there something in it? And if so, how much?

II

Let us begin by outlining the argument that Freud offers us. His narrative focuses our attention on an early memory of Leonardo about a bird. Unfortunately there is an immediate difficulty about this memory that we must clear out of the way. At the beginning of Chapter Two of the essay, Freud writes as follows:

> There is, so far as I know, only one place in his scientific note-books where Leonardo inserts a piece of information about his childhood. In a passage about the flight of vultures he suddenly interrupts himself to pursue a memory from very early years which had sprung to his mind: "It seems that I was always destined to be so deeply concerned with vultures; for I recall as one of my earliest memories that while I was in my cradle a vulture came down to me, and opened my mouth with its tail, and struck me many times with its tail against my lips."

This quotation from Leonardo[2] is the English version of the German translation that Freud used. Unfortunately the German translation from the Italian is defective in two places—as the editor of *The Standard Edition* of Freud's works points out.[3] First, the Italian original ends with the words *"dentro alle labbra."* In the German translation the word *"dentro,"* meaning "within," is omitted. Freud, however, seems to have noticed this and interpreted the original Italian text correctly. The second defect is a serious one. The German translation translates the Italian word *"nibbio"* as *"Geier,"* which means vulture. This is a mistake. *"Nibbio"* is the word for "kite."[4] In this passage Leonardo is talking about kites, not vultures. This mistake of translation has misled Freud and others to some extent. Accordingly, certain parts of his original narrative—parts which are easy to pick out—have to be rejected outright; and his explanation correspondingly modified. Let us suppose, then, that Freud had understood Leonardo correctly to be referring to kites; and let us examine Freud's explanation in the modified form it would then take.

Freud argues that this report of Leonardo resembles the memory phantasies about early childhood produced by patients in the course of being psycho-analysed. Now the report of such a phantasy is a report of an event that never happened. But the patient produces it in the form that he does because, roughly, he has an unconscious adult wish which fixes on some past and related experience of the person when a child, and which now transforms this experience in a way that permits the open but disguised expression of his unconscious wish. Therefore, in producing this phantasy report, Leonardo reveals that an unconscious adult wish is at work in him. What is this wish? Freud claims that Leonardo's report about the kite is yet another instance of a well-known type of phantasy, which patients under analysis have shown to have a clear-cut and well-established significance. Leonardo places his story back in the period when he was in his cradle and still at the breast. Therefore it contains "a reminiscence of sucking—or being suckled—at his mother's breast." This is the past experience that his phantasy has fixed on and transformed. In telling us this story about the kite in his cradle, Leonardo reveals that he has transformed the experience of sucking the breast into one in which a kite opens his mouth and beats about inside it with its tail. In telling us this he reveals that he has an unconscious concern with "the idea of an act of fellatio, a sexual act in which the penis is put into the mouth of the person involved." So Leonardo's story reveals an unconscious wish typical of a passive homosexual, namely, to commit the act of fellatio. The early experience of sucking the breast has been transformed into the report about a kite—the phantasy of a passive homosexual—thereby permitting the open but disguised expression of his homosexuality and his unconscious wish to suck a penis.

But why does Leonardo substitute a kite for his mother? How does the penis, which is the essence of the male, come to take the place of the breast, which is so essentially female and maternal? Why is it that the early experience of the act of sucking at the breast has been transformed by Leonardo into one in which the kite is active and he is inactive? Where have the elements of *passive* homosexuality come from? Because of the mistake of translation already mentioned, Freud was misled into trying to answer the question "Why does Leonardo substitute a vulture for his mother?"; and his answer to his question does not apply to the kite. Hence, the essay does not tell us why a kite takes the place of his mother. The essay answers the second question (How does the penis come to take the place of the breast?) by resorting to Freud's doctrine about infantile theories of sexuality. A small boy believes that his mother also has a penis. His erotic interest in his mother culminates in a longing for her penis, and in the course of his development he may develop a fixation on this object—a fixation that is pathologically manifested in foot-fetishists, in *"coupeurs de nattes,"* and so forth. Therefore, Leonardo's emphasis on the tale of a kite is a way of telling us that there was a time when he was curious about his mother and believed she had a genital like his own. But where does the passivity and homosexuality come from? Psycho-analytical experience has shown that, with one type of male homosexual, the patients have all had as small children a very intense erotic attachment to a female, usually the mother. "This attachment," Freud writes,

> was evoked or encouraged by too much tenderness on the part of the mother herself, and further reinforced by the small part played by the father during their childhood.

But the growing boy is finally forced to repress his love for the mother and he does this in these circumstances by identifying himself with her. The boy is now protected against his love for her, because he now plays the role of mother himself and chooses persons like himself as his love objects. Hence his homosexuality. Freud suggests that this is the fate that overcame Leonardo. When very young, his mother was over-affectionate and his father played a small role in his life. When Leonardo refers in the kite phantasy to the tail striking him many times against the lips, he is referring, not only to the experience of sucking, but also to the experience or memory in which "my mother pressed innumerable passionate kisses on my mouth." Hence, the passive character of the kite phantasy. In it he is expressing the adult wish to play the passive partner in a homosexual act of sucking a penis.

Freud's interpretation of the kite memory is only part, however, of something much more important—namely, his whole attempt to reconstruct the personality of Leonardo. Freud draws attention to what were at the time the known facts about Leonardo's early life; and he notes the following in particular: that Leonardo was an illegitimate child of a woman called Caterina; that he is listed, when five years old, as being among the members of his father's household; that his father married a certain Donna Albiera, and that this marriage was childless; that he later entered Verrocchio's studio as an apprentice; and that at the age of twenty his name appears as a member of the Painters' Guild in Florence.

Freud now offers a hypothetical account of Leonardo's early years which he claims is consistent with these facts. He suggests that his father left Leonardo to be brought up by his mother Caterina in her home. Caterina was over-tender with Leonardo and over-eroticized her relations with him—as the kite memory shows. Somewhere between the age of three and five, Leonardo's tie with his mother was broken. He was returned to his father's household and to the care of a young and childless wife. About this same stage Leonardo had to repress his sexual interest in, and curiosity about, his mother Caterina. This is the normal thing that happens at this time. Because of his close erotic attachment to Caterina, he achieved this repression by identifying himself with her and thereby forcing himself to choose love objects like himself, as we have already seen. But in Leonardo's case the repression of sex interest was severe. No doubt this was due in part to the shattering effect on him of the rupture from the mother who meant so much to him. But it was also due in part to factors in Leonardo's biological make-up about which psycho-analysis cannot speak, and about which in any case nothing is yet known. The effect of this severe repression, however, was to make him sublimate much of his sexual energy and interests into curiosity and a craving for knowledge. So Leonardo entered adolescence with his sexual impulse homosexually directed, but most of it sublimated into his craving for knowledge. The upshot was to reduce his sexual need very greatly, and so make it unlikely that the homosexual bent given to it would lead him into sexual behaviour. In addition, Freud reminds us, "What an artist creates provides at the same time an outlet for his sexual desire." Accordingly, in taking to artistic work Leonardo solved the problem of his adolescence by discharging in this work the upsurging sexual energies of this stage of his life. All this provided a fairly satisfactory solution at the time of his psychological problem. In particular, this solution enabled him to follow the lead of his genius in the fine arts and to use his talents in this field without inhibition at the outset of his career.

Freud points to certain known facts about Leonardo that lend independent support to part of this reconstruction of his personality, namely, the part concerned with his homosexuality. Freud notes the absence of any woman with whom he had any intimacy, physical or mental; as a teacher he surrounded himself with handsome boys and youths; and, whether rightly or wrongly, he was accused and acquitted of homosexual practices when still an apprentice. He was clearly an aesthete and had a love of the refinements of living. His strong repression of ordinary sexuality comes out in one place in his writings where he records his disgust at the whole act of procreation, as he does also in his drawing of coitus. Freud also points to the chaste character of his writings as a whole, and the absence of the obscene drawings one expects among the private papers of artists. "In an age," he writes, "which saw a struggle between sensuality without restraint and gloomy asceticism, Leonardo represented the cool repudiation of sexuality."

III

With the help of this reconstruction of Leonardo's personality, Freud attempts to remove the inconsistencies in his life and work and so makes him understandable. As we have noted, Freud argues that Leonardo achieved a relatively satisfactory solution of his problem in the course of his adolescence. Consequently in his youth he passed through a period of vigorous artistic creation, in which he worked without obvious inhibition. But it is a psycho-analytic discovery that "the almost total repression of a real sexual life does not provide the most favourable conditions for the exercise of sublimated sexual trends." The sexual needs that Leonardo is denying begin to break through. The first thing to happen is that the later, and second, sublimation of his energies into art begins to break down. He finds himself incapable of vigorous and decisive artistic work. He finds himself delaying, hesitating, and becoming incapable of completing anything. A striking example is his work on "The Last Supper." Now all this is like the process of regression that neurotics exhibit. So it is evident that Leonardo regressed from the later position, in which his sublimated energies found their outlet in his art, to the earlier position, in which they were sublimated into the craving for knowledge. At first, Freud reminds us, this interest was still in the service of his art. But as he did not solve his own psychological problem, the regression became permanent and fully developed. His craving for knowledge came to dominate his work, and to develop independently and away from his art. Hence the Janus-like character of Leonardo, part artist, part scientist, and his development from the former into the latter.

Next, let us remember, his father had left him to be brought up by Caterina. Freud supposes that this fact also had an important and shattering effect on the young child in yet another way. It made him come unconsciously to regard his father as a person who had neglected him when a child, who had not cared about him, and who had left him as an undeveloped infant to the sole charge of his mother. Later on in his childhood, Leonardo identified himself with his father in the usual manner. In doing so, he came unconsciously to adopt the same attitude as his father to his own offspring, that is, to the products of his own work. He did not particularly care about them. He found it difficult to sustain his interest in them. He could not bother to finish them, and to see that they were properly developed and completed. Now this early unconscious attitude also played its part in breaking down his adolescent solution of his difficulties. For it helped, along with his regression to the desire for knowledge, to make him indifferent to the fate of his painting and artistic work; and, what is more serious, made it difficult for him to bring *any* of his work to fruition. Hence, also, the unfinished, doodling character of his scientific work. Freud does not actually discuss the influence on his scientific activity of Leonardo's identification with his father. But the suggestion just made is quite consistent with Freud's own narrative; and some such suggestion is necessary if Freud is also to explain the unfinished nature of Leonardo's scientific work.

Freud also attempts to explain some of the content of Leonardo's scientific work and outlook. Leonardo had learnt in his first five years to do without his father's support, and to pursue his sexual researches without his interference. This prepared him later, on reaching maturity, to reject parental and parent-like figures and authority. So he was able to reject the appeal to authority and the ancients, and become the first natural scientist. Likewise, he was able to reject the Christian view of a personal god, as he had no need of an exalted father figure, and was thus able to detach himself from Christian orthodoxy. Leonardo's rejection of authority "simply corresponds to," or symbolizes, his rejection of his father; and Freud implies that the same is true of his rejection of Christianity. Freud notes that a wish to fly in dreams turns out under psycho-analysis to be a longing to be capable of sexual performance. This longing, says Freud, is an early infantile wish. Leonardo's early sexual interests in his mother were frustrated, broken off and then severely repressed. What is worse, he could only deal with the problem of his mother's excessive over-tenderness by adopting a homosexual solution, as we have already seen, thereby incapacitating himself from having ordinary sexual intercourse. Now we know that Leonardo was fascinated by the problems of flight. We can understand this when we regard his interest in this whole subject as a displaced manifestation of his repressed sexuality. His longing to solve the problem of flight and to fly was an expression of his unconscious wish for the sexual performance of which he was incapable.

But what about the content of Leonardo's work as an artist? How does Freud try to explain the special and peculiar character of Leonardo's art? A quick perusal of the essay is enough to show that

Freud only attempts to deal with certain features of Leonardo's paintings which he says are puzzling. For this limited purpose he concentrates on two paintings—the "Mona Lisa" and the "Madonna and Child with St Anne."

Freud makes the supposition that at the age of fifty Leonardo underwent a further development characteristic of middle-age. His sexual impulse "made a further energetic advance." He regressed to a still earlier phase of development, and "still deeper layers of the contents of his mind became active once more." It was at this period that he met and painted Mona Lisa del Giocondo. Freud now cuts through the perennial enigma of the "Mona Lisa" at one stroke. He supposes that, with the deeper layers of Leonardo's mind already stirring, this Florentine woman "awakened in him as a grown man the memory of the mother of his early childhood," and in her smile he saw "his mother's happy smile of sensual rapture." The painting at once becomes understandable. The expression of the face is a perfect representation, Freud reminds us, of "the contrasts which dominate the erotic life of women; the contrast between reserve and seduction, and between the most devoted tenderness and a sensuality that is ruthlessly demanding —consuming men as if they were alien beings." But these contrasts represent precisely how Leonardo was treated by his mother. She over-eroticized her relations with him. In so doing she treated him with tenderness and yet with a sensuality which ended by robbing him of his masculinity. Hence the smile of inner satisfaction and menace, the smile of the cat that has eaten the canary. We know that Leonardo was obviously involved in, and obsessed by, this painting for years. Naturally so, as he was painting one who unconsciously represented a mother from whom he had never really escaped. Leonardo clearly became obsessed by the smile, since it appeared from that date in all his later work. Naturally so, in view of its critical significance for him in his whole life and work.

A little later on Leonardo painted "The Madonna and Child with St Anne." This painting is puzzling, Freud says, because it represents a subject rarely handled in Italian painting, and because St Anne is presented as a young woman of radiant beauty. The puzzle vanishes if we make use of one of Freud's suppositions about Leonardo's childhood. Freud supposed that he was first brought up by Caterina for some years, and then cared for by the young Donna Albiera, the childless wife of his father. The significance of the picture is that it "contains a synthesis of the history of his childhood." It represents for

Leonardo his own childhood—two young mothers of about the same age watching over and caring for him, each endowed with the typical Leonardesque smile. The still later pictures, such as the "St. John," reveal somewhat different features. They still have the familiar smile but they also "breathe a mystical air into whose secret one dare not penetrate"; and they portray androgynous figures—beautiful youths of feminine delicacy and form—who "gaze in mysterious triumph as if they knew of a great achievement of happiness about which silence must be kept." Freud suggests that these figures represent a psychological triumph for Leonardo. Denied of an erotic life, he has represented in these figures the wishes of a boy who was infatuated with his mother. He has fulfilled these wishes by presenting the male and female natures in these figures as blissfully united; and the familiar smile shows us that the secret and mysterious triumph is that of love.

IV

What are we to make of this explanatory narrative?

The first thing is to note where Freud was, or may have been, wrong about certain matters of fact. Since Freud wrote, evidence has come to light, which suggests that Leonardo was brought up in his father's household with Albiera from an early age.[5] This suggestion may make it necessary to modify Freud's narrative. If we suppose that Leonardo was at least breast-fed by Caterina and only left her towards the end of, say, his first year of life, then we would be able, perhaps, to keep the main outlines of Freud's account and merely modify it by supposing that the eroticizing by, and identification with, the mother took place at a much earlier age. Given the general looseness of Freudian theory, such a modification would be quite feasible, and, moreover, in line with current psycho-analytic thinking, which places some of the critical phases of development at much earlier ages than Freud himself suggested. If, however, we suppose that Leonardo was not breast-fed by Caterina but placed at once in the care of Albiera, then it would be more difficult perhaps to keep the main outlines of Freud's own narrative. Psycho-analysts might then be forced into giving quite a different account of Leonardo from that of Freud—one in which the schizoid and depressive features of his personality played a central role. Another possible mistake is this. Freud seriously imagines (in Chapter Three) that the Caterina mentioned in Leonardo's notebooks, and whose burial expenses he records, was his mother. Most contemporary historians seem to think that there is nothing to support this idea. If an analyst wishes to explain the records of the burial expenses, he would be advised to do so in some other way.[6]

Freud makes a different sort of mistake about Leonardo's drawing of coition. In the 1919 edition of his essay he adds in a long footnote part of an article by an analyst called Reitler, including a coition figure said to have been drawn by Leonardo. It is clear that Freud is in general agreement with the tenor of this quotation. Now Reitler's article is based on the reproduction of this coition figure, and the only drawing in Leonardo's corpus which this can represent is on Q III 3 v. (Pl. 70). But the reproduction of this coition figure from Q III 3 v. is wrong —both in Reitler's original article and in *The Standard Edition* of Freud's essay used in this volume. It is wrong in two respects. It presents the two feet—one of the man's and one of the woman's—as complete; in the actual drawing Leonardo does not complete the legs and feet at all. In this reproduction the expression is such that Reitler can describe it as follows:

> The features of the man . . . are marked by a resistance which is positively indignant. His brows are wrinkled and his gaze is directed sideways with an expression of repugnance. The lips are pressed together and their corners are then drawn down.

This face, he concludes, "expresses only indignation and aversion." In the actual drawing, however, the brows are not wrinkled, the gaze is not directed sideways, the lips are not pressed together, and their corners then drawn down. In consequence the whole expression is quite different. It is, if anything, one of peaceful bliss, or calmness, or "strange detachment"—to use Sir Kenneth Clark's words.[7] We need not stay to discuss the origin of this mistake.[8] Freud uses this drawing as an additional item of evidence to support his view that Leonardo had repudiated sexuality, and it is clear that Freud cannot place any weight on it. Moreover, the "remarkable errors" that Freud says are also visible in this drawing can be given another and historical interpretation, which we shall touch on below.

V

Let us, however, ignore Freud's possible and actual mistakes of fact. The next thing to note is that in certain ways Freud's narrative lays itself open to the charge of being quite inadequate and even silly.

(*a*) In two brief passages Freud refers to Leonardo's difficulties as being akin to those of an obsessional neurotic. But Freud leaves it quite unclear how this alleged obsessionalism took its rise, and how it is related to the development and fate of his sexual impulse. Moreover, it is far from clear how large or small a part of Leonardo's conduct his alleged obsessionalism is meant to explain, and how important this part is supposed to be. One seems bound to conclude that Freud did not think out carefully his references to Leonardo's obsessionalism and relate them adequately to the rest of his narrative.

(*b*) We have noted how Freud attempts to explain Leonardo's interest in flying as an expression of his unconscious wish for sexual performance. Now let us suppose that Freud's whole theory of sexuality is correct. It is quite clear that Freud's account of Leonardo's interest in flying is not *sufficient* to explain it. For *all* Freud claims is that this interest has its "roots" in Leonardo's early sexual life—that it is a displaced expression of his repressed sexuality and of his unconscious longing for sexual performance. Freud does not say how this interest developed out of his unconscious wishes—why his repressed sexuality was displaced into an interest in flying, rather than into something else. But as the repression of sexuality is common to all of us on Freud's view, it is evident that Freud is not saying much. The important and interesting thing to know about Leonardo would be the conditions that made his repressed sexuality come out in the displaced form of an interest in flying; and Freud has no explanation to offer of this. At most, therefore, Freud is telling us that an unconscious longing by Leonardo for sexual performance is a *necessary* condition of his interest in flight. But how much does this amount to? It would be a very important contention if this unconscious longing were a necessary condition for an interest in flight *alone*. But Freud does not make this claim, and the perusal of psycho-analytic literature makes it evident that the unconscious wish for sexual performance serves as a necessary condition for all sorts of interests, activities, and personal difficulties. Hence Freud is telling us something which is more trivial and uninteresting than might appear at first sight. Taken by itself, Freud's whole explanation here seems grossly inadequate and lays itself open to the charge of being silly and futile.

(*c*) Freud's attempt to account for Leonardo's rejection of traditional Christianity runs into similar objections. So, too, does his attempt to explain the origin of Leonardo's craving for knowledge and interest in science. It is obviously not sufficient to explain Leonardo's craving as the sublimated outcome of repressing his sexual interest in, and curiosity about, his mother. For, according to Freud, such repression is a normal thing that happens, and yet we do not all develop a craving for knowledge as the result. Nor is it sufficient to explain his craving as the outcome of the *severe* repression of sexual interests, to which Leonardo was subjected on Freud's supposition. This will not do because different people react differently to severe repression, as Freud points out. We want to know why Leonardo reacted as he did; and Freud does not tell us. At best, therefore, Freud is saying that the severe repression of sexual curiosity and interest which Leonardo underwent provided a necessary condition for the development of his craving for knowledge, and so, later on, for his regression into science. But even this limited contention runs into the same objection of relative triviality which, we saw, can be levelled at Freud's explanation of his interest in flight. For, it could be argued, patients under analysis show that the severe repression of sexual curiosity is a necessary condition for all sorts of activities and interests, other than a craving for knowledge. Consequently, in telling us that this is a necessary condition with Leonardo for his interest in science, Freud is really telling us very little indeed.

But this conclusion leaves us uneasy; it seems so exaggerated. Many years ago Professor Broad criticized the "pretentious futility" that, he alleged, was "typical of some of the sillier psycho-analysts," which would "explain" a taste for music as due to repressed sexual desire.[9] In our discussion so far we seem to have convicted Freud of this very pretentious futility that Professor Broad objected to. But we hesitate about accepting this conclusion, because Freud is clearly getting at *something* in his examination of Leonardo's interest in flight and science. He is not just being pretentious and futile. What, then, is he getting at? What is the source of our uneasiness?

Let us notice that there are two different ways of describing what Freud is doing at this point. We can say that he is trying to give an explanation of, for example, Leonardo's interest in flight and science, which is of the same sort as that provided in the natural sciences. Freud himself seems to have accepted as correct this description of what he was doing. Now when an event is fully explained to us in natural science, it will be found that we have also been given the necessary and sufficient conditions for the occurrence of the event. This is a large and important piece of information. It is quite clear, however, that Freud does not give us the sufficient conditions of Leonardo's interest in flight and science, and only draws attention to a necessary condition that tells us very little. If, therefore, we say that Freud is explaining

Leonardo's interest in the way that is done in natural science, we convict him of utter inadequacy, and we expose his explanations as perfect examples of pretentious futility. But because Freud is obviously getting at *something* here, it follows that this description is misleading. It is not right to say that he is just doing a piece of natural science. Once we do say this, we develop the wrong expectations about the essay, and then inevitably convict him of inadequacy.

However, there is another different way of describing what he is doing. We can use the description suggested at the outset and say that Freud is trying to provide a coherent story about Leonardo which removes the inconsistencies in his life and work, and which is true. On this second description, what Freud is primarily concerned to do is to fit together the known facts about Leonardo with the aid of the technical generalizations and concepts of psycho-analysis. Now the known facts may be too sparse, and/or psycho-analytic theory too limited in its scope to enable Freud to provide a narrative which will answer *all* the questions about Leonardo that we should like Freud to deal with. Hence he may not be able to give us a narrative which embodies, for example, the necessary and sufficient conditions of Leonardo's interest in flight and science. But the fact that he cannot do this may not matter much on the second description of his activity. For on this second account of it, all Freud has to do is to fit together this interest of Leonardo with the rest of the data we have about him. He has to show that these are mutually consistent and supporting. Now let us suppose that Leonardo had revealed (*a*) an intense interest in flight and science which looked very much like a symptom of regression; and (*b*) no evidence that his sexual impulses were severely repressed, but, on the contrary, evidence that they were fully and adequately realized and exercised. It would then have been a little difficult for Freud to fit together these two facts about Leonardo. For, on psycho-analytic theory, a regressive interest in flight and science is typically a manifestation of an unconscious wish for sexual performance, and related wishes; and this presupposes that, where such regressive interests are shown, the sexual impulse has undergone considerable or severe repression. Accordingly, it is necessary and important for Freud to show that Leonardo's regressive interest does go along with considerable or severe repression. This is what psycho-analytic theory leads us to expect, and Freud tries to show that this expectation is realized with Leonardo. Thus, he points out, in effect, how the supposition that Leonardo's sexual impulse was subjected to severe repression is supported by all sorts of things in the data, other than his interest in flight and science. This fact indirectly supports Freud's suggestion that Leonardo's interest in flight and science was regressive and a symptom of sexual wishes. Again, Freud points, in effect, to the way in which the data lend this latter suggestion independent support. This fact, in turn, gives added weight to the supposition that Leonardo's sexual impulse was severely repressed. So Freud does succeed in showing that Leonardo's interest in flight and science and the other data we have about him are mutually consistent and supporting. Freud is not really concerned to give us a complete account of the way Leonardo's interest developed out of the severe repression of his sexual impulse and his later sexual difficulties. The fact, therefore, that Freud does not give us the necessary and sufficient conditions of Leonardo's interest does not, in itself, count against the point or adequacy of his story. This gap in his story may not matter much, if at all.

In this way, then, we can save Freud's remarks about Leonardo's interest in flight and science from the charge of silliness and pretentious futility. We save them by making clear that Freud is only explaining Leonardo's interest by providing a coherent story about it; he is not trying to explain it in the sort of way characteristic of natural science. But, of course, we can only save this part of Freud's story at a cost. The cost is that we make his remarks at this point much less important than Freud himself, perhaps, thought they were, and much less impressive than they may seem at first sight to the ordinary, unsuspecting reader. The reason for this is clear. Freud may succeed in giving us a coherent story about Leonardo's interest in flight and so forth, and yet tell us very little indeed about Leonardo. The extent to which Freud's story is genuinely informative and impressive depends largely on the degree to which, in giving us a coherent tale, it also succeeds in giving us the necessary and sufficient conditions of Leonardo's interests. Clearly Freud's story does tell us something about these conditions. But our scientific knowledge of human development and pathology is still very incomplete. Likewise, our knowledge about the particular circumstances and details of Leonardo's development and pathology is very defective. Consequently no coherent tale about Leonardo at the present time—whether Freud's or anyone else's—can tell us much about the necessary and sufficient conditions of his interest in flight and science. Freud's remarks about this interest serve to reveal the extent of our present ignorance and an important limitation of his own narrative.

VI

We can now come closer to the heart of the problem. If Freud's essay is an attempt to provide a narrative which gives a coherent picture or story of Leonardo's life and work, and in which the inconsistencies in it disappear, are there any reasons that make it obligatory for us to accept Freud's narrative rather than some other? Freud himself noted, in effect, that this question could be asked; for he says that his essay has provoked the criticism that he has merely written a "psycho-analytic novel." But he does not do much, if anything, himself to answer this question and meet this criticism.

Now a historian of art may be strongly tempted to assert that a psycho-analytic novel is precisely what Freud has written—at least about topics such as the kite memory, the "St Anne," and the "Mona Lisa." We are not at all obliged, he may argue, to accept Freud's narrative on these topics, because we can explain the oddity of the kite memory and the peculiar features of the "St Anne" and the "Mona Lisa" in another way. We can explain them in the way we ordinarily deal with puzzling items in history. We can remove their inconsistencies by putting them back into their historical context with the help of the psychology of common sense. Resort to the technical apparatus of psychoanalysis is quite unnecessary.

Consider the kite memory.[10] Leonardo's reference to this occurs in a context where he is considering the flight of birds, and the kite is picked out because it is the bird in which one can best observe the mechanics of flight, and in particular the movements of its tail. Leonardo probably got the idea of a kite's tail as a rudder from Pliny's *Natural History,* which he knew and quotes. Further, there was a well-known type of story current at that time about an incident in childhood being an omen of adult fortune or genius—for example, how bees settled on Plato's lips which meant that he would have sweetness of speech. In any case, the connexion of a bird with genius or inspiration was very old, and the mouth was a region significant for wisdom and prophecy. In the Christian tradition, for example, the Trinity was often represented in the Middle Ages with a dove's tail in God's mouth; and in Leonardo's time there was a variant in which the wings of the descending bird reached from the lips of God to those of the Son. It is clear, therefore, that Leonardo's kite memory has nothing odd about it. It is a reconstruction of his own past experience suggested by a current tradition and springing from wishes to be destined for greatness and to become great.

The position is even clearer about the "St Anne." Freud says that this is a puzzling picture because it represents a subject rarely handled in Italian painting and because St Anne is presented as a young and beautiful woman. In fact Freud was mistaken on both points. There had been a widespread and long-standing cult of St Anne and this reached its height in the latter part of the fifteenth century and the beginning of the sixteenth. Anne, Mary, and the Child were worshipped as a more accessible Trinity; and the cult had theological ramifications. Indulgence prayers to St Anne and Mary were issued on sheets with a woodcut of the three; and pictures of them were produced in great numbers—often showing Mary sitting on the lap of St Anne and with the Child on the lap of Mary, an object of tender attentions by both. Furthermore, Anne and Mary had been represented together as young saints long before Leonardo's time. The youth of St Anne is the result of theological idealization, and of the general tendency in medieval and Renaissance art to picture female saints as beautiful and virginal figures. Consequently, as the St Anne is not puzzling in the way that Freud alleged it to be, we do not need to resort to a psycho-analytical story to remove the puzzle.

Freud was also mistaken about the Leonardesque smile. He claims that this dated from the Mona Lisa. In fact the smile appears in what is known as the London cartoon of the St Anne which was drawn in 1500—before he met Mona Lisa. We also see the smile, or something akin to it, in the smiling faces of Verrocchio, and in plaster sculptures of women and men which—it has been claimed—were among Leonardo's earliest works. The smile also appears in Florentine art long before Leonardo. A present-day scholar has the following remark to make about the Gioconda.

> A Frenchman (Robert de Sizeranne, 1896) has observed that Gioconda smiles with only the left part of her mouth—but this is in accordance with the advice given to women in Renaissance times as to how to look most graceful; we read in Agnolo Firenzuola's *Della perfetta bellezza d'una donna,* 1541: "From time to time, to close the mouth at the right corner with a suave and nimble movement, and to open it at the left side, as if you were smiling secretly . . . not in an artificial manner, but as though unconsciously—this is not affectation, if it is done in moderation and in a re-

strained and graceful manner and accompanied by innocent coquetry and by certain movements of the eyes. . . ." This is a precept for ladies of fashion, and we should not overlook the fact that Mona Lisa—who plucked her eyebrows and the hair above her brow—was one of them.[11]

All this suggests that the elaborate fuss Freud makes about the smile of the Mona Lisa is quite unnecessary. We can understand it by putting it in its context and recognizing the obvious truth that it owes its power and charm to the infinite delicacy and subtlety of Leonardo's art.

Let us assume that this criticism from the historian is correct on matters of fact. What is its logical force? If Freud, in his narrative about the kite memory, had claimed that the *sole* or *only* origins of this memory were to be found in the circumstances of Leonardo's childhood, then the criticism from the historian would be incompatible with Freud's narrative; and if it were true, Freud's narrative would be false. But Freud does not make this claim. This becomes clear as soon as one pierces the ambiguities of his narrative here and sees it in the context of his writings and work. What Freud was concerned to do was to point to originating conditions that lie in the early history of the person, and to emphasize their importance. He accepted, and indeed stressed the contribution of subsequent precipitating conditions and of cultural factors in mental functioning. Likewise, if the historian were to claim that the *sole* or *only* origins of this memory are to be found in the literary and scientific traditions of the time, his criticism would be incompatible with Freud's account; and if his criticism were correct, Freud's narrative would be false. But the historian does not claim this either. He merely claims in his criticism of Freud that the kite memory had certain origins in the culture of the time. This view is quite compatible with Freud's hypothesis that the memory had certain origins in Leonardo's relations as a child with his mother. Indeed, it could be argued that the two positions complement each other.

Similarly for the "St Anne." Granted that Freud was wrong in the reasons he gave for thinking that the "St Anne" is a puzzling picture, it is still possible that this picture may have had the psychological significance for Leonardo that Freud maintains. In addition to the religious and contemporary origins of the picture, it may also have had sources in Leonardo's inner and past life that Freud suggested. About the "Mona Lisa," on the other hand, it is clear that, if we accept that the London cartoon of "St Anne" and other earlier works contain the Leonardesque smile, we shall have to modify Freud's story. We shall have to say that, though the smile broke out on earlier occasions, it only came to assume critical significance for him about the time of his crisis of middle-age; and with and after the painting of Mona Lisa, it dominated him. However, apart from some such modification, Freud's story about the Mona Lisa remains intact. The fact that the smile has sources in the artistic and social life of the time is quite compatible with it also having the personal sources that Freud has suggested.

But, we may feel like protesting, this is surely a misleading conclusion. Though the historian's account of Leonardo's two paintings and the kite memory does not refute Freud's story about them, surely it does show that his story is *wholly unnecessary,* and hence that there is no obligation on us whatever to adopt it. We may feel like making this pro-test, because we may be inclined to adopt the general view that, when a personal aberration, or puzzling item in human life, can be explained by common sense or some other rational story, recourse to unconscious motives and the other technical apparatus of psycho-analysis is wholly unnecessary and unjustified.

This position, however, will not do either. Whether it is wholly unnecessary or not to have recourse to a psycho-analytic story when we have *also* provided a commonsensical one depends on the context and purpose. Consider the boy Jones who is caught doing obscene drawings on the walls of the s.c.r. of a conventional public school. The old housemaster may explain to the new head that the execution of these drawings is a prank, traditionally played on the arrival of a new head, and that Jones was secretly selected to do this by his own fellows. In this context and given the purpose of the two schoolmasters, it is wholly unnecessary for the housemaster to produce anything more than this ordinary common-sensical story. But suppose that the school is a therapeutic community for children who are misfits in ordinary schools. It may then be very necessary for the housemaster to say more—to tell the new head, for example, that Jones was probably quite willing to be selected for this job, since he has an obsessional interest in the obscene, an interest which seems to be tied up with his hatred of his puritanical mother and to which the school prank gave a conventionalized outlet. Similarly with Leonardo. If we are only interested in the traditional history of art, we may not require more than the commonsense, historical story about him. But if we are interested in arriving at a coherent picture of his life as a whole, we may then have to say more. We may then find it necessary to resort to the technicalities of psycho-analysis in order to cover all the data about him, and, in particular, to relate his personality to his paintings and to individually curious items like the kite memory. In doing this we would show how his own personal needs made use of the literary and artistic and other traditions of the time, and through them took the opportunity of conventionalized expression. We would thereby show how cultural circumstances and personal factors of a psycho-analytical kind both contributed to produce an item such as the kite-memory.

The historian's narrative, therefore, does not show that Freud's story is wholly unnecessary and without any justification. What it does do is to reveal that there is not as much point in using Freud's story to cover the items of the kite memory, "St Anne," and the "Mona Lisa" as Freud supposed. For in providing an alternative narrative about these items, the historian shows that Freud's story about them is not necessarily compulsory; and that, even if the factors Freud emphasized were at work, their contribution is less than he imagined. It also suggests, moreover, that Leonardo was in general a much less disturbed individual than he appears to be in the picture of him which Freud's essay gives us.

But what is left of this part of Freud's story after the historian of art has finished with it? Does the historian reduce the point of Freud's story *equally* for these three items? Or is there more point left to Freud's interpretation of, say, the "Mona Lisa" than of the kite memory?

We have good independent evidence that Leonardo became deeply involved in, and obsessed with, the painting of the "Mona Lisa" and hence that it had a personal significance for him. The historian's story concentrates on the cultural origins of the smile; it does not give a cultural origin to the disturbing character of the face as a whole. This suggests that the historical account of the "Mona Lisa" does not do much to reduce the point of Freud's story about her, or indeed of any other psychological story about this painting. In contrast, we have no evidence that Leonardo was personally obsessed with the painting of the "St Anne"; and this picture does not engender the disturbed fascination that the "Mona Lisa" does. It looks, therefore, as if the historian's story considerably reduces the point of Freud's account of this painting. About the kite memory, we have no independent evidence that this was psychologically important to Leonardo. The only thing that suggests it was important is the fact that Leonardo recorded it, and that it was the only memory he did put on paper. However, the trouble is that the historian's narrative now suggests a psychological explanation of the kite memory quite different from Freud's. It suggests that this memory is a reconstruction of some past experience of the sort Adlerians emphasize—a reconstruction in which he,

Leonardo, makes use of a current tradition and which springs from his wishes to be destined for greatness and to become great. So the historian's narrative makes Freud's story about this item look rather insubstantial.

The work of the historian also has a bearing on Freud's remarks about Reitler's article on Leonardo's drawing of coition. We have already discussed the errors that Reitler quite mistakenly claims to have found in this drawing. However, Reitler also points to other errors in it, which he claims are evidence of considerable libidinal repression; and Freud appears to accept this claim. Thus, Reitler points to the poor representation of the female genital, in which the vagina is treated as the *portio uteri* and the lines of the uterus are completely confused; as well as to the misrepresentation of the nipple, which is wrongly given as a single excretory duct, not a number of separate ones.

> It is precisely (Reitler says) in the process of portraying the act of procreation that this excessive instinct [of Leonardo] for research has totally failed—obviously only as a result of his even greater sexual repression.

A historian of science may find this contention quite implausible. Thus to O'Malley and Saunders[12] the important thing about this drawing (Q III 3 v.) is that it expresses almost entirely traditional notions on the act of generation, and is an attempt to harmonize the views of Avicenna and Galen. From Galen comes the belief that the sperm is derived from the testes, the "first cause" of man's existence; from Hippocrates through Avicenna comes the idea that the soul, the "second cause" of existence, is infused from the spinal cord, the site of the generative faculty. Consequently, the penis has two canals in the drawing—the upper conducting the animal spirit or soul, the latter allowing for passage of sperm and urine. The corrugated appearance of the uterus reflects the medieval idea that its cavity is divided into seven cells. The uterus itself was supposed to expand during coition, as Leonardo shows, and the cervix to open, according to some Arab authors, to embrace the glans penis. On conception it was believed that the blood of the retained menses was carried by the epigastric veins, as illustrated, to the breasts for the formation of milk. On the same sheet as this drawing are longitudinal and transverse sections of the penis, which are quite fanciful in representing the traditional view that it contains two passages. A drawing of the female genitals (Q III, 1 r.), leaves out the labia minora and clitoris; in a later drawing (Q III, 7 r.) the vulva and labia minora are now shown with greater accuracy and detail. In the famous frontal view of the anatomy of the female (Q I, 12 1.), the anatomical details are drawn for the most part from dissections made on animals, in an attempt to represent the Galenical system. The general view that O'Malley and Saunders take is that the reproductive organs of male and female are treated by Leonardo with a curious mixture of fact and fancy. Most of the figures have some objective basis, which is overlaid, however, by traditional theories on function. Again, and this is common in Leonardo's drawings, the earlier figures reflect primitive, medieval theories of generation which later on are replaced by drawings and text in which Galenical ideas predominate. O'Malley and Saunders also reject, in effect, the common belief that Leonardo did a great deal of dissection on human material. On the contrary, it is not certain that he ever became the possessor of a complete cadaver; his remark that he dissected more than ten bodies does not mean that they were complete bodies; and though he was undoubtedly a spectator at others' dissections, his notebooks only give good evidence that he personally dissected about seven distinct human items. These historians conclude that Leonardo was groping in his anatomical studies, as he sought to escape from a debased medieval Aristotelianism through a corrupted Galenism to the independence of science.

Now this historical account leaves the Freud–Reitler story about the drawing of coition with very little weight. For it is clear that we do not have to appeal to Leonardo's attitude to sex to account for the errors that Reitler pointed out. We can explain these by pointing out that the drawing was primarily a representation of traditional beliefs from which he had not escaped—beliefs that included mistakes about the nature of the uterus, the connexion of the nipples with it, and the behaviour of the uterus and the cervix at copulation. There is nothing surprising about his not doing the dissection of a female cadaver, which would have put him right. He did not do the dissection of a male one either, which would have put him right on the simple matter of the structure of the penis. He did not do any of this partly, no doubt, because he did not have the opportunities, and partly because, like his contemporaries, he had not escaped from a traditional outlook in which fact and fancy were not clearly and carefully distinguished. Hence, as the traditional doctrine stated that the breast milk came via a duct from the uterus, it would not occur normally to Leonardo, or anyone else, to examine cadavers or nursing mothers to find out whether the traditional doctrine was correct or not. So the historical account of his coition figure puts it back into its historical context, and removes its puzzling features in the usual way—by producing a coherent commonsensical narrative about it. The fact that this alternative can be offered reduces the weight of the Freud-Reitler story to negligible proportions.

But in spite of the strength of the criticism from the historians —whether this be directed against Freud's story about the kite memory or his view of the coition figure—Freud's narrative retains certain features which historical criticism does not touch. These features incline us still to cling to it, in whole and in part. Freud's narrative, let us remember, is an attempt to produce a *complete* story about Leonardo, or something approaching one. That is to say, Freud is attempting to cover the whole of Leonardo's life and work, and to fit it together into a coherent picture. Insofar as his story realizes this aim, it has weight and it impresses us. What is more important, the different parts of the whole story, in fitting together, lend one another mutual support. We saw an example of how this worked in our discussion of Leonardo's interest in flight and science. When therefore the historian has done his worst about some one part of Freud's story, such as the kite memory, this part of the story still retains the support that the *rest* of Freud's story gives it; and this fact inclines us to cling to it. Further, Freud's narrative brings Leonardo's life and work into intimate connexion with the inner history of the man, with his private world of unconscious motives, personal experience, and desires. This whole narrative may just be a novel, but it is nevertheless a profoundly interesting and stimulating novel, full of suggestion and insight. In contrast, the narratives of the historians seem flat and superficial. They do not penetrate to the inner recesses of the man; in a way, they tell us nothing about Leonardo—they give us no more understanding of him than we had at the outset. We also cling, therefore, to Freud's narrative because we want the sort of illuminating it offers us. We cling even though we know from the historians that some of this illumination is very probably only apparent and illusory.

VII

The historical narratives that we have considered only cover *parts* of Leonardo's life and work. Freud's narrative attempts to provide *complete* coverage of the data, or something approaching this. What reason, or reasons, are there which make it obligatory for us to accept Freud's complete story about Leonardo, rather than some other story of this same sort?

As Freud's narrative has to present a coherent picture of Leonardo, it follows that, if it is not completely coherent, it is not adequate, and hence less obligatory for us than an alternative story which is free from this defect. Is it, then, a coherent story or picture? Unfortunately, this question is only worth asking where the technical theory used to construct a story is a tight and precisely built one. We are then able to determine the logical consequences of any two statements in the story, and so discover definitely whether these two statements are inconsistent. But the technical theory that Freud uses is not of this sort. It is loosely and imprecisely built, so that it is not really worth while asking whether any story constructed by means of it is free from inconsistencies. The same is true of any other, complete narrative that can be offered at the present time. However, if Freud's story is to be a complete narrative of Leonardo's life and work, then it must cover all or most of the facts about him. Insofar as it does not do so—insofar as it leaves out bits and pieces—Freud's story could only claim to be a coherent narrative about *certain aspects* of his life and work. If we then found some alternative story with fewer omissions and a greater coverage than Freud gives us, we should have a reason for accepting this alternative story in preference to Freud's.

Let us ask, therefore: does Freud's story cover all the known facts about Leonardo or does it leave out any items? To this question it is tempting to give an emphatic answer. There are various aspects of Leonardo's life and work that the story does not cover. Thus, it does not deal with his marked personal fastidiousness. It does not deal with the obvious perfectionism of his art. Though the story does cover some of the content and form of his art, it covers very little of it. For example, it may cover the "Mona Lisa" and her facial expression, but it does not include the fact that she sits with folded hands against a background of rocks. Freud's story may cover the fact that Leonardo painted the "St Anne," but it does not include the fact that the painting takes pyramidal form, or the particular balance of forms which it shows. Nor does Freud's story touch on activities such as Leonardo's drawings of animals (which obviously fascinated him from his early years), his drawings and paintings of nature and of plants and flowers, his essays into architecture and sculpture (for example, the form of the projected monument to Sforza), the vitality and ferocity and animal vigour exhibited in his work for the "Battle of Anghiari," or the whole theme and quality of a work like "St Jerome." Then, if the mysterious smile of the later drawings and paintings conceals a secret of love, as Freud suggests, why the pointing finger, which appears in some of them? Is this not also part of the mystery? And did the finger not first appear very early on in Leonardo's life—in the Louvre version of "The Virgin of the Rocks"—when, according to Freud, Leonardo was still in the full bloom of creative vigour, and long before the libidinal upsurge of middle-age, which gave rise, allegedly, to his androgynous figures with Leonardesque smiles? It looks as if there is an aspect of the Leonardo mystery that Freud's story simply does not cover. Nor, of course, does the story cover the obsession of the older Leonardo with water and cataclysmic destruction; and it passes over such themes in the notebooks as his pessimism and his preoccupation with death. In short, and without going into further details, it is clear that Freud's story is far from providing a complete coverage.

But this tempting and emphatic answer is misleading. The reason is this. If Freud were trying to give us a complete, *scientific* story about Leonardo, *any* failure of coverage would be relevant and worthy of mention. But, as we have already seen, Freud is not trying to do this. He is attempting the less ambitious task of removing the inconsistencies and solving the enigma Leonardo presents. It does not necessarily matter, therefore, if the essay omits to deal with items that a scientific story would have to cover. It only matters if the essay omits to cover items that are concerned with the inconsistencies and enigma that Freud is trying to remove. Thus, it is perfectly true that the essay does not tell us why Leonardo chose to present Mona Lisa with her hands visible (which was a new departure in portrait painting), or why Leonardo was able to represent human flesh as though alive, or why the "St Anne" embodied the particular balance of forms it does. It is true, too, that the essay does not elucidate the important fact that Leonardo became an artist at all—an omission to which Freud draws attention quite explicitly. But these omissions do not matter because they do not contribute much, if at all, to the enigma that Leonardo exhibits. They do not appear to be inconsistent with anything else we know about him. Moreover, *any* psychological story at present would have great difficulty in covering these items. There is no current story that *can* tell us with any confidence why, for instance, Leonardo chose to paint Mona Lisa with her hands visible. Hence these omissions do not help us to distinguish between the worth of Freud's story and the worth of any other. The only omissions that are relevant are those which contribute to the puzzle Leonardo presents. In Freud's story these seem to centre round various aspects of Leonardo's personality, such as his perfectionism, and round the mystery and strangeness of his art. Consequently, though Freud's narrative has gaps in it, this defect is not nearly as serious as it may seem at first sight.

However, it can be maintained, this defect is quite serious enough. The relevant omissions in Freud's story, it could be said, are important enough to make it unwise of us to rely on this story alone. If we did so, we should only gain a very partial understanding of the character and work of Leonardo. Can we, then, employ these relevant omissions, or gaps, in Freud's narrative to distinguish logically between it and any alternative? Again, unfortunately, it seems doubtful whether we can make much use of them. Certainly we cannot use them with any decisive effect. Suppose we try, and we say to a contemporary analyst: "Look, Freud's account of Leonardo leaves out this and that and the other relevant thing. Surely these omissions are good objections to his account?" To this challenge the analyst can make quite a good reply. He can reply by using psycho-analytic theory to fill in and make good these omissions in Freud's essay. In other words, he can defend Freud's story by elaborating and developing it to cover the bits and pieces of relevance and importance that Freud does not deal with. Two different circumstances make it possible for a contemporary analyst to do this. Freud's story is an application of psycho-analytic theory; and this theory, like the typical theory in psycho-dynamics and psychopathology is vague and loosely constructed. Accordingly, it is relatively easy to apply and to extend the theory to cover features of Leonardo's personality that were omitted from Freud's early story about him. What is perhaps more important is that Freud produced his story in the early days of psycho-analysis. Since then developments in psycho-analytic theory have taken place which would enable a contemporary analyst to produce a much more sophisticated and better story about Leonardo than Freud did—indeed, a story in which most of the omissions in Freud's own account are made good. When, therefore, we are feeling critical of Freud's essay, it is just as well to remember that his was an early effort, and that better psycho-analytical stories can now be produced.

Still, we are considering Freud's account in this essay, not any later and better version of it. Do the relevant omissions in it help us to decide on its logical weight in comparison with an alternative? The best way of answering this question is to examine an example of a narrative which is an alternative to Freud's. Moreover, the ordinary person who reads Freud's essay may not be acquainted with any alternative story at all, or aware of how one can be constructed. In his ignorance he may be fascinated by Freud's essay. He may be trapped into letting the story get a monopolistic hold on him that is logically unwarranted. The simplest way to break this monopoly and to free his imagination is to outline an alternative story to the one Freud has given us.

Let us, then, consider a certain alternative which any contemporary psycho-analyst who is not a dyed-in-the-wool Freudian would perhaps agree was an alternative worth considering. For brevity of reference let us call it the "A" narrative or story—"A" being short for "alternative." The "A" narrative, like Freud's, also supposes that certain events occurred in Leonardo's early years which had a great effect upon him. It supposes that in his early years he suffered some great emotional shock or shocks, in which the security he had reposed in some adult or adults was shattered, and his love and affection for them apparently not returned. In other words, it supposes that as a child Leonardo underwent certain experiences which left him bitterly let down, and disastrously hurt and disappointed. These experiences may have centred round Leonardo's removal from Caterina to his father's house, which to him may have been an emotional betrayal and an injustice both by Caterina and his father. But it is not necessary for the "A" story to say, or seriously speculate about, what these traumatic events may have been. Next, the story also supposes that during and after these shattering events, the personal relations inside the family groups concerned were such that the child's deep disappointment was not repaired. For example, the personal relations may have been of a warm-hearted and conscientious, but utterly superficial and unseeing kind, in which the adults failed to make genuine contact with the child. Or, as an only child in a household of adults, his own childish needs may have been swamped and forgotten in an atmosphere that used his own intelligence and precocity to treat him as a little adult, with the consequence that he never had the opportunity as a child to learn how to love adults or children. The family relations, therefore, whatever they may have been, served to entrench or fixate Leonardo's fears of the dangers of expressing himself emotionally at all. Emotionally bitten once or a few times, he became forever shy. Hence his inability as an adult to reveal himself emotionally and develop an affectionate relationship with anyone. Hence his great reserve, his impenetrability, and the personal mystery that he presented to his contemporaries as well as to us. It is not surprising, therefore, that he should write as follows in the *Treatise on Painting*:

> In truth great love springs from great knowledge of the beloved
> object, and if you know it but little you will be able to love it only a
> little or not at all. . . .

Given his distrust of his own feelings, he will have to keep them constantly in check, and one way of doing so is to be distrustful, suspicious,
and sceptical of all those he finds arousing his feelings; to ask himself
whether he knows these people well enough to justify or warrant him
giving them his love, or whether they will not let him down also, as
he was let down in the past.

At adolescence Leonardo is faced by fresh problems. With the
development of the adult sexual impulse, he is threatened by the danger
of personal and emotional involvement. He deals with this in two ways.
First, he completes the development of the severe conscience that he
brings from childhood. This severe and puritanical conscience is revealed
right through his notebooks—for example, in his repudiation of the
struggle for money, and his hatred of cruelty; in the sublime and austere
character of the whole; in his total rejection of sexuality. "Whoso
curbs not lustful desires," he writes, "puts himself on a level with the
beasts. You can have neither a greater nor a less dominion than that
over yourself. It is easier to resist at the beginning than at the end"
(H 119 (24 v.) r.). Leonardo also dealt with the problem of his adolescence by absorbing his sexual energies into his creative work as an
artist, craftsman, and scientific inquirer. As he said himself: "Intellectual
passion drives out sensuality" (C.A. 358 v.a.). The upshot was to make
himself impotent. From his early disappointments he developed into a
sexually negative individual, a man whose genital functioning was
inhibited.

But the aspects of himself that he has denied—the aspects to
which he has failed to do justice—persist in breaking through and coming to the surface. Because he has repudiated the affective side of his
life, his repudiation contributes to make him obsessionally concerned
with it. But as his obsessional interest cannot be directly expressed, it
comes out in displaced and substitute forms. It comes out in the emotionally intense products of his art. It comes out in his obsessional
attempts to grasp and exhibit perfectly the beauty and truth of nature.
But just as he cannot ever achieve what he really needs—namely, love
and inner peace—so this goal of truth and beauty must be placed beyond
the limits of his own powers. Consequently, he always places his standards of perfection beyond his own actual achievements and powers. Hence
his perfectionism—his search for what is to him unattainable. Given

this personal compulsion, he is obviously disposed to adopt an epistemological position that does something to make his search for the unattainable a rational and justifiable enterprise; and indeed it looks as if he did actually come to hold a view of this sort. For in his *Treatise on Painting* he contends with passion that painting is a scientific activity, and it is the business of the painter and artist to present correctly, and therefore perfectly, the truth about nature. But clearly it is logically impossible *not* to abstract from certain features of nature when one paints it. Therefore, his epistemological position sets Leonardo a logically unobtainable goal. It is not possible to present on a piece of paper the whole truth about an item in nature. In this way his articulate attitude about his work—which his obsessional search for the perfect disposes him to adopt—serves in turn to reinforce his obsession.

Given, however, that this is the aim or goal of his work, it follows that he will be frustrated in his attempt to realize it. Therefore his interest in something—his impulse to understand it scientifically and to represent the truth about it visually—will exhaust itself before he has finished with it. He will then move on to something else, in search of fresh stimulus. Hence, in part, the catalogue of unfinished works. He dispersed his energies over a large range of fields, because he was a man of exceptional and many-sided abilities, whose interest could be aroused by almost any problem; and because he lived in an age which still accepted the medieval view that a complete knowledge of nature and spirit was attainable and could be embraced by one man. His gradual transition from art to science was not, as Freud would have us believe, a regression, but the understandable outcome of his obsessional attempts to reach an unattainable goal. When he tries to paint nature in the way he sets himself, he is inevitably frustrated and disappointed. But he is not in a personal position to face up to this fact. So, in effect, he gives up painting and art, and moves over to scientific inquiry. In this way he saves himself from the frustrating disappointment of, to him, unsatisfactory work in art, and yet he preserves his whole orientation, conscious and unconscious, to himself and his work. For in scientific inquiry he can now concentrate on discovering what, in his view, he needs to know about men and things before he is in a position to communicate this knowledge pictorially. In this way he can give scope to his obsessional search for perfection, while avoiding the inevitable pains of trying realistically to end the search in any one product of his genius.

But about 1500 Leonardo came to face the typical crisis of middle-age. Other submerged and denied aspects of his nature began to stir about this time—namely, his need to love and be loved, his need for genuine human affection and sexual satisfaction. When he came to paint Mona Lisa, he was aroused by her; she threatened to bring the submerged aspects of himself to the surface. Leonardo dealt with this danger by using her to symbolize the several-sided character of his difficulties. To him she became an object of loving approach and of frightened avoidance. She was the mother who had loved and nurtured him, and who, having completed her mothering task to her own self-satisfaction, had discarded him. She was the woman who held out the promise of adult love and sexual satisfaction, and yet who dwelt beyond the bounds of the attainable. She was the person who offered him the quiet authority and security of inner peace, and also the threat that he would lose his independence and personal isolation—the menace that she would devour him in the process of loving him and giving him peace. She was the figure who offered him the hope of real intimacy with another soul; and the fear that he would not succeed in realizing this hope of achieving genuine intimacy—the fear that, in spite of his efforts she would remain a being apart, remote, mysterious, and impenetrable. In painting Mona Lisa he put into the picture the different facets of his own personal conflict that she as the model brought to the surface. Leonardo did this in a way that makes the painting the perfect ambiguous figure. This is why it is so remarkable. It arouses in us subtle and endless contrasts of ambivalence about Woman. In this painting Leonardo has created an archetypal image of an *anima* figure—to employ Jung's terms. Hence its fascination for us.

However, to Leonardo the painting also represented a partial solution of his crisis. In putting into it the different facets of his own conflict, he achieved an expression of the conflict, and a measure of detachment from and mastery over it. So the painting of the Mona Lisa helped him to achieve some inner harmony, rather in the way that the patients of Jungians appear to do when they come to produce and articulate mandala-like figures. After this crisis Leonardo went on to express and master his difficulties in a similar manner. In particular, his paintings retained the central feature of the ambiguous Mona Lisa —namely the smile. But the solution he achieved in this way was far from complete. For among the aspects of his personality that he had denied was the craving for sexual experience and union. When this started coming up, he could not master it by means of the Mona Lisa figures and their features—the aid these could give him was not sufficient. He went on therefore to try to deal with this side of his problem by producing the androgynous figures of his later years—works in which male and female were blissfully united.

As we have seen, his obsessional search for the perfection of truth and beauty was bound to be disappointing, intellectually and personally. The chief source of his intellectual dissatisfaction is that, even if he were to communicate the truth and the beauty of nature and of man perfectly, he would not and could not communicate the secret of existence, namely, why God, Nature, and Life are here at all —the ultimate mystery of Being. When his dissatisfaction about this comes to the surface, he expresses and tries to master it in his usual way. He exhibits the mystery of Being in his work. His figures become quite unfathomable, very mysterious and occult; and the finger points to something outside the painting and beyond the limits of our world, to something that neither he nor we can say or solve. The chief source of his personal disappointment lies in the fact that his obsessional search for perfection is a symptom of his own personal tragedy. This search, being a displacement, did not bring him the satisfaction he sought by means of it. So, as old age came on, his unhappiness, his sense of personal failure, came to the surface. He came unconsciously to despair of ever achieving inner peace. Largely because of the way in which the security and happiness of his early years was shattered, he had developed a strong, unconscious dislike of the human race in general—a misanthropy that is revealed in many places in his notebooks. In old age he now lets loose his resentment and his hatred of man. He wishes to die and to destroy the world. This is what is revealed in his drawings of cataclysmic destruction. Here he invokes what he believes to be the most powerful force in nature, namely water. He invokes it to destroy mankind and all its works, and to drown himself and his own despair in the flood of universal chaos.

This, then, is an outline of narrative "A"—an alternative to the one Freud has given us. Clearly, it has affinities with Freud's and it is definitely post-Freudian in nature. But it is not orthodox Freudian psycho-analysis. It is more akin to the sort of narrative that a person influenced by Jung's thought or eclectic psycho-dynamics would provide. It also, perhaps, presents the sort of psychological picture of Leonardo that is implicit in the work of a scholar such as Heydenreich.[13] By outlining this alternative, we may do something to free the ordinary reader from the fascinated hold that Freud's account may have upon him. But how does this alternative help us to decide on the adequacy of Freud's narrative?

It will be evident to anyone who has listened to clinical discussions on ward rounds, in case conferences, and similar places, that there is a close resemblance between the discussion among psychiatrists, and others, over a difficult mental case, and a discussion over the pros and cons of Freud's story about Leonardo and the "A" alternative we outlined. What a psychiatrist does is to try to bring the case in question within the framework of some theoretical scheme or set of concepts and generalizations, or, conversely, to fit the latter to the particular case. Different psychiatrists are apt each to have his own preferred and slightly different scheme or set of concepts. In attempting to fit a particular scheme to the case, what happens typically is that certain features of the case turn out quite easy to fit into the scheme, whereas others prove more difficult; and that the scheme throws up certain illuminating suggestions about the case which may be worth following up, whereas it underplays and even neglects other features that alternative schemes will point to or emphasize. Which particular story about a case a psychiatrist, or other discussant, chooses at a case conference will depend primarily on his theoretical predilections; and in the absence of further new information about the case, rational discussion can only be continued by going on to examine these theoretical predilections themselves.

Similarly with the discussion about Leonardo. Here Freud and a discussant are trying each to fit his own theoretical scheme on to the data of Leonardo. It is clear that each scheme—Freud's and alternative "A"—fits some aspects of Leonardo with ease, omits some and has more difficulties with others, and that each sheds its own limited amount of light. Thus, it is clear that the concepts we use to construct the "A" story are able to deal easily with Leonardo's personal relations and his great reserve, his obsessionalism and perfectionism in art and science, and the misanthropy and despair of his old age. This alternative —at least when fully elaborated—would obviously give a student of Leonardo a great deal of illumination on these aspects of his personality. On the other hand, the concepts used in "A" give us only a thin story about Leonardo's psychological make-up (or "inner dynamics"); and about his erotic and sexual life. In these regions of his personality the "A" scheme is relatively unexciting and unilluminating. In contrast, Freud's theoretical scheme deals more easily with Leonardo's inner dynamics, his erotic and sexual life and the details of his inner development. Freud may be quite wrong in saying that Leonardo was a homosexual, that later he regressed first from art into science, and then—

with "Mona Lisa"—into an art that was a manifestation of his pre-Oedipal stage of development. But what Freud offers us here, though wrong possibly, is detailed and penetratingly suggestive. In any case, it may be easier to cover personal items, such as his fastidiousness, by a development of Freud's story rather than by the "A" alternative, or a development of it.

What Freud has difficulty in dealing with are Leonardo's intellectual and aesthetic interests, the range and the variety of his work, his perfectionism, and the development of his middle and old age. One feels tempted to say that what Freud tells us on these topics is thin and insufficient. On the other hand, Freud uses his concepts to cover the specific item of the kite memory. When we constructed alternative "A," we did not use its concepts to cover this item. By including the kite memory within his narrative, Freud ensures that it both gains and loses in strength. It gains in strength just because it shows that, unlike the "A" story, it can cover a highly specific and singular item such as this memory. It loses because in covering this item Freud is applying his scheme in a way that produces a result which lacks logical weight, and raises doubts about the validity of this application. It is important to emphasize this weakness in Freud's story just because he places so much importance on his interpretation of the kite memory. Of course, we *could* have developed the "A" story to cover the kite memory—by, for example, using the semi-Adlerian interpretation of it we have suggested before. But there is much to be said for not attempting this. The "A" story may be all the stronger just because it does not speculate about this specific item of the kite memory, thereby saving us from the trap that ensnared Freud—the trap of attaching undue importance and weight to the interpretation of this single item. Then, again, alternative "A" has the advantage of being a much *simpler* story than Freud's. It accounts for the central mystery of Leonardo and the puzzling character of his art without resorting to complicated hypotheses about erotic fixation on his mother, repressed sexual curiosity, regression to the oral stage, and the like. Furthermore, alternative "A" is much more commonsensical than Freud's story, and initially much more plausible in consequence. To this, naturally, a Freudian can reply that the simplicity of a narrative is not a necessary condition for its truth. The "A" story is only simple and close to commonsense because it is so superficial. It omits and underplays aspects of Leonardo's life which have to be understood and which Freud does attempt to penetrate.

When we have worked through the points of strength and

weakness in both narratives—where they fit easily and awkwardly, what they can cover easily and what they omit or under-emphasize, where they are suggestive and illuminating and where they are not—there is nothing more we can do. It is evident that the particular story one is inclined to choose about Leonardo will depend on which conceptual scheme, or theory, one prefers. If one's preference is for a classical Freudian scheme, one will opt for Freud's story, or some contemporary elaboration of it. One will then regard as relatively unimportant or insignificant those features of Leonardo's life and work that the Freudian story omits, underplays, finds it difficult to cover, and is not illuminating about. On the other hand, if one prefers a more Jungian scheme, one may opt for the alternative "A" which we outlined, or some variant of it; and again, one will regard the omissions, and so forth, of this story as relatively unimportant. At this point, any further discussion about Freud's essay will have to move on to discuss other things. The two outstanding questions we may then find ourselves discussing are these. (1) What reasons are there for and against these different theoretical preferences? That is to say, what are the merits of the rival schemes or theories? (2) Quite apart from the relative merits of Freud's scheme, how legitimate is it to apply this scheme—derived chiefly as it is from the psycho-analysis of living people and patients—to a dead-and-gone historical figure.

VIII

Let us take up the question of legitimacy first. In applying his theory to Leonardo, Freud relies on an argument from analogy. Consider again the kite memory. Freud's account of it can be exhibited in the following schema:

> Patients who report memories of the kite sort are apt to have homosexual wishes.
> Leonardo reports a kite memory.
> Therefore we have good ground for believing that Leonardo has homosexual wishes.

Likewise with the data as a whole which we have about Leonardo. He tries to apply to this the story he would apply if Leonardo were a patient. The application can be expressed in this schema:

> A patient who exhibits such and such a pattern of data is likely to be a person with a psychological make-up and pathology of this sort, namely . . .
> Leonardo exhibits such and such a pattern of data.

Therefore we have good reason to believe that he has a make-up and pathology of this same sort, namely . . .

How strong is this argument? Let us ignore the difference in logical form between it and comparable arguments in natural science, and therefore pass by the technical difficulties about it that will exercise the logician and the philosopher. The historian of art is likely to say at once that the argument is weak because the analogy is a poor one. It may be the case, for example, that patients who report memories of the kite sort are apt to have homosexual wishes. But there is an important difference between present-day patients and Leonardo, the difference, namely, that the latter, unlike most of the former, was acquainted with similar legends and pictures about kites and birds, as we have already noted. Hence the mere fact that Leonardo reported a kite memory does not make him resemble present-day patients in the other relevant respects. Freud is not entitled, therefore, to argue that we have *good* ground for believing that Leonardo has homosexual wishes. At most he could conclude that we have *a* ground for believing this.

There is another weakness in the argument which disturbs psychoanalysts, psychiatrists, and others in this field. It is doubtful whether Freud's narrative about the kite memory, or about Leonardo as a whole, can satisfy any of the criteria which analysts and others do in practice use to assess the worth of a psycho-analytical narrative about a patient, or about some item in his life. If this doubt is justified, Freud's argument by analogy here differs from the way it is used in the ordinary or standard psycho-analytic context. The consequence of this is to make the whole application of psycho-analytic theory to Leonardo a much more tentative and risky business than the bare bones of the argument from analogy may lead us to suppose.

We can exhibit the nature of this doubt in the following way. Let us imagine that Leonardo was actually a patient of a contemporary analyst, and that he had just produced the kite memory in the course of analysis. Suppose that the analyst at once interpreted this to himself and to us as the manifestation of homosexual wishes, in the way Freud has described. Let us imagine that we challenged him to support this interpretative story. He could defend it as follows. He could say that, if it is true, certain other things will also be true of Leonardo.

(1) A homosexual trend will be revealed in many different types of material in the course of Leonardo's analysis.

(2) The unconscious homosexual trend so revealed will fit together coherently, and so ring true.

(3) This interpretation of the kite memory will be consistent with what is already known in the course of analysis about Leonardo.

(4) This interpretation, when used appropriately by the analyst, will assist the further development of the analysis. It will turn out to be helpful and not obstructive.

These four items are, in effect, four criteria that analysts use in practice to assess the weight of an interpretation.[14] In other words, our analyst could defend his interpretation of the kite memory by saying that the whole and subsequent course of Leonardo's analysis will show whether the interpretation satisfies these four criteria or not. In so far as they are progressively satisfied, we will have better and better reason to accept this interpretation as correct. In so far as they are not progressively satisfied, we will have better and better reason to regard it as mistaken.

Obviously it is very doubtful whether these criteria are applicable to Freud's interpretation of the kite memory. Numbers 3 and 4 are definitely ruled out, because Leonardo is not with us to be analysed. However, it could be argued that, though numbers 1 and 2 are not applicable as they stand, analogues of 1 and 2 may be so. Thus, if we loosen criteria 1 and 2 to allow us to cover the rest of the data about Leonardo which the historical record reveals, we could then ask whether these two analogous criteria are applicable to Freud's interpretation of the kite memory. For we could ask whether a homosexual trend is revealed in the many different types of material contained in the full historical record; and we could also ask whether the unconscious homosexual trend so revealed fits together coherently, and hence rings true. But it is clear that, in this loosened form, these two criteria are rather weak; they serve merely to point to features of Freud's story about the kite memory which are logically inconclusive. Thus, if we try to show that the story satisfies the loosened criterion 1, all we can succeed in doing is to show that it gains support from the fact that other features of Leonardo's record lend themselves to a similar, homosexual type of interpretation. This is far from conclusive, because, as we have seen, the data of Leonardo are open, severally and jointly, to quite a different, non-homosexual type of interpretation. If we try to show that Freud's story about the kite satisfies the loosened criterion 2, all we can succeed in doing is to show that it helps to produce a coherent narrative about the data as a whole that Leonardo gives us. But the *same* claim could, and would undoubtedly, be made for a different interpretation of the kite memory, which formed part of an *alternative* story about Leonardo. Therefore criterion 2 in its loosened form also fails to differentiate logically between Freud's kite interpretation and an alternative.

It is clear that the same sort of conclusion is true of Freud's narrative as a whole. When an analyst deals with a patient, he usually works with and is guided by a tentative, developing, and perhaps not even expressly formulated narrative about the patient's psychological make-up and pathology. If we challenge him over this story, he can support it by means of criteria analogous to the four just considered. But Freud cannot support his narrative about Leonardo as a whole in this way; for it is evident that these analogous criteria are either not applicable to the narrative at all, or are only applicable to it in a weak and inconclusive way. When an analyst, or psychiatrist, or psychotherapist is faced by an actual case which he finds difficult to understand, he and his colleagues may form tentative but alternative stories about the patient. In these circumstances, a story serves to produce all sorts of expectations about the patient; and the alternative stories which are canvassed are apt to produce *different* expectations. Now the living patient in analysis is constantly producing fresh material, and this fresh material may serve to realize some of these expectations about him and not others. The analyst will look to this new material to help him to distinguish between the alternative stories, and so decide which one is to be preferred. But Freud cannot make use of fresh data from analytic sessions to distinguish between his story about Leonardo and an alternative. Indeed, with one exception, neither he nor we can make use of any fresh data at all about Leonardo, as the data are fixed in the historical record. It is quite clear, therefore, that there is this very important logical difference between a narrative about a living patient and Freud's story about Leonardo.

The one exception just referred to is the new material that may be uncovered by further historical research. In order for this to be helpful, the data in the material must be relevant; and the more relevant the more helpful. But the new historical data that may be uncovered in the future are likely to resemble the usual sort of historical material we already have about Leonardo. Now this material—the known facts about him, the notebooks, the paintings, and so on—is very massive and suggestive; but it is not very close to the sort of material that an analyst, psychiatrist, or clinical psychologist would ideally prefer to have about him. What these workers would prefer to have is material sufficiently close to the alternative narratives we can spin about Leonardo to enable them to decide with assurance which narrative is the strongest. But the historical material does not provide the sort of data that a clinical worker would try to obtain from Leonardo—if he were with us—in an attempt to investigate, say, Freud's suggestion that he was a homosexual. It seems unlikely that any fresh historical material will be different in this respect from the old. Hence it is unlikely that any new data will help us to settle the strength of Freud's narrative, in the typical way that fresh material about a patient helps us in analogous circumstances.

The conclusion, then, is that Freud's narrative about the kite memory or about Leonardo as a whole cannot satisfy two of the four criteria analysts apply to their narratives about patients, and only satisfies the remaining two in a form so weak as to make them of little help to us. This means that Freud's application of psycho-analytic theory to Leonardo in this essay cannot be confirmed or disconfirmed in the way that is characteristic of psycho-analytic stories about patients. Consequently, though Freud's essay is based on an argument from analogy of the sort that is typical of psycho-analytic discourse, the essay is a much more tentative and uncertain enterprise than the standard narrative about a patient. All this makes it clear that Freud's essay is not a typical, and therefore good, example of the sort of narrative he usually uses and offers about a patient.

How legitimate, then, is Freud's attempt to apply psycho-analytic theory to Leonardo? How far was he justified in writing this essay? It is tempting to say that Freud was quite justified in giving us his essay, because it is a *jeu d'esprit* which has raised questions of great importance about Leonardo, and which has forced us to look at artists in quite new and exciting ways. No doubt, if we do treat it as a *jeu d'esprit,* we cannot object to it. It becomes a justifiable exercise in intellectual high spirits that has had a great effect. But it is very doubtful if Freud himself, or the orthodox analytic tradition, has regarded the essay in this light. To Freud the essay was an undertaking that "did not perhaps provide any certain results," but clearly it was not just a piece of fun to him. Ernest Jones tells us in his biography that it was one of Freud's favourite works, and refers to one of Freud's letters in which he says that he, Freud, was unmoved by the "horror" people had expressed about it, because he was so pleased with it himself.[15] Ernest Jones himself takes the essay quite seriously; and it has recently been described as a "classic of psycho-analysis."[16] So perhaps it is safer to regard the essay as something stronger than a mere *jeu d'esprit.*

But how much stronger? Some analysts may be tempted to swing to the opposite extreme, and to regard the essay as a diagnostic and psychopathological narrative which has to be treated in exactly the same sort of way as a standard application of psycho-analysis to an individual patient. But we have seen that this essay is very different from the standard psycho-analytic narrative about a patient. Hence, if we view the essay in this light, it becomes an illegitimate application of psycho-analytic theory. On this view, Freud is trying to do with Leonardo what cannot be done, and should not be attempted.

A more cautious analyst, however, may be inclined to take up a more moderate position—which he could explain in the following way. Consider a patient who enters a mental hospital. He is examined and a full psychiatric report drafted about him. This report will include a diagnosis and, where it is deemed relevant, an account of his psychopathology. But if the patient is a difficult case to understand, the report may be very tentative about diagnosis and psychopathology; it may even not include either; or it may include *more* than one story about diagnosis and psychopathology. Suppose that, at the case conference on this puzzling case, an analyst is invited to contribute; and suppose that he spins a psycho-analytic story about the patient. Here the data or material of the case are temporarily fixed or given in the psychiatric report that has been presented to the conference. They are fixed for the time being in this historical record. In these circumstances, the analyst is likely to put forward his story tentatively. He will intend it to be taken seriously, and yet he will admit that he is speculating. He thinks that his story, or something like it, may be true; but he recognizes that it is only one among other alternatives. He concedes implicitly that it may be off the mark; and yet he hopes that it will not be, and that it will turn out to be a fruitful suggestion. In applying his theory to the difficult case in this way, the analyst is doing something that is not only legitimate, but very appropriate and often helpful. Now the moderate analyst can say that *this* is the way in which Freud is applying his theory to Leonardo. What Freud is doing is something very akin to what the analyst did at the case conference. He is offering a speculative story that is meant to be taken seriously.

It is clear that, if we describe Freud's essay in this cautious way, what he did becomes a perfectly legitimate enterprise. But, though we can legitimize the essay in this way, we can only do so at a price. The price is that analysts give up regarding it as the *only* story, or the only *sort* of story, that is or can be correct. They have to recognize that other alternatives can be produced that deserve consideration. Though these may all be post-Freudian alternatives, and in this sense also psycho-analytic in character, they are not alternatives of the sort that Freud himself would have accepted. What therefore analysts will have to give up is Freud's own way of regarding or thinking about his essay. They will have to say that Freud is at fault in supposing that it necessarily provides the only entrée to the truth about Leonardo.

IX

The argument from analogy on which Freud's essay is based moves us for an additional reason which we have not mentioned yet. Consider again the schema of the argument about the data as a whole:

> A patient who exhibits such and such a pattern of data is likely to be a person with a psychological make-up and pathology of this same sort, namely . . .
> Leonardo exhibits such and such a pattern of data.
> Therefore we have good reason to believe that he has a make-up and pathology of this same sort, namely . . .

The strength or weight of this argument depends, in part, on the strength of the major premiss. But the latter is part of the whole classical theory of psycho-analysis which Freud has applied to Leonardo. The strength of the major premiss, therefore, also depends on the weight of the theory to which it belongs. Now the weight of psycho-analytic theory is the additional reason that moves us to accept the argument from analogy. The more weight we are inclined to attach to the theory, the more will we be moved to accept the argument and therefore the essay. What weight, then, should we attach to the classical theory Freud used? As different psychiatrists, analysts, and others, are apt to attach different weights to different theories, and to have different theoretical preferences, what reasons are there for choosing to use classical analysis to understand Leonardo rather than some other theory? Is it more weighty than the others? What, in short, are the merits of the rival theories in this field?

These are very large technical questions which have been much discussed in recent years, but to which no generally accepted answer can yet be given. Accordingly, we shall not attempt to answer them here. We shall merely consider *one* reason for this inconclusive state of affairs—a reason which also throws some further light on the nature of Freud's essay.

The psycho-analytic theory Freud used, like psycho-analytic theory in general, is based chiefly on the evidence obtained from the analysis of patients. This analysis is carried out by means of what we shall call, for brevity, psycho-analytic method. This method has been quite extensively used, in different forms, over the last fifty years or so. But it has not been subjected to a careful scientific investigation in order to determine its validity. It is quite uncertain, therefore, how valid the method is. So naturally the theories that are based on its use are equally uncertain in evidential and scientific status. We can bring out some of the uncertainties about psycho-analytic method by considering the use Freud puts it to in order to explain Leonardo's kite memory.

The kernel of Freud's explanation of this memory is that in it Leonardo reveals to us that he has an unconscious concern with the homosexual idea of an act of fellatio. Freud supports this, as we have seen, by the usual argument from analogy.

> Patients who produce under analysis a memory of this kite type are typically patients with this unconscious homosexual concern.
> Leonardo has produced a kite type of memory.
> Hence he too has this unconscious homosexual concern.

Suppose we now challenge an analyst to produce the evidence to support the major premiss of this argument, namely that patients under analysis who produce a kite-type memory typically have this unconscious homosexual concern. In other words, we ask what is the analyst's evidence for holding that the tail of a kite (or something similar) represents a penis for a patient, and that beating a tail against and within his lips in his cradle (or something similar) represents the insertion and sucking of a penis? To this challenge the analyst could reply: "A memory-report of this sort by a patient is what we call a phantasy. That is, roughly, it is the report of something that did not occur, but which is the transformation of some past experience in accordance with an unconscious wish of the patient. Reports of the kite type are transformations of past experiences at the breast, and reveal an unconscious wish to suck a penis."

But suppose we challenge the analyst again. What is the evidence that the kite type of report is a transformation of some past experience, that the particular experience is one of sucking at the breast, and that the unconscious concern is to suck a penis? To this challenge the analyst might be tempted to offer the usual or typical reply. "The supporting evidence," he might say, "is to be found in the following facts. When in the course of the analysis of a patient, we analysts interpret the kite type of report, and related material, in this way, we find that these interpretations are apt to satisfy the four criteria we have already outlined and discussed; and the patient comes, after a time, to recognize for himself that these interpretations are true, including the hypothesis that he has an unconscious concern with sucking a penis."

Unfortunately, this typical reply from the analyst is far from being conclusive. The chief difficulty about it seems to be this. If the procedure of psycho-analysis were *only* one of discovery, if it simply *revealed the facts* about a patient to us and to himself, then this usual defence by the analyst might be adequate. But there is good reason to believe that the procedure of psycho-analysis is not one of straightforward discovery and revelation, like the standard methods of science. There is good reason to believe that it is a procedure which, whatever else it does, also *transforms* the patient in the direction indicated by the sort of interpretations the analyst uses about him; and that, in doing this, it helps to make the interpretations used about the patient appear to be true of him. The way this happens—though very complex and not yet adequately explored—can be grasped in outline when we take note of two features of psycho-analytic method.

(*a*) The procedure of psycho-analysis is tension-rousing in a way which, during the initial period, disorganizes the patient's beliefs about himself, attitudes in general, and so forth; and therefore makes him labile and hence suggestible.

(*b*) The analyst is concerned, *inter alia,* to understand the mass of material the patient is offering him. He tries to do this by ordering the material in terms of the concepts and generalizations of the particular brand of psycho-analytic theory he prefers. In so doing, he is constantly *seeing in* the material all sorts of subtle cues, fleeting items, nuances of attitudes and conduct, etc., which an analyst from a different tradition and using a different brand of theory might not see in the patient's material. In the light of what the analyst sees in the material, as well as of his own judgement, and so forth, he offers his interpretations to the patient.

Now, in these special circumstances of analysis, these two features, (*a*) and (*b*), have a profound effect. The suggestible patient comes to accept the interpretations offered him and to transform himself in the direction they indicate. These interpretations will then satisfy the four criteria discussed, but this fact is not sufficient to show that they are true. It is only sufficient to show that the analyst and patient are being jointly successful in changing the patient's personality and outlook. The fact that the patient comes to accept the truth of these interpretations is only enough to show that he has been converted to the new point of view about himself, not that they are true of him. But, as the interpretations helped to transform him in a certain direction, they helped to change him into a person of whom these interpretative remarks seem to be correct or true. We are all familiar with the well-known objection to psycho-analysis that Freudian analysts tend to have Freudian patients, Jungian analysts Jungian patients, and so on. The explanation of this and related facts may lie, in part, in the two features of analytic method we have just emphasized, and in the profound effect they exert in analysis.

Now let us return to Freud's interpretation of the kite memory, and the challenge to produce evidence in support of it. It is clear why the typical reply from the analyst is far from conclusive. He is challenged to produce the evidence in support of the generalization that "patients who produce under analysis the kite type of memory typically have the unconscious homosexual concern Freud described." It is not sufficient to reply by saying that in the course of analysis analysts discover that, when they interpret a kite-type memory, and related material, they find the homosexual interpretation of this item satisfies the criteria mentioned, and is accepted by the patient. In other words, it is not sufficient to say that this interpretation helps along the course of the analysis, helps them to spin a coherent psycho-analytical story about the patient and so understand him better, and so forth. It is not sufficient to reply in this vein because the very procedure of analysis itself may contribute to make the homosexual interpretation of the kite memory help along the course of the analysis, make it acceptable to the patient and so apparently true of him. The clinical evidence of psychoanalysis, therefore, does not provide conclusive support for the generalization that patients under analysis who produce a kite type of memory typically have an unconscious homosexual concern. But this generalization is the major premiss of the argument from analogy which Freud uses to support his account of Leonardo's kite memory. It follows that the clinical evidence from psycho-analysis in support of this major premiss is not conclusive, and hence that the whole argument is weaker than analysts normally suppose. Indeed, the position is even worse than this. If the outcome of psycho-analytic method on a patient is even only *in part* the artefact of the method itself, it follows that, unless we know *what* part is not genuine, any generalizations based on the use of psycho-analytic method will be infected with uncertainty. We shall not know what weight to attach to them. At its worst, therefore, it may be that when Freud spins us a story about Leonardo wishing to suck a penis, he, Freud, is himself just the victim or the prisoner of his own method. He may have been trapped by it into a set of beliefs about personality and its development which are delusive, in part or possibly even in whole. In giving us his interpretations of Leonardo's memory, Freud may merely be revealing to us his own delusions about mankind.

The ordinary reader of Freud's essay will probably not be acquainted with the details of psycho-analytic procedure, and of the sort of thing that happens in analysis. Consequently he may be unable to pass any judgment for himself on its validity. However, the essay itself is valuable here, since it throws some light on the sort of thing that goes on. Thus, we have drawn attention to the fact that in analysis the analyst is constantly *seeing things in* the material in the attempt to order and understand it. It is evident to us all, not merely to the psychologist, that this is a hazardous business. For the analyst will see in the material the sort of thing he is on the look-out for. He will read into the material features that an analyst of a different brand will not see there, and that the ordinary person will not see either; and the analyst will go on to use what he sees in the material as the kernel of an interpretation. Now, for reasons connected with the artefact-producing character of analysis, it is difficult usually to pin down examples where the analyst has read things into the material which are just not there, and where, accordingly, the interpretation he offers is just false. But in this essay Freud gives us one excellent example of this very thing, and another example of something close to it.

We have noted that Freud was misled by the German translation he used into supposing that the bird in the kite memory was a vulture. The first example is the "remarkable discovery" that Freud agreed had been made about the "St Anne" by the analyst Oskar Pfister, "even if," Freud acknowledged, "one may not feel inclined to accept it without reserve." Pfister claimed to have discovered the outline of a vulture in the drapery of Mary, and pointed out that the right-hand end of the spread-out tail leads to the mouth of the child. It is clear that, as Freud's whole reference to a vulture is a mistake, it is highly probable that Leonardo did not unconsciously conceal a vulture in the picture at all. Yet a vulture is just what Pfister saw in it; and Freud was sufficiently impressed to call this "a remarkable discovery." In short, Pfister and Freud saw things in the picture which very probably are just not there, and any interpretation that assumes Leonardo had unconsciously concealed a vulture in the picture is almost certainly false. The second example is Freud's interpretation of the vulture phantasy. If Freud is to give a homosexual interpretation of this which is *complete,* one of the things he has to do is to explain how

Leonardo comes to substitute a vulture for his mother. This Freud proceeds to do. He gives us a story the central point of which is that Leonardo was supposed to be acquainted with an ancient fable in which all vultures are females, and which he used unconsciously to produce his phantasy. Now Leonardo may not have had a knowledge of this fable, but Freud is prepared to see in the historical record sufficient evidence to show that he was acquainted with it. Let us presume that Freud is right here, and that Leonardo had a knowledge of it. Freud is also prepared to read into the situation a psychological connexion between this knowledge and the apparent fact of the vulture phantasy. But we know that there was no such connexion whatever, because we know that the phantasy was not in fact about vultures at all. So Freud's story is a piece of speculation which is unnecessary and false. The interpretation he offers us here is just incorrect. We can tell that this is the case in this instance, because we are fortunately placed in having an independent knowledge of the facts. But how can we be sure that *other* parts of Freud's story about Leonardo are not also the outcome of reading Freudian things into Leonardo's life and work, and also, therefore, pieces of speculation which are false? The parts of Freud's essay where he is concerned with the phantasy of the vulture are valuable and instructive to us just because they are wrong. In being wrong, they exhibit clearly and briefly one of the central difficulties about the validity of psycho-analytic method.

We have noted that at the present time there are rival theories or schemes in the field, and that the whole position is still quite inconclusive. One of the reasons for this state of affairs is the present uncertainty about the validity of psycho-analytic method. Because of the doubts about it, we are uncertain what weight to attach to a theory that is based primarily on the data that the method provides. But, of course, *all* psychoanalytic and cognate theories are in the same boat in this respect. Insofar as they rely on psycho-analytic method in some form, they are all of uncertain weight. Given, however, the weakness of all these theories, are there any rational grounds for accepting one of them rather than another —for accepting, say, a Freudian rather than a Jungian scheme? Accordingly, are there any further rational grounds for accepting the Freudian narrative about Leonardo rather than a Jungian one? The short answer is that there are rational grounds available to aid in a decision here, but these are far from being sufficient to settle matters conclusively and to obtain a general consensus. Thus, we can appeal to the simplicity of a particular psycho-analytic theory or scheme in contrast with another; its greater plausibility in the light of biological knowledge and current trends in medicine; its greater clarity; its wider scope and greater power, or richness, in generating clinical expectancies. But these criteria or considerations are not good enough, severally or jointly, to settle matters. For they only work well when the theories concerned are sufficiently developed and constructed to allow the criteria to be clearly and decisively applied. The typical theories, however, in the field we are dealing with are so poorly developed and constructed that the attempt to apply these criteria, far from settling matters, is apt to generate further heat and dissension.

But, naturally enough, a worker in this field usually does make some sort of decision about these psycho-analytic theories for purely pragmatic reasons. He has to handle the materials that the theories are concerned with; and he finds it practically necessary to take some personal stand about them. This decision, however, is largely the outcome of non-rational considerations. The particular stand he takes will depend on things such as his own philosophical position in respect of mind and science, and the sort of language he prefers to talk; the sort of personal psycho-analysis he has had if any; and, more subtly, the influence on him of his own self-analysis. This last is important, since no technical worker in this field can avoid self-analysis in some measure. If, in the course of this analysis, he has been trapped into using one particular psycho-analytic theory on himself, he will be moved to regard this theory as getting at something authentic and important, and better than an alternative theory that he has not found personally helpful.

What is more, the ordinary educated person is also under a little pressure today to take some sort of stand about these alternative theories in the field of personality and psycho-analysis. If he succumbs to this pressure, he too will be influenced by non-rational considerations. In particular, he is likely to be influenced by the personal impact that Freud and others make on him. His reading of psycho-analytical writings will set going some self-analysis; and if he finds some particular theory personally disturbing and illuminating, in whole or part, he will be moved to regard this theory as better than an alternative which does not disturb and illuminate. When, therefore, technical workers and the ordinary person consider the theory embodied in Freud's essay on Leonardo, there is a great deal of room for rational discussion about the merits of the theory and how it compares with alternatives. But a point may be reached when the perceptive among us will recognize that the intellectual conflict about these theories and theoretical preferences is being maintained by non-rational considerations. At this point, we can only take note that these are at work, accept and respect them, and pass on.

X

When we sought to understand our new next-door neighbour, we were in search of a narrative about him which removed the inconsistencies he presented, and which was true. In seeking to understand Leonardo, Freud has tried to give us a narrative of the same sort—one which removes the inconsistencies in his life and work, and which is true. How successful was Freud in this attempt?

It is reasonable to claim that Freud's narrative does seem to remove the inconsistencies fairly well, and to present a story about Leonardo which is coherent and which offers a good coverage of the data. But is it true? Clearly there are some reasons for thinking that, in its main outline, it *may* be true; and some reasons for thinking that parts of the narrative are stronger than others. Because it is apparently coherent, offers good coverage, and may be true, it does throw some light into the darkness surrounding Leonardo, and does do something to dispel the enigma he presents. However, it is also abundantly clear that we have little, if any, reason to believe, or to claim to know, that Freud's narrative *is* true. We are not logically obliged to accept it. What is more, our examination of Freud's narrative suggests that we are not logically obliged to accept *any* all-embracing narrative about Leonardo at the present time. There appears to be no alternative candidate in the field which compels our allegiance either.

What, then, shall we do when we are asked to resolve the enigma of Leonardo—to make him understandable? Shall we say that, as Freud's story or any of the current alternatives is not obligatory for us but is more or less inadequate, we shall refuse to spin *any* of them? Shall we, in other words, just decline for these reasons to offer any all-embracing narrative about Leonardo? Or shall we say that, inadequate though all these narratives are, we shall make use of one or more of them in order to throw what light they can on the puzzle that Leonardo presents? Neither choice is free from difficulties. If we take the former alternative, we lay ourselves open to the charge of being unreasonable. For we are overlooking the help that Freud's narrative, as well as the others, can give us; and we are, in a way, just revealing our personal decision only to use a narrative that we believe or know to be true. If we choose the latter alternative, we shall have to be careful to use our narrative, or narratives, with care. We must guard against falling in love with the one we happen to find most congenial, and, ideally, we should go out of our way to use several narratives to describe Leonardo, in order thereby to bring out their comparative strength and weakness.

The choice we make here is apt to be closely connected with the educational and professional background we bring with us. If we come to Freud's essay from the physical sciences, or experimental psychology, or the so-called "objective" study of personality, or an "objective" clinical psychology, or from an organically oriented psychiatry, or neurology and brain surgery—if we come to the essay from these and similar directions, we are likely to view Freud's story about Leonardo (or any alternative) with great scepticism. We will probably be disinclined to take it at all seriously. On the other hand, if we approach the essay from history or literature, or as a teacher from an eclectic background in psychology, or from functional or dynamic psychiatry—if we approach the essay from these directions, we will probably receive it favourably, and we will be ready to try to explain Leonardo by means of it, or some alternative. The choice we make here is apt to be connected with our educational and professional background for the following reason. If our professional training has been in, let us suppose, one of the physical sciences, or in experimental or objective psychology, we will have learned to use and operate with what can be called "a certain level of satisfactory proof." It is by reference to this level that we distinguish in our own specialism between narratives that are rationally acceptable and those that are not. When, then, we come to Freud's essay from such a direction, we will be apt to bring this level of satisfactory proof with us, and to judge the essay in terms of it. Now this particular level is a high one, and the essay completely fails to reach it. Hence we refuse to touch the essay. We regard it with scepticism and decline to take it seriously. In contrast, if our professional training has been in, say, literature, the level of satisfactory proof which we will have to use will be rather different from, and often lower than, the one we would acquire in the physical sciences. For instance, if we offer an account of Wordsworth's character, the requirements that our narrative will have to satisfy to be rationally acceptable will be less strict and severe than those typical of natural science. Consequently, when we come upon Freud's narrative, we will judge it in terms of a level of rational acceptability, or satisfactory proof, that is much closer to the one Freud himself employed. We will be disposed for this reason to receive it favourably and seriously. Therefore, if we judge the essay in terms of a high level of satisfactory proof, we will reject it, and any current alternative, as unproven. If we judge the essay in terms of a lower level of proof, we may decide that Freud's narrative, or some alternative, inadequate though it is, is good enough to use to throw light on the enigma of Leonardo. But whatever we choose to do, both courses run us into difficulties. If we refuse to use any of these narratives, we meet the objection that we are really only doing concealed propaganda for our own high level of proof, and are just being inflexibly impervious to the subtleties of the conceptual situation. If we are ready to use these narratives, we have to use them with a care and detachment that it is difficult for us to achieve and maintain.

However, whether we accept Freud's essay as unproven, or are prepared to use it, in part or whole, at a lower level of acceptability, there is one thing on which there seems to be general agreement. This is the enormous stimulus that the essay has given to critics and historians of art in their attempts to understand Leonardo. Moreover, the essay also seems to have helped, along with the rest of the Freudian corpus, to transform their general attitude to human nature, and to the work of the artist. This transformation may or may not be justified. But it seems to be a fact, and one that has been stressed in recent years. On the other hand, it also seems to be a fact that the essay has not given much stimulus to the historians of science—in their study either of Leonardo or of creative scientific work in general. Why the essay has failed here, and whether this failure is justified are interesting questions which, perhaps, the historians of science should try to answer.

The influence of the essay on the psychological world has not been large; and at the present time the attitude to it seems to be somewhat uncertain. Psychiatrists, psychotherapists, psychologists of personality, and even analysts themselves will be inclined to see in the essay an intriguing, courageous, but untypical exercise in the application of Freudian theory of the middle period. But they will also be inclined to regard it as having only a historical interest at the present time. To these often hardheaded people, many of them overworked in the day-to-day struggle to improve the mental health of their patients, the study of Freud's essay may seem to be just a piece of antiquarian research with no practical relevance whatever. "What on earth does it matter if Freud was right in supposing that Leonardo remained with Caterina for some years? Or if he and Reitler were wrong about the coition figure?" But this reaction is a mistake. Far from the essay being only a matter of historical interest, it has some contemporary and practical relevance.

It is a fact, no doubt harsh and unwelcome, that psychiatrists, analysts, psychotherapists, and others of this genus, do not yet enjoy a respectable status in the world of science and learning. They have not yet been accepted by their fellow-doctors, psychologists, and others as reputable partners in a joint enterprise. One of the sources of this state of affairs lies in the nature of their work. This work constitutes one of the most perplexing branches of modern science and medicine. An essential and large part of it consists in the attempt to diagnose and treat mental disorders; and an essential part, in turn, of this effort lies in the production and use of interpretations and interpretative narratives about a patient. At the present time, confusion seems to be fairly widespread about the nature of the whole attempt to diagnose and treat, and, in particular, about the character of the interpretations and interpretative narratives used in this work. The problem is complicated by the fact that the material concerned is often private and non-reproducible, complex and evanescent. Obviously it is highly desirable to dispel—as much and as soon as we can—the confusion and uncertainty that surrounds this whole enterprise on behalf of mental health.

Now when we are faced by a complicated problem, one of the recognized ways of opening it up is to consider it in some simplified form. We consider some situation, or condition, or what not, which is simpler than the one our problem is really concerned with, and yet which is relevantly analogous to the situation our problem is about. As it is a simpler situation, we can get to grips with it; as it is relevantly analogous to the one we are really concerned about, we will be able to generalize our results from the simplified situation we have examined to the more complex one we are really interested in. The value of this procedure depends largely on our success in hitting upon a simplified situation which is such that we can investigate it successfully with whatever methods we have at our disposal, and which is relevantly analogous to the one that really concerns us. This procedure, of course, is characteristic of scientific work. It is also, interestingly enough, one of the devices philosophers have learned from Wittgenstein. When philosophers wish to investigate a problem that involves the use of complicated concepts, they sometimes proceed to think of, or imagine, a situation where the concepts and the language they are concerned with can be studied in a simplified form.

What Freud has given us in this essay on Leonardo is a simplified case study. He has asked us to consider a narrative that is less complex than those usually presented by psychiatrists, analysts, and others about a patient. It is less complex in various ways. The data on which the narrative is based contain no material from psycho-analytic sessions, and so the narrative is free from the uncertainty that—as we saw—comes with material from this source. The data concerned are public, acceptable, and fixed by the historical record. Moreover, Freud's narrative, unlike the usual one about a patient, is good enough to reveal that it contains clear-cut mistakes—interpretations that are false. Yet, in a number of relevant respects, his narrative is very like the usual, full story that analysts and others produce about a patient. By examining it, therefore, we are able to get to grips with the complicated problem presented by the narratives used in the diagnosis and treatment of mental disorder. We can use Freud's essay to help us in our efforts to clear up and dispel the confusion that surrounds this work. The essay, therefore, is certainly not of historical interest alone, and the examination of it is far from being just a piece of antiquarian research.

In our study of the essay we have attempted to deal with the doubts and difficulties that the ordinary person is likely to have about it. We have tried, in particular, to make clear what credence we can attach to the essay as a whole and to various parts of it. In the course of doing this, we have also done something to exhibit the character of the sort of interpretative narrative that is central to the activity of many psychiatrists, analysts, and others. We have shown something of the rationale of this sort of narrative, and something of its difficulties, where it is reasonable and can make a contribution, and where its limitations are to be found. Whatever we may think of the value of Freud's attempt to understand Leonardo—whatever we may decide about the substantive answer he provides—we must be grateful to him for his genius and audacity in giving us this simplified case study of Leonardo. By means of it he has thrown light on the nature of the discourse we use about mental disorder, and helped to resolve some of the problems it generates. For this we are all in his debt.

17th November, 1960.

60. Leonardo, *Annunciation.* Florence, Uffizi.
Photo: Alinari-Art Reference Bureau.

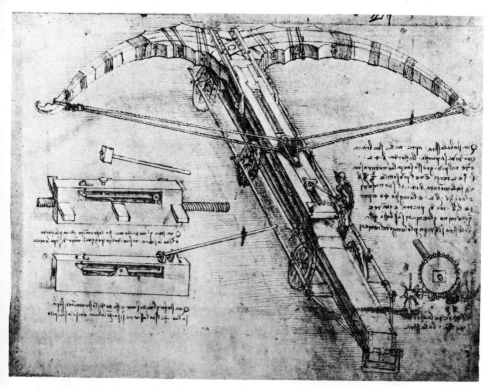

61. Leonardo, *Great Crossbow*. Facsmile of Codice Atlantico fol. 53v-*b*.
New York, Collection IBM Corp.   *Photo: Michael Katz.*

62. Leonardo, *A Study of the Deluge*.
Windsor Castle, Royal Library, No. 12380.

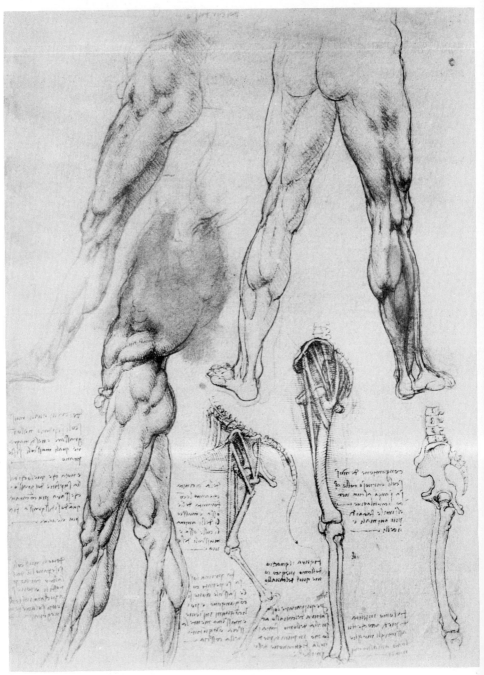

63. Leonardo, *Study of the Anatomy of Legs.*
Windsor Castle, Royal Library, No. 12625.

64. Leonardo, *Study of a Wave*.
     Windsor Castle, Royal Library, No. 12383.

65. Leonardo, *Stratification of a Rock*.
Windsor Castle, Royal Library, No. 12394.

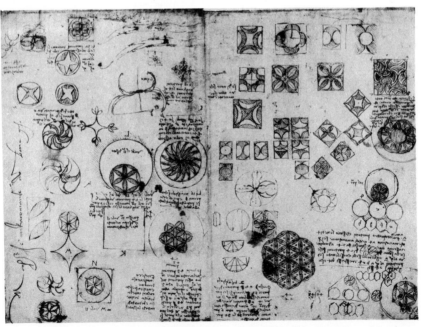

66. Leonardo, *Geometrical Games*. Facsimile of Codice Atlantico fol. 171-a.
New York, Collection IBM Corp.   *Photo: Michael Katz.*

67. Leonardo, *Old Man Meditating and Studies of Moving Matter.*
Windsor Castle, Royal Library, No. 12579r.

68. Leonardo, *Study of Star of Bethlehem.*
Windsor Castle, Royal Library, No. 12424.

69. Peter Paul Rubens, *Drawing After Leonardo's Battle of Anghiari*. Paris, Louvre. Photo: *Alinari-Art Reference Bureau*.

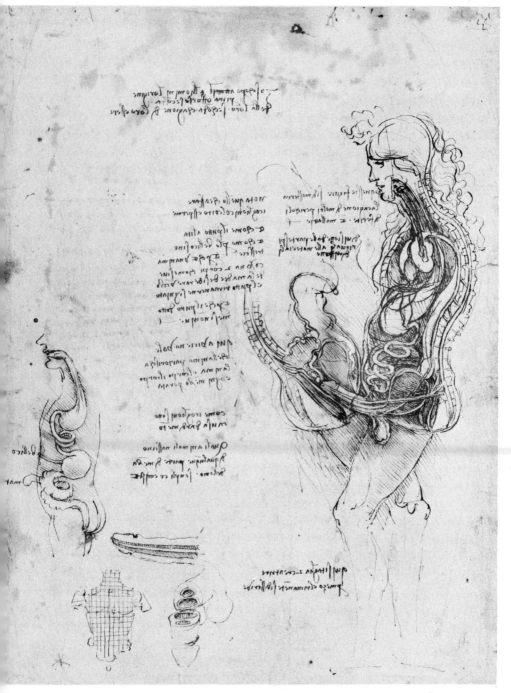

70. Leonardo, *Coition Figure and Other Studies*. Windsor Castle, Royal Library, No. 19097v. Quaderni d'Anatomia III, 3v.

Psychoanalytic Notes

by K. R. Eissler

SOME CONSTRUCTS

HAVE TO GO BACK to my initial construct that Leonardo's basic relationship to the world was a traumatic one, that is to say, that he was almost constantly on the verge of suffering a trauma unless he was geared to counter it by the proper measure. There are two ways of protecting the psychic apparatus against traumatization that are relevant in this context: one is to put the proper guards to the sense organs that are the portals of entrance of external reality; the other is to be capable of predicting the sequence of events and so to eliminate surprise.

PERCEPTUAL STIMULUS AND DEFENSE

For Leonardo the principal portal of entrance was the eye, and he never tires of praising the supremacy and excellency of that organ. To get an idea of how much this organ system was cathected, one has only to listen. He wrote:

> There is nobody so senseless who when given the choice of either remaining in perpetual darkness or losing his hearing will not at once say that he prefers to lose his hearing and his sense of smell as well rather than be blind.[1]
>
> ... whoso loses his eyesight is deprived of vision and of the beauty of the universe and may be likened to one buried alive in a grave where he can move and subsist.[2]

This almost equating of life and sight of itself shows the hypertrophy of the visual function. Indeed, it is necessary to assume a psychobiological factor that endowed Leonardo's eyes with an extraordinary degree of differentiation or sensitivity. The historian of art seems to draw the same conclusion. Thus Clark writes: "There is no doubt that the nerves of his eyes and brain, like those of certain famous athletes, were really supernormal" and on another occasion he speaks of Leonardo's "preternatural sharpness of eye" and inhumanly sharp eye.[3] Heydenreich[4] also believes that the ordinary eye would have been able to see only with the help of optical instruments what this artist's keenness of eye and visual awareness was capable of perceiving.[5]

Whether this is a constitutional factor or a disposition fortified by early stimulation or trauma one can only speculate. Mozart's auditory system seems to have been physiologically endowed with singular capabilities and I am inclined to assume the same about Leonardo's vision. I leave aside other sense systems since the visual was undoubtedly the leading one.

Leonardo's *sfumato* technique, the chiaroscuro, the advice to paint figures in twilight, can be brought into remote connection with attitudes derived from the protective barrier against external stimuli. But hypercathexis of sense organs, constant watchfulness for the minutest changes and details of external reality, do not yet provide a reliable guard against potential trauma. The influx of stimuli may, after all, excite the psychic apparatus unduly unless countermeasures are at hand. Perception may, to be sure, be followed by dangerous consequences: it may convert the self into the object perceived, it may cause destruction. Here I wish to consider the danger only in terms of psychic economy, that is to say, as a potentially unbearable excitation. In Leonardo's case the change aroused by perception is immediately converted into an act of depiction—hence the stream of sketches, of which, I am sure, we have only a small part despite the large number preserved. In going through Leonardo's work one gets the impression of a man who is constantly geared to observation and depiction, the eye and the hand being integrated into a centripetal-centrifugal unit.[6]

Goethe describes how while he is taking a walk a stream of verses goes through his mind, evidently the stream of sense impressions being reflexly converted into verses. I presuppose a like process in Leonardo, but here the medium requires a stream of alloplastic actions in the form of sketches and drawings. The stream of verses going through the mind does not have a discharge value as high as the discharge in the form of drawings and sketches which require, in contrast with auto-plastic thought processes, actual bodily movement.[7]

Despite important similarities between Goethe and Leonardo there is one principal difference: although Goethe too evolved his techniques for withstanding states of high-pitched emotional tension, we observe him for the first four decades of his life falling from one emotional crisis into another. The scanty data on Leonardo suggest a different course.

The impression one gains in Leonardo of a fixation to an opti-mal tension level enforced by hypersensitivity to oscillations is confirmed by the style of Leonardo's notebooks.[8] They are unique in many respects besides the external feature of having been written in mirror script. Hey-denreich characterized them as follows: "His literary remains, numbering thousands of pages, which record the whole of his life as he lived it, down to its daily details, tell us nothing about any strong inclinations, predilec-tions or aversions."[9] The personally intimate, the emotional, the subjective, that is to say, messages about his inner life, are with very few exceptions excluded. Moreover, there is seemingly a great disorder in these notes. Re-marks that seem to be disconnected appear in closest propinquity; repeti-tions are very frequent. The Arundel manuscript in the British Museum starts as follows:

> Begun in Florence in the house of Piero di Braccio Martelli, on the 22nd day of March, 1508. This will be a collection without order, made up of many sheets which I have copied here, hoping after-wards to arange them in order in their proper places according to the subjects of which they treat; and I believe that before I am at the end of this I shall have to repeat the same thing several times; and therefore, O reader, blame me not, because the subjects are many, and the memory cannot retain them and say "this I will not write because I have already written it." And if I wished to avoid falling into this mistake it would be necessary, in order to prevent repetition, that on every occasion when I wished to transcribe a passage I should always read over all the preceding portion, and this especially because long periods of time elapse between one time of writing and another.[10]

Here Leonardo himself ostensibly explains the style of his notes. But the reader whom he introduces occasionally is an illusionary person. Particularly in this instance he serves a rationalization. Somewhere Leo-nardo must have known that he would never publish his notes, but he wanted to justify the peculiarities of his literary work to himself.[11]

Clark characterized Leonardo's notebooks as follows:

However great or trivial a thought, Leonardo could not contain it, down it went at once, to get on as best as it could with cannons and jokes and geology.[12]

It is my impression that Leonardo followed here the same law that his sketches and drawings reveal. He acted under the inner necessity of writing down at the first opportunity whatever came to his mind.[13] A thought, too, as well as a thing seen, may become invested with intense emotional charges and I surmise that the act of writing down had the function of dismissing it, or was, at least, an attempt at achieving this effect or at a reduction to the optimal level of the inner tension that was created by thinking.

Although these notes preserve the logical structure, although they are witnesses of highly elaborate ratiocinations, they still share something, in my opinion, with free associations. Since touching the emotionally explosive was apparently forbidden, this mind had to try to concentrate at all costs on the reasonable. Thus we see it constantly observing and either picturing the content of these observations or digesting them in the form of elaborate ratiocinations that have to be written down immediately. In the course of time or periodically the ratiocinative part absorbs more and more of Leonardo's energy and the last few years possibly are spent without any artistic activity to speak of. Indeed, science is a better protection against trauma than the arts. If everything is known surprise is excluded. Arbitrariness, or what appeared arbitrary, was Leonardo's great enemy, and the finding of a cause reduced the area from which a trauma might arise.

But into how large an area of the unknown can the ratiocination even of a lifetime bring light? When a cause is discovered this requires new explanations, and the mind must not rest since just at such a moment a trauma may arise from the unknown, the unpredicted. But whenever the anxiety is temporarily assuaged by a discovery, by a new assertion that nothing is subjected to arbitrariness, that is an occasion for rejoicing.

Thus he wrote when discussing the meeting of all rays of light at one point such as the eye:

O marvellous Necessity, thou with supreme reason constrainest all effects to be the direct result of their causes, and by a supreme and irrevocable law every natural action obeys thee by the shortest possible process!

Who would believe that so small a space could contain the images of all the universe? O mighty process! What talent can avail to penetrate a nature such as these? What tongue will it be that can unfold so great a wonder? Verily, none! This it is that guides the human discourse to the considering of divine things.

Here the figures, here the colours, here all the images of every part of the universe are contracted to a point.

O what point is so marvellous!

O wonderful, O stupendous Necessity thou by thy law constrainest all effects to issue from their causes in the briefest possible way!

These are the miracles ... forms already lost, mingled together in so small a space, it can recreate and reconstitute by its dilation.[14]

Solmi cites this passage to demonstrate that Leonardo transforms science into a sort of religion, and Freud in agreement with Solmi gives a beautiful account of how Leonardo transforms love and hatred into intellectual interest.[15] "With the persistence, constancy and penetration," Freud continues, "which is derived from passion," he devotes himself to investigation, and at the climax, when the goal is reached, the affect breaks loose and he indulges in ecstatic language.[16] What I wish to stress in this context is that this affect of joy is totally devoted to the idea of absence of arbitrariness in nature and her following a regularity that is enforced by necessity. On occasions of such joy one feels a fullness of passion in Leonardo's words. This may appear like a contradiction to Freud's thesis that Leonardo's capacity to love fully was injured. This free flow of strong emotion when exulting over the predictability of nature seems, however, to confirm Freud's basic proposition about Leonardo's emotional life, since such exultation, passionate though it be, cannot be regarded as a flow of love toward an object.

If this view regarding Leonardo's being under the necessity to combine perception and depiction is accepted, then we shall draw the conclusion that the graphic work with which Leonardo interrupted his dissections did not make his anatomical investigation more difficult, but to the contrary, made it possible. If he had not had the opportunity of discharging the tension evoked by the terrible things he had to see, by re-creating them immediately and rendering them beautiful, he would, in my opinion, have been compelled to accept what Galen and Avicenna had taught, and leave dissection to others, as did the professors in their lofty pulpits.

Thus we see him exploring the whole of the inside of the body, the womb and the child in the womb; and one erroneous traditional assumption after another fell aside under the unswerving scrutiny of his courageous, steady eyes.

The record, however, does not seem to confirm a conclusion Freud apparently drew, namely that Leonardo's unquestionable sexual repressions impeded his scientific inquiry into the subject of sex.[17] Leonardo's anatomical drawings show him exploring the genitourinary system as objectively, eagerly, and successfully as other organ systems.[18] There are at least twelve coition studies in his anatomical drawings, certainly more than in any of our best textbooks of physiology, which shows that the inquiring mind did not stop at investigating that which in his personal life was taboo. To be sure his attitude toward sex would make one rightly expect a grave deficiency in that area, but as genius in general is a phenomenon contrary to expectation and common sense, so here also, in one of his greatest accomplishments, Leonardo contradicts a rule of thumb that seems justified in terms of theory.

HYPERTROPHIED FUNCTION AND STRUCTURE

In looking for a biological equivalent we may, though not quite correctly, compare the production of such extraordinary achievements as abound in the course of Leonardo's life with the immense increase in functional capacity that results from organic hypertrophy. What follows is a speculation about the processes that may lead to such hypertrophies of single functions as we can observe in Leonardo.

It is not probable that the eminent accomplishments of artistic geniuses depend primarily on the contents that are repressed in the course of development. Further research, I can well imagine, may, however, demonstrate that certain repressed contents favor or disfavor the evolvement of artistic abilities. The present perspective of psychoanalytic theory and research rather suggests seeking the specific reasons for artistic accomplishment in the structure of the ego and its relations to reality, drives, and superego. In turning to these relations, again according to the present stand of theory, the defensive functions of the ego are of principal interest.

What is meant by the concept of defense is pretty clear. In order to avoid displeasure (usually in the form of anxiety) or even injury the ego tries to eject totally or partially from its territory anything or everything that may cause displeasure or do harm. If ejection is not possible, compromises are made; the offensive agent may be removed to a part where it is less injurious; it may be converted into a less dangerous agent; it may be isolated, etc. Very decisive in the defensive struggle is the structure of the agency that carries out the defense. In ordinary circumstances the ego, from its genetic inception, develops particular mechanisms, such as repression or identification and others, upon which the task of carrying out the defense devolves. Yet from clinical experience one knows that the ego may use other tools than mechanisms for such purposes.

In the so-called psychopathic states one observes that the ego may use an instinct for the purpose of defense. Thus, a personality type reminiscent of Don Juan indulges in promiscuity in order to combat strong homosexual impulses. His endless amorous adventures can be regarded as having the defensive meaning: "I am sure that I am not a homosexual because I go to bed every night with another woman." He has to display his heterosexual leanings most conspicuously in order to convince others as well as himself that he is without homosexual wishes. The fact that in this type drives are used for the purpose of defense does not mean that defense mechanisms have not been evolved as well. It only means that the array of defense mechanisms is not strong enough or does not work properly to safeguard the ego, and it therefore becomes necessary to engage a drive in the work that would ordinarily be assigned to a specific mechanism or a pattern of mechanisms.

In such an instance, in order to maintain the defense against homosexuality, the ego relies mainly on the gratification of a drive. The advantage of such a defense is that it gains in pleasure, which is lost—at least partly—by the full establishment of a defense mechanism. The disadvantage of a defense by instinctual gratification is evident. The ego is greatly limited in its flexibility and becomes totally dependent on the regular and proper supply of this form of gratification. It may have to spend all its energy and activity on this one function and therefore become very limited in its contact with reality and the evolvement of other functions; and further, since society may disapprove of the defense chosen, a serious conflict may result between community and subject.

Another group in which the insufficiency of defense mechanisms can be observed is the schizophrenic disorders.[19] A comparison taken from biology may illustrate how the defense can lead to severe dysfunction. It seems that in some, though rare, instances of certain infectious disorders antibodies do their work of defense with great rapidity. The toxins excessively liberated in the process of annihilating the invaders damage the host and lead to his death. Older people whose reaction to the infector is slower have in these instances a better chance of survival.

The defenses in schizophrenia also render a poor service to the ego, which must pay a formidable price for the little protection it obtains.[20] Projection, to cite an example, enables the ego to rid itself of an internal source of displeasure by moving it to a point outside of the confines of the self. In schizophrenics this process is so fulminantly carried out that the most important reality functions fail in accomplishing their assigned tasks. The visual and auditory senses, thinking, and other functions carry out the projection and cease to perform their work in the service of the reality principle according to which the correct data of the external world are to be conveyed and digested by reality-adequate thinking. Thus we see in this instance also that when defense mechanisms are weak reality functions tend to be burdened with the task which should have been entrusted to the mechanisms.[21] Yet whereas in the psychopathic states the function carrying the bulk of defense is per se not disturbed but only misapplied or misused or intensified beyond the optimal, we observe in the schizophrenic disorders an actual damage of reality-related functions; they are absorbed in their service of the function of defense to the detriment of their ability to cope adequately with reality.

From the preceding the reader will recognize what I am aiming at. I surmise that the hypertrophy of single functions in Leonardo was caused by the eminently defensive task they had to fulfill.[22] As in psychopathic states and in schizophrenic disorders, the structure of the ego being weak and lacking in the evolvement of solid defense mechanisms, the necessity arises of burdening reality-related ego functions with the task of defense. In a genius like Leonardo it must also be assumed that a deficit in structure not only made the functional hypertrophy possible but made it an absolute necessity. The necessary state of equilibrium would then have depended on the maximal activation of these creative functions.

When Walter Muschg says that the poet's kinship with the criminal and the mentally diseased is unmistakable,[23] he refers to this clinical factor that all three of them have in common. Indeed, we may occasionally observe how creativity, when it does not adequately fulfill the function of defense, may change into either form of psychopathology.[24]

Another point one may find in common is a "fuzziness" between self and object which can best be described in terms of Piaget's research. In an early developmental phase when the infant is on his way to forming a concept of objects but has not yet reached that point, action toward the object per se or the manipulation of the object is equated with the object. "The object is still nothing but a prolongation of the child's activity."[25] In that phase it is impossible "to speak of the object as existing independently of the activity. The objective is in the direct extension of the act. It is as though the child did not dissociate one from the other and considered the goal to be attained as depending on the action alone."[26] This reduction of the objectiveness of objects is definitely encountered in many psychopathic states with their usual hyperactivity and insistence and lack of empathy with objects, and in some schizophrenics in whom not only is the world of objects made dependent on magic gesture or maintenance of certain thoughts, but attention and interest are moved away from objects and concentrated in individually varying ego functions. In the artistic genius in general and Leonardo in particular one can dimly perceive something similar, despite the great devotion to objects, their observation and study, and Leonardo's incessant preoccupation with them. Despite his incredible attachment to the world of things there remains the necessity to re-create them, and, as I will point out later, at times to re-create them in a better shape than they ever existed. The created work of art, be it a simple sketch or an accomplished painting, is necessarily a prolongation of the artist's self, at least in the creative moment and probably for a while thereafter, and the most valuable object, at least the one closest to the creative person, becomes one that is nothing but "the prolongation" of the artist's activity. To be sure, these objects do not exist in reality independently of his activity.

This reduction of the objectiveness of objects is, I believe, a prerequisite to the creation of great art. It is an indispensable admixture of considerable narcissism to ego functions directed toward reality. It probably is essentially related to the initial observation that object-related ego functions have to serve purposes of defense because of a relative weakness of ego structure.[27]

To summarize: we assume that Leonardo's ego was poor in structure, that his defense mechanisms were, for whatever reason, poorly developed or perhaps did not develop at all—which is hardly imaginable— and that therefore defense depended wholly or mainly on the activation of creative functions. This model may tentatively illuminate some of the peculiarities of Leonardo's creativity.

At this point we may rightly raise the question whether anything is known in Leonardo's life that may throw some light on the genesis of the deficit in structure that I have postulated. I would like first to report briefly on an observation I have made in Goethe's development.

In Goethe's life, which is so richly documented, one discovers a process during adolescence that indicates a melting down of ego structure. Whether or not such a process should be called a psychosis is of no relevance here. Suffice it to say that a deficit of ego structure in the adult is not necessarily caused by a slowing down or inhibition of structurization during childhood or the latency period, but may be caused by later processes. In Goethe's case one can observe with some reliability how his poetical talents, already considerable before, more or less suddenly gained in originality after the short-lasting phase of melting down and that he then became capable of producing a new style of poetry that became character-istic of him and led to his greatest lyric achievements. I concluded that this melting down of structure was a turning point that released the activation of functions previously inhibited.

In the light of this observation I was struck by the fact that Sir Kenneth Clark reaches the conclusion that in Leonardo's youth there was a period lasting approximately four years of a well-nigh complete stand-still in artistic creativity. He writes:

> We must assume that Leonardo, like other young men with great gifts, spent a large part of his youth in what is known as doing nothing—dressing up, talking, taming horses, learning the lute, learning the flute, enjoying the *hors d'œuvres* of life, till his genius should find its true direction.[28]

This period of "doing nothing" would cover the years from 1474 to 1478.

It has also been noticed that Leonardo's early paintings, however outstanding they may have been, are not of such quality that one could have anticipated the eminence he later actually attained. Thus Clark writes that Leonardo's "early pictures are less good than we should expect them to be."[29] He excepts the portrait of Ginevra de Benci, in which Leonardo's genius does show itself. However, whereas Clark dates this painting at 1474, others, like Heydenreich and Suida, date it in the period after 1478.[30] If these authors are correct we observe an early period of painting characterized by productions less compatible with Leonardo's later eminence separated by approximately four years from a second, in which Leonardo's pictorial genius showed itself in its full magnitude.

We know of two events that took place during these four years: the birth of Leonardo's first sibling and his denunciations as a homosexual. Now we hear from the historian that the two years before and after these events Leonardo probably spent in doing nothing, that is, did not devote himself seriously to his great mission.[31] I have previously postulated a possible connection between the arrival of a sibling and the suspicion of overt homosexuality. Tentatively I now raise the question whether during these years there took place, as I suggested before, processes that caused the melting down of ego structure. It would help explain—if the Benci portrait was really painted after 1478—why Leonardo, after a compara-tively long period of leisure, more or less suddenly reappears as a painter of unusual stature.

However, Leonardo's dependence on creative and selected reality-related functions in turn made him vulnerable not only to trauma in general but also to stimuli which these functions were unable to cope with. Biographers such as Heydenreich have noticed that Leonardo was compelled to transpose contents into something visual. Mechanics is for him a visual science.[32] Visual representation amounted to accomplished insight. "Leonardo's imagination is a visual one; if a problem is capable of being presented visually, then the presentation amounts for him to scientific proof."[33] Error became inevitable "when he encountered limits beyond which his wholly visual powers of observation could not function."[34] And at times it was not just error but a falling back on authority against which he had so valiantly fought. "When Leonardo reached the limits of his own sensory perception he fell back on traditional theories."[35]

Those authors who claim that science was for Leonardo always visual science seem to me to be very right. The *saper vedere* is the exclusive tool with which the world is to be approached and can be approached. How much Leonardo was aware of his helplessness vis-à-vis the nonvisual world can be fathomed from the following: "Since the eye is the window of the soul, the latter is *always* in fear of being deprived of it."[36] Here we have a documentation of his pervasive fear of trauma, and from his equating death and blindness, as cited earlier, we learn that seeing is the only protection against death. Because of the weakness of the protective barrier against inner stimulation, the mind must be constantly absorbed by external visual stimulation. I have quoted earlier Leonardo's advice to recall at night when lying in bed the forms one has studied during the day.

Voluntary concentration on the recall of recent reality experiences is intended to help in avoiding exposure to internal stimulation. It is necessary to assume that unconscious contents can be kept away from consciousness without the mechanism of repression being fully developed, merely by concentrating all available energy on external contents. This hypercathexis of external reality may impede the intrusion of contents that make up the repressed but which in this instance I cannot rightly call the repressed since I presume that the corresponding mechanism was poorly involved. To be sure, we must presume a fixation to the scoptophilic instinct, but here I am discussing only in what way the visual function assisted the ego in maintaining its organization.

If we consider the utter ruin a breakdown of the visual function would have wrought upon Leonardo's personality, the hypercathexis and constant activation and eminent efficiency of this function may become better understandable. In connection with the relative deficiency I have postulated with regard to the working of defense mechanisms in a genius like Leonardo, I must briefly point to an adjunctive factor. The melting-down process sets in at a time when the ego has to bear increased stress (adolescence in Goethe's instance, delayed adolescence [?] or unknown traumata in Leonardo's). Since the ego proves itself to be unprepared for the solution of tasks imposed upon it we must presume that it has entered this phase in an already weakened condition. I suggest that the cause for this weakness lies in the genius's being possessed of unusual innate talents, which, we may assume, already make themselves noticeable in childhood or even in infancy. I do not think that this necessarily results in unusual achievement but at least in increased interest on the part of the child in the activation of those functions that are favored by the constitutional endowment.[37] If the child's attention and interest are already concentrated upon these functions at an early age, an unduly large preemption of energy by these functions may even then retard the evolvement of solid defense mechanisms. The eminent energic discharge value of these functions must also be considered.[38]

With justification it will be said that, quite independently of the correctness or incorrectness of these views, my hypothesis by centering in the function of defense elucidates the least interesting aspect of creativity. To be sure, my hypothesis does not explain more than the reason why in two subjects with equal endowment only mediocre achievements may be forthcoming in one case and eminent ones in the other. However, if the melting-down process is confirmed, a factor in the etiology of geniushood more relevant than any role that can properly be assigned to the factor of defense may have been found.

At this point one may properly be called upon to demonstrate why in the genius the loss of structure leads to hypertrophy of function, that is to say, the emergence of unique creativity, whereas in the schizophrenic a breakdown and disorganization of the personality is the result. The difference in specific endowment, I believe, is not decisive, for in a relevant number of patients one can observe that even the greatest gifts leave the patient unprotected against the ravages of the disease. For obvious reasons I am unable to contribute an answer to this question, any more than to that of the essence and origin of the psychological factor or set of factors involved in geniushood.

NOTES ON LEONARDO'S ARTISTIC CREATIVITY

Although the factor of communication is stressed in conjunction with creativity in general and Leonardo's drawings specifically, I am inclined to see in it only a secondary motive comparable to the secondary gain in neurotic illness.[39] To be sure, Leonardo himself writes quite frequently about communication. He sets up rules about how an object is to be represented so the beholder will obtain full knowledge of it and even greater knowledge than if he were observing the real object. Many other remarks can be cited that may show the importance of communication as a driving force in Leonardo. And still, when we acknowledge in Leonardo the necessity of observation as primary in order to maintain the coherent organization of his self, we may conclude that the act of depicting was likewise dictated by an equivalent basic necessity.

It seems to me that it was the basic necessity of defense against the fear of death that was strongly involved in Leonardo's stream of graphic creations. "For we part from the body with extreme reluctance, and I indeed believe that its grief and lamentation are not without cause," he wrote.[40]

The connection between creativity and defense against the fear of death is adumbrated in the following:

> O thou that sleepest, what is sleep? Sleep is an image of death. Oh, why not let your work be such that after death you become an image of immortality; as in life you become when sleeping like unto the hapless dead.[41]

This fear of death, translated into abstract psychological terms, amounts to a feeling that the self is under a constant threat of disorganization,[42] and the poignancy with which this fear would be felt is understandable in view of Leonardo's deficient structure, his decreased barrier against inner stimulation, his increased vulnerability to trauma, and his ego's dependence on a limited number of hypertrophied functions. Since the created work is, after all, at bottom a projection of the self, its survival, its enduring beauty, are potent counteragents against the fear of annihilation. Leonardo wrote:

> Behold now the hope and desire of going back to one's own country or returning to primal chaos, like that of the moth to the light, of the man who with perpetual longing always looks forward with joy to each new spring and each new summer, and to the new months and the new years, deeming that the things he longs for are too slow in coming; and who does not perceive that he is longing for his own destruction. But this longing is in its quintessence the spirit of the elements, which finding itself imprisoned within the life of the human body desires continually to return to its source.
>
> And I would have you know that this same longing is in its quintessence inherent in nature, and that man is a type of the world.[43]

This passage in Leonardo's writings is considered a meditation on life and death or a definition of life, whereas I should like to point out its psychological implication.

It strongly suggests that Leonardo may have experienced longing as per se closely connected with death. Longings, as Leonardo so rightly says, imply a dissatisfaction with the speed of time and contain the desire for acceleration of time, that is, indirectly, an earlier approach of death.[44] Yet man, approaching the fulfillment of longings, usually experiences the fulfillment of life, and the associations of longing and death in Leonardo may—despite the fact that similar opinions are expressed by philosophers—betoken his own aversion against longings and satisfactions. "Neither promise yourself things nor do things if you see that when deprived of them they will cause you material sufferings"[45] is again another aspect of Leonardo's fight against exposure to tension created by longings. Creation, however, seems to make an artist of Leonardo's type independent of longings and therefore proves a powerful agent against an accelerated approach of death.

The difficulty inherent in the problem under discussion is quite great and therefore the tentativeness of my inferences may be pardoned. What makes a discussion of the psychology of Leonardo's artistic creativity so difficult is the apparent impossibility of finding a common denominator of the two principal visual arts he was most proficient in: drawing and painting. A large number of drawings from Leonardo's hand are in existence. Most of them are of incredible perfection, the objects limned with a surety and vividness, with a dynamic power that conveys absence of any doubt or hesitation. Most of them were probably turned out with great rapidity. Clark has given us a very able description of the spirit in which they were produced,[46] and it is this part of Leonardo's artistic work that seems to speak strongly in favor of my thesis that depicting was a function ever ready to bring about adequate relief of the fear of "returning to primal chaos."

Yet in direct contrast to the conclusion to which we are prompted by Leonardo's drawings, there seems no doubt that when he was painting a picture Leonardo at times went through long periods of hesitation; in the case of the *Mona Lisa,* tradition has it that he felt he never succeeded in giving it the perfection that he wanted. I refer also to the instances in which there are—or were—several versions of the same subject. These long periods of struggle to find the solution of artistic problems seem to speak strongly against a lowered capacity to bear tension. Here the creative process led to an increase of tension and did not provide that beneficial solution one feels inclined to associate with his drawings. This is confirmed when we hear from a probably reliable though secondhand informant that Leonardo trembled when he set himself to paint.[47] Apparently, creating a painting actually exposed Leonardo to a strain that brought him to the verge of the unbearable.[48]

What was the structure of the ego that could utilize so unerringly and effectively the creative impulse to draw but was so seriously conflicted when it was a matter of painting? In view of everything we know of Leonardo this cannot be attributed to any kind of lack of positive ability.[49]

Clark has tried to trace the sequences that led to final paintings.[50] One of them is the phase of diagrams: "these are usually quite small drawings, done from memory, and are syntheses of the most satisfactory motives." Among his many compositions it was usually these small diagrams that Leonardo carried out in the final paintings. The very small *Leda* sketch Müller-Walde discovered accidentally on a page of the *Atlantic Codex* as mentioned before is one of the impressive examples of this sort[51] (Pl. 72). I have not found an explanation of why these final diagrams are of such small size and I have no doubt there were many reasons. Perhaps it is another manifestation of a general bent in Leonardo which Olschki, in discussing Leonardo's mental work, described as a penchant for the aphorism, an inclination to attempt "to put together a maximum of attributes into the smallest possible space [*ein Maximum von Merkmalen im kleinst möglichen Raum zusammenzufassen*]."[52]

In searching for the unconscious reason why what later would become paintings appear first in the form of these microcompositions, one may raise the question whether perhaps they symbolized for Leonardo the small infants out of which the adult would grow, or even a kind of fetus, in which also the prestages of the later infant can be recognized. If so, this practice would materially confirm how much the work of art was for Leonardo literally a child, as Freud briefly intimated. At the same time, it may provide a factor that interfered with Leonardo's painting and upset the smooth functioning that is supposed to have been characteristic of his drawing. The following passage in the draft of a letter from Leonardo to his brother Domenico (b. 1484) may give the reason thereof:

> My most beloved brother,
> This is sent merely to inform you that a short time ago I received a letter from you from which I learnt that you have had an heir, which circumstance I understand has afforded you a great deal of

pleasure. Now in so far as I had judged you to be possessed of prudence I am now entirely convinced that I am as far removed from having an accurate judgment as you are from prudence; seeing that you have been congratulating yourself in having created a watchful enemy, who will strive with all his energies after liberty, which can only come into being at your death.[53]

Where did Leonardo get his certainty that a son hates his father to such a degree that he looks forward to his death so that he may be free? What he wrote his brother must have been derived from his own experience. Thus children are not only neglected at times by their parents, but also in their turn are "watchful enemies" of their creators. Did Leonardo also displace this conflict upon his paintings and therefore so often hesitate to finish them?

Furthermore, Clark speaks of Leonardo's "inborn distaste for finality." Finality means separation, and separation is often associated in our minds with death. Sketches, drawings, usually do not carry the weight of finality; they are parts of a comprehensive whole and although artistic achievements of the highest order in their own right, they elicit in the artist feelings quite different from those about a finished painting. In Leonardo's case there was, to seek no further, the fact that drawings remained in his possession,[54] whereas his paintings were made on commission and had to be surrendered upon completion. Drawings were free of this inhibitory connotation.

With the paintings, we are dealing with an activity in which depiction did not reduce tension but increased it. Much as such factors as finality and the child-painting identity may have been at work, it is my feeling that there must have been still a deeper reason in his psychic economy for the fact that we have so many "perfect" drawings from his hand and so few perfect paintings.

The demand put upon the psychic apparatus in the painting situation was, as a matter of fact, quite different from that which Leonardo was exposed to, for example, in the effort to invent a flying machine. In that effort he had to study a model of perfection, as represented in the bird. Here his task was reduced to penetrating into the secrets of an object that exists in reality and then transforming his findings into a mechanical instrument. In his superb drawings of plants and beasts and landscapes too he had objects before him to which he could fasten himself, the task being reduced to transposing an image from one medium to another.[55] When he was painting a picture, however, such as the *Adoration* or the *Cenacolo* (*The Last Supper*), he had himself to create the model of perfection. It was no longer a matter of treading the short circuit from percept or inner image to depiction, as it was in the case of drawing. When painting Leonardo had to submit to a task that required a broad synthesis, the construction of a goal whose concretization was far off in the future and which he could approach only very gradually by a series of innumerable little steps. Did the necessity of keeping sight of this far-ahead, visionary goal in the midst of full devotion to a mass of details, which are sometimes detours on the road to finality, burden him with tension that became unbearable? I feel very strongly in favor of this possibility. When Clark says that Leonardo loved diversity more than unity or that he loved accident rather than substance, or speaks of him as "so little concerned with synthesis, so distrustful of abstractions,"[56] he puts his finger on exactly the spots where I think Leonardo's weaknesses were. These were areas where the hypertrophied functions no longer yielded sufficient protection and the psychic apparatus was exposed to grave dangers.

In a genius like Leonardo, as in so many others, one gets the impression that they spend their creative lives as if under an inner necessity or compulsion, that they have no alternative but must create. The model I have devised for Leonardo would approximately explain that inner compulsion. The coincidence of creative function and defense would really have left him no alternative. Creating or not creating was a question of life or death, as was the inner reason that did not permit him to leave off research but drove him relentlessly on and on. This inner necessity, however, may drive a genius beyond what is favorable to his psychic economy, and thus we observe Leonardo exposing himself sporadically to tasks that evidently involved great inner pain. I am not thinking of the pain he suffered in his anatomical work; that seems to have been of a different order. I am thinking of the strain he was subjected to when he was working on his large compositions, when past observations and their concretizations in the form of innumerable sketches were to be synthesized into a material embodiment of a perfect vision he carried in himself or, at least, was groping for. When exposed to such strain he may have felt a revulsion of which possibly we hear when we read Fra Pietro's letter, which, after all, was written at a time when Leonardo was engaged in producing one of his most beautiful paintings.

Thus the following suggestions may be submitted. There came from Leonardo an unimpeded stream of drawings that kept him optimally tension-free since it prevented the accumulation of longings which meant for Leonardo essentially an acceleration of death. This smooth flow was greatly impeded in the case of painting, for several reasons: the final work of art supposedly meant for Leonardo a child; the male child was looked upon by him as a mortal enemy to his father; further, the painting, in contrast to drawings, carried the stamp of finality and thus implied separation, that is, a loss which Leonardo dreaded. Moreover, the strain to which the psychic apparatus was subjected in the course of producing a painting was possibly too great, since it did not allow the copying of an object but presupposed an inner vision that had to be constantly changed and adapted and whose concretization required long detours.

Although these factors may well have been active in Leonardo and have contributed to his trembling when he began to paint, one has the feeling that this frame of reference is not specific enough to clarify the inner resistance Leonardo met. In the following excursus I will make a suggestion as to the area in which the specific etiology may be found.

EXCURSUS ON LEONARDO'S RELATIONSHIP TO PAINTING

In trying to discover the particular psychological difficulty that Leonardo evidently had to overcome in producing a painting we may turn toward the book in which he gives counsel to the painter on how to proceed in such work. A manuscript has reached us which, though not from his pen, reliably reproduces the bulk, if not all, of what he had to say about the subject. The *Trattato della pittura* is a huge mass of notes regarding perspective, color, proportion, etc., in short, a compendium of many items a Renaissance painter needed to know about.[57] The technical part is of less interest here, but there are chapters and remarks that demand psychological interpretation, mainly in that part which is called the *Paragone*.[58]

Among Leonardo's notes on art there are no doubt many that continue a tradition that in some instances goes back before the Renaissance; the type of treatise represented by the *Trattato* was initiated by Leon Battista Alberti (1404–1472). Still, all authors agree upon the originality of Leonardo's ideas about painting and art even though in a substantial part of them he follows Alberti.[59] Conspicuous among the remarks that ask for psychological interpretation are those of an aggressive-defensive nature in which Leonardo extols painting as the foremost science of all and puts poetry, sculpture, and music on a far lower level.[60]

The desire to improve the social standing of artists and to elevate the prestige of painting is also found in Alberti's writings, but nothing of Leonardo's radicalism and exclusiveness is noticeable there.[61] Basic among the objective historical factors that were apt to make an ambitious artist sensitive was the traditional division of the arts into liberal and mechanical, painting being considered to be mechanical. The history of this division and the changing esteem in which painting was held from ancient times through the Middle Ages up to the Quattrocento do not need to be presented here.[62] Suffice it to say that Leonardo put up a fierce struggle for the rehabilitation of painting and reversed the contemporary situation by establishing painting as superior to all other sciences. Alberti's pride in reporting that in ancient Greece slaves were forbidden to learn the art of painting[63] is a close antecedent of Leonardo's endeavor.

In this context it is not superfluous to call attention to the fact that Alberti, like Leonardo, was of illegitimate birth. It seems to me that Leonardo's fight to make out of the "illiberal" art of painting a liberal one is genetically connected with the blemish on his birth. The ambition to rid painting too of a blemish may be seen as a counterpart of his ambition to blot out the stigma of his origin. When Leonardo writes: "And indeed it was not without reason that they have not raised it [painting] to [the rank of] nobility since it ennobles itself by itself without the assistance of other tongues [*e veramente non senza caggione non l'hanno nobilitata, perchè per ser medesima si nobilita, senza l'ajuto delle altrui*],"[64] this may tell us how he overcame a very personal resentment that stemmed from sources quite different from his concern about the art of painting; being as a painter a member of the Guild of St. Luke, he was in a position to repeat a basic issue of his childhood. In fact, the blemish of his birth and the blemish of his profession both stood him in good stead. Indeed Leonardo's youngest half-brother tried to repeat the miracle of nature by marrying a girl from Vinci who was as similar as possible to Leonardo's mother, Caterina, with the effect that Pierino da Vinci, his son, became a noteworthy sculptor.[65]

Turning again to the *Trattato della pittura,* there are two aspects that make one wonder. First it is surprising that in it Leonardo gives advice he never followed himself and which would certainly have threatened his standing as one of the greatest painters if he had. Thus when he wrote about how to depict a battle he suggested that the air should be full of arrows flying in various directions, one ascending, another in descent, and others horizontally; bullets should be accompanied with vapor in the direction of their course;[66] footprints in plain soil should be left filled with blood.[67] If Leonardo had ever tried to practice such gruesome precepts —which, of course, he never did—his paintings would have become, rather than masterpieces, illustrations of how an artist ought not to proceed.[68] Yet in these instances he may have been carried away by his literary genius, so to speak, and in *writing* about painting involuntarily have set forth what a *writer* should describe.[69] Yet the matter becomes more serious when we find Leonardo strongly advocating[70] that the affect or emotion being depicted should be unmixed so that there should be no doubt as to the affect the person represented is possessed by. This is in contrast with Leonardo's actual practice, in which precisely the indeterminateness of affects is an important source of the great power his paintings have over the beholder. I have discussed this feature in regard to the *Gioconda, Leda,* [etc., elsewhere]. It is just the antagonism of opposing emotions that is most characteristic of the human personality, and it was Leonardo who was one of the greatest in the art of intimating by the discreetest shades the presence and interplay of manifold emotions in the same subject. To be sure, he was also capable of presenting an eruption of vigorous one-dimensional passion, as in the *Battle of Anghiari,* but we would not see in Leonardo the artist who knew so much of the human soul were it not for other paintings that present so impressively that sphere of human life where contrasts are not so strictly separated and the quality of the emotion is in doubt. He was a painter of human depth by means of complete mastery of the surface.

A very surprising statement is found in Parte II, 114, where Leonardo counsels how to escape the "calumny" of other painters. He advises that one practice one's art in accordance with a variety of ways so that one will be in agreement, in some part at least, with each of the current opinions that are held about painting.[71] This, though modified in the subsequent paragraph, is a veritable slap to all and everything Leonardo stood for.

The second surprising aspect of the *Trattato* is that it shares with other Renaissance treatises a certain limitedness that has been remarked by the historian.[72] This limitedness can best be summarized as an almost exclusive concern with craft rather than art. That which makes Leonardo's paintings the masterworks they are is not touched upon in the *Trattato.* If his paintings were nothing but the mirror of nature, as he recommends at times, they would be of no greater interest to us than those of any other skillful craftsman. No more need be said than that the greatness of his artistic work derives from an entirely different area, but about that area Leonardo spares scarcely a word aside from generalities.[73] How are we to explain this? It is well known that many a genius has a poor understanding of his own values or of where his true value lies, like most people he has his repressions, prejudices, and is utterly misled about his own psychology.[74] Thus Leonardo may have been honest and sincere in his *Trattato* and may have gone to the limits of his insight. At the same time, there is evidence that a genius may hold back precisely his most personal impressions and insights. A good example is Goethe's apparent reticence regarding the rise of the machine age.[75] Indeed, no reference to it is to be found in his conversations or letters or in the bulk of his writings. Only in his last novel, *Wilhelm Meisters Wanderjahre,* are there passages that demonstrate his awareness of the fundamental changes to which society was being subjected. But there also one encounters his horror at what he envisioned the machine age would do to society and to man. He evidently did not want to ponder on a grave issue for which he saw no path to a solution. Only on this last occasion did he permit himself the minimum of remarks that convey to him who reads between the lines the impact this development had had upon him.

Something similar, it is my impression, may be surmised about Leonardo and the invention and spread of printing which occurred in his lifetime. Sarton finds nothing "more curious and perplexing" than that Leonardo "overlooked two of the greatest inventions not only of his time but of all times: printing and engraving"[76] and he asks: "Did he despise such inventions, as did some Florentine snobs?"

Pedretti recently presented the material in Leonardo's notes that refers to printing.[77] It is evident that Leonardo did not ignore printing, but it is remarkable that he, who was so much interested in machines and technically so very astute, did not pay more attention to it. If one does not read between the lines, one may draw the conclusion that he had a kind of blind spot here and was not foresighted enough to recognize the greatness of an invention that would change as did no other the culture in which he grew up. Again at a place where one would not expect it one discovers a hint that may be suggestive of a hypothesis. In the *Trattato della pittura* one finds a passage in which printing is used as an example to set forth the superiority of painting. Leonardo distinguishes between sciences that are imitable and inimitable. In mathematics the pupil appropriates as much as the teacher presents, but the person who is not favored by nature with special gifts cannot learn painting. One cannot copy a painting as one does writing or as one makes a casting of a sculpture, "It [painting] does not beget infinite progeny like printed books.[78] [*Questa non fa infiniti figliuoli, come fa li libri stampati*]."[79] Here reference to printing is definitely pejorative. For Leonardo, the individualist and the artist, the idea that something so personal and individually characteristic as a manuscript should be multiplied had apparently an offensive implication.[80] The machines Leonardo was occupied with had the function of achieving mastery over physical forces; they multiplied man's physical power to do what he could achieve on a smaller scale unaided. But in printing and engraving the machine arrogated the privilege of the selected few and thus threatened the prerogative of individual culture. We have got accustomed to books, and we are aware of the benefits printing has bestowed, but we overlook the deep injuries this invention has likewise inflicted upon civilization, not only by its facilitating the spread of false-hood as well as truth, but also by the depreciation of mental values it has caused. It is understandable that a mind as aristocratic, in the best sense of this word, as Leonardo's was should have felt offended and pained by the incursion of the mechanical into the live realm of the mind. This, of course, is only a hypothesis. One can feel surer about the reasons for Goethe's silence about the machine age, but whatever the true reasons may have been for the scarcity of remarks about printing in Leonardo's notes, we can be sure it was neither snobbery nor failure to notice or dis-regard. The genius, as this example once more shows, sometimes abstains from explicitly setting forth what possibly is most personal and relevant to him. Consequently we should not be surprised that we must lay aside the *Trattato* without having discovered the specific meaning painting had for Leonardo and the specific goals he pursued by means of it.

A general remark may be interpolated here. Miss Kate T. Steinitz, in a personal communication for which I here take the opportunity to thank her, has cautioned me against forgetting that Leonardo really accomplished a *tour de force* in his defense of the art of painting in the *Paragone*. No doubt he did. But his groping for arguments, his unin-hibitedness in making even quite impossible inferences, the bizarreness of some of his arguments, lead the psychoanalyst to believe that precisely in this area there is a splendid chance of getting hold of direct derivatives of the repressed. However, the motives and meanings we are looking for when we inquire into Leonardo's relationship to the art of painting do not belong strictly to the repressed, although they may have been in-timately connected with it. Clinically it is well known that anxiety in al-most all of its forms is fed by the repressed, but when Leonardo trembled as he set out to paint he must have been hampered also by a content that was part and parcel of his ego, to wit, of its conscious part. Whether this content was actually represented consciously or only preconsciously does not make very much difference in this context. In other words, we are raising the question of what the goals were that Leonardo tried to achieve in painting, for evidently there was something about these goals themselves that was liable to arouse anxiety or cause hesitation or procrastination. If we had an idea as to what these goals were, we might be in a position to draw new inferences regarding the repressed meanings that were attached to his activity as a painter.

The historical relationship between art and art theory or philosophy in the Renaissance has been well studied.[81] Besides this objective historical context there is the subjective one in the artist himself that is of relevance here. The relationship between the two in the artist may have been of various kinds. The artist may have known of certain conceptual frameworks and may have used them consciously in the presentation of allegories or other subjects, or he may even have been in search of a philosophical system that would conceptualize what he was trying to express or present visually.[82] But it may also happen—and possibly this is what has most often been the case—that the artist was not consciously motivated by a theoretical frame of reference. He may have heard of it or even studied it and still it may have slipped into his productions without his conscious awareness. Reflections of contemporaneous philosophy or theory are, of course, observed in works of art without there being a direct connection between the philosophy and the art. The philosopher conceptualizes problems and solutions that have become ripe in his times, and the artist will achieve corresponding solutions in the visual medium. Both are children of the particular historical epoch in which they live, and it is not surprising when one discovers kinship between cultural products of the same period even when these products belong to quite different media. "Art," Max Dvořák said, "consists not only in the solution and development of formal tasks and problems; it is also always and foremost an expression of ideas that dominate mankind; its history, no less than that of religion, philosophy or literature, is part of the general history of thought [*allgemeine Geistesgeschichte*]."[83] I raise a problem here that is eminently complicated and I fear my simplification may make appear almost like a triviality a process the essentials of which are not understood at all and are still as puzzling as when the question first arose. The fact that the artist's responses to stimuli that are not of a personal nature but extrasubjective, such as historical or cultural forces or those of tradition, are usually unconscious has given rise to a tendency to reduce the artist's individuality to a mere medium, and to limit the historian's role to noting the stimuli and responses. Such a concept is adequate when the artist is merely an imitator or when his motives are primarily derived from a sphere extraneous to art. But the great artist responds fully to his own personal subjective world, which is usually replete with conflicts, to a specific area within his historical period, and to some (or all) of the perennial problems of mankind. These areas are not represented separately in the end product, but each element of the work of art and the total configuration contain all of them and more. Since, however, we are not able to discern each single area in every element, it may appear as if some elements contain more or less of one or another area. Such impressions depend on our perspicacity. Behind an apparently objective symbol a most personal conflict may be hiding and go unnoticed—often because we do not know enough about the artist's personal life.[84]

In the search for a motivating theoretical frame (conscious or preconscious) in Leonardo's paintings, one feels inclined to look at Neoplatonism, which had such a great bearing upon Florentine art. Although, as is well known, Leonardo was an avowed opponent of this philosophical system, an internal kinship is not necessarily to be excluded.[85]

What separated Leonardo from any form of Platonism was Plato's turn away from the observation of nature,[86] which was, after all, the mainstay of Leonardo's empiricism.[87] This Platonic aversion to the direct comprehension of natural objects by the senses[88] shows up in the spiritualistic teachings of the Academy of Florence, which degraded or abased nature and banished it to the lowest grade of beings.[89] I should also surmise that the whole circle of literati around Lorenzo il Magnifico, with their stress on poetry and philosophy and a concomitant neglect of the visual arts, must have been repugnant to Leonardo. He may easily have looked upon them as snobs, which they probably were to a certain extent.[90] However, as Cassirer points out, although Leonardo remained quite untouched by Neoplatonism and the Florentine Academy, he found his way to true Platonism *despite* Ficino[91] and the Academy.[92]

However, Leonardo seems to have been strongly under the influence of philosophers, as Duhem's now classic studies prove. So far as I know, this influence has been studied in relation only to Leonardo's scientific and philosophical notes, but not to his artistic work. I wish to demonstrate a significant tie between Leonardo's artistic work and the philosophy of Nicholas of Cusa. Nicholas's bearing on Leonardo as scientist and philosopher has been most ably set forth by Duhem and Cassirer.[93] In presenting this tie, I rely for my account of Nicholas of Cusa's philosophy chiefly on Cassirer's exposition as set forth in his volume on *Individuum und Kosmos in der Philosophie der Renaissance.*[94]

There seems to have been a personal affinity between Leonardo and Nicholas of Cusa (1401–1464). Both are representative geniuses of a time in transition, and therefore are rooted in two historical periods: the Middle Ages and the Renaissance. Both are in substantive ways far ahead of their times: Nicholas to a certain extent anticipated twentieth-century relativity theory,[95] and Leonardo, fulfilling and going beyond the potential inherent in Quattrocento art, anticipated High Renaissance, Baroque,[96] Impressionism to a certain extent,[97] and probably even, as it seems to me, nonobjective art. Both had linguistic difficulties. Leonardo, *uomo senza lettere,* found himself isolated from the crowd that was intellectually fashionable[98] because of his unerudite background—he could not compete with them in their rhetoric performances which were the prerequisite of scholastic standing; Nicholas of Cusa, the German, was clumsy in his Latin, and, as he said, he was incapable of rivaling those that were Latins by birth.[99]

A more striking kinship is noticed when what in Nicholas was possibly only theory but may just as well have been the expression of a subjectively valid truth is compared with what, according to Freud, was in Leonardo the basic interrelationship between self and emotion. When Nicholas finds an inner contradiction in the idea that the affect of love can exist without admixture of cognition, when he declares the true love of God to be *amor Dei intellectualis*[100] and makes cognition a prerequisite of love, then he is anticipating what Leonardo expressed perhaps a shade more radically. "For nothing can be either loved or hated unless it is first known"; and even more strongly: "... love of anything is the offspring of knowledge, love being more fervent in proportion as knowledge is more certain; and this certainty springs from a thorough knowledge of all those parts which united compose the whole of that thing which ought to be loved."[101] Here the historian's search for imitative behavior would, if there ever was imitation, have a better chance of success than when he supposes Leonardo became a vegetarian after studying Porphyry. Was Freud wrong when he made this self-emotion equation a leading pathognomonic sign since we now encounter a similar one in Nicholas of Cusa's philosophy? Did he here at last err by subjectifying a historicosociological trait? The historian probably would be more inclined to agree with the psychologist if Nicholas's proposition was correlated with an appropriate subjective attitude, which I presume can scarcely be proved. Yet even then he might claim that Leonardo was merely following in his view about love and cognition what he presumed to be proper for a man who seriously pursues intellectual goals. Even if we abandon the theory of imitation, it may still be said that Leonardo identified here with the ideal of what he thought a philosopher ought to be and that this type of identification does not necessarily reflect basic psychopathology, that is to say, that Leonardo did not identify with Nicholas of Cusa on the ground of character traits or common psychopathology, but for essentially different reasons, the self-emotion relation being only accessory or incidental.

Notwithstanding the unquestionable feasibility of this explanation, what we know of Leonardo's total emotionality, as far as it can be reconstructed from external evidence and from his notes, speaks rather in favor of Freud's interpretation than of the assumption of accessory identification. If we tentatively assume that this part of Nicholas's philosophy grew out of his own subjective experience, we may observe that the climate of certain historical periods favors the evolvement in certain personality types of above-average talents. It is quite conceivable that the growth of certain cultural patterns requires certain personality types,[102] and since a historical period does not insure the flourishing of all those who have the stuff of genius, it may happen that many a subject's potential genius remains unrealized because the culture of his time does not provide that frame into which the subject could fit the creations of his particular skills. Thus it may have happened that just because of an identical emotional pattern both men had a better chance of their genius being realized in the Quattrocento than they would have had if their self-emotion relations had been different.

In defiance of scholastic theology,[103] Nicholas of Cusa posited the *visio intellectualis* as the principal situation in which man achieves a direct relation to God. This *visio* was not an ecstatic surrender to God but the end result of innumerable intellectual steps. Nicholas calls in mathematics as an instrument on the way to God. *"Nihil certi habemus in nostra scientia nisi nostram mathematicam,"*[104] which again coincides with Leonardo's basic approach. "There is no certainty where one can neither apply any of the mathematical sciences nor any of those which are based upon the mathematical sciences."[105] But the certainty of mathematics cannot provide cognition of God as he is. In defiance of scholastic logic Nicholas maintains that no conclusion except a negative one can be drawn from the finite to the infinite. As long as of a quantity a more or less can be thought, it is qualitatively different from the infinite. The infinite is not a superlative referable to a preceding comparative. No procedure of quantification can bridge the gap between the absolute maximum, the primordial cause of existence, and empirical, finite existence.[106] When Leonardo in his *Trattato*[107] states that no accumulation of points however numerous could ever form a plane, we have an example of how Nicholas of Cusa's philosophy shows up directly in Leonardo's theory of art.

In Nicholas of Cusa's work we find a thought that is particularly striking to the psychologist, though it certainly was not meant as it will be understood by modern man. It can be called the beginning of the subjectivization of the idea of God. Regarding the *visio intellectualis* Nicholas of Cusa states that it is correlated with the nature of the object as well as of the subject. Thus, that which is seen in the *visio intellectualis* partakes of the nature of God but also of the nature of the subject. The two are inseparably intermingled. God is in reality the totality of all the possible individual subjective visions, and therefore the subject in viewing God must consider that the image he can see depends on the location from which he views God and on his own nature, that is to say, the subject can obtain only a partial view of God. Thus Nicholas writes about God:

> Every face that looks into yours, therefore, does not see anything that is different from itself because it sees its own truth.... Who beholds you with a loving look feels your look lovingly directed at himself.... Who beholds you in anger will find your face angry. Who with joy, will find it joyful. For as to the physical eye everything appears red when it looks through a red glass, so does the eye of the mind, in its limitation, see you who are the goal and object of contemplation in accordance with the nature of its own restrictedness. For man cannot judge but humanly. . . . Also a lion if he attributed to you a countenance would ascribe to you that of a lion, the ox that of an ox, the eagle of an eagle. O Lord how miraculous is your countenance that the youth must form youthful, the man manly, and the aged aged if he wants to comprehend it.[108]

I must forgo discussing the consequences of this astounding thought and limit myself to referring to a thought in Leonardo's *Trattato* which is parallel, though in a different context. Simultaneously we shall notice here (for the first time) in Leonardo an attempt at overcoming that restrictedness which Nicholas of Cusa ascribes to man's nature. Leonardo repeatedly warns against what he calls the greatest defect of painters, namely, their inclination to paint what they themselves are.[109] We observe here an aspect of Leonardo that has perhaps not been sufficiently stressed by some of his biographers.[110] Indeed he must have felt well fortified against error by his insistent reliance on empiricism. Otherwise he might well have been fearful of becoming involved himself in self-deception, and hence in deceiving those who viewed his works. How strongly he felt about deceivers may be judged from his well-known outbursts of rage against astrologers and necromancers.

But, at least within the area of creative art, one gets here and there a glimpse of a Leonardo who is quite anxious lest man's subjectivity victimize him and befuddle the objectivity of his judgment. "We know for sure that one recognizes the errors rather in the works of others than in one's own, reprehending the small errors of others and overlooking one's own great ones [*Noi sapiamo certo, che gli errori si cognoscono piu in l'altrui opere che nelle sue, e spesso, riprendendo gli altrui picholi errori, non uedrai li tuoi grandi*]."[111]

Thus he claimed that a painter who has coarse hands will also paint such hands, and that this is true of all the limbs. Only long study will protect a painter from this error. He attributed this inclination of painters to the relationship of mind and body. The mind (*anima*) that was the inventor of its own body, when it has again to make a body by means of the hand, repeats the body it has produced once before.[112] How far Leonardo went in recognizing the effect of what is nowadays called narcissism can well be seen when he adds his observation that one who takes the step of falling in love falls in love with objects that are similar to oneself.[113]

How Leonardo tried to protect himself against the detrimental effect of narcissism is not the question here. It impresses me as important that Nicholas of Cusa described the narcissistic root of religious imagery (though not in psychological, but metaphysical terms) and that Leonardo was aware of the same root in artistic creations. But whereas Nicholas integrated this root and made it a legitimate part of man's relationship to God, Leonardo turns against it, considers it a defect, and tries to eliminate it from art. Leonardo was in general aware of what may "corrupt" an artist's soul. He turned forcefully against avarice and vainglory, all the pitfalls that may pervert the genius's sacred mission in life. This castigating attitude had not only a didactic function; it must also have been a defense against his own temptations. Anna Freud in her inquiry into the psychology of adolescence has described the "antagonism towards the instincts which far surpasses in intensity anything in the way of repression."[114] The adolescent's ascetic attitude alternating with instinctual excesses is a defense directed at the totality of his instinctual desires. In Leonardo, too, ascetic trends are noticeable alternating with exhibitionistic ones (whether there were also instinctual excesses is not known). Thus his discovery of and fight against the temptation to derive narcissistic gratification by painting himself directly into his work may indicate how strongly the narcissistic impulse may have been in himself. But this repudiation of the narcissistic realization likewise indicates a determination not to let the inner cosmos intrude into the painted work of art. Leonardo's aversion against Botticelli and Michelangelo, though it certainly was also based on differences in questions of a purely artistic nature, may have had its subjective root in this area, for Botticelli, and particularly Michelangelo, made their own emotions the center of their art, and what they felt—that is to say, what they were—was "unashamedly" presented to general inspection.

Yet all this does not touch upon the crucial point where Nicholas of Cusa's philosophy became a fulcrum of Leonardo's painting. The possible subjective parentage is not decisive, although it is of interest to observe how frequently, despite an absence of personal acquaintance, intellectual parentage is related with filiation of temperament and character. The part of Nicholas of Cusa's philosophy that must have meant the most to Leonardo was, I presume, the rehabilitation of the senses, their restitution to their own right after their long-lasting past degradation to a status inferior, lowly, or vulgar.[115] Now they became the prime movers of the intellect.[116] Not that this restitution occurred suddenly; it was prepared by previous development. Dvořák, in his unique historical presentation of idealistic and naturalistic trends in Gothic sculpture and painting, has shown how medieval man started to find his way back to the world of things, to the direct observation of his surroundings, after the complete surrender to the transcendency of the Godhead in early Christian art.[117] To be sure, this was neither a return to the classical view and its artistic approach nor did it establish observation in a place comparable to that it held with Leonardo. Gothic naturalism was still in the service of God's transcendency on the principle that Thomas Aquinas formulated as: "God finds enjoyment in all things." Yet in Nicholas of Cusa the transcendent and the immanent worlds are separated, and observation is instituted for the sake of gaining knowledge of the immanent. This world is equally close to or distant from God in all its parts. There are no special contents in the universe that are closer to the fountainhead than others; thus everything that can be observed is equally worthy to be studied and understood. To be sure, man's intelligence is limited and he cannot recognize eternal truth, yet this is not considered by Nicholas as anything like a barrier. It is a value in itself, through which that which is beyond the world can be comprehended.

From this vantage point all religion becomes heterodox. Religion must necessarily be different from God. Truth can be understood by man only by this quality of differentness, and all religions have this very quality in common. Religious institutions and customs are only signs and should not be confused with the referent. Those signs differ in all the various religions, but the referent is always the same [*signa autem mutationem capiunt, non signatum*].[118] We see here how widely Nicholas of Cusa extended the area of relativity. Since man cannot acquire absolute truth, every knowledge can be replaced by a better one. Experience and the resulting insights never go beyond *conjecture,* that is to say, as soon as a hypothesis has been formed, it will be replaced by a better one. Thus there is absolute truth which can reach us only by the quality of different-ness gained from the observation of the immanent world, but all the ex-periental knowledge we gain refers to absolute truth and participates with it in one way or another. Man has to renounce forever the hope of estab-lishing an identity between the two, but the renunciation assures the right to relative knowledge and relative truth.[119] As we can never draw an ideal circle, we may approach it by a polygon. We may improve the poly-gon by breaking down the length of its sides and increasing their number and thus come closer to the ideal image without ever reaching it.

In order to reach God the mind must go through the per-ceptible world which is no longer a mere steppingstone, a place where man, pausing, proves whether or not he is worthy to ascend to God, but has become, besides, a place with values of its own, no less deriving from Heaven, but peculiar to itself. Leonardo, in his artistic work as well as in his scientific, was primarily an empiricist; one is inclined to say that he was addicted to sense data. This, I believe, is one of the reasons for his lag in theory formation, which historians have usually related to shortcomings in the contemporary state of science. That the era was deficient may be quite true, but the similarity with a corresponding lag in Goethe is striking. In Goethe too the prevalence and primacy of the world of sense data, at times almost to the exclusion of corresponding theoretical conclusions, is quite conspicuous. It seems that the person who is eminently endowed with artistic talents has a particular affinity to the perceptible and therefore is impeded in utilizing what may properly be abstracted from observation in order to form theories, but is inclined rather to develop theory as an embodied aspect of the concretely presented observational material. This can be said to be true also of Leonardo, al-though there are passages in his work that ascribe to mathematics its proper function and although in his epistemology he at times differentiated sharply between what is observed and the causes behind it. Thus he wrote:

> . . . although nature begins with the cause and ends with the ex-perience, we must follow the opposite course, namely . . . begin with the experience and by the means of it investigate the cause.[120]

and:

> In nature there is no effect without cause; once the cause is under-stood there is no need to test it by experience.[121]

This, as Cassirer[122] quite rightly states, is an impressive anticipation of principles that underlie modern science; yet, despite such astounding insights into the structure of mind and knowledge, Leonardo, I agree with Olschki in believing, regarded the perceptible world as primary. Cassirer himself notes that from Leonardo's literary work as a whole one may get the impression that Leonardo wavered between two basic principles, in that he sometimes made mathematics and sometimes empiricism (experience) the fundamental measure of certainty.[123] However, when Cassirer concludes that the dualism between the concrete and the abstract did not hold for Leonardo, but that experience and mathematics were both acknowledged and recognized in their mutual dependence, I am inclined to demur. If abstraction and observation had not coincided for Leonardo, he would constantly have been bound to feel defeated, since mathematics occupies an essentially subordinate place in his work[124] and empirical statements certainly constitute the bulk of his notes.[125] From occasional passages it appears that he felt that he was making good progress on the road toward truth by using his outstanding faculty for observation. According to Cassirer's view, he should correspondingly have felt despair over his lack of knowledge of the law or laws that underlay the wealth of observational data, but, despite the occasional aphorisms that imply a modern epistemology, Leonardo's inquisitiveness was satisfied in practice by the minutest observation. However, I do not believe that Leonardo's conflict lay in that area at all. He did not feel perturbed by the paucity, well-nigh absence, of laws in his scientific work, but felt secure and satisfied in making minutest observations of the world that surrounded him.[126] Conflict there was, but we have to turn to a different set of problems to find a discord he probably tried to calm by his efforts.

According to Nicholas of Cusa, as to the rest of the philosophers, there was after all a schism in the realm of existence, that is to say, in the totality of being. The difference between philosophical schools was not as to whether that schism existed or not, but rather as to the relation of man to the two realms of being, the nature of the schism and man's way of grappling with it. Whatever Nicholas said about sense data, experience, and mathematics, there was still absolute being which had no more and no less, which was immeasurable and could never be fully reached by the intellect, which was bound to operate in terms that could be subjected to the idea of a more or less. Nicholas's new idea was that the means of our logic are incommensurate with the task of attaining an understanding of a maximum that no longer permits of addition or subtraction, and that all our inquiries lead only to approximations toward the primordial image or archetype. These primordial images, being infinite, would be nullified by any finite more or less, whereas the images gained by perception and experience can be judged by the degree of closeness they achieve to the primordial image and therefore may properly be measured by a more or less. Nicholas thus postulates a basic separateness between absolute truth and experience, but this separateness is confronted by a mutual participation. The contingent and finite of experience only tends toward the unconditional. Experience obtains determinability only by its participation with or approximation toward that which cannot be determined. Recognition of the limitations of experience was, therefore, prerequisite and cornerstone of its applicability to immanent reality.

But here I also sense the root of Leonardo's conflict. We know his insatiable ambition. He was incapable of acceding to any limitations of his art, as witness his attempt at stamping out any idea that other arts could also make contributions that on their own terms could be equal in excellency with painting. Yet he called painting a science and considered it the greatest of all sciences, while praising now experience, now mathematics, as the conveyor of truth.

Cassirer devotes much thought to the relationship in Leonardo between what we call art and science, how they were identical to him and others.[127] In terms of the analysis of the structure of the historical process this may be correct, but if we try to trace the corresponding psychological process we find a different context. Leonardo rejoices over all the discoveries, all the truth, he obtains by experience, and still, once isolated from these notes, he fights tooth and nail for the supremacy of painting and the visual arts. I believe very strongly that, despite all of Leonardo's rejoicing about the triumph of empiricism, he still believed that painting was essentially superior to all other intellectual or artistic pursuits, because it was in his estimation the only way to pierce through that barrier which separated the immanent world from the transcendent. Painting, when it lived up to its highest standards or realized its full potential, should—so it seems to me he must have felt—depict the transcendent world that is immutable and perfect and is not amenable to a more or less and is beyond the relativity that is a quality of all the things we perceive by our senses and beyond all the empirical observations and hypotheses concerning them.

Thus, for Leonardo, the dichotomy of primordial image and reproductive image would still have had a significant bearing, and in Leonardo's psyche there would have been a cleavage between contents he considered immanent to reality and transcendent contents. As long as he moved within the immanent world, that is to say, as long as he was observing the physical world and the behavior of man as he is, Leonardo could proceed with great alacrity and exuberance and apparently without inhibition. There is the colossal mass of notes and the huge number of drawings, the bulk of which are devoted to studies of what he perceived in the world that surrounded him. Here no inhibitions are noticed. The drawings cannot, of course, be viewed as mere photograph-like reproductions of experiential objects; the goal the artist pursued was the ideal presentation of things, whether this involved properties that are accessible to direct observation or knowledge he had gained about the structure of things such as their organicity, their inner dynamics, etc. In all this he remained within the immanent, and, intense apparently as was his striving toward perfection in representing this immanent world, he seems to have gone ahead without inner conflict. In all this his mind reaches out for properties or qualities that are, openly or hiddenly, still within the terrestrial cosmos that is in principle accessible to man.

Yet I strongly believe that when painting he aspired at making the transcendent world visible, that it was no longer a matter of perfectly realizing the immanent, which he did in his drawings, but of concretizing a totally different sphere of being, which, according to Nicholas of Cusa, by definition could not be made visible. It was possibly this self-imposed demand to make the transcendent visible, which he himself knew to be beyond the capacity of the senses as well as the intellect, that made him tremble when he set out to paint, that caused his constant dissatis-faction, procrastination, and declarations about this or that painting that it had not yet reached the degree of perfection he was aiming at. Thus my hypothesis is that Leonardo was in full agreement with Nicholas of Cusa's philosophy and simultaneously wished to break through the one barrier he found erected in it.

Yet when I discuss the many affinities between Leonardo and Nicholas of Cusa I do not mean that this makes any contribution to the question of whether Leonardo studied Nicholas's treatises or even was acquainted with them, though evidently he was. The relationship I have in mind, aside from the realistic, historical context, is one mainly of kinship within the frame of a history of thought. In Nicholas of Cusa's philosophy we find the embodiment of a conceptual frame of the universe that was also valid for Leonardo, not only as scientist, but also as artist. The various aspects of that philosophy had their bearing on a variety of artistic values; they eased the road toward visual clarification as well as re-creation of the terrestrial universe, but in turn also sowed the germ of conflicts. Nothing would be more erroneous than to treat Leonardo's work as if it were something like painted philosophy. But in Nicholas's writings we find explicitly much of what implicitly also resides in Leonardo's artistic creations.

The unquestionable kinship in terms of the history of thought does not preclude that Nicholas of Cusa's work, so far as it reached Leonardo, may directly have affected him and resulted in a father conflict of the kind referred to earlier, and, prompted by a very subjective motive, Leonardo may have been attempting to carry out a task which his, so to speak, teacher had declared impossible. In three dialogues Nicholas presents the unsophisticated, unerudite layman in an argument with the philosopher, who is defeated because he bases his doctrines on the writings of authors, whereas the layman observes life in the streets, in the market place, and is aware of his ignorance and therefore perhaps more knowledgeable than the philosopher. Cassirer quite rightly points to the similarity of this passage to what Leonardo occasionally said about himself.[128] But it may properly be asked whether Leonardo did not, in the last analysis, make in turn out of Nicholas of Cusa a philosopher, an erudite man, who, though he did not rely on written authority and introduce revolutionary views, still submitted to tradition in one point and denied man's capacity to penetrate into the transcendent. Or did Leonardo perhaps, notwithstanding his full respect for intellectual achievement, keep a reservation regarding what the creative artist is capable of achieving? However much ingenuity, creativity, intuition, may go into scientific discoveries, there is one fundamental difference from art. The scientific discovery can be repeated, whereas no work of art can ever be repeated. If all our scientific discoveries were annihilated, it is extremely probable that later civilizations would reach a point when their knowledge of physics and chemistry and mathematics would include all that had been lost.[129] But the destruction of one work of art constitutes an irreplaceable loss. If one of Shakespeare's plays were lost, the chance of a later culture creating it would be nil.

There are indications that Leonardo was sensitive to this point. It is not directly set forth but strongly enough to be noticed. When he discusses the imitable sciences Leonardo says that painting is the noblest, for in mathematics the pupil can appropriate as much as the teacher proffers, whereas this is not true of painting.[130] Yet he goes even further and almost equates the painting with the Deity it depicts,[131] on the ground that the populace accords to paintings honors reserved to God. Though in general opposed to Church ritual and superstitions, Leonardo here accepts them with approbation to prove his point. He infers that the divine being gives preference to being adored in this form rather than in any other. And further: "The art of painting contains in itself all forms that exist in nature and such as do not exist there."[132] When Leonardo states that (a) the works of nature are of a higher order than those of man, (b) the distance between both is as large as that between man and God, and (c) the art of painting is above nature, as implied by inferences from the adoration of images, conclusions may be drawn regarding the value Leonardo attributed to the person who is capable of creating paintings and to the product itself.

It seems that Leonardo attributed to the artist the potentiality of a God. He can create whatever he feels a longing for: "If the painter wants to behold beautiful things that he will fall in love with, he is the master who can create those things, and if he wants to see monstrous things that terrify, or comical and laughable or even piteous, then he is lord and God over them [*Se'l pittore vol vedere bellezze, che lo innamorino, egli n'è signore di generarle, et se vol vedere cose mostruose, che spaventino, o'che siene buffonesche e risibili, o'veramente compassionevoli, ei n'è signore e Dio*]."[133]

Yet what did Leonardo mean when he claimed that the art of painting contained also the forms that do not exist in nature? Other passages could be cited that show the omnipotence ascribed to the painting artist, not the least being that where Leonardo claims that paintings can be created that will never perish.[134] The godly imagery surrounding the artist follows an old tradition: the relationship God-world or God-man was already in ancient times compared with that of the artist to his creations.[135]

It is more difficult to discover what kind of value Leonardo attributed to paintings or what value he tried to realize in his paintings. I disagree at this point with Cassirer, who has so brilliantly set forth the philosophy of Nicholas of Cusa and Leonardo's kinship with him in the history of thought. Yet Cassirer explicates the values inherent in Leonardo's paintings in terms that, in my opinion, are valid only for Leonardo's drawings but not for his paintings.

To the Renaissance, and foremost to Leonardo, nature had lost the character of the formless that resists the principle of form which it had seemed to have to man of the Middle Ages: nature now appeared a domain perfectly formed throughout in which law and order reigned. Leonardo's burning desire to know this order, to understand it, cannot be questioned. It certainly was the prime motive of his research, and one may observe the same motive in his drawings which are devoted to the study of nature.

But his paintings, or, to be more careful, some of his paintings, go far beyond this limit. There was, after all, that "countenance of all countenances"[136] of which Nicholas of Cusa had written and which no man was capable of fathoming, which the human eye could see only one aspect of, whereas it itself contained all of them, the young and the old, the male and female, and probably also those of all animals. And this was true of all natural objects. Even complete knowledge of them, even insight into their structure, would only mean an approximation to those universal images that contain in one the totality of terrestrial declinations in which types and individual objects exist in nature.

Nicholas of Cusa's philosophy had removed the shackles from inquiry and we see Leonardo turn toward all phenomena of nature. There is no longer a restriction to those that contain the good or the beautiful. Since nature in all of its parts partakes of God, each part is worthy of study. Since the countenance must have contained ugly faces too, Leonardo also studies the human face in its ugliest specimens. Much acumen has been spent on the explanation of these so-called grotesques or caricatures. By hindsight one may even say that, if they had been lost, one should have been able to demonstrate that they once existed. In view of Leonardo's interest in the human body and the face as the most characteristic structure of the human species, he was bound to be attracted just by those extremes in which the filiation, that partaking in God, of all natural objects is most difficult to discover.[137] But most perplexing of all must have been the idea that the countenance of all countenances is to contain even these children of hell, and therefore to advance into the transcendent required just as imperatively that they be studied as the sublime. Leonardo was confronted here by a particularly difficult problem, since the presentation of a face as being simultaneously typically attractive and typically ugly is beyond human ingenuity.[138]

From the artistic point of view Leonardo encountered a more favorable situation when he confronted the dichotomy of sexes that would have to be synthesized into a "countenance of all countenances." His epicene types speak in favor of my thesis that in painting Leonardo tried to realize visually in one the transcendent which contains contrasts. Thus Leonardo's numerous studies, the bulk of his drawings, were the bricks out of which there was to be constructed an edifice whose shape could not be conjectured from the shapes of the variety of bricks used. The difference between the frame into which these studies fitted and that into which some of the paintings did seems essential. One cannot rightly see in those studies prestages of what would be synthesized into the paintings. The drawings aim at a full understanding of the properties of things. The immanent world of things had to be perfectly known and its depiction integrated to such an extent that it could be carried out almost as a matter of routine without the slightest inner or outer difficulty, much as we can handle pen and ink when writing. Since all this was eventually to be used for the presentation of the transcendent, there could be no limit to the study of the immanent world. Therefore Leonardo had in his anatomical research to go far beyond the understanding of surface structures. In the depiction of the transcendent *every* part of an object and every form in which it may appear in nature is to be synthesized; hence Leonardo could not feel satisfied with such partial knowledge as would have sufficed for the ordinary depiction of things and bodies as they meet the eye. This was the principal goal of most Renaissance artists, but I think that Leonardo aimed at something far higher. Man may have the faculty of achieving this goal in the form of a symbol or an allegory. Romanesque art achieved it through the meaning of pure lines. Lines were used independently of what they might convey in terms of representing real objects. They acquired an eminently expressive value by being stripped of meaning that was referable to terrestrial objects.[139] But Leonardo—and this I believe makes him so different from all other artists—was not ready to make a compromise on this score. He insisted that the transcendent should be represented through the images of things as they exist in nature. Even in his last painting, the *St. John,* where the transcendent is set forth most forcibly among all his paintings, the consideration of the natural appearance of the human face is not weakened at all. Quite to the contrary, Leonardo successfully used immanent qualities of the appearance of things in order to reveal a transcendent truth by means that went beyond exaggeration, rearrangement, or patterns of emphasis, and possibly defy specification.

If we compare Leonardo's first painting, the angel's head in the *Baptism of Christ* by Verrocchio, with the portrait of Ginevra de Benci, in which the style of painting that would later make him famous appears for the first time, then we may get a glimpse of what possibly happened during these enigmatic four years in which Leonardo was artistically inactive.[140] The angel's head superbly fulfills the goal of representing immanent qualities, but in the portrait the first flickering of the grasp for the transcendent may be observed. What separated the two phases in time was possibly a process that amounted to a reorganization of the youthful artist's personality and the appearance of a new conceptual frame of artistry in the service of which he spent the rest of his life.[141] From a remark of von Bode's about the Louvre *Annunciation* I take it that the early paintings may have been produced with speed.[142] If it could be shown that Leonardo's habit of painting slowly with the procrastination and doubt that it implies started after the four quiet years, this would increase the probability of my thesis since the intention of reaching out for the transcendent in its pure veracity must necessarily have had the effect of a colossal slowing down.

To prove my thesis it would be necessary to analyze most carefully the paintings in which this new frame of reference appears. This would be beyond my ability as well as outside the scope of this study. Only this may be said: in the *Mona Lisa* and in the *St. John* Leonardo came closest to painting a "countenance of all countenances." The former became the most famous portrait of a woman; the latter has been little esteemed by most critics. One reason for this coldness toward the *St. John* may be that in it Leonardo really came as close to the realization of his goal as is humanly possible. If a genius were actually capable of realizing visually that which Leonardo aimed at, his achievement would be bound to go unnoticed because the ordinary human mind would not be capable of grasping it.

Be this as it may, some of Leonardo's paintings have a degree of finality which must have discouraged many an artist from taking up the same subject. Leonardo's *Cenacolo* and the *Battle of Anghiari* leave a feeling that it is superfluous to look at any other paintings on these themes. Prud'hon is said to have called the former the "masterwork of painting per se." Leonardo's superhuman effort to depict the transcendent through the immanent, that is, the fact that his paintings have their being in two contradictory spheres, may explain why they are more enigmatic than those of others. Clark called Leonardo, quite aptly, the Hamlet of art history.[143] This, too, may be why they affect me at least as being so close and at the same time so distant. There is incredible warmth in them and, strangely, also a frightening icy coldness that often makes it hard to come close to them. It is essentially different with his drawings, most of which are immediately and lastingly captivating.

If Leonardo's paintings are compared with Michelangelo's works, an essential point of the former's art comes to the fore. Almost all of Michelangelo's creations take possession of the beholder on sight.

He is irresistibly drawn into the conflicting emotions that are so powerfully expressed in his creations. This lightninglike effect seems to me to be missing from Leonardo's paintings, which rather inspire awe than enrapture and require long contemplation before their perfection is grasped. A feature of Michelangelo's work will easily account for this difference. To put it into the simplest form, Michelangelo consulted his own emotions in creating his masterpieces. His emotions had free access to what he was forming and the strong effect on the beholder is a reflection of his own titanic emotional conflicts which found their way into the work of art. How strongly his art was subjectively directed can be seen from Benedetto Varchi's lecture in the Academy of Florence in 1546 on two of Michelangelo's poems. There, in a discourse that Michelangelo approved, it was said that art is nothing but the "inward image of the object to be depicted, an image which is in the soul, that is, in the artist's imagination."[144] How far Michelangelo's subjectivity went can be learned from his Victory statue, now in the Palazzo della Signoria at Florence but originally destined for the tomb of Pope Julius II. "The vanquished old man," writes de Tolnay, "would be an idealized portrait of Michelangelo subjugated and enchained by love for the perfect youth kneeling on his back—the idealized image of Cavalieri."[145] Such a state of affairs is unthinkable in Leonardo's painted work. We found this range of problems in one of his allegories, but he would never have permitted himself to let this source of inspiration enter openly the official, final version of his artistic intent. I do not mean to say that this range of problems did not enter his painted œuvre, but it entered it in quite a different way than in Michelangelo's case.

I cited earlier from his Trattato a passage whose psychological meaning clearly declares his repugnance at the idea that the artist may freely let the subjective factor enter into a painting. The momentum of his effort was fully directed toward the outer world, isolated from his own personal conflicts. His ideal of the genius painter, it seems to me, was the representation of the terrestrial world in such a way that we behold through and across it the ideal and immutable images of the transcendent world.[146]

In Michelangelo we must see the genius who, despite all his devotion to the study of objects, represents them after a profound amalgamation with his emotions. The "cosmic forces of life," "the preterhuman sphere where primordial life forces are revealed,"[147] which he represented in his sculptures, are the direct projections of the conflicting feelings, emotions, passions, and impulses that raged in him and to which he lent an attentive and sensitive ear. In Leonardo's work, as has been said, the conflicts show up too, but the actual process that led to his creations was of a different kind. His paintings, in my opinion, compel the supposition of a heroic struggle not to let his passions enter them. The momentum of his creativity goes toward the visible and recognizable world and through it to a transcendent world of generally valid, all-comprehensive images. Lomazzo's report, that in order to paint the image of laughing peasants he gathered a number of peasants and entertained them until they broke out into vehement laughter, impresses me as permitting the conclusion that he would not have felt entitled or, perhaps, even able, to depict his own laughter. Of course, it would be foolish to deny that in the end product of his labor the subjective, personal factor was present. But the preconscious intent was apparently to eliminate it and to devote himself wholly to the service of what is eternally true in the abstract world of ideas.[148] This constitutes possibly the greatest sacrifice of which an artistically creative genius is capable; that it proved worth making may be judged from the fact that he succeeded as far as man can succeed.

A great debt is owed to Berenson for not having hesitated in publishing his adverse criticism of Leonardo's paintings.[149] His frankness has not always been appreciated,[150] but disregarding the detailed points of his opinion one may say that he expressed a reaction that is not only characteristic of him but brings forth an aspect of Leonardo's painted *œuvre*. I find it very significant that his strongest criticism extends to the *Cenacolo,* the *Mona Lisa,* and the *St. John,* and that he can make his peace with the *Adoration,* and *La Belle Ferronnière* (which, by the way, probably was not painted by Leonardo).[151] From my viewpoint I would say that Berenson feels repelled by those paintings in which Leonardo comes the closest to the transcendent, and he feels attracted where the immanent prevails. Indeed, the beholder who is not drawn across the threshold of the immanent world into the realm of the immutable gets stuck, so to speak, in what the painting says literally; he sees only the obviously apprehensible physical aspect and the *Cenacolo* must then become a kind of aggregate of histrionic gesturing.[152] With that attitude it becomes a "composition consisting entirely of figures ending at the waist line, of torsos with heads and arms but no abdomen and no legs."[153] But in his effort to demonstrate Leonardo's inferiority as a painter, the critic makes a remark that may prove the excellency of Leonardo's work, and, oddly enough, contributes greatly to a validation of my theory.

In writing about the *Mona Lisa,* Berenson speaks of the portrait's overmeanings, of which there are "not only as many as there are spectators, but more still, for it will appeal differently to the same spectator at different periods of his life and in different moods."[154] Here Berenson, though with pejorative intent, attributes to the *Mona Lisa* qualities that in certain respects surprisingly coincide with what Nicholas of Cusa had said of "the countenance of all countenances." Consequently it appears that Leonardo's art was, after all, of such excellence that the majority of beholders have reacted to it in accordance with the universal validity that it contained. That the representation of the universally valid was achieved without his having to step outside of nature but with full insistence upon representing the universal in shapes that appear in nature; that this representation was achieved without estrangement from nature; that the natural appearance of beings and objects was preserved in the process of universal validation—this, I believe, is quite unique in the history of art, makes Leonardo different from his peers, and reserves for him the special niche into which the expert as well as the naïve beholder has put him for over four and a half centuries.

Since, probably, every work of art aims at or contains something of transcendency, it may be worth while to specify the Leonardesque transcendency even at the risk of being repetitive. Here it is not a matter of making visible that which exists but is not accessible to human sight, such as the averted side of the moon or events that will take place in the future but are inaccessible in the present, such as the Last Judgment or a religious mood that impresses us as heavenly, as some of Fra Angelico's paintings proffer, or Michelangelo's transcendency inasmuch as he conveys inner processes of man, or the transcendency of the unconscious as presented in most of Goya's portraits, or the casting back of a godship within the terrestrial world in which Rembrandt's work is drenched—it is something far more sober and rational that is essentially divorced from the orectic sphere on the one hand and the actual appearance of objects on the other but is aimed at the visualization of the universally valid which includes in one representation of an object the full range of all possible modes that are or may be encountered within the orbit of reality. One hesitates to use here the concept of "idea," since any intimation that Leonardo was a painter of ideas would do grave injustice to the artistic values of his painted *œuvre.* The beholder is not made to feel any abstract principle and an artistic value is never sacrificed for the sake of an intellectual system; still, behind the forms and objects that appear on the canvas one notices the operation of a relational pattern that I have tried to characterize by certain implications of the new philosophy that had started with Nicholas of Cusa.

After having attempted to reconstruct preconscious and conscious motives that may have had their bearing on Leonardo's internal conflicts when he painted, it may be easier to make a final sensible proposition regarding repressed motives. Freud characterized one aspect of Leonardo's relationship to his father as an urge "to out-Herod Herod." [155] Biographical legend reflects this attitude, as in Vasari's report that Verrocchio, "chagrined that a child should know more than he," gave up painting when he saw Leonardo's superiority.[156] The historical record disproves Vasari's report, but Leonardo's ambition to create the greatest equestrian statue was understood as a successful though ephemeral attempt to outdo his former teacher.[157] Thus it would not be surprising if Leonardo also tried to outdo Nicholas of Cusa and prove to his satisfaction that the impenetrable world of *ideas* can be painted. Yet the concept of the "impossible" has as an unconscious equivalent, the "forbidden." Therefore it may be surmised that Leonardo, by his persistent effort to concretize and to behold that which it was asserted was impossible to concretize and to behold, desired to behold that which it was most forbidden to behold. From the observation of children in Western culture it is known that the strongest taboo extends to observing the genitalia of the parents, particularly of the mother, and to witnessing parental intercourse. No wonder, then, that Leonardo trembled when he set out to create a painting. Yet the impulse of "out-Heroding Herod" that Freud bared in Leonardo, suggests a still more general formulation.

Leonardo's quasi addiction to investigation presupposes the presence of inordinate curiosity. Only an insatiable feeling of curiosity can provide the fuel for a lifelong, equally insatiable investigatory impulse. And here we should recall Freud's statement in his letter of May 27, 1937, to Marie Bonaparte that

> One may regard . . . curiosity, the impulse to investigate, as a complete sublimation of the aggressive or destructive instinct.[158]

Was this sublimation in Leonardo psychologically as complete as we might expect in view of his achievements? Or did his sublimations still preserve some undertones of "the aggressive or destructive instinct" from which it stemmed? If the latter, we may understand why he felt inhibited in publishing the results of his research. Further, may we presuppose an equivalent destructive implication in Leonardo's painting?

After all, the painter arrogates a sector of reality for himself and reproduces it on the canvas.

When Leonardo did research or drew, the result of his labor remained with him. He had control over who would know of it and what. Yet a painting became part of the public domain and if, despite extensive and intensive sublimation, the aggressive-destructive admixtures came to be rejected by the self, the very fact of notoriety might easily have become a source of distress. The factors of hesitation, procrastination, and perfectionism may then be understood as the consequences of these admixtures, inasmuch as the self might have stood under the impact of an alarm that the secret hostility was, after all, not sufficiently eliminated from the product and therefore might be noticeable.

GENERAL REMARKS

These are the observations, conclusions, and speculations that came to my mind while I was working my way through the many materials I was prompted to study by the criticism Freud's Leonardo essay has recently encountered. Before concluding I would like to take up once more a general point which involves a key problem that has been dealt with in quite different ways by various writers on Leonardo.

There is first the question of whether Leonardo should be regarded as a neurotic. How Freud answers this question is not quite clear, but he seems to have leaned toward an affirmative. Clark too speaks of a disease of the will.

That Freud personally regarded Leonardo as a genius there can be no doubt. The 1910 essay conveys this, and when, almost three decades later, he discussed the problem of "great men," that is to say, personalities that move us "beyond the admiration of their grandiose creations," Leonardo is one among the three he cites.[159] Yet Freud's clinical eye discovered certain peculiarities in Leonardo that apparently impressed him as neurotic. There was the particular relationship of the self to emotions, for example; Leonardo's way of mourning; the total absence of heterosexual activity; an inhibition of the capacity to make decisions; regressions that bore upon his vacillation between science and art. However, at most points Freud speaks of that which can be observed in Leonardo as something *to be compared with* what is found in neurotics, which may suggest that Freud did not identify the psychopathology of the genius with neurosis. However, Freud also writes of "the neurotic conflict" in Leonardo, and in a more comprehensive way he stated that

Leonardo may be placed "close to the type of neurotic that we describe as 'obsessional'; and we may compare his research to the 'obsessive brooding' of neurotics."[160] Notwithstanding Freud's qualifications, one gets the impression that he thought of Leonardo as a neurotic. The essence of the problem emerges when we consider Freud's likening of Leonardo's researches to compulsive brooding. That comparison makes us aware of the undeniable similarity of the two phenomena but also of their essential difference: obsessive brooding is an autoplastic phenomenon, whereas Leonardo's researches "soared upwards to the highest realizations of a conception of the world that left his epoch far behind it."[161]

Freud's Leonardo study was written in the light of the clinical experience and observations he had made during the two preceding decades, that is to say, from the perspective of neurosis. As Freud said in his *Autobiographical Study,* with reference to this essay, his aim was to reconstruct "that part of him [the artist] which he shared with all men."[162] In a letter to Dr. Else Voigtländer of October 1, 1911, he wrote that by his Leonardo study he wanted to demonstrate "a particularly glaring example of the effect of the accidental family constellation [*ein besonders grelles Beispiel von der Wirkung der zufälligen familiären Konstellation*]."[163]

Nevertheless, even if the study of genius is limited to what he shares with the ordinary man, it is questionable whether Freud, after he had extended his research into the typology of the personality, would not have categorized Leonardo differently. To what extent would Freud then have stressed Leonardo's similarity with the obsessional *type,* which he characterized as follows:

> its distinctive characteristic is the supremacy exercised by the super-ego, which is segregated from the ego with great accompanying tension. Persons of this type are governed by anxiety of conscience instead of by the dread of losing love; they exhibit, we might say, an inner instead of an outer dependence; they develop a high degree of self-reliance, and from the social standpoint they are the true upholders of civilization, for the most part in a conservative spirit.[164]

or with the narcissistic-obsessional type, which

> represents the variation most valuable from the cultural standpoint, for it combines independence of external factors and regard for the requirements of conscience with the capacity for energetic action, and it reinforces the ego against the super-ego,[165]

or with a combination of both?

At any rate, I presume that in the perspective of Freud's ego psychology the problem of genius reappears as the question: What makes the genius different from the ordinary man? To be sure, one of the elements that make him *prima facie* so different, his outstanding skills, is as impenetrable to psychoanalysis as ever,[166] but, as Freud so rightly said, the problem of the great man is not only that of great skills.[167]

It is not probable that the genius capacity is so profoundly rooted in an innate constitution that, once given, its penetrance would conquer any environment, no matter haw unfavorable. The genius potentiality too needs an adequate habitat. What its structure is, we do not know. We can only retrace in a particular instance of genius some environmental factors which, in view of clinical experience, seem to have favored the development of specific geniushood; we can further try to reconstruct the development and structure of the personality that was prerequisite to transmuting the innate outstanding ability into genius achievement.

In accordance with Freud's theory of complementary series, we may expect to encounter, on the one hand, constitutions with enormous penetrance and little dependence on environmental factors, and, on the other, constitutions that require very favorable environments in order to flourish. However, we encounter here a question that finds no parallel in the study of neuroses and psychoses. Given a certain constitution, there will be several types of environments that will help unfold the potential genius's endowment, but possibly there will be only one that will suit this particular constitution so well that it will lead to the maximum realization. Herein we face an important, well-nigh a decisive, issue.

As Freud stated, Leonardo's illegitimate birth, the asserted separation from his father at the beginning, the closeness to his mother, contributed to what cursorily may be called his neurosis, but it also contributed to his later work. If these environmental factors had been different, he might have been spared his neurosis, but what effect would such change have had upon his later geniushood?

It is no longer disputed that in the study of genius a surprisingly large amount of psychopathology is encountered. The question, however, has not been answered what connection exists between the genius's psychopathology and his achievements. Psychopathology, in general, is looked upon as defect, though most forms of psychopathology have a useful function is so far as they spare the psychic apparatus a damage that would be greater than that caused by the psychopathology (primary gain).

Observation of the genius, however, suggests the possibility that psychopathology is indispensable to the highest achievements of certain kinds. Sarton expressed this indirectly as follows:

> Leonardo's greatest contribution was his method, his attitude; his masterpiece was his life. I have heard people foolishly regret that his insatiable curiosity diverted him from his work as a painter. In the spiritual sphere it is only quality that matters. If he had painted more and roamed less along untrodden paths, his paintings perhaps would not have taught us more than do those of his Milanese disciples. While, even as they stand now, scarce and partly destroyed, they deliver to us a message which is so uncompromisingly high that even today but few understand it.[168]

Before going into the principal point Sarton raises here I wish to refer to a subjective evaluation that implicitly underlies his statement. As is well known, no one has contributed to the enlargement of our knowledge of the history of science as Sarton has, and I agree with him that such knowledge is prerequisite not only for the understanding of science itself, but also of history and culture. Yet there is no doubt that he looks upon science as a good. Whatever favors science is welcome to him, as if the development of science were man's principal function. Sarton may indeed have been right in such an evaluation, but it has not yet been proved and, in the form in which it is found in his admirable work it is still a subjective, personal evaluation that cannot be regarded as binding.

This bias in favor of science may indirectly have led to a weak point in Sarton's argument. Even if Leonardo had given less time than he did, or even no time at all to scientific pursuits, he would never have been capable of painting like a mediocre artist. His earliest works, before he ever became seriously engaged in science, show unmistakably his superiority as a painter, and his first great painting, *The Adoration,* accomplished while he was still in his first stay in Florence, impressed Raphael so deeply that twenty-eight years later he borrowed important elements from it for his own paintings.[169] And this although, at that time, despite his scientific interests, there was as yet no visible schism between art and science.

Thus it may be inferred that once Leonardo had reached manhood he was destined to become one of the greatest painters of his epoch. Sarton's remark definitely sprang from a one-sided evaluation of science. But would Leonardo have been able to paint the *Mona Lisa* or draw the Deluge sketches if he had not "wasted" his time on scientific inquiries?

This is a pertinent question to ask. It is conceivable that after he left Florence his further development might not have carried him to such heights as it did if science had not entered his life extensively.[170]

Sarton's statement has another aspect that seems more pertinent. One may derive from it a strictly deterministic attitude. On this view, genius achievements are so rare and so outstanding that in all circumstances the individual paths that lead to their achievements are the only possible ones and any alternatives in upbringing, working habits, and interests could only work against the excellency of their accomplishments. Thus, if Leonardo had had less scientific interest or had been less compulsive or more heterosexually directed, this would have shown up in a diminution in the quality of his work. Since a person is accorded the distinctive mark of genius only when his works impress us as perfect and cannot be imagined as accessible to improvement,[171] any hypothetical change or alternative of constitutional or environmental conditions can only lead to imperfection.

Indeed, the thesis is quite conceivable that since Leonardo, or any genius, reaches the maximum of what is potentially in him we are to consider relevant environmental factors as causative. This approach would come close to or even coincide with the deterministic principle current in psychoanalysis, where the pathological end product is meaningfully connected with all preceding relevant factors, or, in other words, the symptom is considered to be determined by a manifoldness of causative conditions. With a variation of relevant conditions, the form and content of the symptom would change. Sarton's implication undoubtedly has much in its favor.

I feel strongly inclined toward one aspect of this approach. If we wish to apply seriously to the study of the psychology of genius the principle of psychic determinism, we may have to take his psychopathology into account as one of the factors indispensable to his geniushood. Consequently if what we observed in the genius struck us as neurotic or psychotic or perverse or even criminal, we would then have to reconsider our classification under these accustomed headings. If, for example, an apparently obsessional symptom were observed and it turned out that that symptom was indispensable to geniushood in that case, there would be no sense in calling it a neurotic symptom. Whatever the essence of neurosis may be, the concept of neurosis makes sense only when it is correlated with a deficit. No doubt, neurotic symptoms may facilitate socially approved behavior, or, at least, a person may by means of disease have gained the advantages we actually observe him to be in possession of. Yet, there is no known achievement which would justify the claim that is necessitated by observations in the instance of the genius, namely, that there was no alternative path, for him, to that achievement. During the years of war, for example, I got the impression—rightly or wrongly—that most of those who volunteered for parachute jumping were psychopaths, but it would be profoundly wrong to say that psychopathy is a prerequisite for parachute jumping. Although ability or desire or readiness for parachute jumping may be found more frequently among those who exhibit a selected type of psychopathology, it will be admitted that love of country or sense of duty may likewise induce a person to volunteer for such activity and become proficient in it.

In the case of the genius this is different, as can best be demonstrated in a small documented instance. For a certain period, Goethe, as he relates it in *Dichtung und Wahrheit,* tried each evening to see whether he was capable of committing suicide by stabbing himself. This behavior pattern (and particularly Goethe's rationalization of the choice of method, which I will not report here) is—under ordinary circumstances—characteristic of a deep-seated disturbance and may even announce the onset of a malignant psychosis. Goethe, however, shortly thereafter wrote his famous novel *Werther,* in which the hero of the story ends his life by shooting himself. Rarely have the sufferings of a young man for whom the world's tribulations have become unbearable been so heartbreakingly presented. The biographical evidence compels us to connect Goethe's "neurotic symptom" with his subsequent successful writing of the novel. It can safely be said that only somebody who had repeatedly gone through the throes of preparing for suicide could have presented it so overwhelmingly as Goethe, who was actually accused of having by his novel initiated a wave of suicides in Central Europe.

Here, then, we have a conspicuous example of undeniable pathological behavior that was one of the indispensable prerequisites for the writing of one of the greatest novels. If we continue to call such behavior an indication of a neurosis or psychosis, we make such categories meaningless. I described earlier a sexual pattern I believe represents Leonardo's form of genital release. In ordinary circumstances one would, of course, call such a sexual pattern a perversion. Yet I have tried to show that this pattern may have been indispensable for Leonardo. If he had not formed this pattern—of course only on the assumption that my construction is correct—or if society had interfered and prevented Leonardo from occasional indulgence in this form of sexual release, Leonardo's personality organization might have collapsed and been incapacitated for further production.

I need not go through the equivalent steps to demonstrate that the term perversion, unless used for purely descriptive purposes, would not be applicable to Leonardo either. Whatever its defensive function may have been in Leonardo's case, and no matter what similarities may be adduced between Leonardo's disturbance and that of a clinical pervert, the principal function of this sexual pattern in Leonardo was to provide the minimally necessary release in such a way that the sublimatory processes were not disturbed. It is conceivable that we shall one day recognize that a normal *vita sexualis* is incompatible with certain types of artistic geniushood.

Now just here, where I have myself characterized Leonardo's disturbance as what would ordinarily be called a perversion, the clinician may cite instances within his observation in which psychopathology that unquestionably deserves to be called a perversion has facilitated and even made possible socially approved achievements. Analytic experience, I believe, does not suggest that these achievements become impossible when the perversion has been removed. In the case of the genius, however, as far as one can reconstruct, it does not seem probable that he would be capable of his extraordinary creations if his libido were gratified in an adequate object relation. The energy flow into the object relation would be diverted from the artistic process. Consequently, only the blockage of a permanent object attachment can produce that intense hunger for objects that results in the substitute formation of the perfect work of art.

Therefore I would with a grain of salt say that in the genius all psychic processes that support sublimatory processes are ego syntonic and belong to a special category of psychopathology, which is essentially different from all other forms of psychopathology as set forth in textbooks of psychiatry. This is the psychopathology of genius, which is not amenable to criteria derived from the nongenius.

Yet, to complicate matters, in the genius we also encounter psychopathology that apparently does not support sublimatory processes and to which, consequently, the viewpoint just set forth does not apply. This kind of psychopathology actually drains off energy that otherwise would assist or flow into sublimation, and hence belongs in the categories of psychopathology also encountered in others. The decision as to which of these two types of psychopathology the investigator is confronted by in any particular case is a very delicate one. Probably the nearest one can come to even a rule of thumb is to suggest that if what one is dealing with is psychopathology in the ordinary sense, there will probably be a manifest deterioration in the quality of the created work that is genetically and dynamically connected with it.[172]

After this point, unique to the psychology of genius, has been set forth, one should be prepared to decide whether Freud or Sarton is right. However, I wonder whether the biographical record is rich enough to permit more than speculation. As a matter of fact, despite his eminence Leonardo is one of the geniuses whose works do not in every case live up to the acid test of perfection that I previously asserted. The *Cenacolo* in its original form must have lived up to that standard; in its present form it is a ruin. We may expect from the perfect work of art that its creator will endow it with such longevity as can be humanly achieved.

But just here the antinomy set forth can be demonstrated. I well follow Freud when he describes Leonardo's ambivalence toward his work, but this ambivalence may have been a cornerstone of his creativity. It seems historically well documented that Leonardo's slow way of painting made the use of contemporary fresco techniques impossible. For the technique he invented and which seemed to permit his deliberate ways, he had to pay a terrible price. The *Mona Lisa* too is not as well preserved as other contemporary paintings probably also because of the technique Leonardo used,[173] and his grandiose *Battle of Anghiari* has suffered even more grievously than the *Cenacolo*. But oddly enough the *Cenacolo* became the most representative painting of Christendom and no other portrait matches the *Mona Lisa* in renown. The deliberateness of his working technique, though possibly a derivative of compulsion and ambivalence, may still have been the only pathway on which his creativity could travel and evidently contributed immensely to the unique balance of the whole composition. This deliberateness, whatever its origin and derivation, did not drain the creative effort, but channelized it.[174]

No doubt many illustrations of the psychopathology of the genius can be found in Leonardo, and I have tried to describe the dynamics of some selected samples. Yet one wonders whether precisely in Leonardo, who was certainly one of the most creative minds the world has known, all the psychopathology encountered was really that of the genius and in the service of the creative process. If one equates Leonardo's artistic creative process with his scientific, as an increasing number of historians do since Séailles, then the decision will be rather in favor of Sarton. Freud did not follow this approach, but assumed a conflict between the artistic and the scientific impulse. He was perhaps influenced in this by a comparison with Goethe. At least, in 1930 he wrote:

> In Leonardo's nature the scientist did not get along with the artist; he disturbed him and perhaps crushed him in the end. In Goethe's life both personalities found room side by side; they alternated with each other as to primacy. One does not have to go far to connect Leonardo's disturbance with that inhibition of development which removed from his interests everything erotic and with it also psychology. In this point Goethe's nature was able to unfold itself more freely. [*In Leonardos Natur vertrug sich der Forscher nicht mit dem Künstler, er störte ihn und erdrückte ihn vielleicht am Ende. In Goethes Leben fanden beide Persönlichkeiten Raum nebeneinander, sie lösten einander zeitweise in der Vorherrschaft ab. Es liegt nahe, die Störung bei Leonardo mit jener Entwicklungshemmung zusammenzubringen, die alles Erotische und damit die Psychologie seinem Interesse entrückte. In diesem Punkt durfte Goethes Wesen sich freier entfalten*].[175]

In Goethe there was, however, at times a conscious conflict between the scientist and the artist; his marvelous skill in organizing and synthesizing was able, nevertheless, to get them both into proper balance. It is my impression that Leonardo was not consciously in conflict about the two activities. The climate of his times was, after all, favorable to equating them, although many of his contemporaries wondered about the periods in which he abandoned artistic pursuits. But his teacher, Verrocchio, and others legitimately pursued studies we would call scientific nowadays, and some of Leonardo's collaborators apparently did not take amiss his occasional exclusive devotion to science.[176]

The difference Freud draws between Leonardo the artist and Leonardo the scientist refers, in my opinion, to an unconscious conflict. In the unconscious, the two pursuits may have had a very different meaning and I wish to repeat an earlier suggestion that scientific pursuits perhaps aroused less anxiety in Leonardo than painting, that is to say, science served the function of defense with less conflict than painting. If the biographical record were more complete, we could perhaps reconstruct subjective differences that would permit a final conclusion, as is possible in Goethe's case. Whether Freud, if he had turned, in the light of his ego psychology, toward the problem of what makes a genius different from others, would still have maintained the division between neurosis and sublimation in Leonardo or whether he would have found a synthesis between ostensible disease and creativity, who can say?

The problem before us is to be discussed in still another context. What, in essence, was Leonardo's scientific contribution? It is strange what happens when a great artist also makes research one of his creative pursuits. We find a large number of biographers and historians who extol his scientific achievement and there is usually a lonely voice that disputes his merit. This is very clearly seen in the literature on Goethe as a scientist. One is dazzled when he reads Goethe's scientific publications, and is inclined to agree with those who pay them homage. Yet when a historian of science like Kohlbrugge, who knows the time sequences of scientific discoveries, examines the record he shows item for item that the scientific content of Goethe's writings, to the extent that it proved valid, is surprisingly unoriginal and goes back to earlier sources. He sagaciously adds that this does not detract an ounce from Goethe's greatness.

In the Leonardo literature something similar is to be observed. Notwithstanding Duhem's historical researches, I wish to refer to a doubt that can be discerned in Sarton's lines of praise, if only in the form of the simple question he raises: "Is it possible to ascribe to him [Leonardo] a single discovery, except such as are contained implicitly in his drawings?" Sarton's preliminary answer is:

> In order to receive credit for a discovery it is not enough to make it. One must explain it; one must prove very clearly that one has understood it, one must be ready to defend it. . . . Leonardo's ideas were like seeds that failed to mature.[177]

It is instructive to compare two views on Leonardo the scientist which are both brilliantly set forth, but diametrically opposed—those of Cassirer and Olschki. Cassirer sees in Leonardo a scientist in the full meaning of the word, who has integrated the basic structure and principles of modern science. Olschki disputes Leonardo's scientific eminence; he sees in him a superb observer, technician, and craftsman, but tries to demonstrate that Leonardo was in bondage to visualization, and that this resulted in grave limitations of abstraction when his research is viewed from the point of view of modern science.[178] Wherever research would have required Leonardo to break this bondage he failed.

The difference of opinion between Cassirer and Olschki rests on the interpretation of the numerous aphorismic statements in which Leonardo's notes abound. Are these aphorisms indicators of insight? Olschki shows how they contradict one another, and by analyzing a few examples of Leonardo's practical procedures demonstrates how Leonardo, after recording exact observations, fell into mysticism and abandoned what we would call scientific viewpoints. Cassirer evaluates Leonardo on the basis of the potentiality that was in him; he presents Leonardo's work in terms of an ideal type, whereas Olschki observes the realistic, historicopsychological processes.[179]

I believe Olschki to be right. This lag in Leonardo's scientific development was of the greatest benefit to mankind. If Leonardo had succeeded in what Galileo accomplished about a century later, we would not have his art work. If he had integrated the idea of scientific abstraction and law, his creative impulse toward visualization would necessarily have been weakened. The greatness of his artistic work presupposes a genius to whom visual creation is the supreme outlet. But how could this urge to create visually have competed successfully with the spell that is cast by the mathematical formula, which symbolizes the law of all movements that ever have been or will come to pass?

Was Leonardo's scientific work therefore in vain and waste? It may be worth while to cite here an author of renown who felt compelled to answer the same question in the affirmative with respect to Goethe, who was also distracted from his main mission by a large number of, so to speak, extracurricular activities. It is Ortega y Gasset who rendered devastating judgment on Goethe, whom he considers "perpetually untrue to his destiny" and "whose life was a life à rebours." He was "a perpetual deserter from his inner destiny." "He begins by fleeing from all his real loves. . . . He flees from life as a writer to fall into that unhappy Weimar episode." Further, he reproaches Goethe for his financial security in Weimar, since "a consciousness of security kills life." "Whatever he is, it is neither basically nor wholly: he is a minister who is not seriously a minister, a regisseur, a naturalist who does not succeed in being one." And so it goes on and on, because Goethe did not "enter into an exclusive destiny."[180] I do not wish to deal here with the cacophony of misinformation Ortega spilled out when barking at the moon, but point out how a professor of metaphysics may look at the life of a genius when he subjects it to his idea of destiny. It strikes me that almost everything Ortega says about Goethe could mutatis mutandis be repeated of Leonardo. His "destiny" was the visual arts, and Ortega could just as well have attacked Leonardo by pointing out all his flights from his destiny.[181] The method used by the metaphysician is a simple one. He excogitates a concept of life as it ought to be according to his way of thinking and then forms negative views of anything that does not fit into his conceptual framework. "Consciousness of shipwreck, being the truth of life, constitutes salvation," says Ortega.[182] Goethe did not live the life of the shipwrecked;

therefore Goethe betrayed his destiny. This shows up in his depressions: "Persistent depression is only too clearly a sign that a man is living contrary to his vocation."[183] Depressions, which were not at all persistent in Goethe as Ortega claims, but clearly periodic, we also encounter in Leonardo. There they burst forth in short but all the more impressive outcries: "Di mi se mai fu fatta alcuna cosa [Tell me if anything was ever done],"[184] we hear over and over again.[185] Thus perhaps does the genius express his misery when he feels the discrepancy between his potentiality and his actual realization.[186] This disproportion is always high in the genius despite the most intense creativity, and often low in the talent who turns out one product after another without pause and little conflict.

Thus the conflict about his productions is not atypical either in Goethe's or Leonardo's instance. But, as Olschki has pointed out,[187] Vasari's report that Leonardo on his deathbed expressed "how greatly he had offended God and man in not having worked in his art as he ought"[188] may, despite its legendary origin, reflect a deep psychological truth.[189] Indeed, if one views the whole of Leonardo's creative output, one may regret the imbalance between the artistic and the scientific parts.[190] When, toward the end of his life, he contemplated the results of his research—that is, the scattered notes that had not led to one single integrated text, that contained neither a single formulated law of nature nor the design of that much-desired flying machine—and saw the likeness between these scattered, mortarless building stones of the wonderful edifice he had dreamed of when he set out on his exploratory voyages, and his many unfinished paintings, as well as the ones he had felt capable of creating but had never even started, it may well be imagined that he felt deeply disturbed and depressed and even may have thought of himself as waste and failure, as happens so often precisely with the aging genius.

But even if Leonardo did feel that way, would he have been right? It seems that the function of knowledge in the genius artist is perhaps underestimated. It is true that the knowledge Leonardo amassed about the human body went far beyond what an artist commonly needs in order to be able to depict it. But for the creation of values that go beyond mere verisimilitude, the artist's feeling for his material will be quite different if, besides knowing all one needs to in order to understand the surface structure, he can see through the body and knows the innermost crevices in detail.

This can be shown quite concretely in another instance. Leonardo was obsessed by the study of water with a tenacity which "dismays his most industrious admirers," as Sir Kenneth Clark so rightly says.[191]

Whatever the conscious or unconscious motive of that enduring preoccupation may have been, it cannot be recorded as a waste from the viewpoint of Leonardo's artistic output since something of it, if not all, went into the crowning eleven drawings of the Deluge.

But it may still be objected that even if one relinquishes measurement by the yardstick of surface qualities, his nonartistic pursuits led him into aspects that can by no possible inference be connected with his artistic creations. What was the effect, after all, of his obsession with the flying machine, and where are the paintings in which we can admire the fruits of his anatomical studies? About these last it can be said that they in themselves led to artistic masterpieces in the form of his anatomical drawings; further, a number of his paintings have been lost, and, if all of them were still in existence we would perhaps be able to look upon an original St. John instead of the poor copy[192] in the Louvre which is all we now have, and the nude body of that St. John might demonstrate the final synthesis of Leonardo's lifelong anatomical studies.

In his effort to devise a flying machine he studied the flight of birds. One may say that he went through the process of identification with birds innumerable times, and if we still possessed his original *Leda* painting, we would perhaps be in a position to observe the artistic results of these studies. At least, Berenson says of the swan we know only from copies that it is "too big and real"[193] and the original might have taught us that Leonardo's observations were not a loss to artistic creations in this area either. Also, Leonardo's study of birds developed his feeling for winds and storms, which in turn contributed to his Deluge drawings. Thus we can in Leonardo's case find, in principle, a way back from science to art. But such a conclusion may be too hypothetical to be accepted as valid.

It is true that if Leonardo had not devoted himself so stubbornly to science, the course of science in all probability would not have been essentially altered, that is to say, in investigating the historical process of the development of science we do not find Leonardo as an indispensable link. His destiny, to use Ortega y Gasset's viewpoint, was the visual arts. But approaching Leonardo, not historically, but psychologically, one may discern the possibility that without his scientific pursuits he would not have been able to paint. The knowledge of things, in terms of what he considered (psychologically) satisfactory knowledge, that is, may have been a part of the prerequisite equipment for the adventure of painting, which he evidently approached with some feeling of perplexity. In other words, knowledge may have been the antidote against the anxiety that latently or manifestly was involved when he took up the brush.[194]

Yet withal I have not been able to find the common denominator of Leonardo's apparent neurosis and geniushood. Probably Freud, if his work had taken him back to Leonardo after he had accomplished his research on ego, supergo, and defense, would have given us the solution to this question too.

If I may now return to the question I raised at the outset, I can state that Freud's first major venture, in 1910, into the reconstruction of some relevant psychic processes of a genius of the past stands up quite well in the light of the research that has accumulated during the last fifty years. Still, I am aware that future, particularly archival, research may unearth documents that will disprove beyond question Freud's reconstruction (and, for that matter, also the bulk of my own hypotheses). But even such an outcome, I believe, would not reduce Freud's position as the preeminent, as well as the first, paleopsychopathologist. I feel entitled to coin this term since Freud, when he wrote his study, found himself in the position in which the paleontologist customarily finds himself, namely, of having to reconstruct from a minimum of preserved data a maximum of past entities on the basis of observations made in the present. When Schapiro calls "the habit of building explanations of complex phenomena on a single datum"[195] a weakness of Freud's book, then he rejects one of the most glorious pages in the history of psychology. Quite independently of whether Freud was right or wrong in his reconstruction of one aspect of Leonardo's personality, the personality is a whole, and in principle we ought to be capable of making valid statements about the most complex phenomena on the basis of small knowledge of a single phenomenon. It is not up to me to make a final statement about the progress Freud and psychoanalysis have made in the art and science of paleopsychopathology, but it would be surprising if it really turned out that man's mind is in principle less amenable to scientific inquiry than are physical and biological strata of existence.[196] Freud's Leonardo study should, in my estimation, be regarded as holding unimpaired its pre-eminent historical position as a beacon marking the paths by which psychological insight, actually or potentially, as the case may be, can illuminate man's historical past.

71. Leonardo, *Portrait of a Young Woman (Ginevra Benci)*. Vienna, Liechtenstein Gallery.

72. Leonardo, *Diminutive Sketch of a Standing Leda*. Facsimile of Codice Atlantico fol. 156r. New York, Collection IBM Corp. *Photo: Michael Katz.*

73. Verrocchio, *Baptism of Christ.*
Florence, Uffizi.   *Photo:*
Alinari-Art Reference Bureau.

74. Michelangelo, *Victory.*
Florence, Palazzo della Signoria.
Photo: Brogi-Art Reference Bureau.

75a. Leonardo, *Flying Machine (Ornithopter)*.
Facsimile of Codice Atlantico fol. 276r-*b*.
New York, Collection IBM Corp.

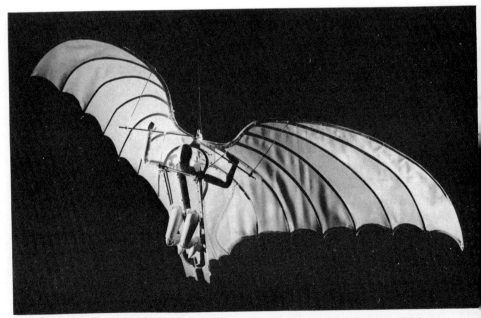

75b. Model of Leonardo's Flying Machine. New York, Collection IBM Corp.

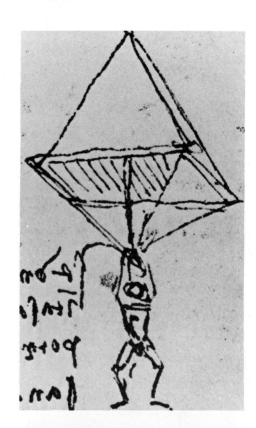

76a. Leonardo, *Helicopter*. Facsimile of
Codice Atlantico fol. 381v-*a*.
New York, Collection IBM Corp.

76b. Model of Leonardo's Helicopter.
New York, Collection IBM Corp.

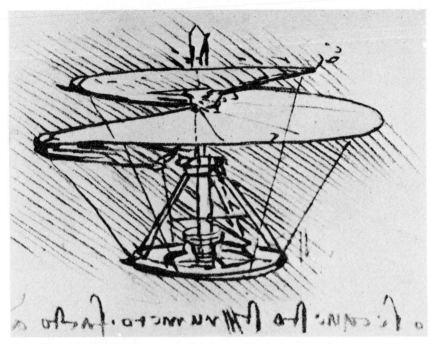

77a. Leonardo, *Helicopter or Aerial Screw*. Paris, Institut de France, Ms.B, fol. 90v. *Photo: IBM Corp., New York.*

77b. Model of Leonardo's Helicopter or Aerial Screw. New York, Collection IBM Corp.

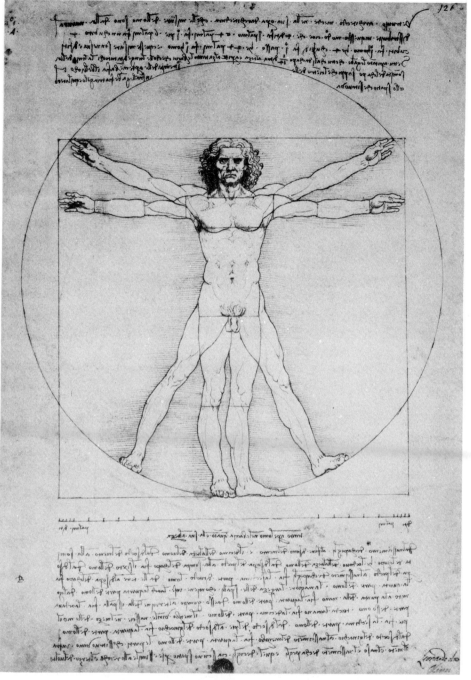

78. Leonardo, *Canon of Proportions*. Venice, Academy of Fine Arts.
Photo: Alinari-Art Reference Bureau.

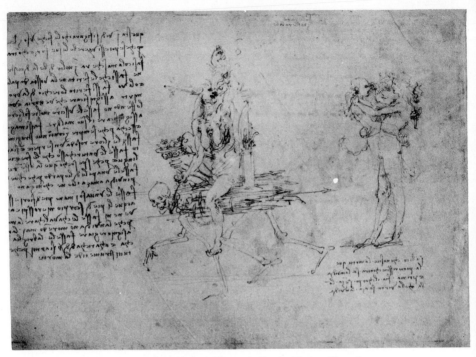

79. Leonardo, *Two Allegories of Envy*. Oxford, Christ Church.
Photo: Art Reference Bureau.

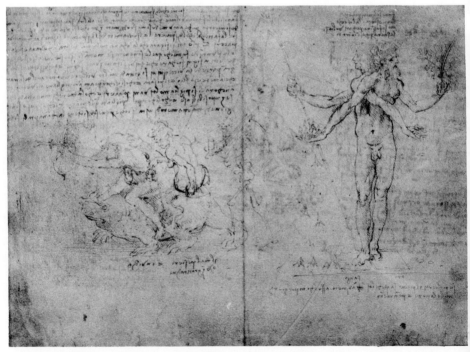

80. Leonardo, *Allegories of Pleasure and Pain and of Envy*. Oxford, Christ
Church. *Photo: Art Reference Bureau.*

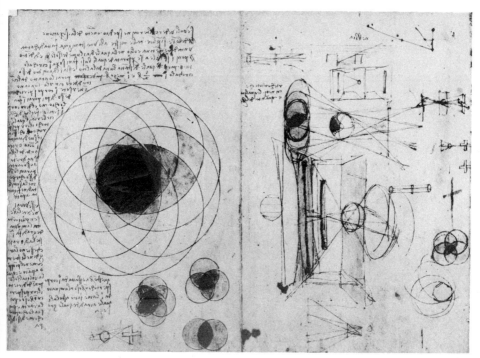

81. Leonardo, *Studies in Gradations of Light and Shade*. Facsimile of Codice Atlantico fol. 187r. **New York**, Collection IBM Corp.   *Photo: Michael Katz.*

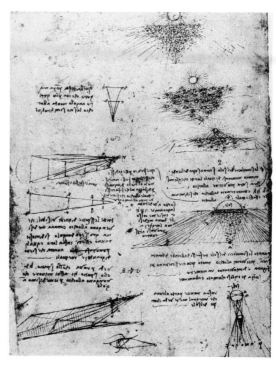

82. Leonardo, *Reflections of the Sun on Water*. Facsimile of Codice Atlantico fol. 208v-b. New York, Collection IBM Corp.   *Photo: Michael Katz.*

5/

THE VISION
BEYOND GRASPING

"It is a sorry master whose work surpasses his judgment; and that master tends toward the perfection of art whose work is surpassed by his judgment."

—from Leonardo's *Treatise on Painting,*
folio 57

Leonardo and the Philosophers

by Paul Valéry

HIS ESSAY was written to serve as preface to a first book by Leo Ferrero, and I cannot let it be reprinted here without saying, to those who never knew the young writer, how much the loss of his person meant to Letters.[1]

Invoking Leonardo da Vinci almost at the beginning of your career, you have placed beneath his name a treatise and meditation on pure aesthetics. Many philosophies have finished or even perished in that field of speculation. Nothing could be nobler than your undertaking, or more venturesome.

With remarkable precision and subtlety you have examined some of the most delicate points in the endless researches that aim to render the Beautiful almost intelligible and to give us superior reasons for being moved by it.

But you are venturing into still more dangerous territory when you ask me to introduce your work to the public. It is not that I have failed to encounter problems of the sort on many divergent paths, or have failed to reflect on them at sufficient length; it is rather that my reflections have echoed one another and that my lights have been confined and confused as if between parallel mirrors. Between nature and artifice, between the pleasures of sight and those of power, the exchanges are infinite. Soon intelligence is lost in a maze. Intelligence, which undertakes

From *Three Masters,* Vol. 8 in the *Collected Works* of Paul Valéry, tr. by Malcolm Cowley. Printed by permission of the Bollingen Foundation.

and continually resumes the task of reorganizing that which exists, while arranging the symbols of all things round itself as the unknown center, grows weary and loses hope in this realm where answers precede questions, where caprice gives birth to laws, where we are privileged to take the symbol for the thing and the thing for the symbol, and where that liberty can serve as the means of achieving an inexplicable sort of rigor.

Uncertain as I am, you would still like me to prepare the minds of others for your dialectic. All I can offer them is the somewhat confused notion I hold of speculations concerning the Beautiful.

It must be confessed that aesthetics is a great and even irresistible temptation. Almost everyone with a strong feeling for the arts has something more than that feeling; he cannot escape the need for going deeper into his enjoyment.

How can we bear to be enchanted by some aspect of nature or by certain works of man without trying to explain this accidental or contrived delight? On the one hand it seems to be independent of the intelligence—*although it may be the principle and hidden guide of the intelligence*—while on the other hand it seems to be quite distinct from our ordinary feelings—*although it may include and transfigure their variety and depth.*

Philosophers could not fail to be puzzled by emotions of this curious type.[2] Moreover, they had a somewhat less naive and more systematic reason for examining such emotions and for searching out their causes, operation, meaning, and essence.

The vast enterprise of philosophy, as seen in the philosopher's own heart, consists, after all, in *an effort to transmute everything we know into what we should like to know,* and the operation has to be effected, or at least presented, or at the very least presentable, in a certain *order.*

Philosophies are characterized by the order of their questions, for, in a philosophic mind, questions do not and cannot exist in complete independence and substantial isolation. On the contrary, what one finds in such a mind, as a sort of ground bass, is the feeling or fundamental *tone* of a latent though more or less close interdependence among all the ideas it contains or might ever contain. Awareness of this deep coherence imposes order; and the order of questions necessarily leads to a sovereign question, which is that of knowledge.

Now, as soon as a philosopher has postulated or founded or justified or depreciated knowledge (whether he has exalted and developed it *ultra vires* by potent logical or intuitive combinations, or whether he has measured knowledge and, as it were, reduced it to limited dimensions by criticism), he always finds himself tempted to *explain*—that is, to express in his system, which is his personal order of comprehension—human activity in general, of which intellectual knowledge is only one of the modalities, although it stands for the whole.

Here we come to a crucial point in any philosophy.

A system of thought that had been so pure and central, one that had actually pursued (whatever its contents and conclusions might have been) the ideal of a *uniform* distribution of concepts round a certain attitude or characteristic preoccupation of the thinker, must henceforth try to recover the diversity, irregularity, and unexpectedness of other manners of thinking; and its order must regiment their seeming disorder.

It must reconstitute the plurality and autonomy of other minds as a consequence of its own unity and sovereignty. It must legitimize the existence of things it had convicted of error and so ruined; it must recognize the vitality of the absurd, the fruitfulness of contradictions; and at times it must even acknowledge that in itself, for all its sense of being informed with the universality from which it seems to proceed, it is no more than a particular production or the individual tendency of a certain person. Here is the beginning of wisdom, and likewise the twilight of a philosophy.

The truth is that other existences are always disturbing to the splendid egotism of a philosopher. He cannot fail, however, to come against the great riddle presented by the inconsequences of others. The thoughts, the feelings, the actions of another always seem to us arbitrary. The partiality we always show to what is ours has been strengthened by our feeling that we are agents of necessity. But *the other* does exist, and hence the riddle is forced upon us. It invades our minds under two forms: one consisting in the different types of conduct and character, the great variety of decisions and attitudes, in all that touches on the preservation of the body and its possessions; the other manifested by the diversity of tastes, expressions, and creations of the sensibility.

Our Philosopher cannot resign himself to not absorbing into his own light all the realities that he would like to assimilate to his reality, or at least reduce to being its possible possessions. He wants to *comprehend,* that is, to comprehend them all in the full meaning of the word. Hence he will dream of building himself a science of the values of action, and another science of the values of expression or of creating emotions—an ETHICS and an AESTHETICS[3]—as if his Palace of Thought would be imperfect without these two symmetrical wings, in which his omnipotent and abstract self could imprison action, passion, emotion, and invention.

Every philosopher, when he has finished with God and the Self, with Time, Space, Matter, the Categories, and the Essences, turns back toward men and their works.

Just as our Philosopher had invented the *True,* so he invented the *Good* and the *Beautiful.* Just as he had invented rules to harmonize isolated thought with itself, so he undertook to prescribe other rules designed to harmonize action and expression with precepts and models that were shielded from everyone's caprices and doubts by the consideration of a unique and universal principle, one that must first of all, and *irrespective of any particular experience,* be defined or designated.

Few events in the history of thought are more remarkable than this introduction of Ideals, in which may be seen an essentially European achievement. The decline of ideals in men's minds coincides with that of the virtues typical of Europe.[4]

We are still rather firmly attached, however, to the idea of a pure science rigorously developed on the basis of *local* evidence, but having properties that may be extended indefinitely from identity to identity. In the same fashion we are still half convinced of the existence of a single Morality and a single Beauty, both independent of times, places, peoples, or persons.[5]

Each day, however, the ruin of this noble edifice is a little more clearly revealed. We are witnessing an extraordinary phenomenon: that the very development of the sciences is tending to weaken the concept of Knowledge. I mean that a seemingly impregnable area of science, one that it shared with philosophy (in other words, with faith in the intelligible and belief in the inherent value of mental acquisitions) is gradually yielding ground to a new fashion of conceiving or evaluating the function of cognition. No longer can the efforts of the intellect be regarded as converging toward an intellectual limit, toward the *True.* A moment of self-examination is enough to reveal in ourselves this modern conviction: that any form of *knowledge,* unless it corresponds to some effective *power,* has only a conventional or arbitrary importance. The value of any knowledge consists only in its being the description or the means of exercising a verifiable power. From this it follows that any metaphysical system and even any theory of cognition, whatever these may be, are ruthlessly cut off and set apart from what is regarded more or less consciously *by all* as the only real knowledge—*payable in gold.*

By the same process and apparently of their own volition, ethics and aesthetics are dissolving into problems of legislation, statistics, history, or physiology . . . and into lost illusions.

Moreover, what excuse could we offer for making and elaborating plans to "do an Aesthetics"?—A science of the Beautiful? . . . Do modern people still use that word as a noun? It seems to me that they never pronounce it without a hint of apology or disdain, unless they happen to be thinking of the past. Beauty is a sort of corpse. It has been supplemented by novelty, intensity, strangeness, all the *shock values.* Raw excitement is the sovereign mistress of recent souls, and works of art are at present designed to tear us away from the contemplative state, the *motionless delight,* an image of which was at one time intimately connected with the general notion of the Beautiful. Art is more and more penetrated by the most immediate and unstable moods of psychic and sensual life. The *un*conscious, the *ir*rational, the *in*stantaneous—which are, as their names indicate, privations or negations of the voluntary and sustained forms of mental activity—have replaced the models *expected by the mind.* Seldom do we encounter anything produced by a desire for "perfection." —Let us observe in passing that this antiquated desire was bound to be destroyed by the blind striving and insatiable thirst for *originality.* The ambition to perfect a work of art comes close to being a project for making it independent of any era; but the effort to be new is also an effort to make the work of art a remarkable event by virtue of its contrast with the passing moment.[6] The former ambition admits and even requires *heredity,* imitation, or tradition, these being stages in an ascent toward the absolute beauty it dreams of attaining. The latter ambition rejects them, while implying them still more rigorously—for its essence is to *differ from.*

In our days a "definition of the Beautiful" has become scarcely more than a historical or philological document. This illustrious word has lost its ancient richness of meaning. Soon the numismaticians of language will put it away in their cabinets, with many another verbal coin that has passed from circulation.

Nevertheless, certain problems remain, and certain others might well arise, that cannot be assigned to any of the well recognized scientific disciplines and have no connection with any particular technique.[7] They have also been neglected by the philosophers, although they keep reappearing—however vaguely or strangely they may be expressed—in the gropings and uncertainties of artists.

Take, for example, the general problem of composition (that is, of the different types of relationship between the whole and the parts); or take the problems resulting from the manifold functions of each element in a work; or the problems of *ornament* that border simultaneously on geometry, physics, and morphology without finding a definite center —although they permit us to glimpse a vague sort of kinship among the forms of equilibrium of physical objects, the figures of musical composition, the structure of living creatures, and the half-conscious or fully conscious productions of human activity when it endeavors to fill an empty space or time, as if in obedience to something like a horror of the void.

Questions of the sort do not obtrude themselves on abstract thinking. They take rise and acquire their strength from the creative instinct, at a moment when the artist has gone beyond the point of setting down what first occurs to him.[8] He begins to look for solutions in a process of meditation that appears to be speculative, even assuming a philosophic form, and he hopes it will lead to some decision that will determine the form and structure of a concrete creation. It may well happen that the artist follows the same path as the philosopher, at least for a time, in his effort to formulate principles than can justify and clarify his intentions by giving them more than a merely personal authority; but what he achieves in this direction is only a biased sort of philosophy, one that aims beyond his principles at a set of particular consequences for the work in hand. The true philosopher regards *what is* as the limit to be attained and the object to be recovered at the extreme point of his mental excursions and operations. The artist, on the other hand, is at home in the possible and makes himself the agent of *what is to be.*

The clearest difference between the aesthetics of a philosopher and the reflections of an artist is that the former proceeds from a system of thinking that regards itself as foreign to the arts and of another essence than the thinking of a poet or a musician—in which respect it may well be mistaken, as I hope to show later. To a philosopher's mind works of art are accidents, or particular cases, or the effects produced by a busy sensibility as it gropes blindly toward a principle that Philosophy sees as a whole and possesses as an immediate and pure concept. The practice of the arts does not seem *necessary* to the philosopher, because its supreme object is one that should belong immediately to philosophic thought, or should be directly accessible to such thought as a result of the attention that philosophers apply to understanding, or to creating a system that jointly explains the perceptible world and the intelligible world. The philosopher does not feel a particular need for artistic activity; he underrates the methods and values of execution and the importance of materials, since he instinctively tends to distinguish these from the *idea*. He finds it distasteful to think of an incessant, intimate, and even-handed exchange between the desired and the possible, between what he judges to be accident and what he judges to be essence, between "form" and content, between consciousness and automatism, between circumstance and design, between "matter" and "spirit." Now, it is precisely the great custom and acquired freedom of making such exchanges; it is the existence in the artist of a concealed standard of measurement applying to elements of radically different natures; it is the inevitable and indivisible collaboration, the coordination *at every moment,* in all his acts, of the arbitrary and the necessary, of the expected and the unexpected, of his body, his materials, his decisions, and even his fits of absence—it is all this that finally enables him to add something to nature considered as a practically infinite source of subjects, models, means and pretexts; to create some *object* that cannot be simplified and reduced to an abstract idea, since it owes its origin and its effect to an inextricable system of independent conditions. *We cannot summarize a poem as we might summarize . . . a "universe."* To summarize a thesis is to preserve what is essential in it. To summarize a work of art, or replace the work with a diagram, is to lose what is essential. When we grasp the implications of this principle, it is easy to see that the analytical work of the aestheticians is largely an exercise in self-delusion.

The fact is that we cannot extract from an object, or from a natural or artificial arrangement, any group of aesthetic characteristics that can be found elsewhere and subsequently used as the basis of a general formula applying to beautiful things. Such an attempt has often been made, but those who make it are unaware that the method applies only to things "already found." Moreover, the object under consideration cannot be reduced to a few of its traits without losing its intrinsic emotive power.

It is hard for a philosopher to understand that the artist passes almost indifferently from *form* to *content* and from *content* to *form;* that a *form* may occur to him *before* the meaning he will assign to it; or that *the idea of a form* is the same for him as *the idea that asks to be given a form.*[9]

In short, if aesthetics could exist as a philosophy, the arts would melt away before it, that is, *before their own essence.*

What I have just said does not apply to technical studies concerned only with methods or particular solution—those aimed more or less directly at the production or classification of works of art, but not proposing to attain the Beautiful *by paths that lie outside its proper domain.*

The truth may be that we cannot form a clear conception of anything unless we might also have invented it. Pascal tells us that he would not have invented painting. He did not *see* the need for duplicating the most insignificant objects by making laborious copies of them. And yet how often this great artist in words took pains to *draw,* that is, to make a spoken portrait of his thoughts! It is true that he seems to have ended by including all desires *save one* in the same gesture of rejection, and by regarding everything but death as something painted.[10]

What was Immanuel Kant really doing when he based his Ethics and his Aesthetics on a myth of universality, on the latent presence of an infallible and unanimous feeling about the universe in the soul of every man coming into this world? And what about all the other philosophers of the Good and the Beautiful?—The answer is that they were creators in spite of themselves, Creators who believed that they were merely substituting a more exact or complete notion of reality for a crude or superficial one, when, on the contrary, *they were inventing*—one by subtle division, another by an instinct for symmetry, and all by a profound desire for a certain state, by a profound love for *that which might be.* What did they do but create when they added problems to problems, entities to entities, and new symbols, new forms and formulas of development, to the existing treasury of intellectual pastimes and arbitrary constructions of the mind?

Philosophy marched out to grapple with the artist, to "explain" what the artist feels and does; but something quite opposite took place and is coming to light. Far from its enveloping and assimilating the whole domain of creative sensibility into the concept of the Beautiful; far from its becoming the mother and mistress of aesthetics, what now appears is that philosophy proceeds from aesthetics and no longer finds its justification, an answer to its qualms of conscience, or even its veritable "depth" save only in its constructive power and its freedom as abstract poetry. An aesthetic interpretation and that alone can shield the venerable monuments of metaphysics from the collapse of their more or less hidden postulates or from the destructive effects of semantic and logical analysis.

At first it may seem quite difficult for philosophers to approach certain problems *as artists* when they were accustomed to thinking about them *as seekers of truth,* or to regard the products of a desperate sincerity as beautiful lies and inherent fictions. "What a splendid past," they will say, "and what a sad present!" They should set their minds at rest about this change, which after all is only a change in customs. I do not look on it as anything more than a reform demanded by the course of events, one for which a sort of model can be found in the history of the plastic arts. There was a time when the likeness of a man or an animal, even if people had seen the craftsman making it, was regarded not only as a living thing, motionless though it was, but as being endowed with supernatural powers. Many of the gods fashioned out of stone or wood did not even resemble men, yet people nourished and venerated these images that were scarcely images. The more formless they were, the more they were adored—a curious fact that is also to be observed in the relation of children to their dolls and of lovers to the beloved; it appears to be a deeply significant trait. (Perhaps we believe that the more life we are obliged to give to an object, the more we receive from it.) But little by little, as the communicated life grew weaker and was withdrawn from such rude images, *the idol became Beautiful.* Impelled by criticism, it lost its imaginary power over events and persons in order to gain a real power over men's eyes. Sculpture became free, and became itself.

Without shocking or cruelly wounding the philosophic sentiment, might I compare its idolized truths—its Principles, its Ideas, its Being, its Essences, its Categories, its Noumena, its Universe, the whole tribe of concepts that seemed indispensable each in its turn—with the idols of which I was speaking?—At present we might ask ourselves what sort of philosophy would stand in the same relation to traditional philosophy that a Greek statue of the fifth century B.C. stands to the faceless divinities of very ancient times.

I sometimes think that little by little, as it becomes possible and permissible to compose with ideas as with tones or colors—to make abstract constructions without having illusions about them and without recourse to hypostasis—it may become evident that this type of untrammeled philosophy is more fruitful and more *true* than the type that attached itself to a primitive belief in explanations, as well as more human and appealing than the type demanded by a rigorous critical aptitude. Perhaps it will then be possible to resume—in a new spirit and with quite different ambitions—the speculative work that was undertaken by the great metaphysicians, whose goals, in the course of time, have been sadly undermined by criticism. An example from another field might prove illuminating. Long ago mathematics made itself independent of every aim that was alien to the concept of itself created by the pure development of its technique and by its awareness of the intrinsic value of that development. Today everyone knows to what extent its freedom as an art, which had promised to carry it far from reality into a world of pastimes, difficulties, and useless elegance, has made it marvelously flexible, besides equipping it to come to the aid of the physical scientists.

An art of ideas—an art of the order of ideas, or of the multiple orders of ideas—is that a wholly vain conception? I find it permissible to think that all architecture does not exist in space, that all music is not heard. There is a certain feeling for *ideas* and their analogies that seems to me capable of acting and being cultivated in the same fashion as a feeling for sound or color; and I might even be inclined, if I had to propose a definition of the philosopher, to make it depend on the predominance in his person of this mode of *sensibility*.[11]

I also believe that one is born a philosopher, as one is born a musician or a sculptor, and that this innate gift, which has always taken the pursuit of a certain *reality* or *truth* as its theme and pretext, might henceforth confide in itself and, instead of merely pursuing, might create. The Philosopher would then expend in full liberty the forces he had acquired through discipline; and there would be an infinite number of questions, an infinite number of forms, on which he could lavish his vigor and the faculty proper to his nature: that of giving life and movement to abstract things.

Thus it would become possible to *save the Noumena*, by simple delight in their intrinsic harmonies.[12]

Finally I might say that there exists an excellent demonstration of what I have so far been proposing in a tentative way. It was no more than a possibility, but we have only to consider the fate of the great philosophic systems to find it already realized. In what spirit do we read the philosophers, and who consults them in the true hope of finding anything else than enjoyment or an exercise for the mind? When we now set out to read them, is it not with a feeling that we are submitting for a time to the rules of an admirable game?—What would happen to these masterpieces of an unverifiable branch of knowledge if it were not that we accepted these conventions out of love for an exacting pleasure? If we disproved a Plato or a Spinoza, would nothing remain of their astonishing constructions? Absolutely nothing—*if there did not remain a work of art.*[13]

Meanwhile, quite apart from philosophy, in certain strategic areas of the search for understanding, there have appeared a few extraordinary beings of whom we know that their abstract thought, highly developed as it was and capable of the greatest subtlety and depth, never lost its concern for figurative creations or tangible applications and proofs of its attentive power. They seem to have possessed I cannot say what inner science that made it possible to effect a continual interchange between the *arbitrary* and the *necessary.*

Leonardo da Vinci is the supreme type of these superior individuals.

What is more remarkable than the absence of his name from the list of recognized philosophers, grouped as such by tradition?[14]

Doubtless the lack of finished texts of a specifically philosophic nature might pass as a reason for this exclusion. Moreover, the quantity of *notes* he left behind is a simultaneous mass of observations that leaves us in doubt regarding the order of questions in his thinking. One hesitates to say which of his curiosities and intentions stood first or last, since Leonardo himself seems to have lavished his ardor on the greatest variety of subjects, depending on circumstances and the mood of the hour—so much so that he gives the not unpleasant impression of being a sort of *coniottiere* in the service of all the Muses turn by turn.

But, as has already been said, the visible existence of a certain order of ideas is characteristic of the recognized philosophers whose qualities permit them to figure in the History of Philosophy (a history that can be written only with the help of certain conventions, including first of all a *necessarily arbitrary* definition of philosophy and the philosopher).

It follows that Leonardo would be excluded for lack of an explicit order in his thinking, and—let us not be afraid to say—for lack of an *easily summarized* statement that would enable us to classify his essential conceptions and compare them with other systems, problem by problem.[15]

But I should like to go farther and distinguish him from the philosophers by more tangible characteristics and for more substantial reasons than these purely negative considerations. Let us see—or imagine —in what respects his intellectual activity differs sharply from theirs, while closely resembling it at moments.

The philosopher, to the eyes of an observer, has a very simple purpose: *to express in speech or writing the results of his meditations.* He tries to constitute a body of *knowledge* that is completely expressible and transmissible by *language.*

But for Leonardo, language is not all. Knowledge is not all; perhaps he regards it only as a means: Leonardo designs, computes, builds, decorates; he makes use of all the concrete methods and materials that are subject to ideas, serve as a test for them, and give them an opportunity to rebound in an unexpected fashion, since the materials offer an alien resistance to ideas and provide the conditions of another world that no previous knowledge or degree of foresight would make it possible to encompass in a purely mental elaboration. *Knowledge* is not enough for this strongly willed and many-sided nature; what matters to him is *power.* He does not separate understanding from creating. He does not like to distinguish theory from practice, or speculative thought from an increase in external power, or the true from the verifiable, or the true, again, from that modification of the verifiable manifested in the construction of works of art and machines.

In that respect, this man is an authentic and immediate ancestor of science as it exists today. Who does not see that science is coming more and more to identify itself with the acquisition and possession of power?[16] Hence I would venture to define it in this fashion—for the definition *is within us,* however we may protest. *Science consists,* I would say, *in all the formulas and all the processes that are always successful,* and it is coming progressively closer to being a *table of correspondences between human actions and the resulting phenomena*—an always longer and more definite table of such correspondences, recorded in the most precise and economical systems of notation.

Infallibility in prediction is, in simple fact, the only characteristic that modern man regards as having more than a conventional value. He is tempted to say, "All the rest is literature"; and the rest would include all explanations and theories. It is not that he fails to recognize their utility, even their necessity, but rather that he has learned to consider them as means and instruments, intermediate operations, steps in the dark, provisional methods that furnish him with logical formulations, with combinations of signs and images, in order to clear the way for the final decisive perception.

In the course of a few decades he has seen the successive and even simultaneous reigns of contradictory theses that proved equally fruitful; of doctrines and methods opposed in principle and making theoretical demands that canceled one another, while all of them produced positive results to be added to his stock of acquired powers. He has heard *laws* described as more or less helpful *conventions;* and he also knows that a great number of those laws have lost their pure and essential character, being reduced to the modest level of simple probabilities—in other words, to rules that apply only in the field of our observations. Finally, he understands the increasing and by now almost insuperable difficulties that inhere in any attempt to represent a "world" that we postulate; a world that imposes itself on our minds, but also a world—revealed as it is in a roundabout fashion by a series of relays and by its indirect effects on the senses; constructed as it is by a process of analysis with disconcerting results when these are translated into common language; excluding as it does any sort of images, since it must be the substance of their substance and must provide, in some sort, a basis for all the categories—*that exists and does not exist.* But all these terrifying indeterminate principles, these inhuman hypotheses, this knowledge incompatible with the knower, none the less leave behind them an always increasing and incorruptible treasure of achievements and modes of producing achievements—in other words, of *powers.*[17]

All the labors of the mind can no longer have as their object a final contemplation, even the mental image of which has lost its meaning (or comes closer and closer to being a theological concept, demanding a contemplator different in essence from ourselves); but, on the contrary, those labors appear to the mind itself as *an intermediate activity connecting two experiences or two states of experience,* the first of which is *given* and the second *foreseen.*

Knowledge of this sort is never separated from action or from instruments of execution and control, without which, moreover, *it has no meaning*—whereas if it is based on them, if it refers back to them at every moment, it enables us to deny meaning to knowledge of any other sort, and specifically to that which proceeds from words alone and leads only toward ideas.

What then becomes of philosophy, besieged and obsessed as it is with discoveries so unexpected as to arouse the greatest doubts concerning the virtues or value of all the ideas and deductions put forward by a mind reduced to its own resources and trying to encompass the world? What becomes of it when—in addition to feeling beset, wounded, and astonished at every turn by the furious activity of the physical sciences —it is also disturbed and menaced in its most ancient, most tenacious (and perhaps least regrettable) habits by the slow and meticulous work of the philologists and semanticists?[18] What becomes of the philosopher's "I think," and what becomes of his "I am"? What becomes, or rebecomes, of that neutral and mysterious verb TO BE, which has described such a vast circuit in empty space? From those modest syllables, to which a strange career was opened by the loss or attrition of their original meaning, very subtle *artists* have drawn an infinite number of questions and answers.

If, then, we take no account of our habits of thought and confine ourselves to what is revealed by a glance at the present state of intellectual affairs, we can easily observe that philosophy as defined by its product, which is *in writing,* is objectively a particular branch of literature, characterized by its choice of certain subjects and by its frequent use of certain terms and certain forms. This very special type of mental activity and verbal production nevertheless aspires to a supreme place by virtue of its universal aims and formulas, but since it is lacking in any objective verification, since it does not lead to establishing any power, and since the very universality it invokes cannot and must not be regarded as a traditional state, as a means of obtaining or expressing verifiable results[19]—we are forced to assign it a place not far from poetry.

But the artists of whom I was speaking fail to recognize themselves as artists and do not wish to be such. Doubtless their art, unlike that of the poets, is not the art of abusing words by putting too great a burden on their resonance and their occult sympathies; yet it gambles on a certain faith in the existence of an absolute value that can be distilled from the meaning of words. "What is reality?" the philosopher asks, or likewise, "What is liberty?" He finds it possible to ignore the partly metaphorical, partly social, and partly statistical origin of these nouns, while taking advantage of their tendency to slip into indefinable meanings, as a result of which his mind will be able to produce combinations of an extreme depth and delicacy. It would not serve his purpose to answer one of his questions with the simple history of a word through the ages, or again with a detailed account of all the misunderstandings, figurative uses, and idiomatic expressions thanks to the number and incoherence of which a mere word becomes as complex and mysterious as a living person, arousing an almost anguished curiosity as a person might do, eluding any sort of definite analysis and—in spite of its being the fortuitous result of simple needs, an age-old device to facilitate social intercourse and the immediate exchange of impressions—sometimes rising to the very high destiny of calling forth all the interrogatory power and all the resources for finding answers of a marvelously attentive mind.[20] This word, this nothing, this chance device created anonymously, altered in form and meaning by nobody knows whom, has been transformed by the meditation and dialectic of a few individuals into an instrument designed to torment the whole group or groups of ideas; it has become a sort of key that can wind all the springs of a powerful intellect, opening long vistas of possibility to the passion for conceiving everything that exists.

Now, every operation of an artist consists in making something out of nothing. Could there be anything more truly *personal,* moreover—anything more significant of a person and his separateness as an individual—than what is done by a philosopher when he inserts a thousand difficulties into a common expression in which those who invented the expression could see none whatever; or when he creates doubts and perturbations, discovers paradoxes, and disconcerts the minds of others by overawing them with an imposing interplay of substitutions—could there be anything more personal under the appearance of being universal?

The word, that means an end of the philosopher; the word, that handful of dust into which he breathes life, was for Leonardo only the least of his resources. We know that he even regarded mathematics, which, after all, is essentially a language with exact rules, as little more than a provisional device. "Mechanics," he said, "is the paradise of the mathematical sciences." The idea is already quite Cartesian, as is also his unending concern with the physics of physiology.[21]

From that point he went forward along the path in which our minds are now engaged.

But he belonged to an age less interested than ours, or at any rate less practiced, in identifying the useful, or the comfortable, or the exciting with *that which induces a state of resonance and of harmonic reciprocity among sensations, desires, movements, and thoughts.* What seemed most desirable to men of Leonardo's day was not something to increase the comfort of the body, save it time, and spare it from fatigue;

or something to surprise and stimulate merely the soul of the senses; rather it was anything that multiplied sensual enjoyment by means of intellectual artifice and calculation, while adding to such a rare delight by the introduction of a certain specious and delightful "spirituality." Between fauns on the one side and angels on the other, the Renaissance had mastered the art of making very human combinations.

And that brings me to the most difficult point for me to explain, one that may also prove the hardest to understand.

Here, then, is what means to me more extraordinary in Leonardo, something that both opposes him and joins him to the philosophers in a much stranger and deeper fashion than anything I have so far alleged of one or the others. Leonardo was a painter: *I say that painting was his philosophy.* The fact is that he said so himself, if not in exactly those words, and he talked painting as others talk philosophy, which is to say that he made everything depend on it.[22] He formed an excessively high opinion of this art, which seems so specialized in comparison with abstract thought and so far from being able to satisfy the whole intelligence: he regarded painting as a final goal for the efforts of a universal mind. So it was in later days with Mallarmé, who held the curious notion that the world was made to be expressed, and all things would eventually be expressed, by the methods of poetry.

To paint, for Leonardo, was an operation that demanded every form of knowledge and almost all the scientific disciplines: geometry, dynamics, geology, physiology. A battle to be portrayed involved a study of whirlwinds and clouds of dust, and he refused to depict such phenomena before observing them in a scientific spirit, with eyes that had been impregnated, so to speak, with understanding of their laws. A human figure was for him a synthesis of researches extending from dissection to psychology.[23] With exquisite precision he noted the bodily attitudes according to age and sex, as he also analyzed the movements proper to each trade. All things were as if equal before his will to perceive and grasp forms through their causes. It seems to have been the outward appearance of objects that set his mind in movement; then he reduced, or tried to reduce, their morphological features to systems or forces; and only after those systems had been learned—*felt*—and reasoned out did he complete or, one might better say, resume the movement by executing the drawing or painting, as a result of which act he reaped the harvest of his toil. In this manner he projected or recreated an aspect of his subjects by means of analyzing all their properties in depth.

But what part did language play in this process?—It served him only as an instrument, just as numbers did. It was no more than an accessory means, a working auxiliary, one that advanced his passionate enterprises in much the same way that sketches in the margin sometimes help *those who write* to sharpen a phrase.

In short, Leonardo found in the painted work all the problems that could be proposed to the mind by an effort to make a synthesis of nature—and many other problems as well.[24]

Then was he or was he not a philosopher?

If it were merely a question of the word! . . . But there is much else involved besides the choice of a rather vague appellation. What stops me at the point where the high title of philosopher might or might not be conferred on one whose name was rendered illustrious by so many works *not in writing,* is the problem of the connection between the total activity of a mind and the mode of expression it adopts—the connection, that is, of the mind with *the sort of work that gives it the most intense sensation of its power* and with *the forms of external resistance it accepts.*

The particular case of Leonardo da Vinci offers one of those remarkable coincidences that demand a reconsideration of our intellectual habits and something like a rebirth of awareness in the midst of ideas that had been passed on to us.

It can be affirmed of him, I think with some degree of assurance, that the place occupied by philosophy in the life of other minds—with the profound need to which it bears witness, the generalized curiosity that accompanies it, the hunger for facts to be retained and assimilated, and the constant search for causes—is the exact place occupied in Leonardo by his lasting preoccupation with painting. Here is something to disturb us in some of our long-standing distinctions, while tormenting both philosophy and art under the forms in which they had figured separately in our thinking.

Compared with what we are used to seeing, Leonardo appears to be a sort of monster, a centaur or a chimera, because of the hybrid species he represents to minds that are bent on dividing our nature into compartments. Philosophers, to them, are lacking in hands or eyes, and artists have such small heads that there is no room in them for anything but instincts.

We must make an effort, however, to grasp what is implied by this strange adoption of the cult of a plastic art as a substitute for philosophy. Let us start by observing that there can be no question here of arguing about the more subjective states or occurrences, since, in the depths or at the moment of psychic life, the difference between the philosopher and the artist are plainly indeterminate or even non-existent. We must therefore have recourse to what can be seen and distinguished "objectively"; and at this point we again meet with the essential problem of the part played by language. If philosophy is inseparable from its expression in words, and if that expression is the goal of every philosopher, then Leonardo, whose goal is painting, is not a philosopher in spite of his meeting most of the other requirements. But having offered this judgment, we are obliged to accept all its consequences, some of which are far-reaching. I shall try to suggest what they might be.

The philosopher *describes* what he has thought. A system of philosophy can be reduced to a classification of words or a table of definitions. Logic is only our method of using such a table in its permanent form.[25] We take this condition for granted, and as a result of it we cannot but accord a quite special and central place in our intellectual life to articulated language. There can be no doubt that the place is deserved and that language, although composed of innumerable conventions, is almost *ourselves*. We can scarcely "think" without it, nor can we direct, preserve, or recapture our thought, or above *all . . . foresee* it in some measure.

But let us look at the matter a little more closely; let us consider it in ourselves. At the moment when our thinking starts to go deeper—that is, when it comes closer to its object, trying to operate on things in themselves (so far as its activity might be regarded as things), instead of on signs that merely suggest a superficial idea of things— at this moment when we start to live our thinking, we feel that it is drawing apart from any conventional language. No matter how closely woven into our lives the language may be; no matter how densely its "chances" are distributed, or how sensitive this acquired organization may prove in ourselves, or how quick it may be to intervene, still, by a process of *enlargement,* or under the pressure of *continued attention,* we are able to separate it from our mental life of the moment. We feel that words are lacking, and we know there is no reason why words should be found to answer us, that is . . . *to replace ourselves*—for the inherent power of words, from which comes their utility, is to carry us "into the neighborhood" of states already experienced; to systemize, or to establish, repetition; whereas at this point we are penetrating into a mental life *that never repeats itself.* Perhaps that is the real nature of "thinking deeply," which does not mean thinking more usefully, accurately, or totally than we usually do; it is simply thinking far, *thinking as far as possible from verbal automatism.*[26] We feel at such moments that vocabulary and grammar are alien gifts: *res inter alios actas.* We have the direct perception that language, organic and indispensable as it may be, can fully express *nothing* in the world of thought, where there is *nothing* that corresponds to its nature as an intermediary. Our rigor and our fervor both set us against it.

The philosophers, notwithstanding, have tried to bring language into a closer relation with their deepest feelings. They have tried to reorganize it, adding new words and meanings to meet the needs of their solitary experience, so as to make language a more flexible instrument, better adapted to cognizing and recognizing their cognition. We might picture philosophy as the attitude of concentration and restraint owing to which someone, at moments, thinks his life or lives his thinking in a sort of equivalence, or in a reversible state, between *being* and *understanding*—while he tries to suspend all conventional expression and waits eagerly for a combination much more precious than the others to take shape and reveal itself, a combination of the reality he feels impelled to offer with the reality he is able to receive.[27]

But the nature of language is not at all in keeping with the happy outcome of this great endeavor to which all the philosophers have devoted themselves. The strongest of them have worn themselves out in the effort to *make their thoughts speak.*[28] In was in vain that they created or transfigured certain words; they could not succeed in transmitting the inner reality. Whatever the words may be—Ideas or Dynamis or Being or Noumenon or Cogito or Ego—they are all ciphers the meaning of which is determined solely by the context; and so it is finally by a sort of personal creation that their reader—as also happens with readers of poetry—gives the force of life to writings in which ordinary speech is tortured into expressing values that men cannot exchange and that do not exist in the realm of spoken words.

It can be seen that by basing all philosophy on verbal expression, and at the same time refusing it the liberties and even the inconveniences proper to the arts, we run the risk of reducing it to the different sorts of *brayer* offered by a few admirable and lonely figures. Moreover, we have never known, nor can we even imagine, two philosophers compatible with each other, or a doctrine open at all times to only one interpretation.

There is still another point to be noted about the relation between speech and philosophic activity, a simple matter of fact I should like to mention.

Merely by looking about us we can observe that the importance of language is steadily diminishing in every field of activity in which we also observe an increasing degree of precision. Common speech will doubtless continue to serve as the initial and general instrument for establishing relations between external life and internal life; it will always be the means of teaching us the other languages that have been consciously created; it will accommodate those potent and accurate mechanisms to the use of still unspecialized minds. But gradually, by contrast, it is coming to be regarded as a first crude means of approximation. Its function is being restricted by the development of purer systems of notation, each better adapted to a single purpose, and any new step in this direction leads to a further shrinking of the ancient horizons of philosophy.[29] . . . Everything that becomes more precise, in a world where everything tends toward precision, escapes from its primitive means of expression.[30]

Today, in a number of truly remarkable cases, even the expression of things by means of discrete signs, arbitrarily chosen, has given way to lines traced by the things themselves, or to transpositions or inscriptions immediately derived from things. The great invention that consists in making the laws of science visible to the eyes and, as it were, readable on sight has been incorporated into knowledge; and it has in some sort overlaid the world of experience with a visible world of curves, surfaces, and diagrams that translate qualities into lines we can follow as they rise or fall, so gaining an impression of values in transition. The *graphic method* has a continuity of movement that cannot be rendered in speech, and it is superior to speech in clearness and precision. Doubtless it was speech that commanded the method to exist; doubtless it is now speech that assigns a meaning to the graphs and interprets them; but it is no longer by speech that the act of mental possession is consummated. Something new is little by little taking shape under our eyes; a sort of ideography[31] of plotted and diagramed relations between qualities and quantities, a language that has for grammar a body of preliminary conventions (scales, coordinates, base lines, etc.), and for logic the relative size of figures or portions of figures and their situations on a chart.

An altogether different system of representation, but one that has certain analogies with the graphic method, is offered by the art of music. We know what an untold depth of resources exists in the "universe of sounds"; we know what *immediate presence* of all the affective life—what intuitions of the labyrinthine patterns and superpositions of memory, doubt, and compulsion; what forces, what lives, and what fictive deaths—are communicated, are imposed on us, by the artifices of the composer. Sometimes the design and modulation are so in accord with the inner laws of our changing moods that they make us dream of their being exact *auditive formulas* of those moods, capable of serving as models for an objective study of extremely subtle subjective phenomena. In this type of research, no verbal description could approach the effects produced by these *auditive images,* for they are transformations and restitutions of the vital states they transmit, even if they are presented— *since we are dealing with an art*—as the arbitrary[32] creations of an individual.

From such examples we see that simultaneous groups and continued series of auditive sensations can be linked with what are supposed to be the "deepest" modes of philosophic thought—that is to say, those farthest from language. And we see that the most previous part of all that might be contained or perceived by philosophic thought—the part it communicates so imperfectly—is if not transmitted at least suggested by what are not in the least its traditional methods.

Philosophy has always sought, however, and will put forth greater and greater efforts, to protect itself against *the danger of seeming to have a purely verbal aim.* "Consciousness of the self," which, under various names, is its principal means of existence (as well as an always convenient occasion for skepticism and a gateway to perdition), keeps reminding philosophy of its inner vigor and necessity, but also keeps revealing the weakness from which it suffers as a result of its dependence on speech. That is why almost all philosophers insist, in their different manners on distinguishing their thoughts from any accepted convention. Some, being particularly sensitive to what is produced and continually transformed in their inner worlds, are concerned with a region on the hither side of language, where they discover the nascent inner form that can be described as "intuition"—for our apparent real spontaneity includes among its other contributions a number of immediate *illuminations,* leading to instantaneous solutions and unexpected impulses or decisions. Other philosophers, less inclined to consider the eternally changing than intent on *that which endures,* try to entrench their thought in the language itself.[33] They put their trust in formal laws, finding in them the true structure of the intelligible; and they hold that this is the source from which any language borrows its discontinuity and the typical forms of its propositions.

The first sort, if they further developed their tendency, might imperceptibly be carried toward the art of time and hearing; they are the musicians of philosophy. The second sort, who give language a framework of reason and a sort of well defined plan; who contemplate, one might say, all its apparently simultaneous implications and try to reconstruct it on a new foundation, or to complete this product of everyone and no one as though it were the work of one man—those other philosophers might be compared with architects.

I do not see why both sorts should not adopt our Leonardo, for whom painting took the place of philosophy.

The Tortoise and the Hare:
A Study of Valéry, Freud, and
Leonardo da Vinci

by Roger Shattuck

N BERTRAND RUSSELL's *Wisdom of the West,* one comes upon two superbly chosen illustrations on facing pages. On the left Marie Curie stands erect in her austere laboratory, waiting to resume work with her electrical equipment. On the right Sarah Bernhardt poses amid the bric-a-brac of her histrionic sensibility, her handsome head tilted in an expression of infinite longing and infinite boredom. We chuckle over the neatness of the juxtaposition and comprehend the opposition it represents of two sensibilities, two ways of reckoning with life. The history of this split has not yet been written. St. Paul and St. Augustine and St. Thomas Aquinas all distinguish three orders of being: body, mind, and spirit. Descartes reduces the three to two: body and mind, in almost total separation. It was Pascal who reopened a subtle fissure in the midst of thought by distinguishing between *l'esprit de géométrie* and *l'esprit de finesse*—an untranslatable distinction not at all clear in his work but long remembered nevertheless.

The eighteenth century sailed along seemingly unperturbed by the fact that things might be coming apart, and then the nineteenth century seriously took up the task of dividing the human mind into opposing faculties. Cartesian rationalism congealed into positivist theory with its idea of science and history as a growing collection of facts that would reveal their own significance in the shape of law and order. Professor Henry Morgenau makes the point about positivism in a lucid article, "The New

From *The Origins of Modern Consciousness,* ed. by John Weiss (Detroit: Wayne State University Press, 1964). Reprinted by permission of the publisher, Wayne State University Press, and the author.

Style of Science." "Science, then, according to this pristine understanding, is an aggregate of facts, often of trivia, put together with a suffusion of majesty about their mere factualness." Next to this idea of scientific fact, romanticism spawned a tradition that declared the only true values are feelings—the passions and inner responses that tell us what and how and why we are. Out of this conviction Madame de Staël could write in *De l'Allemagne*: "In effect, when we abandon ourselves completely to reflections, images, and desires that surpass the limits of our experience, then only do we begin to breathe freely." The old conflict between faith and reason gives way to a new conflict about the very faculty with which we should encounter experience: reason or instinct, thought or feeling, intelligence or sensibility. The opposition is attributed shakily to Rousseau, affirmed by Matthew Arnold and Rimbaud and the decadents and D. H. Lawrence, and given social status in the purported alienation of the artist from the bourgeois values of the era.

The two photographs of Marie Curie and Sarah Bernhardt come to stand less for two types of women than for a division in the mind, a necessary choice between the forces of reason and the forces of feeling. Ample evidence for the division can be mustered. One can hear an army of professors haranguing their classes on the dangers of specialization, the anti-intellectual as a political force, the symptomatic significance of Bergson, and the tragic isolation of the artist in our time. A recent formulation by R.-M. Albérès in the introduction to *L'Aventure intellectuelle du XXe siècle* carries the story down to the present:

> The European sensibility in the twentieth century is characterized by the belief that there exists a divorce between the intelligence on the one hand and, on the other, reality, truth, or instinct. The very term *intelligence* creates a problem, something like what we commonly call a "complex." Before 1860 the question did not arise; neither Voltaire nor Stendhal used the word "intelligence" very often. By a tendency toward self-punishment, perhaps, Europe has created and invented within itself a rending apart of "intelligence."

Such a statement brings us to a crossroads in the forest through which pass Gourmont's "dissociation of sensibility" appropriated by T. S. Eliot, Eric Heller's "disinherited mind," C. P. Snow's two cultures, and a whole flock of images to express the drawing up of frontiers between positivistic science and romantic sensibility during the nineteenth century. A further stage in the separation is sometimes detected around the turn of the century in the form of new discoveries in physics (relativity and quantum theories) and the toppling of the arts into expressionism and nonfigurative modes.

Our two ladies illustrate this great divorce as the *fin de siècle* imagined it. One wonders whether the furniture of history was not also being moved about in order to accommodate the new arrangement. Which great thinkers or artists out of the past were receiving attention? Aristotle? Jesus? Dante? Montaigne? Goethe? All of them, of course; we know no reliable method of measuring esteem so as to ascertain the culture heroes of an era. Yet one of the most elementary means of discovering about whom people were thinking, writing, and reading is to inventory the titles of books published. My investigations have yielded this hard result: between 1869 and 1919, an average of one full-length book per year was published in Europe on the subject of Leonardo da Vinci. (The number excludes the numerous editions of Leonardo's own writings, and also excludes translations and the flood of articles in reviews.) The list of some fifty items includes the following names: Bernard Berenson, Jakob Burckhardt, Pierre Duhem, Sigmund Freud, Arsène Houssaye, Edward MacCurdy, Dmitri Merejkowski, Walter Pater, Péladan, Smiraglia-Scognamiglio, Gabriel Séailles, Edmondo Solmi, Paul Valéry, and Lionello Venturi. If we set aside the institutionalized figure of Jesus, no other human being, historical or imaginary, appears to have received so much systematic and widely disseminated attention from Western culture during the fifty years under scrutiny.

Now here is a raw piece of information to fit into place. But the job is not easy. In most of these writings, and in the books that have continued to appear about him in slightly diminished numbers, Leonardo emerges as the great ambiguous figure of all time. The impression one comes away with is something like a cross between Benvenuto Cellini and St. Francis of Assisi. What was Leonardo's sex life? Was his real preoccupation magic, or science as we know it? Was he the mere creature of his patrons or a great independent mind? Do his notebooks give us the fragments of a supremely organized consciousness or the best efforts of a distraught talent? Does his art serve his science or his science his art? In his restless career and spottily preserved work, should we read triumph or tragedy? I shall not attempt to answer these questions. In the face of so great a bulk of publication on Leonardo, my attention gravitates irresistibly to two books that are the shortest on scholarship yet the most revealing of a particular strain of thinking—in Leonardo's mind, in their authors' minds, and in the climate of an era. The names Paul Valéry and Sigmund Freud stand for two of the most independent, courageous, and productive intelligences of recent times. What they wrote about the great Italian, apparently unaware of each other's work, carries us off on two fruitful expeditions that reach adjoining countries by different routes.

Paul Valéry wrote and published his earliest poems before he was twenty, while still a law student in Montpellier. His mind had been attracted very early to the study of architecture, painting, mathematics, and physics, and to works of Poe, Huysmans, and Mallarmé. Through the writer Pierre Louÿs, he came to know Mallarmé, then entering his fifties, and Gide, just Valéry's own age. In 1892 at the age of twenty-three he underwent a kind of conversion in reverse, a period of profound self-doubt leading to a night of turmoil in Genoa. Subsequently he turned away from poetry toward further study in the sciences and history. It was twenty years before he returned to literature with a succession of poems, essays, notes, translations, introductions, and plays that made him the leading poet of France in the thirties and forties. He bore the major responsibility for keeping the French Academy free of taint during the German occupation. His elaborate state funeral in 1945 symbolized the country's resolve, following the liberation, to reaffirm its great intellectual and artistic traditions. Valéry wrote six different texts on Leonardo at approximately even intervals throughout his career. The first two are the most important, *Introduction à la méthode de Léonard de Vinci,* begun in 1894 soon after his detachment from poetry, and *Note et digression,* added to the previous text when it was republished in 1919. In 1929–30 he wrote extensive marginal notes to these two early texts and to a third written in 1928, so that today they appear as a palimpsest, the apt representation of a mind that could endlessly develop and transform any subject just by bringing attention to bear on it.

Valéry opens the *Introduction* by stating flatly that neither the biography nor the personality of Leonardo concerns him. Rather he will examine a method of thinking or a "creature of thought" to whom, because it appears the most appropriate, he assigns the name Leonardo. In prose so dense that one can feel the sustained cerebration that formed it, Valéry describes an elevated, universal, and perpetually self-correcting Mind. Its secret is to grasp "relations . . . between things whose principle of continuity escapes the rest of us." Thus, for both Leonardo and Napoleon, "at the crucial moment they had only to act." This hypersensitive ability to see connections is rendered bearable by a compensatory mechanism of "foresight" that carries every train of thought instantaneously to its limit, a heightened capacity for compression and comparison. Valéry is somewhat hard put to explain the operation of this form of consciousness. What he says about how thought organizes undifferentiated impressions resembles Taine's theory of *hallucination vraie*. He seems to be on firmer ground in considering the two complementary faculties of universal thought: to identify with individual things—a strong sense of particularity in the world—and to recognize regularities in the world: continuity, similarity, periodicity. The truly great mind exercises these faculties at a speed so high as to appear instantaneous, yet remains at least partially conscious of the mental operation taking place within it.

Valéry's reflections (reflexions) on the nature of thought and subjectivity make difficult reading. In a curious way, though Valéry's theory of mind is diametrically opposed to that of biologically-oriented behaviorists and sociologists, what he writes often sounds like an elaborate restatement of the dictum: "Mind is minding." But the cross-hatch and chain-stitch of his style convey Valéry's perpetual refinement of such an equivocation. The pure activity, the mere free play of mind is as exciting and as productive as any externally imposed purpose or special discipline. This in fact is the point with which he begins the later essay, *Note et digression*. He swoops back down on Leonardo as the "leading actor in the intellectual comedy which never to this day has found its poet." In a less clotted, more transparent prose, Valéry reaffirms this judgment of the "integrity" of Leonardo as a mind, never torn between a naturalistic and a spiritualistic sense of man. But another, more subtle division lurks within, for which Valéry offers the expression, "presence of mind." He illustrates the delicate circular equilibrium of this self-awareness with two metaphors: first, the swirling drafts that form a smoke ring, and second, the stage of a theater surrounded by a hidden but distinctly real audience. Finally these two easily grasped figures are plunged together to a deeper level of discourse and of mind:

> The character of man is consciousness; and the character of consciousness is a perpetual emptying, an unremitting unsparing detachment from everything that appears, no matter how it appears. An inexhaustible act independent of the quality or number of things that present themselves, and by which the *man in the mind* [*l'homme de l'esprit*] must knowingly restrict himself to being an indefinite refusal to be anything at all.

Before this endless self-repulsion of mind, all things are equal. What survives, the pure impersonal self of consciousness, sounds to Valéry like the very bass note of our existence. Leonardo represents this intensified and complex presence of mind, as much the result, Valéry concludes, as the cause of his works.[1]

In these two texts and the later ones, Valéry has composed variations on a single theme: the miraculous variety of Leonardo's work springs from a highly developed singleness of mind or unity of thought. Examined in itself, apart from the works it strewed along its path, this astonishing mind reveals the nature of the self, not personality or biography but pure consciousness beholding an infinity of relations in what it sees and perpetually backing away from what it sees in the very act of beholding.[2]

At the end of the first essay on Leonardo, Valéry quotes a sentence in which, he submits, Leonardo has expressed a purely modern concept:

> The air is full of infinite, straight, radiant lines crossing and interweaving without one ever entering the path of another, and they represent for each object the true FORM of its cause.
>
> L'aria e piena d'infinite linie rette e radoise insieme intersegate e intessute sanza ochupatione luna dellaltra rapresantano aqualunche obieto lauera forma della lor chagione.

Valéry relates this sentence to the undulatory theory of light, to the old absurdity of "action at a distance" in gravitational theory, and then successively to the work of Faraday, Maxwell, and Lord Kelvin. Remember, this is a disaffected poet aged twenty-three writing in 1894 when the results of the Michelson-Morley experiment six years earlier had not yet gained universal acceptance. He was discovering in Leonardo da Vinci an early formulation of field theory, something that had not yet taken clear shape out of Maxwell's electro-magnetic theory published twenty years before. Edmund Wilson has pointed out in *Axel's Castle* the evident vanity in Valéry's parading of scientific materials in much of his writing. But here Valéry sums up in one all-encompassing idea the various aspects of consciousness that he has brought out earlier: rigor, continuity, compression, contrast, symmetry, regularity. Himself of course an outstanding example of the mentality he was exploring, Valéry saw the relation between the infinity of visible connections between all things apparent to a supremely attuned imagination like Leonardo's, and the infinity of physical connections between all things soon to be established by field theory. This essay on a Renaissance subject is less historical than prophetic.

The word that chants the refrain in Valéry's series of texts on Leonardo is *continuity*. And in the quoted passage expressing a vast unity of creation, Valéry is expanding and refining into scientific terms the now commonplace doctrine of *correspondences.* Its recent history goes back to Swedenborg, Fourier, Novalis, Blake, Baudelaire, and Yeats. But Valéry made bold to transpose the idea of discontinuous and analogical correspondences, parallels between different things, into the idea of a continuum, a single medium or field displaying modifications that we call "things" yet not separable into different entities. The mind is one in this text as, some ten years later, space and time would be affirmed as one in the special theory of relativity. And Valéry concludes the 1919 text with a reference to the problem of the existence of intelligences outside our own as being "comparable to the physical problem of relativity."

Until 1910 Freud's theory of mind had stressed the division between primary or instinctual thought processes operating according to the pleasure principle, and secondary or inhibitory thought processes observing the reality principle. The last chapter of *The Interpretation of Dreams* gives the best systematic account of the two processes, and one still hears in this text, finished in 1900, the professional neurologist both urging on and cautioning the vigorous young analyst. The chapter in question, once it has established the two thought processes and the areas of consciouness and unconsciousness they rule, pays lengthy attention to the principle that guards the frontier: repression or censorship. Gradually, however, Freud shifted his attention from separation to communication between these areas. The last of the Clark lectures, delivered in 1909, contains at its close a fine paragraph that recognizes the previously little-mentioned process of sublimation as psychically and socially valuable. "It is probable that we owe our highest cultural successes to the contributions of energy made in this way to our mental processes." Within a few months Freud began to work on Leonardo.

Freud was over fifty when he wrote his first and only psychoanalytic biography. The subject was not new to him. "Perhaps the most famous left-handed individual was Leonardo," he had written in a letter in 1898, "who is not known to have had any love affairs." A questionnaire in 1907 revealed that Merejkowski's novel, *The Gods Reborn: Leonardo da Vinci,* was one of Freud's favorite books. Then in 1909, right after the Clark lectures, he was consulted by a patient whose temperament strongly resembled that of Leonardo, though without the Italian's genius. Impelled from so many sides toward Leonardo, Freud bought several works on him and began extensive reading. It was only at this point that he discovered the text of Leonardo's remarkable childhood recollection. That brief passage provided the framework for the study entitled *Leonardo da Vinci and a Memory of His Childhood.*

The disclaimer with which Freud begins differs from Valéry's. The fact that he is studying Leonardo, Freud tells us, does not suggest that the great Italian genius was a pathological case, nor even represent any desire to detract from his fame. Freud affirms he is concerned with "laws which govern normal and pathological activity with equal cogency." The problem Freud first poses is the apparent interference that occurred between Leonardo's investigative activities and his painting, between scientist and artist. The first and longest of the six sections advances the thesis that Leonardo's truly exceptional capacities as an experimental investigator, unimpeded by the authority of either church or antiquity, can be traced in great part to his childhood, through the theory of sublimation. "After his curiosity had been aroused in infancy, he succeeded in sublimating the greater part of his libido into an urge for research." His notes and his behavior show that he felt compelled "to love in such a way as to hold back the affect, subject it to the process of reflection." This instinct for knowledge, though it channeled his genius, in the end affected the free play of his artistic expression. What was left of his childhood sexuality, Freud supposes, expressed itself as sublimated homosexuality.

The remaining pages flesh out this hypothesis with a brilliant, though often factually unsupported, demonstration. Freud quotes from a German translation the famous sentence from the *Codex Atlanticus* given by Scognamiglio:

> It seems I was always destined to be so deeply concerned with vultures; for I recall as one of my very earliest memories that while I was in my cradle a vulture came down to me, and opened my mouth with its tail, and struck me many times with its tail against my lips.

Freud interprets it as a passive homosexual phantasy of fellatio transferred to infantile suckling. Unfortunately "vulture" is a mistranslation of *nibio,* which means kite; part of Freud's more elaborate bird and mother symbolism collapses as a result. He reconstructs a plausible but unprovable portrait of the illegitimate infant Leonardo alone with his doting mother and then adopted by his father, married but as yet without legitimate children. In his father's prosperous household Leonardo was further indulged. These pages give one of the earliest discussions of the origins of homosexuality in narcissism: desiring to reinforce his mother's love for him and to identify with it as an extension of his self-love, the son indulges his love for her to the point of substituting himself for her, looking for a male partner, and thus remaining faithful to his mother. Freud attributes the mysterious blend of reserve and seductiveness we call "Leonardesque" to the painter's having been reminded of his mother by the model for the "Mona Lisa." Thenceforward that ambivalent expression characterizes all his female figures, including the two in "Virgin and Child and St. Anne." In that composition Freud detects a recollection of Leonardo's two young mothers, the real and the adopted. After associating Leonardo's great preoccupation with flight —bird flight and human flight—with a throwback to his childhood sexual researches when he was alone with his mother, Freud concludes with a reaffirmation that Leonardo's extreme case of inhibition was not pathological or neurotic but obsessional and healthy. Freud concedes the insufficiency of the material evidence on which to construct a case, the need "to recognize here a degree of freedom" in Leonardo's choice of actions, and the "limits which are set to what psychoanalysis can achieve in the field of biography." Yet he believes that the key to Leonardo's great and mysterious genius lay in his capacity to direct and transmute the deep feelings aroused in him during childhood.

The reservations that have to be made about hanging so much mass of interpretation on a single sentence can be found elsewhere.[3] The passage on which Freud's argument pivots occurs about ten pages after the opening. He states in effect that what might be seen as two separate problems in Leonardo must be interpreted as one:

> There is only one way in which the peculiarity of this emotional and sexual life can be understood in connection with Leonardo's double nature as an artist and as a scientific investigator.

The "one-way" means of course sublimation, in this case accompanied by narcissism and homosexuality. But the last two items are far less important than the central hypothesis that in Leonardo we witness a mind that succeeds in defending its integrity and defeats the censor, even if at some final cost in dispersion of talent.

This would seem a long way to come if these two highly individual books have little in common but their subject and their total inadequacy as systematic biographies. But the reason for the comparison should begin to assert itself. Valéry, whom we think of as an artist, gives most of his attention to Leonardo's notebooks and to his methodology as a thinker. Freud, whom we think of as a scientist, at least by training, refers briefly to the notebooks and then elaborates the greater part of his argument on the basis of the painting and the life. Valéry cites no historical persons, dates, or places, and attempts only to illustrate a theory of self-consciousness; Freud obviously believed he could contribute to Leonardo's biography and to biographical method by bringing to bear on an enigmatic and eminent life the new science of analysis. Yet by the time we reach the end of Freud's study, Leonardo's personality interests us less than the process that permitted him to come to terms with himself and the world. Not the individuality but the generality of his case emerges from these pages. His personality has melted away into a set of carefully described responses.

Why, then, if neither author wrote a biography but was really concerned with something quite apart from Leonardo's individual life, did they compose these two books nominally aimed in his direction? The first answer is quite easy. They both identified with Leonardo—admired him, understood something of him, and could understand something of themselves in examining him. Though Valéry's first article was commissioned, the subject was far from new to him. He makes little effort to hide the fact that what he writes of Leonardo is in effect the fruit of introspection. And he wrote at far greater length on Leonardo than on any other person, including his master Mallarmé. Freud's interest in Leonardo went back at least a dozen years and probably more, and the work remained one of his favorites. Ernest Jones tells us that Freud particularly admired two historical figures: Moses, the wise leader who guided his people to a new land and a full life, and Leonardo, who combined the talents of an artist and the knowledge of a scientist in creating some of the greatest artifacts of Western culture. There is nothing very rash in saying that both Valéry and Freud felt in themselves the double temperament, the twin genius that tradition attributes to Leonardo. Furthermore Leonardo's apparent irresolution and perpetual shift of focus in his work probably struck a responsive cord in each of them. Valéry had just gone through a personal crisis that was to divert the channel of his writing for many years: he came to value a completed work less than the state of mind that permits creation. Freud, though well established in his central field of inquiry when he wrote on Leonardo, had been very much at loose ends for a time about what calling to follow. After deciding against law, a slow and somewhat erratic progress had carried him through physiology, medicine, teaching, neurology, and psychopathology to psychoanalysis. He was always profoundly attracted to literature and the arts, and wrote to the novelist Schnitzler that he felt their temperaments were very similar.

But more important than any personal reasons for writing of Leonardo, the conclusions of their studies show more similarity than we might have expected. I have suggested earlier that the books contribute to a discernible pattern that reveals Leonardo as a culture hero for the era.

Yet these two works, weak as they are biographically, help us understand why so many other authors were studying Leonardo without shedding much new light. From their very different cultural vantage points, Valéry and Freud glimpsed something behind Leonardo they could approach through him. For both of them, Leonardo stood for a form of consciousness they admired—a new equilibrium of faculties that could be fully recognized and appreciated only four hundred years after the fact and on slender evidence. Their essays describe a case that has particular relevance to our modern situation, like Eliot writing of Donne, or Baudelaire writing of Poe. I feel that in the end, for Freud as much as for Valéry, the name Leonardo is reduced to an exemplary case, a convention, a pure symbol, a term like "Socrates" as traditionally used in the syllogisms that start "Socrates is a man." Someone has to represent humanity, if possible at its best. But subtracted from his life, what does Leonardo stand for? Does anything remain beyond Vasari's appealing myth of a restless genius releasing birds, blowing up bladders, and painting an occasional picture?

Three semi-parenthetical remarks will clear the ground a little around these questions. To begin with, Valéry's *Note et digression* carries one of the most merciless and concise attacks on Pascal (his name is not mentioned in the text) that has ever been composed. It is too good to miss:

> [Leonardo] had not the least knowledge of that gross and ill-defined opposition which, a century and a half later, was declared between *l'esprit de finesse* and *l'esprit de géométrie* by a man entirely insensible to the arts, who could not conceive of that natural but delicate blending of talents. It was he who lured us into a wager that gobbled up all finesse and all geometry, and who, having changed his new lamp for an old one, wasted his time sewing little notes into his pockets, when the moment had come to bring to France the glory of having discovered infinitesimal calculus. . . .

No, Leonardo was not wasting his time on dividing the mind against itself and setting odds on immortality. The passage is significant. Secondly, nothing in Freud's analysis of Leonardo's tendency to abandon his painting for elaborate, fragmentary, and often mysterious scientific studies inclines in the slightest toward the concept of schizophrenia. On the contrary, this double man, distracted as he may have appeared on the outside, incapable of finishing much of what he started, and careless of the fate of what he did finish, exemplified a high level of inner integration. "Our aim remains that of demonstrating the connection along the path of instinctual activity between a person's external experiences and his reactions."

Here at the end of the essay Freud affirms for the second time that Leonardo made these connections very well indeed.

The last remark concerns the French mathematician Poincaré, who began publishing in the nineties a series of articles on the intuitive, unconscious nature of mathematical imagination, on the distinction between fact and hypothesis, and on the significance of the new physics. Though these writings found a large audience only when they appeared in book form (1902–09), Valéry read the articles as they appeared, consulted Poincaré personally on a mathematical point, and cited him for support in the first text on Leonardo. A year later Valéry wrote André Gide that he was thinking of composing a literary portrait of the mathematician. "Poincaré is hard to do without knowing the man. He interests me very much, for he hardly does anything now but psychological articles on mathematics. That's exactly to my taste." And he regrets not knowing Poincaré well. Evidently the "novel" about an imaginary personage, *Monsieur Teste,* the *Introduction* to the hypothetical mind of Leonardo, and the unwritten study of the contemporary mathematician turned psychologist all represent one preoccupation, in effect one work. We discover also that Freud received from Maria Bonaparte a copy of Poincaré's *La Valeur de la science* (1905), a book which he read with interest and sympathy because it corroborated his conviction that science could never replace religion. Science teaches not to have faith but to doubt the things about which we feel most certain. Freud's letter to Maria Bonaparte makes it clear that psychoanalysis had particular reasons to keep its doubts about itself.

Valéry's attack on Pascal's irresponsible dividing of the mind into two parts, Freud's reluctance to see Leonardo as a man at odds with his own most precious talents, and their common interest in Poincaré's psychology of scientific and creative thinking—these circumstances reinforce what should already be clear about the coincidence that Valéry and Freud both wrote about an Italian painter and thinker who lived four hundred years before their time. They did not see in him a universal genius who represents the variety of human faculties vying with each other in a great divergence of roles and activities. His versatility led them in another direction. Their two highly contrasting books relentlessly trace the multiplicity and contradiction of Leonardo's activities back to a mind. And above all, that mind is one, an integrity of scientist and artist, of sensibility and intelligence. All Valéry's terms (method, invention, central attitude, presence of mind) grant to that master mind a tremendous freedom to see from a single vantage point the continuity of all things around it.[4] Freud's elaborate apparatus for describing two cities in the mind (or three, if one counts the preconscious along with the conscious and unconscious) gradually vanishes as he approaches Leonardo. And the lesson of the book is that a single, all-encompassing power, an incredible integrity of mind, can result from a mingling of previously separated energies. One can distinguish different directions for investigation (sex, science, art), but the "case" of Leonardo displays not different drives or instincts but a single common activity of mind that gives rise to all these.

And thus, along with Pascal, a whole tradition of dualism in the mind comes a cropper if we draw the full conclusion. Valéry did; his precocious certainty about the indivisibility of the mind probably explains the coyness with which he indulges in interdisciplinary by-play in some of his writings. But his vision was steady. Freud unfortunately never tested his theories against another mind equal to Leonardo's and turned increasingly to culture and society as his subject. His dualistic terminology has remained, but I maintain that his essay on Leonardo lets us see how strongly Freud felt drawn toward an interpretation of mental activity as one, only artificially divisible. At the very moment when, we are usually told, Western consciousness was hardening into a division between reason and feeling, two of the greatest contemporary minds were saying precisely the opposite in terms that recapitulate the history of modern European thought. They assert, in effect, that the experience of four hundred years tells us urgently and insistently not to divide up the mind. For to oppose one faculty to another implies that the drift toward specialization has its source in our thinking, a kind of racism of the mind prone to segregation. Furthermore they avoid the error of Vico and Comte and finally Lévy-Bruhl, who affirmed the existence of primitive thought as an essentially different functioning of mind from our civilized thought.[5] No one has ever satisfactorily demonstrated that the "savage" makes associations and forms conclusions about his animistic or god-ridden world any differently than we do. Nor—to take an extreme example—need the "logic" of Rimbaud's *Les Illuminations,* or of *Alice in Wonderland,* or of a nightmare, be any different from the "logic" that should be connecting one proposition to another on this page.

Valéry and Freud do not indulge in any suggestion that the superiority of Leonardo's mental organization, his power to perceive relations and find pleasure in experiment, removed him from humanity. On the contrary, an image they both use displays their awareness of the risks run by so powerful a mind if aware of its own power. Valéry's exposition never withdraws from the dilemma of self-consciousness, so that every metaphor for thought or attention ("the dream of the waking sleeper," "detachment," "repulsion") signifies a perpetual spiraling out of the self in order to see the self—which is no longer there to be seen. Throughout his poetic production, Valéry reverted to the figure of Narcissus to express this problem of the fugitive self: and narcissism is precisely the psychoanalytic concept to which Freud gave one of its earliest elaborations in the Leonardo text. The metaphor does not serve the same purpose for the two of them; but in both cases its meaning reaches far into the ambiguous area where the mind, trying to catch sight of itself in action, discovers that nothing is there but a perpetual movement of recoil or afterthought. Narcissus attests not to a division but to a contortion of mind. Freud points out very shrewdly that nothing seemed to escape the notice of Leonardo's investigations. "Yet his urge for knowledge was always directed to the external world; something kept him far away from the investigation of the human mind. . . . There was little room for psychology." In other words, Leonardo would never have written either Valéry's or Freud's book.

So limited a demonstration as this could never "prove" that all thought is one. Nor could it hope to flatten the barriers that have grown up between a long series of artificial opposites, not the least of which is the inseparable pair: theory-fact. And even if the theory-fact of the unity of thought is accepted as demonstrated in the specific instances of Valéry and Freud looking at Leonardo, the problem remains of why we cling to different words for such versions as patient observation, discursive logic, intuition, a flash of inspiration, reverie, and the like. Or more specifically, how is it Freud associates wit-work, dream-work, and artistic creation and treats that cluster of activities as distinguishable from the thought patterns that direct our ordinary living? And then there is the even more troubling question of why certain forms of presumably rational thought, such as the implications of quantum and relativity theory, or theories, about time and entropy, bear a close resemblance to their decreed opposites, dream and fantasy. The answer, I believe, lies close at hand in the pacing of mental events. Both Freud and Valéry speak of rapidity and compression.

Our thinking, in a manner no one has yet described satisfactorily to my knowledge, has a widely variable speed. The same operations of association and dissociation take place slowly in activities we refer to as "reasoning it out" or " systematic analysis," and with infinitely greater speed in dream and hunch and wit. However, it is ridiculous to assume—as we usually do—that our minds work at a nearly uniform rate in any given interval. Inspiration or intuition comes in the midst of the dullest analysis. The dross that surrounds the vividness of a remembered dream probably just goes unrecorded. In the superb essay, *Mathematical Invention,* Poincaré describes how he discovered Fuchsian functions not during the long hours spent sitting at his work table but one morning as he was stepping into a bus. It sounds like a page out of Proust. Nevertheless those seemingly fruitless hours were necessary, for the solutions they eliminated and for the inner expectancy they built up. Valéry describes the composition of his poem, "La Cimetière marin," in the same fashion. Scientists or poets, we do not know the very timing of our minds.

Reasoning by analogy is a very dangerous procedure. Yet the experimenter as much as the artist proceeds on faith—the faith that his mind can truly come to terms with reality and that there is always a higher order of things for him to discover. (That faith is often called doubt.) I wish to argue from one of the most ambitious theories of orderliness in nature back into the jungle of the mind. Einstein's special theory of relativity was given graphical expression almost immediately by Minkowski, whose four-dimensional geometry does an enormously helpful job of representing physical reality. In the figure below, the *x* axis represents the three dimensions of space and *t* axis represents time measured by a free (i.e. unaccelerated) observer at *O*. In this geometry a diagonal *OC* separates time-like curves (more vertical than horizontal) from space-like curves (more horizontal than vertical) and this diagonal represents energy moving at the speed of light, *c*.

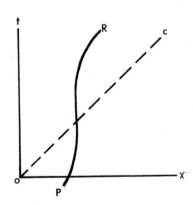

The world line of a single particle, say PR, must be time-like, and as it approaches the limiting speed of light it contracts so enormously as to cease to have the properties of matter. To "jump" into the diagonal it would have to change from matter into energy, according to Einstein's formula, $E = mc^2$. A space-like curve is really a map of points in space which cannot be reached by any one particle's world line. In the xt plane, called space-time or Minkowski space, the velocity of light c is of crucial importance and is assigned some very special characteristics. For example, the world line of energy traveling with this velocity has zero length and is perpendicular to itself. But the significant point is that all this represents a single space, a *continuum*, both connected and articulated by the mysterious diagonal $x = t$ or c. The "light" that travels with unalterable speed is the most commonplace and miraculous element in our environment. What "travels" in time or "stays put" in space is one, energy or mass, according to how you look at it or, more revealingly, according to its velocity.

So it is, I submit, with thought: one entity, one faculty, one process. But of various velocities. What Minkowski space suggests by analogy is the possibility of a critical velocity. In this idea of a frontier not between two things but between two speeds or two states, I suggest we have a working definition of consciousness itself. Below a certain speed, thought seems observable and its coherence verifiable; its trajectory lends itself to expression in discursive forms of language. Above a certain speed, thought outruns any continuous observation, appears incoherent, and finds expression in extremely elliptical or disjointed forms. When he dealt with dream and psychosis and wit, Freud described this high-velocity activity in terms of compression and displacement. They are probably as good working terms as we shall have in some time.

I do not wish to imply a fixed constant of consciousness for all individuals at all times, in the fashion that the constant velocity of light has turned out to be the Rock of Ages in physics. All of us have direct experience of the fluctuations in our own consciousness according to physical and psychical states. Inevitably I am speaking out of my own experience, remembering those exalted yet awkward moments of stumbling onto a mountain-top in the mind from which one beholds the majesty of everything properly in place. In particular, one evening while reading an article on physics after an exhausting day, I suddenly felt an almost physical release within me. Flanked by others I did not recognize, two images flashed vividly into my mind: an early cubist painting by Braque I had seen several months earlier, and the haunting mystery of Poe's stories read many years earlier. And it all came clear. The necessity of anti-matter, the necessity of mirror symmetry, the necessity of the psycho-literary myth of the double, and above all the necessity of myself seeing it thus—all that literally struck me, at once and as one. I found no words to record the blow then; it seemed miraculous yet very familiar, as if I had known it for a long time. Still, the ceiling of consciousness had to lift in order for me to glimpse it. What lures mankind into experimentation with drugs is probably not a direct sensual pleasure but the fact that they can raise (or lower) the critical velocity below which our mental processes reveal themselves. Slow motion effects, geometric music, massive coilings and uncoilings—these drug experiences show the mind, rather than the cosmos, laid bare. Censorship and repression, the processes so roundly criticized by Sartre, could be described anew as measurements of distance and the velocity of thought rather than as a separate faculty. Of course just as Minkowski geometry, like any representation of space-time, must include a location for the hypothetical observer, so a representation of consciousness leaves us in the quandary of showing an observer, an *"I"* beholding the trajectory of my own thought. This duality in identity is vastly more real and significant than the false one we started with between intellect and sensibility.

For one very elementary lesson, then, we may look back a medium range of sixty-odd years to the turn of the century. Amid the surprisingly large number of writers in Europe devoting their attention to Leonardo da Vinci, two thinkers discovered the opportunity to approach the most universal subject of all: the nature of the human mind. A little distance beyond the place where their explicit commentary stopped, one can discern a significant agreement. The division we have begun to lament publicly between two climates of thinking, scientific and humanistic, between opposed methods of inquiry, cannot be traced to any corresponding division between regions or faculties in the mind. At the origin is unity; we have imposed the separation upon ourselves, possibly to lighten our burden. For it is an onerous responsibility to live both inside and alongside the thoughts that we are—almost.

There is more than we ever knew in the story of the tortoise and the hare. Just look again. You will see not two animals but one, traveling at different speeds. .

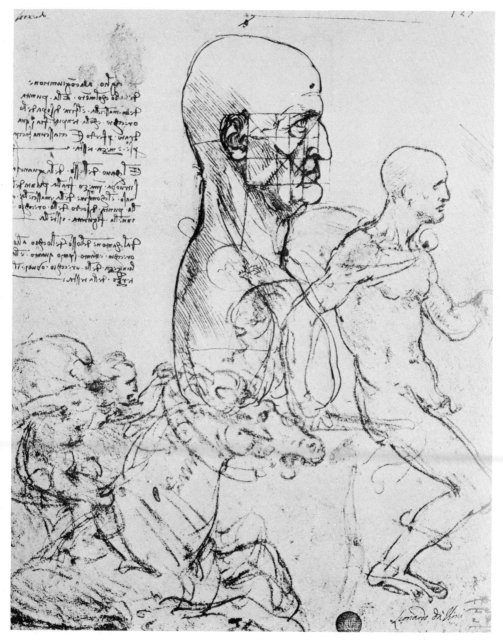

83. Leonardo, *Profile of a Man Squared for Proportion.*
Venice, Academy of Fine Arts.

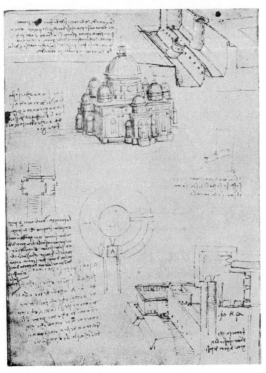

84a. and 84b.
Leonardo, *Designs for a Centralized Building*. Paris, Institut de France,
Ms.B, fol. 18v and 19r.   *Photos: Agraci-Art Reference Bureau.*

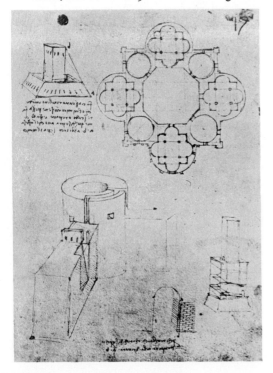

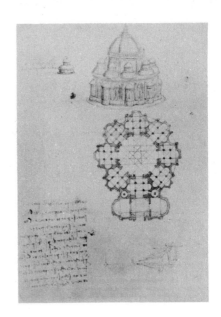

85. Leonardo, *Circular Domed Church with Eight Chapels*. Paris, Institut de France, Cod. Ash. II, fol. 5v.
Photo: Agraci-Art Reference Bureau.

86. Leonardo, *Plan for an Ideal City*. Paris, Institut de France, Ms.B, fol. 16r.
Photo: Agraci-Art Reference Bureau.

87. Leonardo, *Figures of Combatants with Cross Section of a Projectile.*
Paris, Ecole des Beaux Arts.
Photo: IBM Corp., New York.

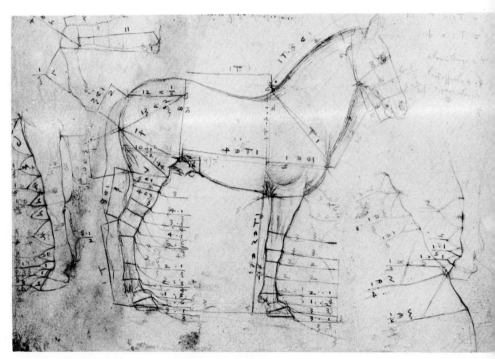

88. Leonardo, *Measured Drawing of a Horse.*
Windsor Castle, Royal Library, No. 12319.

89. Leonardo, *Studies of Struggle Between Horse and Dragon.*
Windsor Castle, Royal Library, No. 12331.

90. Leonardo, *Whole Length of an Old Man in Profile to the Right.*
Windsor Castle, Royal Library, No. 12582.

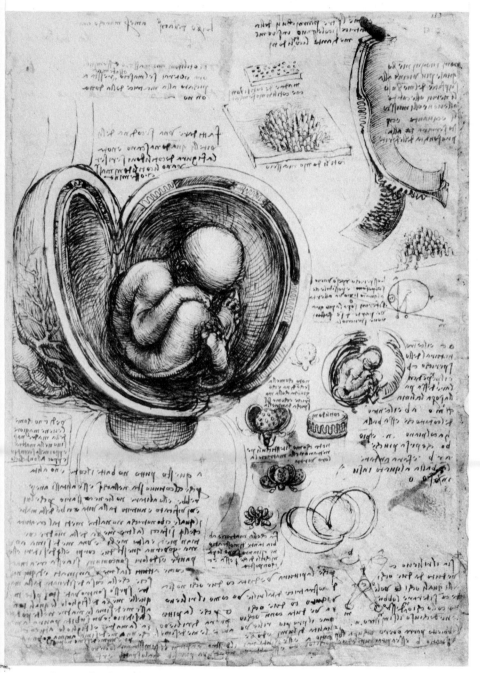

91. Leonardo, *Drawings of an Embryo in the Uterus.*
Windsor Castle, Royal Library, No. 19102.

92. Leonardo, *Bird's-eye View of Tuscany*.
Windsor Castle, Royal Library, No. 12683.

93. Leonardo, *Snow-covered Mountain Chain*.
Windsor Castle, Royal Library, No. 12410.

Leonardo Chronology

The scientific achievements of Leonardo can hardly be dated because they stretch over long periods of time. The following chronology will enable readers to locate his artistic creations within the frame of his life. Very few of his innumerable notes are dated, and these few are more often than not insignificant. The paintings and some drawings can be dated more or less; critics do not always agree as to their authenticity or their exact date. Sometimes we know the date of beginning but not that of completion.

My main authorities are Sir Kenneth Clark, *Leonardo da Vinci. An account of his development as an artist* (222 pp., 68 pls., Cambridge University Press, 1939), Germain Bazin, editor, *Hommage à Léonard de Vinci* (142 pp., ill., Paris: Musée du Louvre, 1952), and Jean-Paul Richter, *The Literary Works of Leonardo da Vinci* (2 vols., Oxford University Press, 1939). Richter refers to the original Mss.

I. YOUTH IN FLORENCE, 1452–82

1452. April 24 (N.S.) Leonardo's birth in Vinci, the son of a Florentine notary, Ser Piero, and a country woman, Caterina (*Isis*, 43: 125).

1466. Leonardo enters the *bottega* of Verrocchio, Via del Agnolo in Florence, and remains there about twelve years. He may have entered the *bottega* a little later.

1472. Leonardo is admitted as a master painter in the Guild of St. Luke, in Florence.

1472–73. He paints the angel in Verrocchio's *Baptism of Christ* (Uffizi).

1472–73. *The Annunciation* (Uffizi).

1473. August 5. First dated drawing, landscape of Val d'Arno (Uffizi).

c.1474. Portrait of *Ginevra de' Benci,* a Florentine lady married in January 1474 (Liechtenstein Gallery, Vienna). Its ascription to Leonardo is doubted by some critics.

1476. April 8. Leonardo and other painters are accused of homosexuality; he is exonerated. Later, the accusation and exoneration were repeated.

1478–80. The *Benois Madonna* (Hermitage). Authorship uncertain. Drawings for it are unquestionably by Leonardo (e.g., *La Vierge aux fruits,* Louvre).

From *Six Wings* by George Sarton (Bloomington, Ind.: Indiana University Press, 1957). Copyright © 1957 by Indiana University Press. Reprinted by permission of the publisher.

c.1480. The *Madonna Litta,* in profile (Hermitage). Difficult to appreciate because it was badly repainted at least twice. Study for it in the Louvre.

1481. The Monastery of San Donato orders a painting for its high altar, *The Adoration of the Magi.* Two incomplete studies (Uffizi, Louvre). Leonardo is now working in his own studio.

c.1482. Letter to Lodovico Sforza il Moro offering his services (Richter no. 1340). His services are accepted and he moves to Milan.

II. FIRST MILANESE PERIOD (1483–99) DURING THE RULE OF LODOVICO IL MORO

1483. April 25. The Confraternity of the Immaculate Conception, Milan, orders a painting which became *The Virgin of the Rocks* (Louvre). The order was given to Leonardo and the brothers Evangelisto and Ambrogio da Predis.

c.1483. *St. Jerome* doing penance in the desert with lion, drawing (Vatican).

c.1483. Portrait of Cecilia Gallerani, one of Lodovico's mistresses (Czartoryski Gallery, Cracow). Is this by Leonardo, Boltraffio, or some other? This "lady with a weasel" in her arms looks very much like the *Belle Ferronnière* in the Louvre (see 1495–96).

1485. March 16.[1] Leonardo observes a total eclipse of the sun.

c.1485+. *Portrait of a musician,* head finished, body not (Ambrosiana, Milan).

1488. Verrocchio's death.

1488–90. Studies for the Sforza equestrian monument (Windsor).

1491. January 26. Drawings for a tournament in honor of Lodovico il Moro and his wife, Beatrice d'Este.

1493. November 30. Model of a horse of gigantic size, exhibited in Milan to celebrate the wedding of Bianca Maria Sforza with the Emperor Maximilian I. The marriage took place at Innsbruck on March 16, 1494.

1495–96? Portrait traditionally called *"La belle ferronnière"* (Louvre). If not by Leonardo, it is a work of his school. It is probably a portrait of Beatrice d'Este (she died on January 2, 1497). Surprising likeness to the "lady with a weasel" (see c.1483).

1497. *Last Supper* (*Cenácolo*) in Santa Maria delle Grazie (Milan).

1498. February 9. Luca Pacioli praises Leonardo in his dedication of *Divina Proportione* to Lodovico Sforza. Leonardo provides geometric drawings for that book, which was not published until eleven years later (Venice: Paganinus, 1509). Leonardo must have drawn these figures without instruments, for they are inaccurate.

c.1498. Cartoon of the *Virgin and Child with St. Anne and St. John the Baptist* (Burlington House, London).

1499. October 6. The armies of Louis XII enter Milan.

1499. December. Leonardo goes to Mantua at the invitation of Isabella d'Este.

was probably then that he drew her portrait (cartoon in the Louvre). She was then 25. Isabella (1474–1539) and Beatrice (1475–97) were two sisters, daughters of Ercole I d'Este.

III. VARIOUS PLACES, CHIEFLY FLORENCE, 1500–05

1500. April. Back in Florence.

1502. In the service of Cesare Borgia, Leonardo inspects the fortifications of Romagna.

1503–1506. Portrait of *Mona Lisa.* Born in 1479 in Florence, she married, in 1495, Francesco di Bartolommeo di Zanobi del Giocondo of Florence (la Gioconda, la Joconde). She was 24 in 1503. It was one of the three paintings which the cardinal of Aragon saw in Cloux in 1517. There are at least 61 old copies of it.

1504. January 24. Leonardo gives his advice about the best location for Michelangelo's David.

1504. May 4. Contract between the Signoria and Leonardo for the wall painting, *The Battle of Anghiari,*[2] to decorate the Salone del Cinquecento (*gran consiglio*) in the Palazzo Vecchio (P. della Signoria) in Florence. Leonardo did his work in 1504–1505, then abandoned it; the unfinished painting was eventually destroyed but is known from ancient copies.

1504. July 9, Wednesday. Death of Leonardo's father, Ser Piero, notary at the Palazzo del Podestà, Florence. He was 80 years old and left behind him ten sons and two daughters (Richter nos. 1372, 1373A, 1373).

IV. SECOND MILANESE PERIOD (1506–13), UNDER FRENCH RULE

1506. May. Leonardo returns to Milan at the request of the French governor, Charles d'Amboise, count of Chaumont (d. 1511).

1506–1508? *Virgin of the Rocks* (National Gallery, London). A copy of the Louvre painting by Leonardo, or a member of his school. See 1483.

1506–1509. *Bacchus,* first known under the name *St. John in the Desert* (Louvre).

1507. May 24. Louis XII visits Milan; Leonardo helps to organize festivities at the Castello Sforzesco.

1507. July 24. Louis XII appoints Leonardo as his painter and engineer. Leonardo spends six months in Florence for the legal defence of his patrimony.

1508–10. *St. Anne, Virgin and Child* (Louvre). Leonardo was thinking of such a composition since 1498. There are 27 known copies.

1509+. *St. John the Baptist* (Louvre). See 1515?

1510. Leonardo expects to complete his "anatomy" in the winter (Richter no. 1376).

1511–12. Studies for the Trivulzio monument (Windsor).

1513. September 24. Leonardo leaves Milan for Rome with Francesco Melzi and others.

V. ROME 1513–16

1513. December 1. Arrives in Rome, the guest of Giuliano de' Medici, elder brother of Giovanni (Leo X), at the Belvedere, Vatican. He remained there until 1516 (Richter no. 1376B).

1515. January 9. Giuliano de' Medici leaves Rome to be married in Savoy. On the same day Louis XII dies. Leonardo's own note *ad hoc* (Richter no. 1377).

1515? *St. John the Baptist* (Louvre). See 1509+.

1516. Autumn. Poorly treated by the Pope, who preferred his rivals, Michelangelo and Raphael, Leonardo leaves with Francesco Melzi on his way to France, via Milan.

1516. Self-portrait, drawn with red chalk (Torino). As Leonardo looks like a very old man, this can hardly have been made before 1516, when he was 64.

VI. AMBOISE, 1517–19

1517. Leonardo and Francesco Melzi are the guests of François I at the little chateau of Cloux, in the royal domain of Amboise. Leonardo receives a pension of a thousand "écus soleil" and Francesco one of four hundred. "Ascension Day at Amboise 1517 in May at Cloux" (Richter no. 1377B).

1517. October 10. Cardinal Luis d'Aragon and his secretary, Antonio de Beatis, visit Leonardo at Cloux (Antonio's account of the interview is extant).

1518. June 24. "St. John's Day at Amboise in the palace of Cloux" (Richter no. 1378).

1519. May 2. Leonardo dies at Cloux at the age of 67. According to Vasari, François I was at his bedside. This is not true; the king was not in Amboise at that time.

1519. August 12. Leonardo is buried at Amboise.

Notes

HAUSER / THE RENAISSANCE ARTIST

1. Kenneth Clark: *Leonardo da Vinci*, 1939, pp. 11–12.
2. Cf. for the following: M. Wackernagel: *Der Lebensraum des Kuenstlers*, pp. 316 ff.
3. Albert Dresdner: *Die Entstehung der Kunstkritik*, 1915, p. 94.
4. Gaye: *Carteggio inedito d'artisti dei sec. XIV–XVI*, 1839–40, I, p. 115.
5. M. J. Jerrold: *Italy in the Renaissance*, 1927, p. 35.
6. H. Lerner-Lehmkuhl: *Zur Struktur u. Gesch. des florent. Kunstmarktes im XV. Jahrhundert*, 1936, pp. 28–9.
7. Ibid., pp. 38–9.
8. Ibid., p. 50.
9. M. Wackernagel: *Der Lebensraum des Kuenstlers*, p. 355.
10. Robert Saitschick: *Menschen und Kunst der ital. Renaiss.*, 1903, p. 199.
11. Paul Drey: *Die wirtschaftlichen Grundlagen der Malkunst*, 1910, p. 46.
12. Ibid., pp. 20–1.
13. H. Lerner-Lehmkuhl, op. cit., p. 34.
14. R. Saitschick, op. cit., p. 197.
15. H. Lerner-Lehmkuhl, op. cit., p. 54.
16. A. Dresdner, op. cit., pp. 77–9.
17. Ibid., p. 95.
18. Joseph Meder: *Die Handzeichnung. Ihre Technik und Entwicklung*, 1919, p. 214.
19. Leonardo Olschki: *Gesch. der neusprachlichen wiss. Lit.*, I, 1919, pp. 107–8.
20. A. Dresdner, op. cit., p. 72.
21. J. P. Richter: *The Literary Work of Leonardo da Vinci*, 1883, I, No. 653.
22. R. Saitschick, op. cit., pp. 185–6.
23. Cf. Bandello's description of Leonardo's discontinuous method of working on "The Last Supper"; quoted by Kenneth Clark, op. cit., pp. 92–3.
24. Edgar Zilsel: *Die Entstehung des Geniebegriffes*, 1926, p. 109.
25. Cf. Dietrich Schaefer: *Weltgesch. der Neuzeit*, 1920, 9th edit., pp. 13–14.—J. Huizinga: *Wege der Kulturgeschichte*, 1930, p. 130.
26. Julius Schlosser: *Die Kunstliteratur*, 1924, p. 139.
27. Joseph Meder, op. cit., pp. 169–70.
28. Karl Borinski: "Der Streit um die Renaissance und die Entstehungs geschichte der hist. Beziehungsbegriffe Renaissance und Mittelalter," *Sitzungsberichte der Bayr. Akad. d. Wiss.*, 1919, p. 21.
29. Ernst Walser: *Gesammelte Studien zur Geitesgeschichte der Renaissance*, 1932, pp. 104–5.
30. K. Borinski, op. cit., pp. 32–3.
31. Philippe Monnier: *Le Quattrocento*, 1901, II, p. 229.

32. Wilhelm Dilthey: *Weltanschauung u. Analyse des Menschen seit Renaiss. u. Reformation. Ges. Schriften*, II, 1914, pp. 343 ff.

33. Adolf Hildebrand: *Das Problem der Form i.d.bild. Kunst*, 1893.

34. Cf. for the following: Erwin Panofsky: *Die Perspektive als "symbolische Form,"* Vortraege der Bibl. Warburg, 1927, p. 270.

35. Ibid., p. 260.

36. Cf. Jacques Mesnil: *Die Kunstlehre der Fruehrenaissance im Werke Masaccios,* Vortraege der Bibl. Warburg, 1928, p. 127.

37. The speed of the execution is also praised in Aretino's letters to Tintoretto (1545–46).

38. E. Zilsel, op. cit., pp. 112–13.

39. E. Walser, op. cit., p. 105.

40. Cf. J. Huizinga: *Erasmus*, 1924, p. 123.—Karl Buecher: "Die Anfaenge des Zeitungswesens." In *Die Entstehung der Volkswirtschaft*, 1919, 12th edit., I, p. 233.

41. Hans Baron: "Franciscan Poverty and Civic Wealth as Factors in the Rise of Humanistic Thought," *Speculum*, XIII, 1938, pp. 12, 18 ff. Quoted by Ch. E. Trinkaus: *Adversity's Noblemen*, 1940, pp. 16–17.

42. Alfred v. Martin: *Sociology of the Renaissance*, 1944, pp. 53 ff.

43. Julien Benda: *La Trahison des clercs*, 1927.

44. Ph. Monnier, op. cit., I, p. 334.

WÖLFFLIN / THE NATURE OF HIS "CLASSIC" ART

1. Leonardo, *Trattato della Pittura*, Ludwig's Italian-German ed., No. 73. [English translation in McCurdy, *Notebooks of Leonardo da Vinci*, II, p. 256.—*Trans.*]

2. *Trattato* No. 70 [McCurdy, op. cit., p. 262] on light and shade melting into one another, "like smoke" (an earlier expression). The same passage has the injunction to observe where lines "are heavy and where they are fine."

3. The edges of Leonardo's picture do not coincide with the limits of the room depicted; there is a considerable amount of space imagined above the upper edge of the picture. This division of space is one of the means by which it is possible to compose large scale figures in a small space without their appearing confined. The Quattrocentisti were in the habit of rendering interiors with sidewalls and the whole of the ceiling—cf. Ghirlandaio's *Birth of St. John* or Castagno's *Last Supper*.

4. Goethe's error, widely repeated since his day, must here be corrected. He thought St. Peter had struck Judas in the side with a knife, which could explain the sudden movement.

5. The Albertina pen-drawing (Fischel, *Raffaels Zeichnungen*, 387) now correctly attributed to G. F. Penni, cannot be accepted as a preparatory drawing for this Marcantonio engraving as it is quite different in composition.

6. Poliziano, *Giostra*, I, p. 50, *"lampeggiò d'un dolce e vago riso."*

7. Baldassare Castiglione, *Il Cortegiano*, 1516. In the first Book it is stated that men imitated women in plucking the eyebrows and forehead (*pelarsi le ciglia e la fronte*).

8. When Lucrezia Tornabuoni nei Medici, the mother of Lorenzo the Magnificent, sought a bride for her son among the Roman nobility, she wrote to her husband

finding fault with the carriage of the Roman women as being less upright than that of the Florentines (Reumont, *Lorenzo magnifico*, I, 272).

9. *Cf.* the Raphaelesque so-called *Drawing for the Maddalena Doni* in the Louvre.

10. *Trattato della Pittura* (Ludwig's Italian-German ed. No. 128). [Several of these theories may be found in McCurdy's edition of the Notebooks.—*Trans.*]

11. It has long been felt that the *Belle Ferronnière* (Louvre) has no place in Leonardo's work. This fine picture has recently been tentatively ascribed to Boltraffio, but this is not convincing.

12. The cartoon is lost and the picture may have been executed considerably later; *cf.* Cook, *Gazette des Beaux-Arts*, 1897.

13. The impression made on contemporaries can be clearly gauged in a report from Fra Pietro da Novellara to the Marchioness of Mantua on 3 April, 1501, where he speaks of this aspect, *"e sono queste figure grandi al naturale, ma stanno in piccolo cartone, perchè tutte o sedono o stanno curve, et una sta alquanto dinanzi all' altra."* (*Archivio storico dell' arte*, I.) ["These figures are life-size, but in quite a small cartoon, since they are all seated or bent forward and one rather in front of the other." *Cf.* also Sir Kenneth Clark, *Leonardo da Vinci*, 1940.— *Trans.*] The Cartoon in London (Royal Academy) is of a group of two women and two children, less beautiful, and may well be a somewhat earlier and less fluent composition. Its effect on Leonardo's School may be seen in Luini (Ambrosiana).

14. Vasari (ed. Milanesi, IV, p. 21).

15. Vasari (ed. Milanesi, III, p. 297). *Cf.* the drawing in Munich (Berenson No. 1908).

16. On the questions of the Milanese monument and a second, later, equestrian project with a tomb below it for General Trivulzio, see Müller-Walde in the *Jahrbuch der preussischen Kunstsammlungen*, 1897 and 1899. Since then, Müntz's great book has appeared (*Léonardo de Vinci*, Paris, 1899) which gives exhaustive information on all matters of fact. [The English reader is again referred to Sir Kenneth Clark's book, cited above.—*Trans.*]

17. I do not venture an opinion on Ruben's authorship of the Louvre drawing: Rooses is emphatically in favour of it. At any rate, Rubens knew the composition—his *Lion Hunt*, in Munich, and other works attest this.

18. [For this use of the word "unclear," *cf.* Wölfflin, *Principles of Art History.*— *Trans.*]

19. *Cf.* Müller-Walde, *Beiträge zur Kenntnis des Lionardo da Vinci, Jahrbuch der preussischen Kunstsammlungen*, 1897. Müller-Walde discovered a minute pendrawing of the figure in the *Codex Atlanticus*. *Cf.* Müntz, *op. cit.*, pp. 426 ff.

20. The picture is in the Galleria Borromeo, Milan, and should be compared with Leonardo's *Mona Lisa*, a version of which, even in his own life-time (and perhaps by Leonardo himself) was transformed into a nude. *Cf.* Müntz, *op. cit.*, p. 511.

VALENTINER / LEONARDO AS VERROCCHIO'S COWORKER

1. W. Suida, *Leonardo und sein Kreis*, Munich, 1929.

2. The suggestion of Suida (p. 26) of a possible connection of the female portrait

in the Uffizi, a work in the style of Piero Pollaiuolo, with Leonardo's early works does not seem to me to be convincing, still less the attribution of the portrait of a goldsmith by Franciabigio to Leonardo (A. Venturi, in *L'arte*, 1924, p. 197).

3. Among all the Leonardo investigators he distinguishes himself by a remarkable animosity toward the opinions of others.

4. Berenson also has recently designated the Liechtenstein portrait as a work of Verrocchio or Leonardo (*Dedalo*, 1926, p. 638).

5. The most important works which deal with our subject are the following: B. Berenson, *The Drawings of the Florentine Painters*, 1903; *idem*, *Study and Criticism of Italian Art*, III, London, 1916; W. von Seidlitz, *Leonardo da Vinci, der Wendepunkt der Renaissance*, Berlin, 1910; J. Thiis, *Leonardo da Vinci*, London and Boston, 1913; A. Venturi, *Leonardo da Vinci, pittore*, Bologna, 1920; *idem., Storia dell'arte italiana*, VIII, 192–; W. von Bode, *Studien über Leonardo da Vinci*, Berlin, 1921; Aldo de Rinaldis, *Storia dell'opera pittorica di Leonardo da Vinci*, Bologna, 1922; E. Hildebrandt, *Leonardo*, Berlin, 1927; O. Sirén, *Leonardo da Vinci*, Paris, 1928; W. Suida, *Leonardo und sein Kreis*, Munich, 1929; R. van Marle, *Italian Schools of Painting*, XI, The Hague, 1929.

6. The most comprehensive work on the subject is F. Malaguzzi-Valeri, *Leonardo da Vinci e la scultura*, Bologna, 1922.

7. As everyone knows, Verrocchio, Leonardo, and Lorenzo di Credi were equally active as painters and sculptors; but one may also assume Francesco di Simone to have been active in both fields, at least his sketch-book with picturesque scenes of cavalry battles or religious representations with landscape backgrounds argues for his activity as a painter.

8. The assumption made by Berenson, that Lorenzo di Credi had executed the first sketch—that preserved in the Victoria and Albert Museum—is according to the date (1474) improbable; Credi was at that time only fifteen years old. Miss Cruttwell's suggestion that the London sketch is a modern forgery, I believe to be inconclusive.

9. This has been pointed out by Miss Cruttwell in her excellent work on Verrocchio, London, 1904, Chapter XI.

10. W. Suida, *op. cit.*, pp. 250–255.

11. E. Hildebrandt, *op. cit.*, p. 30, designates, without foundation, the year 1466 as "documentarily testified."

12. R. van Marle, *op. cit.*, p. 498.

13. As a kind of documentary evidence that Leonardo worked in Verrocchio's work-shop before 1471 we may take the mention of the method by which the Palla for the cathedral at Florence was melted together: "Remember," he says (MSS, fol. 84v.), "the means by which the Palla of S. Maria del Fiore was soldered to-gether." The order for the Palla was received by Verrocchio in 1468; the Palla was fastened to its place in 1471.

14. In the question of the date compare the thorough researches of Müller-Walde, in *Jahrbuch der preuss. Kunstsammlungen*, 1897, pp. 146 ff.

15. Cf. G. Gronau's excellent biography in Thieme-Becker's Künstler-lexicon.

16. See the detailed illustrations of van Marle, *op. cit.*, XI, p. 510.

17. A. Popp, *Old Master Drawings*, I, 1926.

18. In spite of this fact E. Hildebrandt has published in his work under the name

of Leonardo several obviously right-handed drawings, which also for stylistic reasons can scarcely be by Leonardo's hand. In Miss R. A. Taylor's imaginative book, *Leonardo the Florentine,* 1928, several reproductions which have been carelessly retouched by the publisher (e.g., pp. 244, 256, 274) appear as if done by a right-handed artist, although the originals are left-handed drawings.

19. People have often wracked their brains over why Leonardo practiced mirror writing. The reason seems to me to be simply that it is more comfortable for the left-handed writer if he can write from right to left instead of from left to right. Only if he writes from right to left can he lay his hand upon the unused part of the paper as comfortably as can the right-handed person.

20. Reproduced by Suida, *op. cit.,* p. 36, no. 57.

21. This has been pointed out by G. Gronau in his article on Lorenzo di Credi in the Thieme-Becker lexicon, and by O. Sirén, in his *Leonardo.*

22. A. Chiapelli, in *Arte del Rinascimento,* 1925; *idem,* in *Bolletino d'arte,* 1925; J. Thiis, *Leonardo,* p. 177, etc.; R. van Marle, *op. cit.,* p. 536.

23. Illustrated by Suida, *op. cit.,* no. 58.

24. This has been denied by Thiis in a quite incomprehensible manner (p. 267).

25. That the drawing was used later by Marco d'Oggiono, as Suida demonstrates, is not opposed to its early origin, for the Milan pupils repeatedly used Leonardo's Florentine sketchbook, which he had naturally taken with him to Milan.

26. Cf. reproductions in E. Hildebrandt, *op. cit.,* nos. 186, 187, 240.

27. See recently Sirén, *op. cit.*

28. For the connection of similar vases of flowers with the architectural pilasters of related profiles, compare also the drawing in the *Codex Atlanticus* illustrated by J. P. Richter, *The Literary Works of Leonardo da Vinci,* II, p. 104.

29. *Studien über Leonardo da Vinci,* 1921, p. 19.

30. J. P. Richter, *op. cit.,* II, no. 1383.

31. Printed and annotated by C. Fabriczy, in *Archivio storico italiano,* 1893. See also G. Calvi, *I manoscritti di Leonardo da Vinci,* Bologna, 1923, and E. McCurdy, *Leonardo da Vinci's Notebooks,* in *Burlington Magazine,* 1925, p. 260.

32. It seems to me very probable that Leonardo has represented Cesare Borgia in a drawing at Turin (Pl. 50), which shows the same person seen from three different views (J. P. Richter, *op. cit.,* pl. 120, who considered it as a study after an Oriental; Berenson, no. 1085). If we compare the features with the best authenticated portrait of Cesare Borgia in Paolo Giovio's *Elogi* (Pl. 51), the profile, even down to the curled point of the beard, has much similarity. No certain *en face* portrait of Cesare Borgia exists; if Leonardo's drawing should prove to represent him, it would be of special interest, since it allows a full study of the type from all sides. The view from the front makes it comprehensible that Cesare was regarded as the most handsome man in all Italy. This criminal type has here almost a superficial likeness to the features with which Christ used to be represented in the Renaissance; only the unevenly formed eyes, placed narrowly together, betray the sly and dangerous character. In the side views the bull-like neck, the upturned nostrils, and the disagreeable form of the ear, reveal more clearly the brutality of the man. The similarly formed, unusual ear is to be found also in the supposed profile portrait of Cesare Borgia in the Museo Correr, Venice, reproduced by A. Venturi, *Storia dell'arte italiana,* VII, 2, p. 84.

33. W. Bode, *Studien über Leonardo*, p. 73.
34. *Op. cit.*, p. 172.
35. J. P. Richter, *Leonardo*, 1880, p. 97.
36. *Archivio storico*, 1893, p. 87.
37. P. 34.
38. Reprint of the correspondence between Lorenzo de' Medici and the council of Pistoja by M. Cruttwell, *Verrocchio*, pp. 127 and 257.
39. *Archivio storico*, p. 89.
40. *Ibid.*, p. 92.
41. Aldo de Rinaldis, *op. cit.*, p. 38, reprints the contract with Piero Pollaiuolo and Leonardo.
42. Not on January 1, as is given by Milanesi, Müntz, and others. Compare Müller-Walde, in *Jahrbuch der preuss. Kunstsammlungen*, 1897, p. 126, and Aldo de Rinaldis, *op. cit.*, p. 38.
43. Berenson (*The Drawings of the Florentine Painters*) has already pointed out this influence, especially through Leonardo's Adoration of the Kings. Compare, also, my notes on a predella by Filippino Lippi and his use of Leonardo drawings, in *Bulletin of the Detroit Institute of Arts*, April, 1930.
44. Published by G. Pauli in *Zeichnungen alter Meister in der Kunsthalle zu Hamburg*, 1927, but dated too late (90's). The type of Phyllis is the same as that of the Madonna in one of the studies for the Madonna with the Cat in the Uffizi while the figure of Aristotle is quite Verrocchiesque and shows close connection with one of the soldiers in the relief of the Villa Careggi.
45. Compare H. Thode, *Michelangelo*, I, p. 13.
46. Bode has devoted one of his last books to the interesting artist, *Bertoldo und Lorenzo Medici*, Freiburg, 1925.
47. I have since found that Malaguzzi-Valeri (*Leonardo da Vinci e la scultura*, p. 34) has also pointed out the similarity of the motive of Bertoldo's relief and Leonardo's designs of cavalry battles, more, however, in order to prove that other artists besides Leonardo were also occupied with related artistic representations and without thinking of any personal connection between the two artists.
48. Bertoldo's statuette of the Bellerophon in the Museum in Vienna precedes in the position of the springing horse Leonardo's Trivulzio monument.
49. G. F. Hill, in *Burlington Magazine*, 1910, p. 143; *idem*, *Medals of the Renaissance*, 1920, p. 57.
50. P. Schubring, *Die Plastik Sienas im Quattrocento*, 1909; *idem*, in *Handbuch für Kunstwissenschaft*, 1919; *idem*, in *Monatshefte*, 1916; F. Hartlaub, *Matteo da Siena*, 1910; W. R. Valentiner, *The Italian Renaissance Sculptures of the Widener Collection*, in *Art News Supplement*, 1926.
51. P. Schubring, *op. cit.*, 1907, p. 175.
52. Schubring also regards this as a possibility.
53. W. Bode in *Amtliche Berichten der Berliner Museen*, 1916, p. 104.
54. P. Schubring, *op. cit.*, p. 175.
55. That Francesco di Giorgio was not a professional medalist is evidenced by this medal as well as by the one coined for Federigo, for both are preserved as poorly coined specimens only, besides which the characters on one of the specimens are not very skillfully done, while on the other one the inscription is missing entirely.

56. A further connection between Leonardo and Francesco di Giorgio may be established by the comparison of Leonardo's St. Jerome in the Vatican, which was created about 1480, and the relief with the same representation in the Widener collection, if my attribution of this work to Francesco—as it is treated in a much too picturesque fashion to be considered as a work done by Desiderio—proves correct. Suggestions of Leonardo's compositions are to be found not only in the type of the face, but also in the landscape.

57. *Una terracotta di Verrocchio a Careggi*, in *L'arte*, 1904, p. 59. As a work by Verrocchio it has been further described by W. Bode, *Denkmäler der Renaissance*, p. 178; A. Venturi, *Storia dell'arte italiana*, VI, p. 708; F. Malaguzzi-Valeri, *Leonardo e la scultura*, p. 15.

58. *Verrocchio*, pp. 57–61.

59. We may form an idea of the shape of the bronze chandeliers from the two chandeliers of the Donatello school which are preserved in the cathedrals of Pistoja and Prato. The one in Pistoja has recently been attributed by L. Planiczig (*Jahrbuch der preuss. Kunstsammlungen*, 1928, p. 200) to Bellano. He dates it tentatively within the years 1467–1469, which is exactly the time when Verrocchio executed his. The documents refer to Verrocchio's chandelier with the words *"in similitudine di un vaso."* This unusual motive is found in both the chandeliers in Prato and Pistoja, i.e., the middle piece of the chandelier is shaped like a large vase. If Verrocchio used this Donatellesque motive, it would agree with the opinion of those who consider him a pupil of Donatello. In the chandelier in Pistoja is the naturalistic treatment of the rising arms rather in Verrocchio's early style; it permits a comparison with the ornamentation found on the tomb of Piero and Giovanni de' Medici.

60. Published for the first time by C. v. Fabriczy, *Il Verrocchio al servizio dei Medici*, in *Archivio storico dell'arte*, 1895.

61. Compare F. Malaguzzi-Valeri, *Leonardo da Vinci e la scultura*, 1922; and Raymond S. Stites, *Leonardo da Vinci, Sculptor*, in *Art Studies*, 1926, p. 103. Mr. Stites in his interesting essay convincingly links the terra cotta group in the Camondo collection in the Louvre with Leonardo's Battle of Anghiari—the attribution to the Pollaiuoli is indeed impossible—but it appears to me less certain whether it was created as early as he assumes—before 1506—and not rather about the middle of the century. The cartilaginous and baroque formation of the muscular system and the repetitions of contraposed positions seem in my opinion to go beyond Leonardo's time; furthermore, the repetition of the motive of the wide-open mouth in *all* five figures, whose type has besides hardly varied at all, does not seem to speak especially for an ingenious master like Leonardo who distinguishes himself by the greatest variation of individual forms. To my mind the execution is very close to the Paduan workshop of Andrea Riccio.

62. M. Cruttwell, *op. cit.*, pl. VII.

63. *Storia dell'arte italiana*, IX, 1, p. 51.

64. See W. Suida, *loc. cit.*, p. 250.

65. Raffaelino del Garbo also used the composition of the Careggi relief for his Annunciation in the Academy in Florence. The sleeping youth is taken over from it almost literally, if somewhat farther removed toward the background.

66. Reproduced by H. Mackowsky, *Verrocchio*, 1901, p. 32.

67. T. Cook, *The Signa Madonna*, 1919. Contrast F. Malaguzzi-Valeri, *Leonardo e la*

scultura, p. 27. A second, better preserved stucco relief of the same composition, to which my attention was first called by Dr. U. Middeldorf, belongs to Professor Piero Tozzi, Florence (Pl. 47). I had lately in New York the opportunity to compare the reliefs, placing them side by side. The comparison proved conclusively that both were cast from a third original, most likely from a lost marble relief by Verrocchio. They have exactly the same size; the Signa relief is, however, more rubbed off than the other and does not show the marks of the knife with which the artist worked it over after the casting.

No more convincing is Professor F. J. Mather's attribution to Leonardo of a terra cotta relief representing the Madonna and Child from the school of Verrocchio, which I once purchased for the Metropolitan Museum, New York. He dates it "about 1465" (*History of Italian Painting,* p. 48) and compares it with the drawing in the Uffizi, mentioned above (Pl. 37), which, however, no one else has dated earlier than 1478. "Both the relief and the drawing breathe the feeling of Verrocchio's David of 1465 and should not be much later" (F. J. Mather, Jr., in *Art and Archaeology,* 1916, p. 122). In 1465 Leonardo was thirteen years old! And where does Professor Mather get the exact date 1465 for Verrocchio's David? The statue is first mentioned in documents in 1476, and since it was executed for the Villa Careggi and most likely for Lorenzo de' Medici, who presented it later to the City of Florence, Verrocchio in all probability received the order not before 1469, when Lorenzo de' Medici inherited the Villa Careggi. Also from stylistic reasons it would be difficult to place the David earlier than the first half of the 70's.

68. Reproduced in A. Marquand's excellent books on the della Robbias. The Braunschweig St. Michael (Vieweg collection) has been sold recently.

69. Another external feature points to the relation of Andrea della Robbia's St. Michael in Braunschweig, created for S. Michele Archangelo at Fænza about 1475–80, to the Verrocchio workshop. The cuirass with lions as shoulder pieces and plant tendrils upon the breast must have been an atelier piece in Verrocchio's workshop as it resembles the one in the silver relief of the cathedral workshop by Verrocchio and was also drawn by Leonardo (drawing in Windsor, reproduced by F. Malaguzzi-Valeri, *Leonardo e la scultura.* Wherever we encounter this suit of armor, as in Cosimo Rosselli's altarpiece of St. Barbara in the Academy in Florence, or in the terra cotta bust of a young man in armor in the Widener collection, we may infer a connection with the Verrocchio workshop.

70. To attribute the terra cotta reproduction in Roman possession to Leonardo, as Venturi does (*L'arte,* 1927) seems to me, however, unsatisfactory. Just as little am I able to recognize Leonardo's style in the insignificant relief of David in the Lanckorowski collection in Vienna.

71. Most recently by E. Hildebrandt, *op. cit.,* p. 332, who compares the profile of the bronze David and that of the doubting Thomas with Leonardo's profile drawings. The connection between the head of David and the drawing in Weimar (Hildebrandt, *op. cit.,* p. 333), to which E. Müntz first pointed, is indeed obvious, but unfortunately the drawing is not by Leonardo, but by one of his followers. Compare also the drawing of Leonardo's reproduced by Thiis, *op. cit.,* p. 153, with the profile of David.

72. F. Malaguzzi-Valeri, *op. cit.,* pp. 16–18.

BERENSON / AN ATTEMPT AT REVALUATION

1. Also known as "Adoration of the Magi."—*Ed.*
2. Reproduced, p. 79, G. Gronau's "Leonardo" (London, Duckworth). This inexpensive little book contains adequate illustrations of nearly all the other paintings and drawings mentioned here. The text can be recommended as informing, appreciative, and free of humbug and re-echoing nonsense.

READ / THE ILLUSION OF THE REAL

1. *Gothic Art and Scholasticism* (Latrobe: Archabbey Press, 1951), p. 26.
2. A work on perspective by an English scholar, John of Peckham, was very popular in the thirteenth century and was probably known to the brothers Van Eyck. It was printed in Milan in 1494. Cf. Joseph Kern, *Die Grundzüge der linearperspektivischen Darstellung in der Kunst der Brüder van Eyck und ihrer Schule* (Leipzig, 1904). For a masterly summary of the whole question of perspective in relation to the art of this period, see Erwin Panofsky, *Early Netherlandish Painting* (Cambridge: Harvard University Press, 1953), especially the introduction, pp. 1–20.
3. *Early Netherlandish Painting,* pp. 16–17.
4. Cf. Paul Henri Michel, *La pensée de L. B. Alberti* (Paris, 1930).
5. "Die Perspektive als symbolische Form," *Vorträge der Bibliothek Warburg* (1924–25), pp. 258 ff.
6. *The Note-Books of Leonardo da Vinci,* trans. Edward MacCurdy (London and New York, Jonathan Cape, 1908), I, p. 134.
7. *Note-Books,* I, pp. 167–168.
8. Cf. R. H. Thouless, "Phenomenal Regression to the Real Object," *British Journal of Psychology,* 21, pt. 4; 22, pts. 1 and 3 (1931–32).
9. *Note-Books,* II, 266.
10. Ibid, II, 257–258.
11. Ibid, II, 364.
12. Ibid, II, 374.
13. Ibid, II, 529.
14. Ibid, II, 528.
15. For a penetrating analysis of this transition, see M. H. Abrams, *The Mirror and the Lamp* (New York: Oxford University Press, 1953).

KOYRÉ / THE BEGINNINGS OF MODERN SCIENCE

1. Leonardo's was the typical drawing of the engineer. Thus be introduced rollers to minimize friction between the heavy bodies and the inclined planes on which they were placed.

SARTON / ART AND SCIENCE

1. This is a free translation of my lecture delivered in French at the Palais de la Découverte in Paris on the Fourth of July, 1952, and published in *Léonard de Vinci et l'expérience scientifique au seizième siècle* (Paris: Presses Universitaires

de France, 1953), pp. 11–29. I delivered substantially the same lecture, in English, at the Pierpont Morgan Library on October 16, 1952. I take advantage of this first publication in English [1957] to thank the sponsors of these lectures in Paris and New York for the opportunities which they so kindly opened to me.

2. For the reader's convenience, each quotation is identified by the number given to it in Richter's edition. This one is Richter 886. Jean-Paul Richter, *The Literary Works of Leonardo da Vince* (2d ed., 2 vols., Oxford University Press, 1939; reviewed in *Isis,* 35: 184–87). Richter refers to the original Mss.

3. The fragment is Richter 1363. Sigmund Freud, *Eine Kindsheiterrinerung des Leonardo da Vinvi* (74 pp., Leipzig, 1910).

4. In 1916 I was invited to deliver six lectures at the Lowell Institute in Boston on science in Leonardo's age. After that I spent two more years analyzing every one of Leonardo's thoughts. My ideas and plans were then set forth in various writings, such as "Une encyclopédie léonardesque" (*Raccolta Vinciana,* 10: 235–42, Milan, 1919). I then realized that my knowledge of ancient and mediaeval science was insufficient, and I decided to undertake an elaborate study of this subject, which bore fruit in my *Introduction to the History of Science*. I had to end my story not in 1900, as I had planned, but in 1400. In spite of thirty-five years of diligent work, I was not yet back to Leonardo.

5. For a discussion of the birth date see *Isis,* 43: 125 (1952).

6. The best known visitors of Verrocchio were il Perugino, Sandro Botticelli, young Lorenzo di Credi, and the brothers Pollaiuoli.

7. When Cardinal Luis d'Aragon visited Leonardo at Cloux in 1517 his secretary, Antonio de Beatis, noticed that Leonardo could not use his right hand for painting and concluded that it was paralyzed. Was not that a wrong interpretation of Leonardo's left-handedness?

8. The years between the end of his stay with Verrocchio (c.1477) and the beginning of his residence in Milan (1483) are rather obscure. If Leonardo traveled to the Near East (Egypt, Armenia, Taurus Mountains), it was possibly during this period. Richter, 2: 315–23.

9. Never did the wheel of fortune turn more furiously than in the case of Lodovico Sforza, also called Lodovico il Moro. Born in 1451, he was duke of Milan from 1481 to 1499, a great patron of the arts, but he joined a league against the French in 1495 and was defeated by Louis XII in 1499. He spent the rest of his life imprisoned and died in his last prison, the castle of Loches (23 miles southeast of Tours) in 1508.

10. Luca Pacioli was dealt with in Wing Two [of *Six Wings*], when I spoke of his best known work, the *Summa de arithmetica geometria,* etc. (Venice: Paganinis, 1494). Another work of his, *Divina proportione* (same printer, 1509) was illustrated with geometric figures drawn roughly by Leonardo (Richter, 1: 243–44).

11. Marcantonio della Torre (1478–1511); see below, note 30.

12. Giuliano de' Medici (1478–1516), the elder brother of Giovanni de' Medici (1475–1521) who became Pope Leo X (1513–21); they were the sons of Lorenzo il Magnifico and like him great patrons of arts and letters.

13. Raphael was also working in the Vatican at the same time. He was painting frescoes, the Disputa, the School of Athens, etc. Michelangelo was completing the ceiling of the Sistine Chapel. An extraordinary conjunction of major stars!

In 1514 Leonardo was 62, Michelangelo 39, and Raphael 31. The oldest and the youngest were nearest to death; they had but 5 and 6 more years to live, but Michelangelo was to live another 50 years, more than the whole of Raphael's span.

14. John the maker of mirrors (Richter no. 1351–53).

15. Cloux was a part of the royal domain of Amboise on the Loire. The congress organized in 1952 by the French government to celebrate the fourth centenary of Leonardo's birth ended on Sunday, July 14, in Amboise. The royal estate now belongs to the Comte de Paris, who offered a dinner; a solemn mass had been celebrated in the morning in the church of Amboise. The main officiant was the parish priest of Vinci.

16. The identification of this portrait with the Mona Lisa cannot be proved but is considered probable by Germain Bazin: *Hommage à Léonard de Vinci* (Paris: Musée du Louvre: 1952), p. 24. The three paintings have remained together since 1515 and are now in the Louvre.

17. Francesco Melzi was a young gentleman of Milan (Richter no. 1566) born in 1493 (hence 41 years younger than Leonardo). He inherited all of Leonardo's manuscripts and took them to Vaprio d'Adda (Milan), where Giorgio Vasari saw them in 1565. He died in Vaprio, c.1570. Very little of his work is extant. A very attractive portrait of him drawn by Giovanni Antonio Boltraffio (1467–1510), another of Leonardo's disciples, is preserved in the Ambrosiana; the curators of that museum vouch for its authenticity.

18. Shio Sakanishi, *The spirit of the brush, being the outlook of Chinese painters on nature from Eastern Chin to Five Dynasties, 317–960* (Wisdom of the East Series, London: John Murray, 1939; reviewed in *Isis*, 31: 220). See also *The essay on landscape painting (Lin ch'üan kao chih)* by Kuo Hsi (c.1020–90), translated by S. Sakanishi (Wisdom of the East Series, 1935; reviewed in *Isis*, 25: 461–64), and the *Chieh-tzŭ-yüan hua ch'uan,* translated into French by Raphael Petrucci (Paris: Laurens, 1918; reviewed in *Isis*, 4: 345–47).

19. The three outstanding equestrian statues of the Renaissance are: first, the one of Erasmo Gattamelata in Padua, made by Donatello, c.1444; second, that of Bartolommeo Colleoni in Venice, made by Verrocchio after 1479 (Leonardo witnessed its composition and planning); third, that of Francesco Sforza, duke of Milan (1447–66), Lodovico's father, made by Leonardo, who had devoted considerable thought to it. See his notes concerning the casting (Richter nos. 710–15). It was destroyed by Gascon archers during their occupation of Milan (1499–1512).

20. In my *Introduction* (vol. 3) I have given a list of some fifteen authors of technical books of the fifteenth century. Three of these are Italians; it is not necessary to assume that Leonardo had seen their texts and drawings, but he certainly followed the same oral and manual traditions.

21. I do not refer to the observations made in our own time by means of ultra-rapid photography. This made it possible to see details that no human eye could observe.

22. Richter, no. 1155.

23. In my Harvard lectures on the history of science I came back to Leonardo and Vesalius every other year, and tried to explain the technique of their dissections, how they cut and separated integuments and tissues with various knives and

sometimes with their nails. I did it one day with so much realism that a student felt nauseated and was obliged to leave the auditorium at great speed. I have often wondered how the early anatomists managed to escape infection.

24. See *Introduction*, 3: 1584. Leonardo's ideas *ad hoc* are shown in his drawing of the Accademia of Venice, often reproduced. The Greek canon was fixed by Polycleitos (fl. 452–412 b.c.).

25. Galen (II–2). See my little book *Galen of Pergamon* (University of Kansas Press, 1954; reviewed in *Isis*, 46: 296–97), p. 47.

26. *Quaderni d'Anatomia* I, 3r; II, 3 (*Isis*, 35: 186). These *quaderni* were very well edited by Ove C. L. Vangensten, A. Fonahn, and H. Hopstock (6 vols., folio, Christiania, 1911–16). Richter, 2: 419.

27. From that point of view the method of *"plis cachetés"* practiced by the Académie des Sciences in Paris seems unfair to me. A member is permitted to announce a discovery in a sealed envelope, the date of which is authenticated, but which will be opened and published only when the member wishes it. Can this establish any valid priority? If the member had no faith in his own discovery until it had been confirmed by later events, he did not really make it. He cannot have it both ways.

28. Richter, 1: 5–7.

29. These figures may not be exact, but they will suffice to prove the point.

30. Vasari defined Leonardo's collaboration with Marcantonio as follows "aiutato e scambievolmente aiutando." Marcantonio, who died at thirty without having given anything to posterity, is immortalized by Leonardo's references to him and by the bronze bas-reliefs which Andrea Riccio executed for San Fermo Maggiore in Verona (now in the Louvre). See note 11.

31. In fairness to him it must be added that in this case he was the victim of circumstance. The statue was to be of very large size; the model of the horse only was 7.2 meters high and the weight in bronze would have been of the order of 200,000 pounds. The model was destroyed by Gascon soldiers. It would have cost a very large amount of money to cast the monument in bronze, and Leonardo was criticized by many, including Michelangelo. The bronze needed for the statue was given to Lodovico il Moro, but he had it cast into guns (Richter, 2: 3).

Toward the end of his life Leonardo planned an equestrian statue of the famous captain, Gian Giacomo Trivulzio (died Chartres, 1518), but nothing came of this (Richter, 2: 9).

32. Many young painters worked in Leonardo's studio, chiefly when he was in Milan; they were apprentices and servants and their names appear in Leonardo's notebooks in such brief manner (say, Giulio, Bonifazio, Arrigo, Lorenzo, il Fanfoia) that identification is impossible. Others are better known, such as Giacomo Salai, Francesco Melzi, Cesare da Sesto, Ambrogio de Predis (c.1455–1508), Andrea Solario (1458–1509+), Giovanni Antonio Boltraffio (1467–1516), Gaudenzio Ferrari (c.1484–1546). The greatest, or at least the most popular, of those epigoni was Bernardino Luini (c.1475–c.1532). Leonardo's influence was felt not only by Milanese or Lombardese artists but also by other Italians and by some of the Flemish painters who visited Italy.

33. Italian typography began at Subiaco (not far from Rome) in 1465; the first

Roman edition dates from 1467, those of Venice from 1469, those of Florence and Milan from 1471. Before the end of the fifteenth century printing was one of the main industries of Venice.

34. He refers to definite books but it is impossible to know whether his references apply to manuscript or printed copies.

35. *Anatomical Mss., A,* 8b, Paris, 1898.

36. Pietro of Arezzo (1492–1557), poet, satirist, and blackmailer.

37. Albrecht Dürer (1471–1528) was a little younger than Leonardo (1452–1519), but he did not live as long (57 years instead of 67). One might compare Leonardo also with Raphael of Urbino (1483–1520), who lived only 37 years, yet produced an incredible number of paintings.

38. The first of these three books (1525) was soon translated into Latin (Paris: C. Wechel, 1532, 1534, 1535) and again by Joachim Camerarius (Nuremberg, 1534); the second (1527) was translated into Latin (Paris: C. Wechel, 1535); the third (1528) was translated into Latin by Joachim Camerarius (Nuremberg, 1532), into French by Loys Meigret (Paris: Périer, 1557) and into Italian by G. P. Gallucci (Venice, 1591–94).

39. There is no absolute incompatibility between art and business, and Dürer was not the only artist to be a good business man; we think of Titian, Rubens, and Van Dyck, or even of Chopin.

40. Drawn with red chalk, kept in the Library of Torino. It is the only portrait of him which I can trust to be genuine.

41. Richter 1210, "l'amore di qualunche cosa è figliuolo d'essa cognitione e l'amore è tanto piu fervente quanto la cognitione è piu certa."

DE SANTILLANA / MAN WITHOUT LETTERS

1. In his "Questions" (1368) on Aristotle's *De Caelo,* Albert mentioned that his anonymous master had expressed a belief in the earth's daily rotation.—Trs.

2. I admit this is an impressionistic way of dealing with the earnestness of Leonardo's search and of Duhem's research, a way which might well be accused of frivolity if it were not taken with a grain of salt. I have only been trying to make clear by contrast the difference between the ways of studying of the scholar sunk in his books, and the uncertain inquiries of the craftsman "without letters," polarized on a world of realities.

CLARK / LEONARDO'S SCIENCE AND HIS ART

1. J. P. Richter, *The Literary Works of Leonardo da Vinci,* Oxford, 1939 (originally published 1883).

2. The drawings of machines in the MSS. of Francesco di Giorgio may be a year or two earlier than Leonardo's earliest, i.e., before 1480. Leonardo owned one such MS. by Francesco di Giorgio and annotated it, but at a later date.

3. *Corpo nato della prospettiva/di leonardo vinci discciepolo de/la sperientia.* The word *prospettiva,* as used in the Renaissance, cannot be rendered in English by the word perspective. The *Codice Atlantico* is the name given to a huge scrapbook of his notes and drawings in the Ambrosian Library, Milan.

4. Gabriel Séailles, *Léonard de Vinci, L'artiste et le savant,* Paris 1892.

5. Painted in Florence in about 1506; taken to Fontainebleau and lost or destroyed. Known from copies, of which two are in the present [1952] exhibition at Burlington House, nos. 255 and 259.
6. In the Louvre. Painted c.1482.

FARRELL / ON FREUD'S STUDY OF LEONARDO

1. Clark, Kenneth. *Leonardo da Vinci.* Harmondsworth (Penguin Books), 1958, p. 159.
2. Codice Atlantico, 66 v. This is usually written: C.A. 66 v. (on page 118 of this edition) Freud gives the reference inaccurately as "65 v." In subsequent references to Leonardo's words the following abbreviations will also be used:
Q = Quaderni Anatomia,
H = an MS. in the Library of the Institut de France.
SKM = Codices Foster in the library of the Victoria and Albert Museum.
   The student can consult Leonardo's writings in J. P. Richter, *The Literary Works of Leonardo da Vinci,* compiled and edited from the original manuscripts (rev. ed., 2 vols., London, 1939). For a selection from the writings, see Edward McCurdy, *Leonardo da Vinci's Note-Books,* London (Duckworth), 1906; and Irma A. Richter, *Selections from the Notebooks of Leonardo da Vinci,* London, (O.U.P.), 1952.
3. Farrell, Brian. Introduction to *Leonardo da Vinci and a Memory of His Childhood* by Sigmund Freud, tr. by Alan Tyson. Harmondsworth, England (Pelican Books, Ltd.), 1963, pp. 8–9.
4. Leonardo spelt the word "nibbio" with one "b."
5. Möller, Emil. "Der Geburtstag des Lionardo da Vinci," *Jahrbuch der preussischen Kunstsammlungen,* 60 (1939), 71–5.
6. Thus, Freud supports his argument by one text (p. 146*n.* below) which is incorrect. It should read: "Giovannina has a fantastic face, lives at Santa Caterina, at the hospital." (SKM II 3r; I. Richter, op. cit., p. 322; and J. P. Richter, op. cit., Vol. II, p. 352). Clearly this does not refer to the woman Caterina. Further, the burial expenses are given by J. P. Richter in soldi, not florins (op. cit., Vol. II, p. 379, 1522).
7. Clark, Kenneth, op. cit., p. 143.
8. The history of the mistake seems to be as follows. The original drawing is on Q III 3 v. (see p. 103 of this edition [of Freud's *Leonardo da Vinci*]; a collotype reproduction appears in the definitive edition of the *Quaderni d'Anatomia* by Ove C. L. Vangensten, A. Fonahn, and H. Hopstock, 6 vols., Christiania, 1911–16). This was reproduced, in an engraving by Bartolozzi, in Chamberlain's *Royal Collection of Drawings,* 1812. This reproduction was inaccurate. Bartolozzi put in the feet, and put them in wrongly; he shaded in the eye; and he introduced lines on the forehead and on the side of the mouth. But he left the general expression of the face detached or reposeful. Next came a volume whose shortened title and reference reads: *Tabula Anatomica Leonardo da Vinci,* Lunaeburgi, 1830. This volume contains a lithograph by Wehrt, which purports to be a reproduction of the original drawing, Q III 3 v. Now there is no evidence that Wehrt ever had access to the original; and when one places his lithograph alongside Bartolozzi's engraving, it is clear on inspection that the former is a

copy of the latter—Wehrt obtained the lithograph by copying Bartolozzi. This is clear not only from a study of the coition figure, but also from a study of the other drawings and the handwriting on the same sheet. In making his copy Wehrt incorporated the errors that Bartolozzi had already committed, and added others of his own. In particular, he so changed the face as to give it the expression that appears in the Freud–Reitler reproduction. The next step in the history appears to have been a work by Eduard Fuchs with the following title and reference: *Illustrierte Sittengeschichte vom Mittelalter bis zur Gegenwart.* Renaissance, Ergänzungsband. Privatdruck, Albert Langen, München (Date of Preface: 1909). This book reproduces the coition figure as it appears in Wehrt's lithograph; and it is this book that Reitler gives as his source of Leonardo's drawing in his article ("Eine anatomisch-künstlerische Fehlleistung Leonardos da Vinci," *Int. Z. Psychoan.*, 4, 205). The history of the Freud–Reitler mistake becomes patent to the eye when one places the three reproductions alongside one another in order of date—the original drawing, in the collotype of Vangensten *et al.*, the Bartolozzi engraving, and the lithograph by Wehrt.

9. Broad, C. D. *The Mind and its Place in Nature*, Ch. I. London (Kegan Paul), 1925.
10. The argument which follows is largely a summary of the case made about the whole essay by Meyer Schapiro (1956), "Leonardo and Freud: an Art-Historical Study," *Journal of the History of Ideas*, vol. xvii, 17, no. 2, 147–78.
11. Goldscheider, Ludwig. *Leonardo da Vinci*. London (Phaidon Press), 1959, p. 157.
12. O'Malley, C. D., and Saunders, J. B. de C. M. *Leonardo da Vinci on the Human Body*. New York (Schuman), 1952.
13. Heydenreich, Ludwig H. *Leonardo da Vinci*. London (Allen & Unwin), 1954.
14. [Cf. Ruth L. Munroe, *Schools of Psycho-analytic Thought Etc.*, Ch. Two. London (Hutchinson Medical Publications), 1957.]
15. Jones, Ernest. *Sigmund Freud Life and Work*, Vol. Two. London (The Hogarth Press), 1955.
16. Wohl, R. R., and Trosman, H. "A Retrospect of Freud's *Leonardo*, An Assessment of a Psychoanalytic Classic." *Psychiatry*, 18, 27–39. 1955.

EISSLER / PSYCHOANALYTIC NOTES

1. J. P. Richter (1883), *The Literary Works of Leonardo da Vinci*, 2 vols. London-New York-Toronto: Oxford University Press, rev. ed. by I. A. Richter, 1939, Vol. I, p. 66, No. 30. H. Ludwig, ed. (1882), *Lionardo da Vinci. Das Buch von der Malerei*, 3 vols. [Quellenschriften für Kunstgeschichte und Kunsttechnik des Mittelalters und der Renaissance, Vols. XV, XVI, XVII]. Wien: Braumüller, Vol. I, p. 55.
2. Richter, *Literary Works*, Vol. I, p. 67; Ludwig, *Lionardo*, Vol. I, p. 57.
3. K. Clark (1939), *Leonardo da Vinci*. London: Cambridge University Press, pp. 130, 134, 179.
4. L. H. Heydenreich (1954), *Leonardo da Vinci*, 2 vols. New York: Macmillan; Basel: Holbein, Vol. I, p. 129.
5. The biology of genius is a challenging topic. It is fascinating to observe how in the one instance the exquisiteness of a biological apparatus makes it possible for an equally exquisite mind to create supreme values, how in others the ex-

quisiteness of a biological function leads to unusual but mediocre or trivial achievements, and then again to observe an exquisite mind impeded in the creation of corresponding values by the dearth of biological endowment (P. Greenacre [1957], The Childhood of the Artist. In: *The Psychoanalytic Study of the Child*, Vol. 12, pp. 47–72. New York: International Universities Press).

6. This has been observed by almost every writer on Leonardo.

7. The recoil of the drawn picture or sketch is also to be considered. Most of the verses that percolated through Goethe's mind were forgotten as quickly as they emerged.

8. See Berenson for an important remark regarding the imbalance of verbalization and visualization in Leonardo, which is a key issue in the structure of personality (B. Berenson [1903], *The Drawings of the Florentine Painters Classified, Criticized and Studied as Documents in the History and Appreciation of Tuscan Art with a Copious Catalogue Raisonné*, 2 vols. New York: Dutton, p. 147). Cf. M. Johnson (1949), *Art and Scientific Thought*. New York: Columbia University Press, pp. 147f.

9. Heydenreich (1954), *Leonardo*, Vol. I, p. 19; see also Clark (1939), *Leonardo*, p. 179.

10. E. MacCurdy, ed. (1956), *The Notebooks of Leonardo da Vinci*. New York: George Braziller, pp. 58f.; B.M. 1 r.

11. Cf. G. Sarton (1953), Léonard de Vinci, ingénieur et savant. In: *Léonard de Vinci et l'expérience scientifique au seizième siècle* [Colloques internationaux du Centre National de la Recherche Scientifique, Paris, 4–7 juillet 1952]. Paris: Presses Universitaires de France, p. 18.

12. K. Clark (1929), A Note on Leonardo da Vinci. *Life and Letters* (London), Vol. 2, p. 128.

13. Cf. Olschki for a theory that integrates Leonardo's attitude into the basic aim of his research (L. Olschki [1919–27], *Die Geschichte der neusprachlichen wissenschaftlichen Literatur*, 3 vols. Heidelberg: C. Winter; Leipzig: L. S. Olschki; Halle a/S.: Niemeyer, Vol. I, p. 391).

14. MacCurdy (1956), *Notebooks*, pp. 238f.; C.A. 345 v. b.
Leonardo's triumphant rejoicing at this point is perhaps referable to the confirmation of a secret imagery about an "all-seeing" eye. The occasion, after all, was given by the meeting of all rays in the eye.

15. Sigmund Freud (1910), Leonardo da Vinci and a Memory of His Childhood. *The Standard Edition of the Complete Psychological Works of Sigmund Freud*, 24 vols. London: Hogarth Press, 1953–   , Vol. 11, p. 75. This is, to my knowledge, also the first instance in psychoanalytic literature in which the sublimation of the aggressive drives is described.

16. Freud (1910), Leonardo, Vol. 11, pp. 74f. Yet compare this passage with that on p. 133 where Freud speaks of Leonardo's research as seemingly having contained "some of the features which distinguish the activity of unconscious instincts—insatiability, unyielding rigidity and the lack of an ability to adapt to real circumstances."

17. Cf. Freud's account of the vicissitudes of the instinct of research (1910, Leonardo, pp. 79f.). By the third type, which "avoids any concern with sexual themes" (p. 80) despite the free growth of intellectual interests, evidently Leonardo was

meant. Cf. also Freud's footnote of 1919 and the beginning of the quotation from Reitler (p. 70).

18. Cf. E. Belt (1955), *Leonardo the Anatomist.* Lawrence: University of Kansas Press, pp. 41–67.

19. H. Hartmann (1953), Contribution to the Metapsychology of Schizophrenia. In: *The Psychoanalytic Study of the Child,* Vol. 8, pp. 177–98. New York: International Universities Press.

20. For the double aspect of defense mechanisms, their necessity, and assistance on the one hand, their noxious effects on the other, see Sigmund Freud (1937), *Analysis Terminable and Interminable. Collected Papers,* Vol. 5, p. 340.

21. For a subtle analysis of two instances of disturbance of sensory functions by their serving primarily purposes of defense, see M. Katan (1950), Schreber's Hallucinations about the "Little Men." *International Journal of Psycho-Analysis,* Vol. 31, pp. 32–5. M. Katan (1952), Further Remarks about Schreber's Hallucinations. *International Journal of Psycho-Analysis,* Vol. 33, pp. 429–32.

22. However, see M. Klein (1948, *Contributions to Psycho-Analysis 1921–1945.* London: Hogarth Press, pp. 97f.) about Leonardo for a hypothesis of libidinized ego tendencies and subsequent protection against repression in favor of sublimation.

23. W. Muschg (1948), *Tragische Literaturgeschichte.* Bern: Francke, p. 108.

24. For case histories referring to genius, psychopathy, and psychoses, see W. Lange-Eichbaum (1927), *Genie, Irrsinn und Ruhm,* 4th ed. rev. W. Kurth. München: Ernst Reinhardt Verlag, 1956, pp. 256–450. However, I do not agree with Lange-Eichbaum's clinical approach. To my way of thinking genius and mental disorder are disparate, although the latter may arise when the former is blocked or decays.

25. Hartmann (1953), Metapsychology, p. 181.

26. J. Piaget (1937), *The Construction of Reality in the Child.* New York: Basic Books, 1954, p. 12.

27. Although I agree in the main with Dr. Greenacre's view of the artist's love affair with the world (1957, Childhood, p. 57, et passim), still there are narcissistic elements that are specific to geniushood and as indispensable as the object-related elements. When Dr. Greenacre writes that "the compelling drive of creativeness . . . may give the creative activity the semblance of a special kind of addiction for which there is no cure" (p. 69), I believe she is referring collectively to narcissistic components.

28. Clark (1939), *Leonardo,* p. 16.

29. *Ibid.,* p. 24.

30. Heydenreich (1954), *Leonardo,* Vol. II, p. iv. W. Suida (1929), *Leonardo und sein Kreis.* München: Bruckmann, p. 26. See also W. von Bode (1921), *Studien über Leonardo da Vinci.* Berlin: Grote, p. 40.

31. However if Valentiner is right in his conception of Leonardo's relationship to Verrocchio, one may obtain a different impression of the four allegedly silent years (W. R. Valentiner [1930], Leonardo as Verrocchio's Coworker. *Art Bulletin,* Vol. 12, pp. 43–89). The process of melting down of psychic structure in Leonardo's youth, as suggested by me, would not have had to cover such a long period. In Goethe's instance this process occupied only a few weeks. The critical

episodes as reconstructed in these two instances appear to have a structure essentially different from the identity crisis and various moratoria Erikson describes in the life of George Bernard Shaw (E. H. Erikson [1956], The Problem of Ego Identity. *Journal of the American Psychoanalytic Association,* Vol. 4, pp. 58, 66f.).

32. Heydenreich (1954), *Leonardo,* Vol. 1, p. 115.
33. *Ibid.,* p. 112.
34. *Ibid.,* p. 148.
35. *Ibid.,* p. 142.
 Olschki adopted the most extreme views regarding Leonardo's limitations imposed by the hypertrophy of the visual system (*Die Geschichte,* Vol. I, pp. 343ff. et passim). Within the framework of the history of thought Olschki describes the very process I try to explicate in terms of psychology. For a different view, see E. Cassirer (1927), *Individuum und Kosmos in der Philosophie der Renaissance.* Leipzig & Berlin: Teubner, p. 171.
36. MacCurdy (1956), *Notebooks,* p. 232; italics added; C.A. 119 v. a.
37. For tentative suggestions regarding the artist's childhood development, see Greenacre (1957), Childhood.
38. For other reasons of delay in the structurization of the personality in the gifted child, see Greenacre (1957), Childhood, pp. 58–60, 64.
39. For a viewpoint that stresses the motive of communication and assigns to it a central value in Leonardo's work, see Olschki, *Die Geschichte,* Vol. I, p. 327.
40. MacCurdy (1956), *Notebooks,* p. 80; Fogli A 2 r.
41. *Ibid.,* p. 63; C.A. 76 v. a. Cf. the two remarks quoted earlier, "Shun those studies in which the work that results dies with the worker" (MacCurdy, p. 80; Forster III 55 r.), and "In life beauty perishes and does not endure" (*Ibid.,* p. 91; Forster III 72 r.).
42. Anna Freud (1936), *The Ego and the Mechanisms of Defence.* New York: International Universities Press, 1946, p. 63. R. Waelder (1936), The Principle of Multiple Functioning: Observations on Overdetermination. *Psychoanalytic Quarterly,* Vol. 5, pp. 47f.
43. MacCurdy (1956), *Notebooks,* p. 75; B.M. 156 v. For an interpretation of this passage different from mine, see E. Panofsky (1939), *Studies in Iconology. Humanistic Themes in the Art of the Renaissance.* New York: Oxford University Press, p. 182.
44. A view regarding the passage of time seemingly contradicting this opinion is found in the following: "Wrongly do men lament the flight of time, accusing it of being too swift, and not perceiving that it is sufficient as it passes; but good memory, with which nature has endowed us, causes everything long past to seem present" (Richter, *Literary Works,* Vol. II, p. 244, No. 1170; C.A. 76 r.). This sounds to me like a consolation, as if Leonardo were saying: "Even if time passes, it is not lost, for all the past can become present again at any moment and at will."
45. MacCurdy (1956), *Notebooks,* p. 81; Fogli B 21 v.
46. Clark (1939), *Leonardo,* pp. 20, 121. See also Berenson (1903, *Drawings,* Vol. I, p. 148) for a superb description of Leonardo's graphic function.
47. Lomazzo, quoted by Freud (1910), Leonardo, p. 66.

48. Berenson's accounts of the drawings and paintings are of great help in pointing up the essential differences between the two categories of Leonardo's work (1903, *Drawings;* 1916, Leonardo da Vinci, An Attempt at Revaluation. In: *The Study and Criticism of Italian Art.* Third Series. London: G. Bell, pp. 1–37).

49. The late Professor Heinrich Glück used to cite Leonardo as the only artist who was acknowledged as genius during his lifetime *and* whose prestige persisted unabated throughout the centuries independently of changes of style, fashion, taste, and art theories. See also von Bode (1921), *Studien,* p. 3.

50. Clark (1939), *Leonardo,* p. 20.

51. See also the sketch for *Anna Metterza* (A. E. Popham [1945], *The Drawings of Leonardo da Vinci.* New York: Reynal & Hitchcock, Plate 175).

52. Olschki, *Die Geschichte,* Vol. I, p. 342.

53. MacCurdy (1956), *Notebooks,* pp. 1137f.; C.A. 202 v. a.

54. Cf. E. Hildebrandt (1927), *Leonardo da Vinci. Der Künstler und sein Werk.* Berlin: G. Grotesche Verlagsbuchhandlung, pp. 224f.

55. Cf. Berenson (1903, *Drawings,* Vol. I, p. 151) about one of Leonardo's drawings: "It is perhaps as near an approach to the actual transfer to paper of a visual thought as man has ever achieved."

56. K. Clark (1929), *Note,* pp. 130, 126.

57. The most complete and reliable manuscript is the *Codex Vaticanus (Urbinas)* No. 1270 titled: *Libro di Pittura di M. Leonardo da Vinci, Pittore et Scultore Fiorentino* (Ludwig). Panofsky has discovered in the Codex Huygens, Codex M.A. 1139 at the Morgan Library, a part that is an exact copy of otherwise unknown notes and drawings by Leonardo that belong to this subject (E. Panofsky [1940], *The Codex Huygens and Leonardo da Vinci's Art Theory.* London: Warburg Institute). For a history of all the manuscripts involved and a complete bibliography, see K. T. Steinitz (1958), Leonardo da Vinci's "Trattato della pittura." Preface by Elmer Belt. Copenhagen: Munksgaard.

58. Literally, "Comparison," a title used for the first time by Guglielmo Manzi in 1817.

59. K. Clark (1944), Leon Alberti on Painting. Annual Italian Lecture of the British Academy. In: *Proceedings of the British Academy,* 30. London: Humphrey Milford, pp. 16f.

60. Ludwig, *Lionardo,* Vol. I, pp. 3–103.
    The first part of Leonardo's *Trattato,* the *Paragone,* in which the rivalry of the various arts is presented, is also found in Richter, *Literary Works,* Vol. I, pp. 31–101.

61. Cf. H. Janitschek, ed. (1877), *Leone Battista Albertis kleinere kunsttheoretische Schriften* [Quellenschriften für Kunstgeschichte und Kunsttechnik des Mittelalters und der Renaissance, Vol. XI]. Wein: Braumüller, p. 146.

62. For an excellent summary of this history and for the specific goals Leonardo pursued in his defense of painting, see Richter's introduction to the *Paragone,* Vol. I, pp. 14–30.

63. Janitschek, *Leone,* p. 96.

64. Ludwig, *Lionardo,* Vol. I, p. 72.

65. Pierino da Vinci (Pier Francesco di Bartolomeo del Ser Piero da Vinci), sculptor and silversmith, born 1530 in Vinci, died 1553 in Pisa, one of the most im-

portant Florentine followers of Michelangelo (Thieme-Becker [1907–50], *Allgemeiner Lexikon der bildenden Künstler von der Antike bis zur Gegenwart.* Ed. H. Vollmer. Leipzig: E. A. Seemann, Vol. XXXIV, pp. 364f.).

66. Ludwig, *Lionardo,* Vol. I, p. 191. Cf. what Lessing had to say about the limitations of painting (G. E. Lessing [1766], Laokoon oder über die Grenzen der Malerei und Poesie. *Lessings Gesammelte Werke.* Leipzig: Tempel Verlag, n.d., Parts XV and XVI).

67. Ludwig, *Lionardo,* Vol. I, p. 287.

68. There are also remarkable contradictions between specific pieces of advice he gives to the beginner. At one point he recommends work in solitude (Ludwig, *Lionardo,* Vol. I, p. 107); shortly thereafter he considers it preferable to draw in company (Ludwig, *Lionardo,* Vol. I, p. 131). Compare also Leonardo Parte II 56 with Parte III 407 (Ludwig, *Lionardo,* Vol. I, p. 111 and p. 399). In both instances Leonardo discusses how the use of a mirror may help in achieving the best results in painting, but in one instance he castigates the artist who takes a walk for the sake of physical refreshment whereas in the other he recommends rest periods. For Alberti's counsel to interrupt work and rest, see Janitschek, *Leone,* p. 158. For the question of whether or not Leonardo knew of Alberti's writings, cf. Clark (1944), Leon Alberti, pp. 16f., and Richter, *Literary Works,* Vol. I, p. 23. Pedretti recently published a passage that shows Leonardo in his later years succeeded in making a synthesis between the two above-cited contradictory pieces of advice. Thus he wrote (C.A. 184 v. c.): "And his [the painter's] companions should resemble him in a taste for these studies, and if he fail to find any such he should accustom himself to be alone in his investigations, for in the end he will find no more profitable companionship" (C. Pedretti, ed. [1959], Leonardo's Last Drawings. *Italian Quarterly,* Vol. 3, p. 47).

69. Cf. Olschki, *Die Geschichte,* Vol. I, p. 359.

70. Ludwig, *Lionardo,* Vol. I, pp. 209, 317, 363.

71. *Ibid.,* p. 165.

72. *Ibid.,* Vol. III, pp. 109f.

73. Cf., however, Clark: "The finest passages in the *Trattato* are those in which Leonardo describes the springs of the painter's genius" (1939, *Leonardo,* p. 34). "The springs of genius," I think, can be observed only after psychological interpretation of some statements. The overt content of the *Trattato,* aside from the *Paragone,* is concerned with technical advice on problems of the craft.

74. Occasionally one hears that only a genius is capable of understanding a genius. To be sure, a genius may have a better understanding than even the best of critics of the values of another genius's creations, but this is a limited area if measured against the comprehensive scope of geniushood. Moreover, even within this narrow area many a genius has committed grievous errors. Furthermore, while there is no doubt that some geniuses have a degree of self-knowledge that is quite outstanding, this is rather the exception than the rule. The principal source for the study of the creative process is by no means to be found in what geniuses have said about their own geniushood or that of others.

75. W. von den Steinen (1949), *Das Zeitalter Goethes.* Bern: Francke, p. 12.

76. G. Sarton (1957), *Six Wings. Men of Science in the Renaissance.* Bloomington: Indiana University Press, p. 229.

77. C. Pedretti, ed. (1957), *Studi Vinciani. Documenti, analisi e inediti Leonardeschi.*

In appendice: saggio di una cronologia dei fogli del "Codice Atlantico." Geneva: Librairie E. Droz, pp. 107–17.

78. If we consider that Leonardo avoided even potential opportunities of progeny, we will fathom the full meaning of the metaphor.

79. Ludwig, *Lionardo,* Vol. I, p. 10.

80. Engraving, of course, came frighteningly close to the area dearest to his heart, since it made possible the copying of drawings and even paintings.

81. See: E. Panofsky (1924), "Idea." Ein Beitrag zur Gegriffgeschichte der älteren Kunsttheorie. *Studien der Bibliothek Warburg,* ed. F. Saxl. Leipzig & Berlin: Teubner. Panofsky (1939), *Iconology.* R. W. Lee (1940), *Ut pictura poesis.* The Humanistic Theory of Painting. *Art Bulletin,* Vol. 12, pp. 197–269. Cassirer (1927), *Individuum.*

82. Panofsky gives an example of this. He writes: "Michelangelo resorts to Neoplatonism in his search for visual symbols of human life and destiny, as he experienced it" (1939, *Iconology,* p. 182).

83. M. Dvořák (1923), *Kunstgeschichte als Geitesgeschichte.* München: Piper, p. x.

84. For a presentation of the plurality of approaches in the interpretation of art, see A. Hauser (1959, *The Philosophy of Art History.* New York: Knopf), which came to my attention after this book was written.

85. In his book on Neoplatonism and the Renaissance, N. A. Robb (1935, *Neoplatonism of the Italian Renaissance.* London: Allen & Unwin), however, tries to prove a closer relationship of Leonardo to Neoplatonism than is commonly supposed. Cassirer has set forth the point where Leonardo and true Platonism merge (Cassirer [1927], *Individuum,* p. 177). For a sociological remark regarding the effect of Neoplatonism on Leonardo and Michelangelo, see Olschki, *Die Geschichte,* Vol. I, pp. 259ff.

86. Cassirer (1927), *Individuum,* p. 176.

87. Here and in what follows I use the term *empiricism* in a sense not strictly in accord with that which it usually has in the history of philosophy. When I speak of Leonardo's empiricism I mean only that he used sense data, observation, and experience in his scientific inquiry, and relied on his senses for gaining insight into the structure of things.

88. For the position of art in the system of Plato see E. Cassirer (1922–23), Eidos und Eidolon. Das Problem des Schönen und der Kunst in Platons Dialogen. *Vorträge der Bibliothek Warburg,* ed. F. Saxl, 2 (1):1–27. Leipzig: Teubner, 1924.

89. Cassirer (1927), *Individuum,* p. 149.

90. Olschki, *Die Geschichte,* Vol. I, pp. 259ff.

91. In the exposition of Ficino's philosophy by Kristeller, it becomes quite clear why Leonardo was bound to be repelled by Florentine Neoplatonism (P. O. Kristeller [1943], *The Philosophy of Marsilio Ficino.* New York: Columbia University Press).

92. Cassirer (1927), *Individuum,* pp. 177f.

93. P. Duhem. (1909–13), Nicholas de Cues et Léonard de Vinci. In: *Etudes sur Léonard de Vinci, ceux qui'l a lus et ceux qui l'ont lu,* 3 vols. Deuxième série. Paris: Librairie scientifique A. Herman, Vol. II, particularly pp. 4–53, 146–85. Cassirer (1927), *Individuum.*

94. For what follows, see also Panofsky (1924), "Idea."

95. R. Klibansky (1953), Copernic et Nicolas de Cues. In: *Léonard de Vinci et l'expérience scientifique au seizième siècle* [Colloques internationaux du Centre National de la Recherche Scientifique, Paris, 4–7 juillet 1952]. Paris: Presses Universitaires de France, p. 233.

96. von Bode, *Studien*, p. 145.

97. At least a remark by Clark may be interpreted in this sense (1939, *Leonardo*, pp. 157f.). Popham is more outspoken on this point (*Drawings*, p. 44). Cf. also Berenson (1903), *Drawings*, Vol. I, p. 159. But for a contrary view, see von Bode, *Studien*, p. 145.

98. G. de Santillana (1953), Léonard et ceux qu'il n'a pas lus. In: *Léonard de Vinci et l'expérience scientifique au seizième siècle* [Colloques internationaux du Centre National de la Recherche Scientifique, Paris, 4–7 juillet 1952]. Paris: Presses Universitaires de France, p. 45.

99. Cassirer (1927), *Individuum*, p. 20.

100. *Ibid.*, p. 13.

101. MacCurdy (1956), *Notebooks*, p. 88; C.A. 226 v. b; *Ibid.*, p. 83; Q. II 14 r.
    Cf. the *Trattato*, where the same idea is also expressed in the negative: "If you know it [the loved object] only little, then you will be able to love it but little or not at all [*Se tu no'la cognoscerai, poco o'nulla la potrai amare*] (Ludwig, *Lionardo*, Vol. I, p. 136).

102. A. L. Kroeber (1944), *Configurations of Culture Growth*. Berkeley & Los Angeles: University of California Press.

103. For the place of cognition in the system of Meister Eckhardt, whose work had influence on Nicholas of Cusa, see J. Chevalier (1956), *Histoire de la pensée*. Vol. II: La Pensée Chrétienne. Paris: Flammarion, pp. 452–7.

104. Cassirer (1927), *Individuum*, p. 15.

105. MacCurdy (1956), *Notebooks*, p. 619; G 96 v. In view of the foregoing, Leonardo is consistent when he introduces his above-quoted opinion regarding knowledge and love with a praise of mathematics.

106. Cassirer (1927), *Individuum*, pp. 21f.

107. Ludwig, *Lionardo*, Vol. I, pp. 4f.

108. Cassirer (1927), *Individuum*, p. 34.

109. Ludwig, *Lionardo*, Vol. I, pp. 155, 159, 161, 491.

110. See Kris for a discussion of this factor (E. Kris [1936], Comments on Spontaneous Artistic Creations by Psychotics. In: *Psychoanalytic Explorations in Art*. New York: International Universities Press, pp. 87–117).

111. Ludwig, *Lionardo*, Vol. I, p. 398. Cf. also Alberti when he advises the artist to ask others for their opinions and to listen to everyone who is ready to express his views (Janitschek, *Leone*, p. 160).

112. "...*hauendo co'le mani à rifare un corpo humano, uolontieri rifa quel corpo, di ch'essa fu prima inuentrice*" (Ludwig, *Lionardo*, Vol. I, p. 490).

113. "...*et di qui nasce, che chi s'inamora uolontieri s'inamorano di cose à loro simiglianti*" (*ibid.*).

114. Anna Freud (1936), *Ego*, p. 169.

115. This degradation of the senses has been described repeatedly but no more convincingly than in the following: "St. Anselm, writing at the beginning of the twelfth century, maintained that things were harmful in proportion to the num-

ber of senses they delighted, and therefore rated it dangerous to sit in a garden where the.: are roses to satisfy the senses of sight and smell, and songs and stories to please the ears (K. Clark [1950], *Landscape Painting*. New York: Scribner, p. 2).

116. Cassirer (1927), *Individuum*, p. 47.
117. Dvořák (1923), *Kunstgeschichte*, pp. 43–147.
118. Cassirer (1927), *Individuum*, pp. 31f.
119. *Ibid.*, p. 24.
120. Richter, *Literary Works*, Vol. II, p. 239, No. 1148A; E 55 r.
121. *Ibid.*, 1148B; C.A. 147 v.
122. Cassirer (1927), *Individuum*, p. 177.
123. *Ibid.*, p. 163.
124. According to Olschki (*Die Geschichte*, Vol. I, p. 386), Leonardo conceived of mathematics only as a concrete method of computation, thus limiting its use to practical application without conception of its function as a construct.
125. Olschki has persuasively and ably presented this view. His demonstration of the primacy of the visual world, of the barrier to theory formation, in Leonardo is convincing (*Die Geschichte*, Vol. I, pp. 341f., 344). His characterization of Leonardo as a *forschender Magier und Mystiker* [a magician and mystic who does research] (p. 404) is apropos.
126. This, of course, should not imply that Leonardo was devoid of imagery regarding the world behind his observations. Yet this area is dominated by fantasy and without insight into laws as conceived of by science. Cf. Clark: "Leonardo's mind passed without warning, and almost without consciousness, from fact to fantasy, from experience to imagination" (K. Clark [1952], *Leonardo da Vinci; A Note on the Relation between His Science and His Art. History Today* [London], Vol. 2, p. 303).
127. For an elaborate treatise on art and science with special reference to Leonardo, see Johnson (1949), *Art*.
128. Cassirer (1927), *Individuum*, p. 52.
129. Here I cannot spell out the conclusions that I have implied in the above statement. In contrast to works of art in which each element is potentially psychologically relevant, scientific statements, inasmuch as they are correct, are more or less psychologically non-relevant. Rostand expressed a similar idea in the following: "Scientific errors . . . generally bear the individual stamp of their perpetrators" (J. Rostand [1958], *Error and Deception in Science*. New York: Basic Books, 1960, p. 12).
130. Ludwig, *Lionardo*, Vol. I, p. 11.
131. *Ibid.*, p. 13.
132. "...la pittura...è *contenitrice di tutte le forme, che sono, e di quelle, che non sono in natura"* (*Ibid.*, pp. 62, 64).
133. *Ibid.*, p. 18.
134. Cf. also Parte II, 133 (Ludwig, Vol. I, p. 181) where Leonardo states that drawing should not be called a science but a deity [*una deità*]. It is remarkable that Leonardo overrules *prima-facie* evidence when he discusses the superiority of painting. Much as paintings have been the objects of religious reverence, statues have been so even more frequently. Also the claim that images are imperishable

—Leonardo specifies how they may become so—is an illusion necessitated by inner conflict.

135. Cf. Panofsky (1924, "Idea," p. 20) for the traditional comparison contained in the terms *deus artifex* and *deus pictor*. What was in the Middle Ages nothing but a metaphor to explicate a quality in God and by no means in the artist seems to have become for Leonardo a literal truth related to the artist. Cf. also Kris (1952, *Psychoanalytic Explorations,* pp. 79, 150).

136. Cassirer (1927), *Individuum,* p. 34.

137. A psychological inquiry into these caricatures is one of the most challenging tasks. Perfunctory examination suggests that an attempt at demonstrating the bizarre or monstrous as a special manifestation of the laws that are valid also of other faces, that is to say, the monstrous in conformity with the species, was one of Leonardo's goals. Therefore I believe it is misleading to call these drawings caricatures at all. For the psychology of caricature, see E. Kris and E. Gombrich (1938), The Principles of Caricature. In: Kris (1952), *Psychoanalytic Explorations,* pp. 189–203.

138. The drawing in which Leonardo disposed caricatures around a "normal" face (Pl. 41, W. 12495 r.) is important since there they appear like variations of effects which Leonardo considered ugly and which were imprinted upon the human face by old age.

139. E. Panofsky (1924–25), Die Perspektive als "symbolische" Form. *Vorträge der Bibliothek Warburg,* ed. F. Saxl. Leipzig & Berlin: Teubner, p. 274.

140. Cf. Clark (1939), *Leonardo,* p. 16.

141. This proposition, in my opinion, does not contradict my earlier suggestion that a loss of structure occurred during the quadrennium. A reorganization may be made possible by a melting down of ego structure.

142. von Bode (1921), *Studien,* p. 18.

143. Clark (1929), Note, p. 122; (1939), *Leonardo,* p. 179.

144. C. de Tolnay (1943–54), *Michelangelo,* 4 vols. Princeton: Princeton University Press, Vol. I, pp. 117f.

145. *Ibid.,* Vol. IV, p. 59.

146. Cf. Hildebrandt (1927), *Leonardo:* "That which is incomparable in his [Leonardo's] achievement resides in that he knew how to transport thoughts of the most transcendental content into the full tangibleness of spatial-corporeal reality" (p. 33).

147. de Tolnay, *Michelangelo,* Vol. I, pp. 64, 115.

148. Cf. W. Pater (1873), *The Renaissance.* London: Macmillan, 1922, pp. 113, 112: "To others he seems to be aiming at an impossible effect, to do something that art, that painting, can never do," and particularly: "His [Leonardo's] problem was the transmutation of ideas into images."

149. B. Berenson (1916), Leonardo da Vinci, An Attempt at Revaluation. In: *The Study and Criticism of Italian Art.* Third Series. London: G. Bell, pp. 1–37.

150. See, for example, von Bode, *Studien,* p. 146.

151. Berenson (1916), Leonardo: *Cenacolo,* pp. 2, 15, 29; *Mona Lisa,* pp. 2f., 11; *St. John,* pp. 5, 14; *Adoration,* p. 7; *La Belle Ferronnière,* p. 6.

   See for a discussion of authorship of the portrait, Clark (1939), *Leonardo,* p. 50. Berenson (1916, Leonardo, p. 6) believes Boltraffio to have painted it.

152. Berenson (1916), Leonardo, p. 2.
153. *Ibid.*, p. 29.
154. *Ibid.*, p. 11.
155. Freud (1910), Leonardo, p. 121.
156. G. Vasari (1568), Life of Leonardo da Vinci, Painter and Sculptor of Florence, tr. A. B. Hinds. In: *Leonardo da Vinci,* ed. L. Goldscheider. London: Phaidon, 1944, p. 7.

    See E. Kris and O. Kurz (1934, *Die Legende vom Künstler.* Wien: Krystall Verlag, pp. 41, 126) for this typical motif in the biography of artists.
157. Even if Valentiner's (1930, Leonardo) hypothesis of an extremely rich and mutually fertilizing teacher-pupil relationship is accepted, this would not disprove the existence of profound ambivalence as indirectly suggested by the biographical legend. Other and more direct evidences of ambivalence toward male authority are found in Vasari's biography. When Leonardo studied mathematics "he made such progress that he frequently confounded his master by continually raising doubts and difficulties" (Vasari, Life, p. 5). Also, the afore-mentioned episode of succeeding in frightening his father by means of the painted Medusa head deserves attention here. Although violent outbreaks of rage, so characteristic of Michelangelo (R. Sterba and E. Sterba [1956], The Anxieties of Michelangelo Buonarroti. *International Journal of Psycho-Analysis,* 37:325–30), are not known from Leonardo's dealings with authority and he apparently succeeded by and large in getting along with his noble employers, a longitudinal section of his biography nevertheless shows his ambivalence in the form of easy and rapid changes of loyalty and allegiance. However much such ambivalence may have corresponded to the "spirit of the time," one is justified in seeking also an individual basis for it.
158. E. Jones (1953–57), *The Life and Work of Sigmund Freud,* 3 vols. New York: Basic Books, Vol. III, p. 464.
159. S. Freud (1937–39), *Moses and Monotheism.* London: Hogarth Press, 1951, p. 172.
160. Freud (1910), Leonardo, pp. 105, 131. At one point Freud writes: "We must expressly insist that we have never reckoned Leonardo as a neurotic or a 'nerve case,' as the awkward phrase goes" (1910, p. 131), but this statement seems to have been meant rather as a defense against any pejorative implications the reader might infer from Freud's study through incautious acceptance of the vulgarized stereotype connoted by these words.
161. *Ibid.*, p. 134.
162. S. Freud (1925), An Autobiographical Study. *Standard Edition,* Vol. 20, p. 119.
163. I owe thanks to Dr. Bernard L. Pacella for his kind permission to quote from Freud's letter which he presented before the Annual Meeting of the American Psychoanalytic Association in May, 1956.
164. S. Freud (1931), Libidinal Types. *Collected Papers,* Vol. 5, p. 248.
165. *Ibid.*, pp. 249f.
166. Freud (1925), Study, pp. 119f. (1933), Foreward to *The Life and Works of Edgar Allan Poe,* by Marie Bonaparte. London: Imago Publishing Co., 1949, p. xi.
167. Freud (1937–39), *Moses,* pp. 171f.
168. G. Sarton (1948), *Life of Science.* New York: Schumann, p. 81.

169. Clark (1939), *Leonardo*, p. 31.

170. For a most sensitive analysis of the problem of art and science in Leonardo's life, mainly in terms of historical background but by no means with a neglect of psychology, see Clark (1929), Note.

171. G. Bychowski (1951), From Catharsis to Work of Art: The Making of an Artist. In: *Psychoanalysis and Culture. Essays in Honor of Géza Róheim,* ed. G. B. Wilbur & W. Muensterberger. New York: International Universities Press, p. 407.

172. I have tried to demonstrate the occurrence of such psychopathology in Goethe. His *Chromatology* is the work which, in my opinion, exhibits the reduced quality that resulted from it. Of course, the mental scientist is in danger here of basing his findings on more or less arbitrary value judgments, which Schapiro (1956, Leonardo and Freud: An Art-Historical Study. *Journal of the History of Ideas.* Vol. 17, p. 177) has warned against. Nothing prevents the scholar in other fields from discovering for himself that the quality of the product has deteriorated, as indeed has happened in the case of the *Chromatology;* the mental scientist is then freed of this onus. Still, anyone who knows how far short the humanities are of providing an objective yardstick for evaluating cultural products will also be aware of how great the risks are that the psychologist must run in this area.

173. C. de Tolnay (*Revue des Arts,* 1952, pp. 18ff), however, claims that the conservation of the *Mona Lisa* is much better than commonly assumed.

174. Clark (1952, Leonardo, p. 303), however, takes a quite different stand regarding Leonardo's faulty technique of fresco painting.

175. S. Freud (1930), Ansprache im Frankfurter Goethe-Haus. *Gesammelte Werke, Chronologisch geordnet,* 18 vols. London: Imago Publishing Co., 1940–1952, Vol. 14, p. 547.

176. From Clark's essay in 1952 one may get the impression that he no longer sees a dichotomy between Leonardo's science and art.

177. Sarton (1957), *Six Wings,* p. 228.

178. Cf. also Johnson (1949), *Art,* p. 152.

179. Also Clark (1952, Leonardo, p. 302) seems to doubt Leonardo's greatness, as a scientist. He weighs the possibility that most of Leonardo's drawings of machines were largely copies of machines already in existence on which Leonardo elaborated or which he extended.

180. Ortega y Gasset (1932), *In Search of Goethe from Within.* In: *The Dehumanization of Art.* Garden City, N.Y.: Doubleday, n.d., pp. 145, 146, 149, 151, 153 (italics by the author).

181. Ortega sees Goethe's mission as one "to be the German writer on whom it devolved to revolutionize his country's literature and, through it, the literature of the world" (p. 148). This, however, Goethe did not do. The great genius exhausts the possibilities of the new forms he has created and makes it impossible for those who come after him to continue to use them without inevitably seeming servile imitators, even when their imitations are extremely talented. German literature became different through Goethe's creations, but it was a long time before successors appeared who were able to throw off the livery of epigoni. Nietzsche rightly raises the question of what German prose literature deserves to be read over and over again aside from Goethe's writings

(F. Nietzsche (1880), Der Wanderer und sein Schatten. In: *Menschliches, All-zumenschliches,* 2 vols. Leipzig: Kröner. 1930, No. 109, p. 227). Cf. Berenson, in his discussion of the negative effect Leonardo had on Italian painting: "No Tuscan painter or sculptor born after Leonardo's death produced a single work with the faintest claim to general interest" (1916, Leonardo, p. 23).

182. Ortega y Gasset, *Goethe,* p. 127.

183. *Ibid.,* p. 144.

184. Richter, *Literary Works,* Vol. II, p. 343, No. 1365.

185. Clark (1939), *Leonardo,* p. 164.

186. Clark, in accordance with historical sources, limits these expressions of despair to a period of Leonardo's old age when conditions were adverse for him in Rome and refers them to Leonardo's despair over the ultimate inconclusiveness of his research. I feel more inclined to see in them the verbalization of a depressed mood which I feel justified, on clinical grounds, in assuming to have occurred sporadically throughout his life.

187. Olschki, *Die Geschichte,* Vol. I, pp. 412f.

188. Vasari, Life, p. 12.

189. An instance of intentional and successful fabrication of a legend about an artist is recorded by Kris and Kurz (1934, *Die Legende,* p. 124). The fabricator was so intuitive that Panofsky (1924, "Idea," p. 56), unaware of the hoax, was able to use the forged document perfectly for his presentation of art theory of mannerism.

190. Cf. Olschki (*Die Geschichte,* Vol. I, pp. 260f.): "Leonardo remained to the end a hybird nature [*Zwitternatur*] and his science ended in an omnium-gatherum of sharply observed facts and imaginative reveries."

191. K. Clark (1935), *A Catalogue of the Drawings of Leonardo da Vinci in the Collection of His Majesty the King at Windsor Castle,* 2 vols. London: Cambridge University Press, Vol. I, p. xvii.

192. However, Clark (1939, *Leonardo,* p. 175) doubts that that painting goes back to an original by Leonardo.

193. Berenson (1916), Leonardo, p. 16.

194. At this point I do not need to repeat what I have stressed over and over again in the foregoing: that the artist's knowledge of and about things has its direct effect on the visual presentation of them. Here also is the point at which Ortega y Gasset shows his obliviousness of the genius's creativity. Some of the most beautiful portions of the second part of *Faust,* of the *Wilhelm Meister* novels, and many others could never have been created by a writer who did not have firsthand knowledge of all sectors of the society in which he was living. Goethe was a type of writer who could never have created out of the abstract by imagining things, so to speak, behind his desk; the contents that were subjected to artistic elaboration had grown out of concrete experiences, actual observations, the broadest knowledge and expertship in a breath-taking number of functions and activities. Likewise I suggest that Leonardo's Deluge drawings would never have been possible unless the artist had gone through the grinding work of innumerable observations and investigations of water in all its shapes —rivers, streams, lakes, and seas—as well as of air, winds, storms, clouds, rocks, mountains, etc.

195. Schapiro, Leonardo and Freud, p. 177.
196. In a recent publication, however, Waelder envisions this possibility (R. Waelder 1960, *Basic Theory of Psychoanalysis.* New York: International Universities Press, pp. 6–13).

VALÉRY / LEONARDO AND THE PHILOSOPHERS

1. While [Leo Ferrero] was making a long trip abroad, a motor-car accident deprived us of that precious life. I have known few minds as precocious as his, and very few more subtle, quick, or sensitive. Depth, with the Italians, is not at all incompatible with liveliness and high spirits. That combination of qualities—not so much opposed to each other as they are rarely united in certain cultures—was strongly developed in Leo's case. He had a thoroughgoing knowledge of our language and an intuitive understanding of French authors and French ways of thought. Paris was adopting him as a son, when misfortune would have it that he must visit America, and there he was overtaken by death—of which he had written, *"It is the thing that happens only to others."*

2. We might define the philosopher as a *specialist* in the *universal,* his function being expressed by a sort of contradiction.

   Moreover, this "universal" appears only in a verbal form.

   These two considerations naturally lead to our classifying the philosopher under the species "artist." But this artist will not admit to his being one—and here begins the drama, or the comedy, of Philosophy.

   Whereas the painters and the poets have only their rank to quarrel about, philosophers quarrel with one another about their *existence.*

   Does the philosopher think that an *Ethics* or a *Monadology* is something more serious than a *Suite in D Minor?*

   It is true that certain questions presented by the mind to the mind are more general and more *natural* than most works of art, but there is nothing to prove that the questions are the right ones to ask.

3. —which are invariably the weak points of a philosophy.

   In my opinion, every philosophy is a question of form. It is the most comprehensive form that a certain individual can give to the *whole* of his internal and external experience—and this *without respect to the knowledge he might possess.* In his search for this form, the closer he comes to finding a more individual expression, one better adapted to his own nature, the farther he will be from the deeds and works of others.

4. Leonardo is one of the founders of a distinct Europe. He resembles neither the ancients nor the moderns.

5. It is clear that the "Good" and the "Beautiful" have gone out of fashion.

   As for the "True," photography has shown us its nature and limits. The recording of phenomena by means of the phenomena themselves, with as little human intervention as possible—such is "our Truth."

   To this I can testify.

6. It must be admitted that a positive or "practical" conception of life leads inevitably to a search for immediate effects and to the end of craftsmanship. We are living in the Twilight of Posterity.

7. There is nothing more surprising to the innocent mind than certain problems

that philosophers insist on placing foremost—nothing except the absence of other problems that the innocent mind would regard as being of fundamental importance.

8. I mean to say: when an artist undertakes to produce a work that is so vast or complicated, or so new to him, that his plans for it and his choice of methods are not immediately determined by their mutual compatibility, he often starts by inventing a "theory" that appears to have a general application. He explores the resources of abstract language to find an authority opposed to himself, one that will simplify his task under pretense of subjecting it to universal conditions. Anyone who lives among artists and listens to what they say can observe this phenomenon, besides hearing many a wise precept.

9. A type of sentence may precede the sentence as written. The masses of a picture may be established before the artist has decided on a subject.

10. It is quite easy to demonstrate by a certain chain of reflections that all is vanity. Pascal was finding new words to adorn the subject of countless sermons. What lies behind it is usually no more than a feeling of revulsion that is purely physiological in its origin, or a wish to make a resounding impression at no great expense.

It is as easy to evoke a horror of life, to picture its fragility, its hardships, and its folly, as it is to arouse erotic ideas and sensual appetites. All one needs is a different vocabulary. (But we can take for granted that the first exercise is of a nobler sort.)

I might add (if only for some) that the determination not to let oneself be manipulated by words has something to do with the goal to which I gave, or thought I was giving, the name of *pure Poetry*.

11. That is why courses in philosophy—unless they also teach the freedom of every mind not only with regard to doctrines but even with regard to the problems themselves—impress me as being antiphilosophical.

12. In the intellectual life—so it seems clear to me—philosophical works occupy the same place for those who admire them that works of art occupy for those who admire them. There are art lovers of Spinoza, just as there are of Bach.

Sometimes we find significant resemblances between the two species—as note Wagner and Nietzsche.

13. For that matter, what else could be *hoped for* by thinkers of that grand sort?

14. Nor is Montaigne in that same list.

He would give the same answer, "I do not know," to all the questions in a philosophical catechism, and therefore he could hardly be called a philosopher. And yet . . .

15. Let us not forget that the broadest fame is based on the sort of merit that can be called to mind in a few words.

16. Science in the *modern sense* of the word consists in making knowledge depend on power. And it has reached the point of subordinating the intelligible to the verifiable. Our confidence in science is entirely based on the assurance that a certain phenomenon will be produced again or observed again as a result of certain well defined *acts*. As for the manner of describing the phenomenon—of "explaining" it—that is the arguable, changeable, and perfectible part of the development or exposition of science.

17. Such is the foundation of what we regard as true knowledge. The propositions of this true knowledge should be simply directions for performing certain acts: Do this, do that. All this amounts to *power,* in other words, to an assured external transformation that depends on a conscious internal modification.

18. This is an age when metaphysics has been surprised by the sudden changes in science, some of which have produced a truly comic dismay.

Hence it has sometimes occurred to me that, if I were a philosopher, I should apply myself to making my philosophic thought independent of all forms of knowledge that might be overturned by some new experiment.

19. —but demands to be taken as an end in itself.

20. It seems to be characteristic of the greatest philosophers that they add problems of interpretation to the immediate problems raised by observation.

Each of them imports a terminology, and there is no case in which the terms they introduce are so definite that the argument about the value of their principles can be clearly separated from the other argument about their meaning.

21. The idea of the animal as a machine expressed by Descartes and forming a remarkable element of his philosophy had been carried farther by Leonardo, who reveals it not only *in verbo* but *in acto.* I doubt whether anyone before his time had thought of observing persons with the eye of a mechanical engineer. For him the support of the body, its propulsion, and its respiration were problems in mechanics. He was more the anatomist and more the engineer than Descartes. The dream of creating a mechanical man and hence of achieving knowledge by construction was paramount in his thinking.

22. For it was a condition of his painting that he should make a minute preliminary analysis of the objects he planned to represent, one that was not in the least confined to their visual properties, but went deep into their organic life, involving questions of physics, then physiology, then psychology—so that finally his eye would, as it were, *expect* to perceive the visible accidents resulting from the hidden structure of the model.

23. Benvenuto Cellini tells us that Leonardo was the first to *admire* the adaptation of organic forms to mechanical functions. He revealed the special type of beauty possessed by certain bones (the omoplate, for example) and articulations (like that of the arm with the hand).

A very modern system of aesthetics is based solely on this principle of functional adaptation. The Greeks had thought chiefly of optical effects, and they did not isolate the pleasure resulting from the virtual function of forms. Yet the men of every age have created *perfect* weapons and utensils.

24. When circumstances led me to consider da Vinci, I approached him as the archetype of those who perform each task so consciously that it becomes both art and science, inextricably mingled; as the exemplar of a system of art founded on *general* analysis and demanding that every *particular* work should be created only out of verifiable elements.

As a result of Leonardo's analysis, his desire to paint merged into a curiosity about all phenomena, whether or not they were visual; he felt that nothing was alien to the art of painting, which in turn seemed precious to perception in general.

Another characteristic of Leonardo is the extraordinary reciprocity between making and knowing, as a result of which the second is guaranteed by the first. This reciprocity stands opposed to any purely verbal science and has become dominant in the present era—to the great detriment of philosophy, which now appears to be something incomplete, *speech without action.*

25. Logic has only a limited value when it employs ordinary language, that is, a language without absolute definitions.

26. It also consists in reconsidering the values of our thinking as originally given —by extending the conscious *duration* of the given thoughts.

27. All thinking involves taking one thing for another: a *second* for a *year.*

28. There is not a single problem in philosophy that can be stated in such a form as to banish all doubt concerning the existence of the problem.

29. Although it must be observed that the accommodation is often very far from being satisfactory—as note the definitions of *point, line, relation,* etc.

30. There has been no philosophy (till now) that could withstand a *precise* examination of its "definitions."

31. —as well as a sort of "analogistics."

32. There is much to be said about *the arbitrary.*

   Everything we do that is arbitrary in our own eyes—as, for example, letting the hand make *random* designs on a scrap of paper—is a more or less separate activity of some organ. Thus, we close our eyes in order to draw a card from a hat *at random.* Such acts, in which the attention is relaxed, are in contrast with our supervised activities.

   A briefer way of saying the same thing is to remark that the degree of consciousness required by an act can be measured by the *number* of independent conditions imposed on it.

33. They have never done so, however—or not to my knowledge—by starting with an analysis of language that would reduce it to its statistical nature, and hence would permit them not to attribute verbal creations (including "problems") to "the essence of things"—when their origin may have been innocence, or the poetic sentiment, or the gropings and fumblings of generations.

   A disregard of these humble beginnings is doubtless the precondition of more than one philosophic problem.

   In particular the existence of "notions" capable of being interpreted in different fashions, or the accidental coexistence of terms created independently of one another, opens a way for antinomies and paradoxes that favor a rich development of misunderstandings and highly "philosophic" subtleties.

SHATTUCK / THE TORTOISE AND THE HARE

1. Anyone who has read *Being and Nothingness* will perceive the extent to which Valéry's idea and vocabulary in this passage anticipate Sartre's description of the *pour-soi.* Jean Hippolyte was the first to notice the unexpected resemblance. ("Note sur Paul Valéry et la crise de la conscience," *La Vie intellectuelle,* March, 1946.)

2. An earlier treatment of this theme appears in *An Evening with Monsieur Teste.* Of this text about another "master of his own thought," Valéry later wrote: "I think there is also in it a kind of transposition out of art and a unification of Leonardo da Vinci and Mallarmé." The figure of Descartes also lurks behind

both figures. The best treatment of the literary and philosophical value of these two works by Valéry is in Francis Scarfe's book.

3. The most thoroughgoing criticism is Meyer Schapiro's "Leonardo and Freud: An Art-Historical Study," in *Journal of the History of Ideas,* April, 1956.

So far as I know no one has undertaken to correct Professor Schapiro's extreme position in two matters. Freud did not accept Pfister's "discovery" of a vulture hidden in the St. Anne painting as confirmation of his theories. The 1919 note says the discovery "is of remarkable interest, even if one may not feel inclined to accept it without reserve." And the one new document Professor Schapiro cites about Leonardo's ten godparents supports his own thesis of a hostile mother no more strongly than Freud's. Both these matters arise at the start of the article; the remainder of it and the conclusion seem to me very judicious, and his documentation invaluable.

[In an amiable letter of rejoinder to my essay, Mr. Schapiro insists that he nowhere committed himself to the theory of the hostile mother, but rather wished to suggest a possibility Freud ignored. On this point I readily yield. However I cannot agree with Mr. Schapiro that the pronoun "one" in the 1919 footnote refers only to the "sceptical reader" and does not include Freud's own mixed feelings. The question has not been allowed to rest there. Several important commentaries on Leonardo's life and Freud's version of it have appeared since this essay was written: a lengthy monograph by K. R. Eissler in 1962; Brian Farrell's tendentious introduction to the Penguin edition of Alan Tyson's translation of Freud's text; and a remarkable review article by E. H. Gombrich (*New York Review of Books* in February 11, 1965) which brings out Freud's debt to Merejkowski's novel based on Leonardo.]

4. A passage often quoted from *Note et Digression* runs thus: "I sensed that this past master of all disciplines, this adept at drawing, at illustration, at mathematics, had found the central attitude from which the undertakings of knowledge and the operations of art are equally possible; the exchange between analysis and action, singularly probable: a marvellously exhilarating mind."

In the years to follow, Valéry did not remain alone. In the *Second Surrealist Manifesto* André Breton writes as follows in 1929: "Everything leads us to believe that there exists a certain vantage point of the mind, from which life and death, the real and the imaginary, past and future, the communicable and the incommunicable, high and low, cease to be perceived as contradictory. Now, it would be useless to look for any other motive in surrealist activity than the determination of this point."

5. The burning question of how "savages" think has begun to provide a focus for such varied disciplines as linguistics, anthropology, psychology, taxonomy, logic, literary criticism, and mathematics. Some recent and general treatments: Claude Lévi-Strauss, *La Pensée sauvage,* Paris, 1962; Aimé Patri, "La Pensée Sauvage et la notre," in *Preuves,* February, 1963; and the group of articles in *Esprit,* October, 1963.

LEONARDO CHRONOLOGY

1. The date March 16 is Julian; the extrapolated Gregorian date would be March 25. This eclipse was conspicuous in western and central Europe (it ended in

Russia); the track of totality passed through France into Bavaria and Austria (A. Pogo).

2. Victory of Florentines over Milanese in 1440 at Anghiari, eastern Tuscany, northeast of Arezzo.

Notes on Contributors

BERNARD BERENSON, born in Lithuania in 1865, was, as a child of ten, taken to Boston by his parents. He remained there till his graduation from Harvard in 1887, when he made his first journey to Italy. Although he made frequent trips back to the United States, he lived from 1900 on in his famous villa, I Tatti, at Settignano, near Florence. Here he brought together his own fine collection of paintings and an extraordinary library. His rise to a position of pre-eminence in the field of art history began in 1894 with the publication of the first of his many books on Italian art, which have become classics in their field. Of these, *The Italian Painters of the Renaissance* is perhaps the best known. Berenson died in October 1959.

SIR KENNETH CLARK was born in 1903. He was educated at Winchester and Oxford, and worked for two years with Bernard Berenson in Florence. He was appointed Director of the National Gallery at the age of thirty and remained there until 1945. He was Slade Professor of Fine Art at Oxford from 1946 to 1950. Sir Kenneth has been Chairman of the Arts Council since May 1953 and was appointed Chairman on the setting up of the Independent Television Authority. His first publication, written at the age of twenty-two, was *The Gothic Revival,* and many others have followed. *Leonardo da Vinci* (1939), *Landscape into Art* (1949), and *The Nude* (1956).

K. R. EISSLER was born in Vienna in 1908 and received his Ph.D. and his M.D. from the University of Vienna. Since serving in the U. S. Army in World War II, Dr. Eissler has had a private practice in psychoanalysis in New York City. He is the author of *The Psychiatrist and the Dying Patient* (1955); *Leonardo da Vinci: Psychoanalytic Notes on the Enigma* (1961); *Goethe: A Psychoanalytic Study—1775–1786* (1964); and *Medical Orthodoxy and the Future of Psychoanalysis* (1965).

BRIAN FARRELL was born in Cape Town in 1912. He was educated at the universities of Cape Town and Oxford. A onetime lecturer in the Department of Philosophy, the University of the Witwatersrand, he is now Wilde Reader in Mental Philosophy, Fellow of Corpus Christi College, Oxford University. His articles have appeared in *Mind, Proceedings of the Aristotelian Society, International Journal of Psycho-Analysis, British Journal of Medical Psychology, Inquiry,* and other journals.

434

ARNOLD HAUSER was born in Hungary and studied in the universities of Budapest, Vienna, Berlin, and Paris. Following World War I, he spent two years in Italy doing research in Classical and Italian Art. In 1921, Dr. Hauser returned to Berlin to study economics and sociology under Werner Sombart and Ernst Troeltsch. Between 1924 and 1938 he lived in Vienna; from 1938 to 1959 in London; and since then in the United States, where he has taught at Brandeis University. He is the author of *The Social History of Art* (1951), *Philosophy of Art History* (1959), and *Mannerism* (1965).

ALEXANDER KOYRÉ, born in Taganrog in 1892, studied in Göttingen and at the École Pratique des Hautes Études in Paris, receiving his Ph.D. from the University of Paris in 1923 and becoming Docteur es Lettres in 1929. He taught at the University of Montpellier from 1930 to 1931 and at the Sorbonne beginning in 1932. He was a member of the faculty of the New School for Social Research in New York from 1942 to 1945 and has been a member of the Institute for Advanced Study in Princeton since 1955. His publications include *The Philosophy of Saint Anselm* (1923), *Discovering Plato* (1945), and *From the Closed World to the Infinite Universe* (1957).

SIR HERBERT READ was born in 1893. After service in the British Army during World War I, he commenced his career as a critic. He has written extensively in fields of both art and literature and is also a distinguished poet. His most important works are: *Reason and Romanticism, Art Now, Art and Society, Education Through Art, Wordsworth, Art and Industry,* and *The Philosophy of Modern Art.*

GIORGIO DE SANTILLANA, born in Rome in 1902, was graduated from the University of Rome in 1925 and taught there from 1929 to 1932. He came to the United States in 1936, lecturing first at the New School for Social Research, then at Harvard from 1937 to 1939, before becoming a member of the faculty of the Massachusetts Institute of Technology in 1941. Among his works are *A History of Science* (1933) and *The Crime of Galileo* (1955).

GEORGE SARTON, born in Ghent, Belgium, in 1884, studied at the University of Ghent. He came to the United States in 1915, as lecturer on the History of Science at George Washington University. Since 1916 he has been Professor of the History of Science at Harvard University. His publications include *Introduction to the History of Science* (1927, 1931), *The Life of Science* (1948), and *Science and Tradition* (1951).

ROGER SHATTUCK, born in New York in 1923, did his undergraduate work at Yale University; he was a junior fellow of the Society of Fellows at Harvard University from 1950 to 1953. He was instructor in French Literature at Harvard until 1956, when he became a member of the faculty of the University of Texas. He is the author of *The Banquet Years* (1958) and *Proust's Binoculars* (1963).

W. R. VALENTINER, born in Karlsruhe in 1880, studied at Leipzig and Heidelberg. He was Curator of Decorative Arts at the Metropolitan Museum of Art from 1908 to 1914; adviser to the Detroit Institute of Arts, and subsequently its Director from 1924 to 1944. He wrote works on Rembrandt, Michelangelo, and David before his death in 1958.

PAUL VALÉRY was born in 1871 in Cette and studied law at the University of Montpellier. There, influenced by a visit from Loüys and Gide, he decided to go to Paris and devote his life to writing. Leon Daudet commissioned him to do "Introduction to the Method of Leonardo da Vinci" for his *Nouvelle Revue,* and the following year *Centaur* published "An Evening with M. Teste." For the next seventeen years he published almost nothing until Gide asked him to collect his earlier scattered poems, which were finally published as *La Jeune Parque.*

HEINRICH WÖLFFLIN, born in 1864, is said to have found art criticism a subjective chaos and left it a science. In 1893 he succeeded Jacob Burckhardt in the Chair of Art History at the University of Basle. His first book (apart from a thesis on the psychology of architecture) was *Renaissance and Baroque* (1888). This was followed ten years later by *Classic Art: The Great Masters of the Italian Renaissance;* and in 1915 by the first edition of *Principles of Art History.* The effect of that work has been so extensive that it would not be inaccurate to say that every art critic after his time has been influenced by Wölfflin's contributions. He died in 1945 at the age of eighty-one.

Index

437